Defending the Breast Cancer Malpractice Case

Defending the Breast Cancer Malpractice Case

CAMPBELL F. WATTS, M.D.
DAVID M. ELDERKIN, J.D.

WITH INVITED COMMENTARIES BY
DAVID PLOTKIN, M.D.,
FRANCIS G. BLANKENBERG, M.D.,
ALBERT E. CRAM, M.D., F.A.C.S.,
JOHN W. CANADY, M.D.

PRENTICE HALL LAW & BUSINESS

Printed in the United States of America

Library of Congress Cataloging-in-Publication Data

Watts, Campbell F. (Campbell Franklin), 1918-
Defending the breast cancer malpractice case / Campbell F. Watts, David M. Elderkin.
p. cm.
Includes bibliographical references and index.
ISBN 0-13-349598-1
1. Physicians—Malpractice—United States. 2. Oncologists—Malpractice—United States. 3. Breast—Cancer—Patients—Legal status, laws, etc.—United States. 4. Breast—Cancer—Law and legislation—United States. 5. Defense (Civil procedure)—United States. I. Elderkin, David M. II. Title.
KF2905.3.W32 1994
346.7303′32—dc20 94-34048
[347.306332] CIP

TABLE OF CONTENTS

CHAPTER 3
MOTIONS

CHAPTER 4
DISCOVERY

CHAPTER 5
TRIAL STRATEGY

PART II
MEDICAL SECTION

CAMPBELL F. WATTS, M.D.

CHAPTER 6
MORTALITY AND INCIDENCE RATES OF BREAST CANCER: A 63-YEAR OLD ENIGMA

CHAPTER 7
THE EVOLUTION OF OUR PRESENT DAY CONCEPT OF THE NATURAL HISTORY OF BREAST CANCER

CHAPTER 8
NATURAL HISTORY OF BREAST CANCER

CHAPTER 9
CAN BREAST CANCER BE CURED?

CHAPTER 10
METASTASIS: WHEN DOES IT OCCUR?

CHAPTER 11
TUMOR SIZE

CHAPTER 12
LYMPH NODE STATUS: CLINICAL SIGNIFICANCE

CHAPTER 13
AXILLARY NODE METASTASES: DELAY IN DIAGNOSIS?

CHAPTER 14
THE CAMOUFLAGED TUMOR

CHAPTER 15
TUMOR THRESHOLD SIZE

CHAPTER 16
THE CANCER CONTROL WINDOW

CHAPTER 17
THE INTERVAL TUMOR

CHAPTER 18
THE TNM STAGING SYSTEM HAS MANY LIMITATIONS

CHAPTER 19
DOUBLING TIME DEFENSE

CHAPTER 20
LIMITATIONS OF EARLY DIAGNOSIS

CHAPTER 21
SCREENING INTERVALS AND FOLLOW-UP

CHAPTER 22
BIASES

CHAPTER 23
PROGNOSTIC FACTORS

CHAPTER 24
SILICONE GEL BREAST IMPLANTS

CHAPTER 25
SILICONE AND PUBLIC HEALTH: PLASTIC SURGEONS' VIEWPOINT

by Albert E. Cram, MD, FACS and John W. Canady, MD

ABOUT THE AUTHORS

David M. Elderkin (*left*) **and Dr. Campbell F. Watts**

Dr. Campbell F. Watts is a diplomate of the American Board of Surgery. He obtained his M.D. from the University of Iowa College of Medicine and his postgraduate training in general surgery at the Mayo Clinic. He received his M.S. in surgery at the University of Minnesota.

The author was engaged in the private practice of general surgery in Cedar Rapids, Iowa, for 35 years. Over the years he developed a special interest in breast cancer and ultimately a large portion of his practice was limited to diseases of the breast. Through his career he was a part time clinical instructor and lecturer in the Cedar Rapids Hospitals education program. He is Past President of the Iowa Clinical Surgical Society and the Linn County (Iowa) Medical Society. He is the recipient of St. Lukes (Cedar Rapids) Health Care Foundation Founders Award for significant involvement, impact and leadership for the benefit of Eastern Iowans. He received the ''Golden Cane Award'' from his medical colleagues and the C.E.O. of Mercy (Cedar Rapids) Medical Center for 1992.

Since retiring in 1985, he has focused his medical research on the role of biology and the determination of the outcome of breast cancer. In addition to authoring this book with Mr. Elderkin and writing a book (*Malpractice Defense: Breast Cancer*, Medical Economics Books) in 1990, he has continued to research and lecture on the molecular biology of breast cancer. Recently he has been interested in the role of angiogenesis in invasion and metastasis and as a possible target for the treatment of breast cancer.

David M. Elderkin is the senior member of the firm of Elderkin & Pirnie, P.L.C., Cedar Rapids, Iowa. He received his J.D. degree from the University of Iowa Law School and other than time spent in military service during World War II, has since engaged in the practice of law in Cedar Rapids, Iowa. His practice has encompassed virtually all types of litigation, but particularly in the field of medical and hospital malpractice defense. He is a Past President of the Iowa State Bar Association and the recipient of its Lawyer of the Year Award. He is a Past President of the Iowa Academy of Trial Lawyers and in 1991 was named Dean of the Academy. He was a longtime member of the Iowa Supreme Court Advisory Committee on Evidence and Rules of Civil Procedure. He is a recipient of the Award of Merit of the Fellows of the Iowa State Bar Foundation. He is a Fellow of the American Board of Trial Advocates and a Fellow and former State Chairman of the American College of Trial Lawyers. He is a charter member of the American College of Hospital Attorneys and has written and spoken extensively on trial practice over a period 50 years.

Contributors

Invited Commentary -
Is Breast Cancer Curable?

David Plotkin, MD
Associate Clinical Professor of Medicine, UCLA
Associate Clinical Professor of Medicine, USC
Director, Memorial Cancer Research Foundation of Southern California, Los Angeles, California

Francis G. Blankenberg, MD
Acting Assistant Professor of Radiology
Stanford University, Palo Alto, California

Invited Chapter -
Silicone and Public Health - Plastic Surgeons Viewpoint

Albert E. Cram, MD, FACS
Professor of Surgery and Director,
Division of Plastic and Reconstructive Surgery
University of Iowa Hospitals
University of Iowa College of Medicine
Iowa City, Iowa

John W. Canady, MD
Assistant Professor of Plastic and Reconstructive Surgery
University College of Medicine
Iowa City, Iowa.

PREFACE

A 39-year-old mother of two children consulted her family doctor regarding an aching in his left axilla. Examination by both the family doctor and a surgeon noted that the left breast was slightly tender, but there was no palpable mass. Mammograms revealed a 5 mm cluster of 10 micro calcifications, smooth and thought to be benign. Follow-up mamograms in six months revealed no change. Nine months following the initial workup, the patient discovered a painful mass in her left breast. The surgeon found a 2 cm tender mass in the left breast at the 6 o'clock position just inferior to the areola, the same area in which the cluster of calcifications was first located. Biopsy indicated a carcinoma, and a left modified radical mastectomy was performed. Post operative course at the end of 10 months indicated pain in left arm and forearm; two years following surgery the plaintiff died of breast cancer.

It goes without says that this factual situation has the ingredients of a lawsuit. In today's atmosphere, all physicians run the risk of being sued for malpractice, and this is particularly true in breast cancer cases.

There has been a growing tendency by the courts to treat all passive injury medical malpractice cases by different rules than those guiding other negligence actions. Causation, which is treated as an all or nothing proposition in the run of the mill negligence actions, has been relaxed in the majority of jurisdictions, particularly those following the loss of chance doctrine which either lessens the plaintiff's burden of proof on causation or is considered as a separate cause of action.

Physicians often find themselves defending cases simply because the patient fails to improve or where serious disease processes are not arrested. This is true in any cancer case, but is particularly true in breast cancer cases, which bring to the tragic scenario an enormous emotional component. As was stated by Dr. Murray H. Seltzer:

> The unique role of the human female breast throughout history must be appreciated prior to attempting an understanding of the emotions related to a disease such as breast cancer or related to litigation involving the diagnosis and treatment of this disease. This gland, in contradistinction to other bodily glands, is related to both sexuality and nurturing. *This is the only part of the human body that is capable of sustaining the newborn nutritionally. *While disease of any part of the body poses a threat to the patient, cancer of the breast poses a special threat in that not only is health and survival threatened, but also sexuality, nurturing and self image are threatened.

M. Seltzer, Remarks at the Meeting of the American Bar Association Tort and Insurance Practice Section (August 3, 1993).

Quoting Dr. Dominique Gross of Straasbourg, Dr. Alexander Walt of Wayne State University School of Medicine states:

> When the breast, a taboo organ, is affected by cancer, a taboo illness, reactions from both the individual and from society deal more with emotions than with reason.

Speaking to *physicians*, Dr. Walt stated:

> *It is vital that *we* recognize that the baggage *we* carry may be heavy with emotions and fears rather than facts.

Mayo Foundation, May Alumni, Spring 1992, at 12-27.

Over 27,000 medical articles have been written on breast cancer since 1966 with half of these being written since 1987. In 1993 there have been over 1,500 medical articles published relating to breast cancer. As Dr. Seltzer points out, a relatively new term "the politics of breast cancer" Langer, J., 47 Am. Women's Med. Assoc. 207 has arisen which involves addressing research and public attitudes towards breast cancer as well as research funding procedures. This politics of breast cancer ingredient is seen in the over-propaganda by the American Cancer Society as hereinafter discussed.

Breast cancer is the leading cause of cancer related death in women ages 15 to 55, is the second leading cause of such death in women ages 55 to 74 (lung cancer is first) and is the third leading cause of such death in women above 75 years of age (colon-rectum first, lung second). In the year 1993 approximately 182,000 developed breast cancer and 46,000 will die from it. The age-adjusted mortality rate has not changed in the last 63 years, despite improved diagnosis, surgery and treatment.

There is no way to know exactly how many of these deaths, or other unfortunate results in breast cancer cases will result in litigation. A breast cancer study by the Physician Insurers Association of America in March of 1990 reported that breast cancer medical malpractice suits are the second most common type of medical malpractice cases after brain damaged baby cases, and also reported that they were the most costly of all medical malpractice cases.

Even though breast cancer is less common in younger women, it is younger women who are the most common plaintiffs, usually women in their thirties. The second largest group of plaintiffs are in their forties with relatively few plaintiffs in their fifties.

A comprehensive review of the jury verdicts in New York State over a six-year period (1985–1991) shows that in 94% of the cases studied, a delay in diagnosis of breast cancer was involved, the time interval in the presumed delay ranged from one month to three years, the average being 11.6 months (figures of the Physicians Insurance Association study computed the average delay in their study as 13 months). Of these cases, 10.8% were because of purported misinterpretation of mammograms. Mammograms were not obtained in 50% of the cases or were interpreted as negative in 37.5% of the cases. The most common speciality sued was obstetrics and gynecology, followed by internists and surgeons. Verdicts ranged from $185,000 to $2,750,000. The most common scenario for litigation was a delay in the treatment of a (presumed) palpable mass which was alleged by the plaintiff to have decreased the changes of survival. Dr. Mitnick, Vasquez, J.F., Pesser, M.P. and Roses, D.F. *Murrayhill Radiology and Mammography*, Tisch Hospital, New York University Medical Center, New York, and Murray Hill Radiology and Mammography. Statistics gathered by Kenneth A. Kern, et al., nationwide; (*Causes of Breast Cancer Malpractice Litigation*, Arch. Surg. Vol. 127, May 1992) are roughly comparable. See also Kern, *Medical Litigation Analysis, Surgical Oncology of North America*, Vol. 3, No. 1, Jan. 1994).

To ask a blunt question: while plaintiffs in the cases reported were compensated for an obvious tragedy, and while many plaintiffs whose cases are now pending or will be started in the future will also be rewarded, how many of these are based upon reasonable medical certainty and how many have been at the expense of some conscientious physician, surgeon, radiologist or pathologist?

The emotion surrounding the agony of a breast cancer or a breast cancer death as brought to the courtroom is often permitted to conceal the fact that the patient brought this disease to the doctor's office, it was not the doctor who created it.

> In no other human cancer has there been such enormous research and clinical effort made to understand the disease and modify treatment according to current clinical presentations and research findings.

Bland and Cady, *Breast Cancer: Strategies for the 1990's I*, 70(4) Surgical Clinic North America (preface) (August 1990).

During 1992, 46,000 women died of breast cancer because they harbored viable distant metastasis or inoperable local or regional disease at the time of diagnosis and treatment. Substantially the same number died in 1993. (Chapter 6) Why, despite all efforts of medical science to diagnose and cure? Basically, because of the problems of biologic determination and tumor camouflaging 46,000 breast cancers spread to distant sites before they could be detected by any method, including mammography, and both entities are completely beyond the control of the clinician who screens for breast cancer. Despite this fact, physicians will continue to be sued in some 3,000 to 4,000 lawsuits per year.

Admittedly, there are some physicians who are guilty of ignorance and carelessness. This book does not seek to justify or excuse such physicians, but does assert that they are far fewer in number than are accused in the judicial setting. So often, so very often, lawsuits against physicians are based upon outcome and, unfortunately, all too many are successful.

The factual situation presented at the outset is not hypothetical, but real, and a lawsuit was filed charging the surgeon and radiologist with failure to make a timely diagnosis of breast cancer. The claim was that a 2 cm palpable mass in the left breast should have been discovered at the time of the original workup nine months prior and that if it had been then surgically removed, the patient would have had a substantial possibility of survival.

The defense preparation began with a careful evaluation of the pathology and clinical history which revealed that this was an infiltrative duct cell carcinoma, one of the most common and one of the most malignant types. It was a classic example of a camouflaged, highly lethal tumor which metastasized early in its life cycle, certainly more than 9 to 12 months prior to the time the patient was first seen by the defendants. Fortunately, the defense was successful.

It is the intent and hope of the authors that this book will aid more such defenses. To be successful in any defense of a breast cancer malpractice case, defendant must overcome several obstacles. One, of course, is the emotion factor, already discussed. Another is the mass of statistics thrown around with abandon.

While some of the literature is good, some of it is worthless because everyone's publication differs on the sample of patients examined; in some instances the patient selection is poor, the series too small, and the follow-up too short. The prediction of 5-year survival rate as 85%, for example, doesn't tell what risk of dying the plaintiff has. Some cancers simply don't metastasize and are, therefore, easily "cured" while others cannot be cured because they metastasize early.

Plaintiff's expert testimony always speaks retrospectively, seldom upon any scientific opinion, usually upon speculation. For example again, there is absolutely no way anyone can establish the tumor size or survival rate 12 months before it was diagnosed and removed. Some plaintiffs' experts attempt to do so by using the doubling time theory in reverse, which has both errors and limitations. (Chapter 19).

A formidable obstacle to the defense is the over-promotion by the American Cancer Society as to the benefits of early diagnosis while ignoring its limitations. As spread by the media, this has resulted in many, if not most, people assuming that early diagnosis guarantees cure. That early diagnosis is important is true, but it must be remembered that all cancers are not alike. For example, basal cell carcinoma of the skin grows slowly, is locally invasive, lacks the ability to metastasize and is easily cured by simple excision. Carcinoma of the uterine cervix has a long, precancerous phase, remains local for a considerable period of time, can be diagnosed easily by a Pap smear, and surgery and radiation are effective treatments. (See §19.05).

There are other cancers, such as small cell cancers of the lung, in which distant metastases are present before the cancer can be detected by chest x-rays. Chronic lymphocytic leukemia is never cured, no matter when the diagnosis is made. Malignant brain tumors such as glioblastoma multiforme, have a cure rate close to zero. Early diagnosis of breast cancer does not guarantee cure. Yet, this has been the propaganda, and it has resulted in most people, including most jurors, of course, believing that breast cancers are easily found, if not by palpation, at least by mammography, which will provide an early diagnosis and surgical intervention will then effect a cure. There is no scientific study which justifies those claims.

Dr. Susan Love, Director of the Faulkner Breast Cancer Center in Boston, Mass. (now at the University of California, Los Angeles), spoke on behalf of the Breast Cancer Coalition before a senate committee on labor and human resources in Washington, D.C. She testified as follows:

> We have spent a lot of time, energy and money touting "early detection" and presenting it as if it were the answer. Unfortunately, we have misrepresented the situation through wishful thinking or just an attempt at simplification. We have acted as if all tumors go through progression from 1 cm to 2 cm and so on and as if all tumors have the potential to be detected at a small size and therefore could be cured. Would that that were true. What we are dealing with is a combination of a tumor and an immune system. Some tumors are very aggressive and will have spread before they are palpable. Thirty percent of non-palpable tumors are found to have positive lymph nodes. Some tumors are very slow growing and will not spread even though they have reached a large size.
>
> Mammography screening when optimally applied in women over 40 will reduce the mortality from breast cancer by 30%. This is certainly an advance, but it means that 70% of post menopausal women will get regular mammograms and still will not benefit either because they (the cancers) are so fast growing that the tumor will have already spread or because they are so slow growing that it doesn't matter. And this doesn't even count the premenopausal women where mammography is less useful. This is not to say that we sould abandon mammography, but that we should not over-emphasize its benefits. Mammography is not prevention, it is only detection. (Chapter 7)
>
> Thus, we must dispel the notion that early diagnosis invariably results in cure and the failure to cure is unvaryingly secondary to the failure to make a timely diagnosis. The public must understand that our currently available diagnostic modalities are imperfect and that even the most astute clinicians fail to detect many breast cancers before they become incurable. To do this, we must, in simple terms, "educate" the public regarding the role of biology and the clinical behavior and outcome of breast cancer."

In 1987 the General Accounting office in refutation of the National Cancer Institute claims of progress in curing breast cancer, observed that there was in fact no clear evidence that current diagnostic techniques and therapies had produced any impact on breast cancer survival. (General Accounting office *Cancer Patient Survival: What Progress Has Been*

Made, P.E.M.D. 87-13 Mar. 1987) (Report to the Chairman, Subcommittee on Operations, House of Representatives).

Spratt not only agrees, but goes further and describes the propaganda as "*over promotion that skirts on scientific fraud. Such propaganda gives rise to false expectations which, in turn, creates medical liability claims.*" *Geometry Growth Rates and Duration of Cancer and Carcinoma in Situ of the Breast Before Detection by Screenings*, 46 Cancer Research 970-74, (1986).

The basis for the propaganda appears to be rooted in a doctrine long since discredited scientifically, but carried over by virtue of the politics of breast cancer, as referred by Dr. Seltzer. Some time between 1890 and 1910, Dr. William Halsted postulated that breast cancer spread via the lymphatics through the breast and tissue planes to the regional lymph nodes and then to distant sites via the perivascular lymphatics. It was logical to conclude, therefore, that early diagnosis and radical surgery would cure breast cancer. Following this, Dr. Halsted and Dr. Meyer popularized the radical removal of the breast, the underlying muscles and the regional lymph nodes in continuity. Yet, this failed to cure 50% of women with operable breast cancer, which led to questioning the validity of the Halsted doctrine. It became recognized that breast cancer spreads not only through the lymph glands, but also through the bloodstream and that many cancers become systemic with viable metastasis before they can be detected by mammography or by any other known means. (Chapter 7).

The National Cancer Institute has issued a statement supporting the theory that breast conservation provides survival equivalent to radical surgical removal on the basis that breast cancer is a systemic disease from its beginning by its consensus statement promoting the use of systemic chemotherapy in women with Stage I, node-negative breast cancer. (*Treatment of Early Stage Breast Cancer NIH Consensus Development Conference Consensus Statement*, A:18-21, 1990).

This book presents a concise summary of the biology and natural history of breast cancer, showing that there is no relationship between the stage and the rapidity of the growth of the tumor, and that the tumor itself determines at what size it is possible to detect it. In short, that the unfortunate outcome (death) of the patient is due to the biology of the cancer, rather than any fault on the part of the physician.

This defense is not new, although often used in connection with the doubling time theory, which is somewhat controversial. (Chapter 19).

The defense has also been somewhat sneeringly referred to as the "so what" defense, a term that is not only untrue, but unfair. Much the same type of disdain was shown by those physicians who questioned the Halsted doctrine that breast cancer spread only through the lymphatics, breast and tissue planes to the regional lymph nodes and then to distant sites via the paravascular lymphatics. The same disdain was also held for those physicians who disputed the fairly recent assertion that trauma caused breast cancer. Worker's compensation awards for "traumatic cancers" were made by the thousands without any credible study of the biological mechanism. As the saying goes, the experts who testified in these cases were wrong, but certainly not in doubt and were contemptuous of those who felt otherwise.

Q. *Is it not possible that something else (than trauma) contributed to the breast cancer?*

A. *Within the knowledge of man, I think not.*

Menarde v. Philadelphic Transport Company, 103 A.2d 681 (Penn. 1954).

Yet today there is no claim that single trauma can create cancer. (Monkman, G. R., Ivans, J. C. *Trauma and Oncogenesis*, Mayo Clin. Proc. 49:157-163, 1974). Scientific standards shifted and litigation of traumatic cancer ended.

As demonstrated by the medical part of this book, there have been evolving biological paridigms about cancer and most modern day scientists agree that the biology of the tumor determines survival time. To assert the hypothesis of tumor biology in the defense of breast cancer malpractice cases no longer can be termed the "so what" defense, and the appellation was never deserved. No cases can be found where a defendant physician, dragged into what has been described as the "cold and inhospitable halls of justice" brings the cancer to the patient. Most physicians are devastated by the death of a patient and it is neither fair nor accurate to picture a defendant physician, upon the death of a patient, shrugging his or her shoulders and saying "so what."

Despite the massive educational programs concerning the benefits of monthly breast self-examinations, mammography and early diagnosis and treatment, despite the improved quality of medical education, despite the explosion of knowledge of the molecular biology of the cancer cell, and despite the widespread use of mammography and other diagnostic modalities, the age-adjusted mortality rate of breast cancer has not decreased during the past 63 years. During the year 1993, 46,000 women died of breast cancer and they did not die because of some physician's alleged failure to diagnose. They died because they harbored viable but distant metastasis or inoperable local or regional disease at the time any diagnosis could have been made. As will be repeatedly emphasized throughout this book, it is the biology of the tumor that affects survival, not the time of diagnosis.

Campbell F. Watts
David M. Elderkin
November 1994

Acknowledgments

If it were not for the many generous individuals who gave their time, expertise and encouragement to the project of this book, it could not have been completed. From the medical side, the contributions of Malcolm Beinfield, Associate Professor of Surgery, Yale University, and Julie Mitnik, Associate Professor of Clinical Radiology, New York University Medical Center, were critical in importance. Both reviewed early drafts of the entire manuscript, made many excellent suggestions, and encouraged us to continue this project. Dr. Curt Hass, a Cedar Rapids, Iowa, radiation oncology and Director of the Eastern Iowa Cancer Center, provided an excellent peer review of the more difficult chapters. Dr. Dean Gesme, a Cedar Rapids, Iowa, medical oncologist and Assistant Director of the Eastern Iowa Cancer Center, provided a critical review of chapters 6-10 and offered many excellent suggestions. Dr. Allen Cram provided a peer review for the chapter on silicone gel implants and agreed to prepare an "invited commentary." It is appreciated. David Russell, a Cedar Rapids, Iowa, radiologist and mammographer, related his experiences regarding the detection of implant rupture and carcinoma of the breast in women with silicone gel implants.

Dr. Richard Quetsch, a Cedar Rapids, Iowa, internist and a grammarian at heart, meticulously reviewed the manuscript for errors in grammar and punctuation. Dr. William Price, a retired urologist, examined early drafts in the manuscript and made most helpful suggestions.

From the legal side, we are enormously grateful for the outstanding lawyers that reviewed the legal part of the book, notably Tom Allen, Helaine Heydemann and Sally Olson of Wildman, Harrold, Allen & Dixon, Chicago, Illinois, Robert V. P. Waterman of Lane and Waterman, Davenport, Iowa, Tom Riley, and Frank Mitvalsky of Cedar Rapids,

Iowa, Kenton W. Elderkin of Boston, Massachusetts, and Ansel Chapman, Retired District Court Judge, Iowa City, Iowa. An appreciation also to Robert H. Taylor, Consulting Actuary.

Our special thanks to Sister Mary Augustine Roth, Ph.D. of Mount Mercy College, Cedar Rapids, Iowa, for her review and to Linda Armitage, Librarian for Mercy Medical Center of Cedar Rapids Iowa, who cheerfully provided research material. And finally to a most competent, efficient and patient legal secretary, Carma Kucera.

We are grateful for the patience of our editor, Noah Gordon, who tirelessly reviewed the many drafts of our manuscripts and with great skill and professional competence, blended the legal and medical manuscripts into a useful and coordinated tool for the defense attorney. Lastly we thank our Production Editor, Kelly Warsak, for skillfully formatting our book and the entire staff of Prentice Hall Law & Business for making preparation of this book such a pleasant experience.

Campbell F. Watts, M.D.
David M. Elderkin, J.D.

How to Use This Book

Claim of failure to diagnose breast cancer has come to be one of the most successful lawsuits against physicians. These suits are not easily defended, primarily because the benefits of early diagnosis have been grossly over-promoted while the limitations have been largely ignored. The only defense is to present the truth by helping the jury to understand the actual facts regarding the natural history of breast cancer.

In this connection, the medical aspects presented in Part II of this book, commencing at Chapter 6, are the most important. These chapters are based upon an exhaustive study of breast cancer, which demonstrates that the majority of poor outcomes (death) from breast cancer are directly or indirectly secondary to its inherent biology, to tumor camouflaging or the limitations of clinical and technical diagnostic modality. All of these factors are entirely beyond the control of the physician. THROUGHOUT THIS BOOK THESE TRUTHS ARE STATED MANY TIMES, IN DIFFERENT WAYS. THE REPETITION IS INTENTIONAL.

While the medical section is the most important, Part I, the legal section, Chapters 1 to 5, should be read first. Its purpose is to aid defense counsel in understanding the medical section, leading counsel into it and using it in trial.

Part I is not by any means intended to be either a general primer on trial tactics or a general treatise on malpractice law. Legal literature abounds with advice covering every aspect of a lawsuit. It is assumed that the lawyer defending a breast cancer malpractice case is an experienced advocate and this book is designed only to help him or her present the defense supported by the medical section. Extensive cross-referencing from the legal section to the medical section should enable defense counsel to easily locate specific medical topics, and vice versa. In addition, the medical section contains highlighted practice pointers which provide counsel with strategies and tactics for the best use of the medical information presented in a particular section. Finally, several of the chapters have helpful appendixes and exhibits that contain sample questions, visual aids, and other materials for use in preparing for and at trial.

PART I

LEGAL SECTION

David M. Elderkin, J.D.

CHAPTER 1: THE LAW

CHAPTER 1

THE LAW

Theoretically malpractice actions may sound in contract as well as in tort, and in some instances a combination of both. Prosser points out that the fundamental difference between tort and contract lies in the nature of the interests protected. The duties of conduct which give rise to torts are imposed by the law, based primarily upon social policy and not necessarily upon the will or intention of the parties. Contract obligations are imposed because of conduct of the parties manifesting that consent and the damages recoverable for a breach of the contract duty are limited to those reasonably within the contemplation of defendant when the contract was made. In a tort action a much broader measure of damages is applied. *Law of Torts 4th Ed.*, p. 613, Prosser, William L., (1971). See also *61 AmJur2d 461.*

There are times when a patient and a physician enter into an express contract in which a particular result is assured and if the result is not obtained, a cause of action for breach of contract results, entirely separate from one of malpractice. The same case, however, may also give rise to a tort action resulting from negligent treatment. Yet while the old law school intellectual exercise of when to ''waive the tort and sue in assumpsit'' is stimulating, the question of contract or tort rarely arises in malpractice actions. Under modern code pleading, claims under both contract and tort may be made in the same pleading.

- A party may also state as many separate claims or defenses as the party has regardless of consistency and whether based on legal, equitable or maritime grounds.

F.R.C.P. Rule 8(e)(2).

Inasmuch as damages recoverable are much broader in tort cases, most malpractice actions are brought in tort and the essential elements are basic tort law. The defense must be aimed at these.

In the ordinary malpractice case the plaintiff must prove by a preponderance of the competent, credible evidence that the defendant physician violated the general standard of care, which is the requirement that the physician apply that degree of skill, care and learning ordinarily possessed and exercised by other physicians in similar circumstances. 61 AmJur2d 329, p. 486. Except in cases where the deviation from this standard of care is so obvious as to be a matter of common understanding, it must be supported by substantial expert evidence. *68 AmJur 349, p. 513*; Tiffany, F. B. *Death by Wrongful Act* #189 at 426 (2d Ed. 1913); *Johns Hopkins Hospital v. Genda,* 255 Md. 616, 258 A.2d 595 (1969); *Waffen v. U.S. Dept. of Health and Human Services,* 799 F.2d 911 (4th Cir. 1986).

After establishing negligence it becomes incumbent upon the plaintiff to also prove by a preponderance of the evidence that the negligence was a proximate cause of the injury. Unless this also is obvious, it, too, must be supported by expert evidence.

The issue thus posed relates to the doctrine of causation. Some legal students distinguish the doctrine of causation from the doctrine of proximate cause, but most courts do not, and for the purpose of this discussion, we shall treat them as the same. The test for causation is the commonly known "but for" or "sine qua non" standard. It means that the plaintiff has the burden of proof to establish that it was more likely than not—that it was probable—that the injury would not have occurred but for the defendant's negligence.

In the ordinary negligence case, including the ordinary malpractice case, the definition of causation is easy to recognize and easy to apply. In failing to diagnose breast cancer cases, (and other cases involving passive injuries), causation becomes more difficult and there is a wide variance among the various jurisdictions about its applicability.

In passive injury cases, the defendant physician does not create the plaintiff's condition—the cancer does. The charge is that the defendant physician, by reason of a delay in diagnosis or improper treatment combines with the cancer to cause the ultimate injury. The historic rule required proof that the defendant's failure to properly treat the pre-existing condition had to be a probable cause of the resultant injury. This rule has been relaxed by different theories, such as the "substantial possibility" or loss of chance rules. (See cases cited in §§1.01-1.04, inc.)

§1.01 THE TRADITIONAL RULE— CAUSATION

The traditional rule treats causation as an all or nothing proposition. Expert testimony is required that but for the defendant's negligence, the patient would probably have survived. *Rewis v. United States*, 503 F.2d 1202, 1205 (5th Cir. 1974) (applying New Mexico law); *Bryant v. Rankin,* 468 F.2d 520 (8th Cir. 1972); *Davis v. Kemp*, 225 Ark. 925, 481 S.W.2d 713 (1972); *Schenck v. Roger Williams Gen. Hosp.*, 382 A.2d 514 (R.I. 1977); *Morgenroth v. Pacific Medical Center, Inc.*, 126 Cal. Rptr. 681, 688-89 (1976); *Gooding v. University Hospital Building, Inc.*, 445 So. 2d 1015, 1018-20 (Fla. 1984); *Walden v. Jones*, 439 S.W.2d 571, 576 (Ky. Ct. App. 1968); *Cornfeldt v. Tongen,* 295 N.W.2d 638, 640 (Minn. 1980); *Nieman v. Refugio County Memorial Hospital,* 855 S.W.2d 94 (Tex. Ct. App. 1993); *Nelson v. Kelson-Seybold Clinical P.A.* No. A14-92-00931 (Tex. Ct. App. April 8, 1993); *Clayton v. Thompson,* 475 So. 2d 439, 445 (Miss. 1985); *Cooper v. Sisters of Charity of Cincinnati, Inc.,* 272 N.E.2d 97, 104 (Ohio 1971); Note, *Negligence—Medical Malpractice—Should Lack of Diligence in Diagnosis Resulting in Loss of Chance to Live Be a Compensable Injury? —Cooper v. Sisters of Charity of Cincinnati, Inc.,* 3 Seton Hall 505 (1972); *Budd v. Nixen,* 6 Cal.3d 195, 98 Cal.Rptr. 849, 491 P.2d 433 (1971); *Jones v. Ortho Phar. Corp.,* 163 Cal.App.3d 396, 309 Cal.Rptr. 456 (1985). As stated in the *Gooding* case:

> Relaxing the causation requirement might correct a perceived unfairness to some plaintiffs who could prove the possibility that the medical malpractice caused an injury but could not prove the probability of causation but at the same time it could create an injustice. Health care providers could find themselves defending cases simply because a patient fails to improve or where serious disease processes are not arrested because another course of action could possibly bring a better result. No other professional malpractice defendant carries this burden of liability without the requirement that plaintiffs prove the alleged negligence probably, rather than possibly, caused the injury.

Gooding at 1019-20.

In the *Cooper* case, the expert testimony placed a chance of survival at 50 percent; the court spelled the causation standard it had in mind: *"Some place around 50% is not a probability because 'probable is more than 50 percent'."* *Cooper* at 104.

§1.02 THE RELAXATION OF THE TRADITIONAL RULE

Medical malpractice cases, particularly cancer cases, carry with them a strong, intuitive sense of humanity which emotionally directs certain conclusions. In recent years many courts have become caught up in the feeling that because of the difficulty of proving injury in certain types of medical malpractice cases, they should apply a standard of causation more flexible than that used in conventional tort claims. *Herkovitz v. Group Health Co-Op,* 664 P.2d 474, 491 (Wash. 1983); *Estep v. Pope,* 842 P.2d 360, 362 (Okla. App. 1992). Professor King, 90 Yale L.J. 1353, 1377, observed that the all or nothing approach "subverts the deterrence objectives of tort law by denying recovery for the effects of conduct that cause statistically demonstrable losses." *Thompson v. Sun City Community Hospital, Inc.,* 141 Ariz. 597, 688 P.2d 605 (1984), stated that the all or nothing approach placed "a premium on each party's search for the willing witness," one who will utter the "magic words" 51% rather than 49%.

In any event, the problem has been addressed by many courts and commentators resulting in a wide variety of suggestions for avoiding the perceived injustice of the traditional rule. Two rules have been widely adopted by the courts, the "substantial possibility" test and the "loss of chance" doctrine. While they each have the same purpose and tend to overlap, there is a distinct difference. The "substantial possibility" test reduces the commonly accepted standard of causation in tort cases and it is substituted for the "but for" test where the harm is produced by concurrent causes. (See W. Keeton *Prosser and Keeton on Torts,* ¶41 at 266-68 (5th Ed. 1984), Malone *Ruminations on Cause and Effect* 9 Stan. L.Rev. 60, 88-90 (1956)).

Courts are divided as to whether the "loss of chance theory" is a new test of causation, a new cause of action, or a different measure of damages. King, 90 Yale L.J. 1353; *Waffen v. U.S. Dept. of Health and Human Services,* 799 F.2d 911 (4th Cir. 1986); *Cooper v. Hartman,* 533 A.2d 1297, 311 Md. 265; *Dumas v. Cooney,* 1 Cal.Rptr.2d 584 (Cal.App. 6th Dist. 1991). (See §1.04).

However construed, it lessens plaintiff's traditional burden of proof.

[a] The Substantial Possibility Rule

This standard requires the jury to determine whether the deviation alleged, in the context of the pre-existing condition, was sufficient significance in relation to the eventual harm to satisfy the requirement of proximate cause.

In applying the standard most courts have based their holdings on the language of §432(2) of the Restatement (Second) of Torts 1965, referring to a ''substantial possibility'' test. The Restatement refers to a ''substantial factor in bringing about harm'' and the leading case advancing this standard was *Hicks v. United States,* 368 F.2d 626, 632 (4th Cir. 1966) (applying Virginia law):

> When a defendant's negligent action or inaction has effectively terminated a person's chance of survival, it does not lie in the defendant's mouth to raise conjectures as to the measure of the chances that he has put beyond the possibility of realization. If there is any substantial possibility of survival and the defendant has destroyed it, he is answerable.

Actually the statement in *Hicks* was dictum; the issue of whether a relaxed standard of causation should be adopted was not presented. *Hicks* is thus questionable authority for modifying the traditional rule of causation. Nevertheless, it has been so used.

But while the ''reasonable possibility'' rule as a substitute test of causation is easy to adopt, it is less easy to apply. What is the definition of ''substantial'' and how can it be valued? In *DeBurkarte v. Louvar,* 393 N.W.2d 131 (Iowa 1986), the court defined substantial as a party's conduct that has such an effect in producing the harm as to lead a reasonable person to regard it as a cause. *Kroll v. U.S.,* 708 F.Supp. 117 (D. Md. 1989), concluded that the plaintiff must prove with reasonable certainty that a substantial chance of survival was lost, defining a substantial chance as being more than de minimis, but less than 50%.

Conduct is a substantial factor where it is of sufficient significance in producing the harm as to lead reasonable persons to regard it as a cause and to attach responsibility. *Sharp v. Kaiser Foundation Health Plan,* 710 P.2d 1153 (Colo.); see also Restatement (Second) of Torts §431, Comment A (1965). W. Prosser and W. Keeton *Torts,* ¶42 (5th Ed. 1984). An instruction that permitted recovery of damages because of a mere diminishment of the ''chance of recovery'' was held erroneous in *Clayton v. Thompson,* 475 So.2d 439 (Miss. 1985). Michigan law defines substantial possibility as a "fairly good" chance, according to *Bell v. United States,* 854 F.2d 881 (Ca. 1988). A number of courts have used the expression "loss of an opportunity for a more favorable result as distinguished from an unfavorable result." *Falcon v. Memorial Hospital,* 462 N.W.2d 44 (Mich. 1990). In *Ehlinger v. Sipes,* 454 N.W.2d 754 (Wis. 1990), the court held that the plaintiff only needed to show that the treatment omitted more probably than not could have lessened or avoided the plaintiff's injury and submitted to the trier of fact the problem of deciding whether this was a substantial factor in causing the plaintiff's harm. In *Delaney v. Cade,* 756 F.Supp. 1476, the court held that a 5% loss of chance was not an appreciable chance, stating that if the court were to recognize the same as substantial, virtually any medical decision which resulted in a less than ideal outcome would be subjected to second guessing and tort liability. To the same effect is *Waffen v. United States Department of Health and Human Services,* 799 F.2d 911 (4th Cir. 1986) and *Bryant v. Rankin,* 468 F.2d 510 (8th Cir. 1972), both of which held in effect that more is required by way of proof of harm than testimony that the sooner you find an injury, the better the chance of getting a good result. But see cases such as *James v. United States,* 483 F.Supp. 581 (N.D. Cal. 1980), holding that no matter how small a chance might have been, no one can say that the chance of prolonging one's life or decreasing suffering is valueless. Cases dealing with the substantial possibility rule include the following: *Maltempo v.Cuthbert,* 504 F.2d 325 (5th Cir. 1974); *Hoeke v. Mercy Hospital of Pittsburgh,* 445 A.2d 140, 144-45 (Pa. 1982); *Sharp v. Kaiser Foundation Health Plan of Colorado,* 710 P.2d 1153, 1156 (Colo. Ct. App. 1985) (increased risk was 20 to 25%); *Evers v. Dollinger,* 471 A.2d 405, 408-09 (N.J. 1984); *Herskovits v. Group Health Cooperative of Puget Sound,* 664 P.2d 474, 479 (Wash. 1983); *Ehlinger v. Sipes,* 454 N.W.2d 754 (Wis. 1990); *Bell v. United States,* 854 F.2d 881, 890 (6th Cir. 1988); *Hamil v. Bashline,* 392 A.2d 1280 (Pa. 1978); *Scafidi v. Seiler,* 543 A.2d 95 (N.J. 1988); *Falcon v. Memorial Hospital,* 462 N.W.2d 44 (Mich. 1990). In *Richmond County Hospital Authority Operating University Hospital v. Dickerson,* 356 S.E.2d 548 (Ga. Ct. App. 1987), the patient had a less than 50 percent opportunity of survival. In *Morales v. United States,* 642 F. Supp. 269 (D.P.R. 1986), survival was a "possibility." In *Cloys v. Turbin,* 608 S.W.2d 697, 700 (Tex. Civ. App. 1980), the court said that a plaintiff must establish a "reasonably close causal connection between the defending party's conduct and the resulting injury to the complaining party." *Kallenberg v. Beth Israel Hospital,* 357 N.Y.S.2d 508 (1974), aff'd 337 N.E.2d 128 (N.Y. 1975). Although a confusing case, it would appear that a mere 2 percent chance of survival represented a substantial possibility. See also Restatement (Second) of Torts §431, Comment A (1965); W. Prosser and W. Keeton *Torts,* ¶42, 5th Ed. 1984); *Thompson v. Sun City Community Hospital, Inc.,* 688 P.2d 605 (Ariz. 1984); Green *The Causal Relation Issue,* 68 Mich. L.Rev. 543 (1962); Malone *Ruminations on Cause in Fact,* 9 Stan. L.Rev. 1956; *Boody v. U.S.,* 706 F.Supp. 1458 (D. Kan. 1989); *Shumaker v. U.S.,* 714 F.Supp. 154 (M.D. N.C. 1988); Rosati *Causation in Medical Malpractice: A Modified Valuation Approach,* 50 Ohio St. L.J. 469 (1989). Note: *Medical Malpractice: The Increased Risk Rule: Establishing "Probable" Causation Through Mere Possibility,* 27 Ariz. L.Rev. 257 (1985).

[b] Loss of Chance

A growing number of courts have adopted what has become known as a "loss of chance" theory. The purpose is the same as that behind the "substantial possibility" rule—to avoid the perceived injustice of the probability standard. *James v. United States,* 483 F.Supp. 581 (N.D. Cal. 1980), *Waffen v. United States Department of Health and Human Services,* 799 F.2d 911 (4th Cir. 1986), and other cases hold that this theory does not change or lower the traditional standard of causation, but simply creates a new cause of action. It would appear that King also considered it such. Under his theory, the causation issue was avoided—or "satisfied"—under the traditional standard—because the injury being compensated was the loss of a chance of avoiding the harm and not the harm itself. King *Causation, Valuation and Chance in Personal Injury Torts Involving Pre-Existing Conditions and Future Consequences,* 90 Yale L.J. 1353 (1981). Other courts have described King's loss of chance theory as leaving the traditional rules of causation intact, but treating the loss of chance as a way of approaching damages. *Cooper v. Hartman,* 533 A.2d at 1297 (311 Md. 265); *Weimer v. Hetrick,* 525 A.2d 643 (Md. 1987).

> A claim under that theory does not involve the creation of a new tort, but rather involves a redefinition of damages involved in the claim.

Weimer, supra

Historically the theory came from the English case of *Chaplin v. Hicks,* 2 K.B. 786 (1911) wherein the plaintiff, an actress, lost an acting engagement because her manager negligently failed to notify her that she had been selected as a candidate for 12 available positions. Loss of chance in the area of malpractice law is relatively new, developing from the man overboard doctrine in maritime law where the captain of a vessel has the duty to search for a seaman who has been lost overboard. *Gardner v. National Bulk Carriers, Inc.*, 310 F.2d 284 (4th Cir. 1962). Where the seaman was lost overboard and the master of his ship failed to reverse the ship's course to conduct a search for the missing seaman, the master was held liable on proof that the master's omission destroyed a reasonable possibility of rescue even in the absence of a specific showing that the lost seaman could have been saved had the ship's course been reversed and a search conducted. Obviously, upon application of this doctrine, the liability of physicians and hospitals was broadened.

The doctrine has been most clearly articulated and advanced by Professor King, supra.

Prof. King stated that all too often examination of causation is not accompanied by analysis of its companion concept of valuation, the process of identifying and assessing the value of the interest destroyed. Even when valuation is considered with causation, understanding often is inhibited by a tendency to commingle the concepts. Causation refers to the cause and effect relationship that must be established between tortious conduct and a loss before liability for that loss can be imposed.

According to Prof. King, causation has for the most part been treated as an all or nothing proposition. Either a loss was caused by the defendant or it was not. Inexplicably the all or nothing approach of the causation inquiry has been allowed to slip its analytical moorings, influencing the identification and valuation of losses in cases involving pre-existing conditions and claims for future consequences. A plaintiff ordinarily should be required to prove by the applicable standard of proof that the defendant caused the loss in question. What caused the loss should be a separate question for the nature and extent of what the loss is. Most courts have misperceived the nature of the interest destroyed by failing to identify the destroyed chance itself as a compensable loss.

King, in support of his argument, postulated a game of chance in which the wheel gave the player 10 chances of winning and 9 chances of losing. The defendant tortiously prevented the plaintiff's hand from placing a bet. Since the defendant's conduct deprived the plaintiff of a probable win, the traditional rule would award the plaintiff the entire jackpot. If the plaintiff have 50/50 odds, however, i.e., 10 chances of winning and 10 chances of losing, the plaintiff would recover zero. King proposed this as an obvious inequity:

> A better method of valuation would measure a compensable chance as a percentage probability by which the defendant's tortious conduct diminished the likelihood of achieving some more favorable outcome. *Id.*

Although the courts have not always clearly stated the basis for recognizing the loss of chance theory, many, if not the majority, have adopted it in one form or another. *DeBurkarte v. Louvar,* 393 N.W.2d 131 (Iowa 1986); *McBride v. United States,* 462 F.2d 72, 75 (9th Cir. 1972) (applying Hawaii law); *O'Brien,* 443 F.2d at 1018 (applying Iowa law); *Jeanes v. Milner,* 428 F.2d 598, 604-605 (8th Cir. 1970) (applying Arkansas law); *Hicks v. United States,* 368 F.2d 626, 632-33 (4th Cir. 1966) (applying Virginia law); *Mays v. United States,* 608 F.Supp. 1476, 1482 (D.Colo. 1985) (applying Colorado law); *James v. United States,* 483 F.Supp. 581, 587 (N.D. Cal. 1980) (applying California law); *Thompson v. Sun City Community Hospital, Inc.,* 141 Ariz. 597, 688 P.2d 605, 616 (1984); *Sharp v. Kaiser Foundation Health Plan,* 710 P.2d 1153, 1156 (Colo. App. 1985); *Northern Trust Co. v. Louis A. Weiss Memorial Hospital,* 143 Ill.App.3d 479, 97 Ill.Dec. 524, 529-30, 493 N.E.2d 6, 11-12 (1986); *Roberson v. Counselman,* 235 Kan. 1006, 686 P.2d 149, 159-60 (1984); *Glicklich v. Spievack,* 16 Mass.App. 488, 452 N.E.2d 287, 292, *reh'g denied,* 454 N.E.2d 1276 (Mass. 1984); *Aasheim v. Humberger,* 695 P.2d 824, 828 (Mont. 1985); *Evers v. Dollinger,* 95 N.J. 399, 471 A.2d 405, 415 (1984); *Kallenberg v. Beth Israel Hospital,* 45 App.Div.2d 177, 357 N.Y.S.2d 508, 510-11 (1974), *aff'd,* 37 N.Y.2d 719, 374 N.Y.S.2d 615, 337 N.E.2d 128 (1975); *Morrison v. Stallworth,* 73 N.C.App. 196, 326 S.E.2d 387, 393 (1985); *Jones v. Montefiore Hospital,* 494 Pa. 410, 431 A.2d 920, 924 (1981); *Sherer v. James,* 286 S.C. 304, 334 S.E.2d 283, 285 (App. 1985); *Truan v. Smith,* 578 S.W.2d 73, 76-77 (Tenn. 1979); *Cloys v. Turbin,* 608 S.W.2d 697, 701 (Tex.Civ.App. 1980); *Brown v. Koulizakis,* 229 Va. 524, 331 S.E.2d 440, 446 (1985); *Herskovits v. Group Health Cooperative,* 99 Wash.2d 609, 664 P.2d 474 (1983). See Comment: *Recovery for "Loss of Chance",* 59 Wash.L.Rev. 981 (1984).

Some courts have limited the loss of chance theory to cases involving loss of chance of survival. *Delaney v. Cade,* 756 F.Supp. 1476. *Blank v. Southern Maryland Hospital Center, Inc.,* 320 M.D. 776, 580 A.2d 206

(1990). Other cases, however, have not. *Jones v. Montefiore Hospital,* 494 Pa. 410, 431 A.2d 920 (1981); *Thompson v. Sun City Community Hospital, Inc.,* 141 Ariz. 597, 688 P.2d 605 (1984); *Ehlinger v. Sipes,* 155 Wis.2d 1, 454 N.W.2d 754 (1990); *Herskovits v. Group Health Cooperative of Puget Sound,* 99 Wash.2d 609, 664 P.2d 474 (1983):

> It is not necessary for the plaintiff to introduce evidence to establish that the negligence resulted in the injury or death, but simply that the negligence increased the risk of injury or death.

See also Annotation, *Medical Malpractice: "Loss of Chance Causality",* 54 ALR4th 11 (1987).

While the law differs in the different jurisdictions, the loss of chance concept seems to be increasingly accepted, conditioned upon the companion rule of allowing damages for the loss of chance only. (See Damages, §1.03, supra).

§1.03 DAMAGES

In the ordinary tort case where there is proof that defendant's tortious conduct caused the plaintiff's injury, the damage question is relatively simple, or at least simple by definition. In medical malpractice cases where the defendant is not alleged to have caused the injury but only charged with reducing the chance of the plaintiff avoiding the injury, the problem becomes more difficult. As Prof. King has pointed out:

> In these cases courts have historically had difficulty in separating the issues of causation and evaluation of damages.

Under the more probable, measured as more than the 50% approach, the plaintiff who establishes that she had more than a 50% opportunity of not suffering physical harm if the defendant had not acted negligently receives 100% of the damages. The better than even opportunity is compensated as if it were a certainty, even though plaintiff's chances of a better result are significantly less than 100%. See *Falcon v. Memorial Hospital,* 462 N.W.2d 44 (Mich. 1990).

Under the reasonable possibility or loss of chance theory, to permit damages based on the underlying injury, the unfairness is even more pronounced. See *Kallenberg v. Beth Israel Hospital,* 357 N.Y.S.2d 508 (1924); *Thompson v. Sun City Community Hospital,* 141 Ariz. 598, 688

P.2d 605 (1984). Under the reasoning of these cases a patient can recover all damages resulting from an injury for which the defendant may be only partly responsible. See also *Daniels v. Hadley Mem. Hosp.*, 566 F.2d 749 (D.C. Cir. 1977); *McBride v. U.S.*, 462 F.2d 72 (9th Cir. 1972). This is an extreme position. See Note, 27 Ariz. L.Rev. 257, 262-63 (1985).

The majority of cases formulate a new legal injury—risk exposure—and hold that the defendant is liable if the plaintiff proves that there was such a risk exposure and the defendant was a cause of it. Since the injury on which damages are based is the risk exposure that led to the injury rather than the injury itself, liability is limited to the proportion of the manifested injury that is equivalent to the increase in risk that the defendant caused. This position has been supported by Prof. King:

> The defendant should be subject to liability only to the extent that he tortiously contributed to the harm by allowing a pre-existing condition to progress or by aggravating or accelerating its harmful effects or to the extent that he otherwise caused harm in excess of that attributable solely to pre-existing conditions. The effect of pre-existing conditions should depend on the extent to which such conditions affect the present and future value of the interest lost.

King, supra.

One court, holding that recovery could only be for the lost chance of survival reasoned as follows:

> To illustrate, consider the case in which a doctor negligently fails to diagnose a patient's cancerous condition until it has become inoperable. Assume further that even with a timely diagnosis the patient would have had only a 30% chance of recovering from the disease and surviving over the long term. There are two ways of handling such a case. Under the traditional approach, this loss of a not better than even chance of recovering from the cancer would not be compensable because it did not appear more likely than not that the patient would have survived with proper care. Recoverable damages, if any, would depend on the extent to which it appeared that cancer killed the patient sooner than it would have with timely diagnosis and treatment and on the extent to which the delay in diagnosis aggravated the patient's condition, such as by causing additional pain. A more rational approach, however, would allow recovery for the loss of the chance of cure even though the chance was not better than even. The probability of long term survival would be reflected in the amount of damages awarded for the loss of chance. While the plaintiff here could not prove

> by a preponderance of the evidence that he was denied a cure by the defendant's negligence, he could show by a preponderance of the evidence that he was deprived of a 30% chance of cure.

DeBurkarte v. Louvar, 393 N.W.2d at 137 (Iowa 1986).

Interestingly, the Iowa Court's adoption of the lost chance theory in *DeBurkarte* was gratuitous as far as the facts in the case were concerned. The expert testimony was that the plaintiff had probably lost a 50-80 chance of survival and the loss of chance issue was never really in the case. While the court stated the instructions limited plaintiff's damages to the lost chance, this is less than clear.

The same reasoning, however, is found in *Cudone v. Gehret,* 821 F.Supp. 266 (D. Del 1994) and *Falcon v. Memorial Hospital,* 462 N.W.2d 44 (Mich. 1990). See also Wagner and Hart, *Making A Long Shot Longer,* Brief, 12 & 37 (Spring 1990), Andel, *Medical Malpractice: The Right to Recover for the Loss of a Chance of Survival,* 12 Pepperdine L. Rev. 973, 974 (1985). For a detailed discussion, see Annotation, *Medical Malpractice: Measure and Elements of Damages in Actions Based on Loss of Chance,* 81 A.L.R.4th 485 (1990).

In *Mays v. United States,* 608 F.Supp. 1476, 1482 (D. Colo. 1985), the court found that the malpractice reduced the patient's opportunity of survival from 40% to 15%. The court spelled out that in computing damages, the opportunity lost, 25% (40% less 15%) would be multiplied by the net pecuniary loss to determine the damages.

A case discussing the causation and damage issues at length is the case of *Scafidi v. Seiler,* 574 A.2d 398 (N.J. 1990), which added a new twist by holding that in cases where the damages are apportionable between the pre-existing condition and defendant's negligence, the defendant has the burden of proving what part of the harm is not attributable to his negligence. *Id.* at 401. The general rule, of course, is that the burden of proof rests upon the plaintiff to prove recoverable damages flowing from an alleged act of negligence. *Prosser and Keeton on Torts,* 41 at 269 & note 1 (5th Ed. 1984). In this connection, *Scafidi* has not been generally followed.

See *Johns Hopkins Hosp. v. Genda,* 258 A.2d 595 (1969) and *Weimer v. Hetrick,* 525 A.2d 643 (Md. 1987). For extensive discussion of damages permitted by the different jurisdictions under the several forms of causation, see *Causation in Medical Malpractice: A Modified Valuation Approach,* Rosati, Jack, Ohio State L.J. Vol. 50:469 (1989); also Christine A. Carolan, Rutgers L.J. Vol. 23:169 (1991). An interesting article is *Causation Responsibility, Risk, Probability, Naked Statistics and Proof; Pruning the Bramble Bush by Clarifying the Concepts,* Wright, R.W., Vol. 73 Iowa L.Rev. No. 5, 1001 at 1067.

In applying or instructing upon the proper method of arriving at damages, courts have taken different approaches. The court in *Borgren v. United States,* 723 F.Supp. 581 (D. Kan. 1989), held, for example, that it would determine plaintiff's damages by arriving at a compensatory figure which would justify and adequately compensate the claimant for her damages rather than by taking the value of claimant's life and multiplying it by the percentage chance of survival loss. It quoted Judge Theis in *Boody v. United States,* 706 F.Supp. 1458 (D. Kan. 1989) as holding that:

> One could calculate damages by taking the value of plaintiff's life and multiplying it by the percentage of the chance of survival loss with the resulting amount being the compensation for the loss of chance of survival.

It disagreed with Judge Theis, stating that there was no real difference between this method and arriving at a compensatory figure which would justify and adequately compensate the plaintiff for damages. Both, said the court in *Borgren,* are subjective. But see *Delaney v. Cady,* 873 P.2d 175 (Kan. 1994).

While this may be true, the fact is that most courts in arriving at damages under the loss of chance approach do, as the court did in *Mays v. United States,* supra, compute damages by taking the net pecuniary loss of plaintiff's life and multiplying it by the opportunity lost.

> The finder of fact should take into account both the plaintiff's chances of survival if properly treated and the extent to which the plaintiff's chances have been reduced by the claimed negligence.

Roberson v. Counselman, 686 P.2d 149 (Kan. 1984).

Should plaintiff be required to quantify the chance allegedly lost? Should damages be restricted to loss of an appreciable chance and, if so, what is appreciable? 10%? 5%? It is conceivable that a 1% chance of survival recovery would be appreciable.

The court in *James v. United States,* 482 F.Supp. 581 (N.D. Cal. 1980), seemed to think so, holding that no matter how small a chance might have been, no one can say that the chance of prolonging one's life or decreasing suffering is valueless. In the case of *Kallenberg v. Beth Israel Hospital,* 357 N.Y.S. 508 (1974), plaintiff was allowed to recover wrongful death damages for a 20 to 40% chance of survival for a 3-day delay in treatment. Yet, most courts have recognized that the loss of chance, to be compensable, must be substantial, something beyond just any chance. *Delaney v. Cade,* 756 F.Supp. 1476 (U.S. D.C. Kan. 1991), specifically rejected a 5% chance as de minimis. See also *Waffen v. U.S. Dept. of Health and Human Services,* 799 F.2d 911 (4th Cir. 1986).

As all experienced trial lawyers know, the question of damages in any case has its difficulties, particularly in cases where juries are faced with a quagmire of statistical evidence. To apply statistical chances of survival before a negligent treatment, then subtract the statistical chance of survival after the negligent treatment, then multiply these figures times the value of the loss of life is no easy thing. Juries are more often than not left in a morass of confusion and their answer is guesswork. It has to be guesswork because the evidence of the loss of chance they are attempting to evaluate is in itself guesswork. Always. (Chapters 10 and 11).

§1.04 CRITICISM OF SUBSTANTIAL POSSIBILITY AND LOSS OF CHANCE RULES

Traditional tort law is based upon probabilities. Where it is alleged that the defendant directly caused injury or death, the plaintiff has the burden of proof to establish that it was more likely than not—that it was probable—that the injury would not have occurred but for the defendant's negligence.

This is also the rule in medical malpractice cases where it is alleged that the defendant physician directly caused the injury or death of the patient.

When, however, it is admitted that the physician did not create the injury, but that the same was a pre-existing condition, under the substantial possibility or loss of chance rule, a different situation exists—the plaintiff is then permitted a lower standard of causation or handed a new cause of action. See *Evers v. Dallenjer,* 471 A.2d 405 (N.J. 1984).

Thus a defendant physician under either the substantial possibility or loss of chance concept can and is held liable for damages resulting from the death of the patient when it was the pre-existing condition that caused the death. To hold a defendant physician liable on the theory that the physician's negligence deprived plaintiff of, for example, a 30% chance of recovery, ignores the fact that it was 70% probable it did not. As stated by the court in *Gooding v. University Hospital Building, Inc.* 445 So.2d 1015 (Fla. 1984):

> No other professional malpractice defendant carries this burden of liability without the requirement that the plaintiffs prove the alleged negligence probably, rather than possibly, caused the injury.

As the court observed in *Atkins v. Clein,* 3 Wash.2d 168, 100 P.2d 1 (1940):

> The physician serves a vital function in our society, a function which requires the assumption of a duty to the patient. Yet his profession affords him only an inexact and often experimental science by which to discharge his duties. Moreover, the tendency to place blame on a physician who fails to find a cure is great. Thus, policy considerations do not on balance weigh in favor of abandoning the well established requirements of proximate cause. Yet, both the "substantial possibility" and "loss of chance" rules do exactly this.

The motive in changing the traditional rule is to make it easier for unfortunate plaintiffs, suffering from a vicious and sometimes incurable disease to obtain, or make it easier to obtain compensation in a particular class of cases from a particular group of defendants.

From a plaintiff's point of view, the effort is laudable. From a defendant's point of view, it is not. And the support given for the relaxation of the traditional rule does not stand scrutiny, either logically nor legally.

In *Roberson v. Counselman,* 235 Kan. 106, 686 P.2d 148, the Supreme Court of Kansas justified its recognition of the loss of chance theory in cases involving a less than a 50/50 chance of recovery on the basis that without it a physician might simply ignore a critically injured person simply because that person had a less than 50% chance of surviving. To follow the probability doctrine, "would declare open season on the critically ill." If the loss of chance doctrine is to be based upon medical ethics, some rebuttal might be in order.

Some courts, as does *Thompson v. Sun City Community Hospital, Inc.,* 141 Ariz. 597, 688 P.2d 605 (1984), argue that requiring a plaintiff to prove her case on the basis of probability—more than 50%—places "a premium on each party's search for the willing witness." (*Thompson,* at p. 615).

Actually, a reading of the advertisements in *Trial* magazine or even the *American Law Journal* indicates that willing witnesses are readily available in any field, including cancer. It is quite true that it is often difficult for a plaintiff to find expert witnesses who will give a professional opinion under oath that in a cancer case it was more probable that the physician killed the patient than the cancer. However, this isn't because witnesses are not readily available nor does it mean that they are any less willing, it simply means that current medical knowledge (Chapter 6, et seq.) will seldom support such an opinion. This is conceived as being hard on an ''innocent'' patient. The harshness, however, comes from the scientific fact that it is more likely than not that the plaintiff's death or injury was caused by the biology of the disease rather than any act on the part of the physician. (Chapter 10). But instead of accepting this scientific fact, the majority of courts have either reduced the ordinary causation requirements in this particular kind of action or have adopted a loss of chance cause of action on the premise that it is the purpose of tort law to compensate for lost chances. This abandons the truth seeking function of the law. If the acts of the defendant did not actually cause plaintiff's injury, then there is no rational justification for requiring the defendant to bear the cost of plaintiff's damages.

As stated in the chapter on the ''substantial possibility'' rule (§1.02 [a]), most courts have based their holdings on the language of §432(2) of the Restatement (Second) of Torts (1965) referring to a ''substantial possibility'' test. The Restatement refers to a 'substantial factor in bringing about harm'' and the leading case advancing this standard was *Hicks v. United States,* 368 F.2d 626, 632 (4th Cir. 1966).

> When a defendant's negligent action or inaction has effectively terminated a person's chance of survival, it does not lie in the defendant's mouth to raise conjecture as to the measure of the chances that he has put beyond the possibility of realization. If there is any substantial possibility of survival and the defendant has destroyed it, he is answerable.

But the statement in *Hicks* was dictum; the issue of whether a relaxed standard of causation should be adopted was not presented. *Hicks* is thus questionable authority for modifying the traditional rule of causation.

In the same manner a number of courts have adopted the loss of chance doctrine on the basis of the Restatement (Second) of Torts, p. 323(A), 135 (1965) reading:

> One who undertakes to render services to another which he should recognize as necessary for the protection of the other person or things is subject to liability to the other for physical harm resulting from his failure to exercise reasonable care to perform his undertaking if (a) his failure to exercise such care increases the risk of harm.

This section does not deal at all with causation. It elaborates only on the scope of the duty on the part of those who undertake to render services to another. As Professor Wright in his article on *Causation Responsibility, Risk, Probability, Naked Statistics and Proof: Pruning a Bramble Bush by Clarifying the Concepts,* 73 Iowa L.Rev. 1001 (1988) states:

> The Restatement provision does not indicate any intention to depart from the ordinary requirements for approving causation which are covered under Sections 431 and 433B of the Restatement.

Probably the greatest reliance by the courts adopting the loss of chance theory has been on the article by Professor King, *Causation, Valuation and Chance in Personal Injury Torts Involving Pre-Existing Conditions and Future Consequences,* 90 Yale L.J. 1353 (1981), as discussed in the section on loss of chance, §1.02[b], supra.

> The plaintiff ordinarily should be required to prove by the applicable standard of proof that the defendant caused the loss in question. What caused the loss should be a separate question for the nature and extent of what the loss is. *King,* supra.

Not all courts are agreed on what Prof. King's loss of chance theory does. Some have stated that it leaves the traditional rules of causation intact, but creates a new cause of action. *James v. United States,* 483 F.Supp. 581 (N.D. Cal. 1980); *Waffen v. United States Department of Health and Human Services,* 799 F.2d 911 (4th Cir. 1986).

Other courts have stated that the theory leaves the traditional rules of causation intact, does not create a new cause of action, but treats the loss of chance as a way of approaching damages. *Cooper v. Hartman,* 533 A.2d 1297 (311 Md. 265); *Weimer v. Hetrick,* 525 A.2d 643 (Md. 1987).

But see *Dumas v. Cooney,* 1 Cal. Rptr.2d 584 (Cal.App. 6th Dist. 1991):

> Finally the lost chance theory is, in reality, focused on causation rather than injury or damage.

Whatever label applied to the loss of chance theory is of no moment. However described, it is subject to logical as well as legal criticism.

> Because loss of chance recovery is based on statistical probabilities, it might be appropriate to examine the statistical probabilities of achieving a "just" result with loss of chance damages. In Brennwald, *Proving Causation in Loss of Chance Cases: A Proportional Approach,* 34 Cath. U.L.Rev. 747 (1985), the author, citing Orloff and Stedinger's article *A Framework for Evaluating the Preponderance of the Evidence Standard,* 131 U.Pa.L.Rev. 1159 (1983), attempted to analyze statistically the errors produced using traditional tort recovery as compared to the errors produced by loss of chance recovery.
>
> To compare the two rules, assuming a hypothetical group of 99 cancer patients, each of whom would have had a 33-⅓% chance of survival. Each received negligent medical care and all 99 died. Traditional tort law would deny recovery in all 99 cases because each patient had less than a 50% chance of recovery and the probable cause of death was the pre-existing cancer, not the negligence. Statistically had all 99 received proper treatment, 33 would have lived and 66 would have died; so the traditional rule would have statistically produced 33 errors by denying recovery to all 99.
>
> The loss of chance rule would allow all 99 patients to recover, but each would recover 33-⅓% of the normal value of the case. Again, with proper care, 33 patients would have survived. Thus, the 33 patients who statistically would have survived with proper care would receive only ⅓ of the appropriate recovery while the 66 patients who died as a result of the pre-existing condition, not the negligence, would be overcompensated by one-third. The loss of chance rule would have produced errors in all 99 cases.

Fennell v. Southern Maryland Hosp., 580 A.2d 206 (Md. 1990).

The *Fennell* court also observed that another factor weighing against adoption of a loss of chance damages approach is its practical application in civil jury trials.

> Probabilities and statistical evidence comprise a substantial portion of the evidence submitted to the trier of fact in loss of chance actions. This evidence will generally be in the form of opinions based on statistics that show chance of survival of other individuals similarly situated to the victim. The use of statistics in trial is subject to criticism as being unreliable, misleading, easily manipulated and confusing to a jury. When large damage awards will be based on the statistical chance of survival before the negligent treatment, minus the statistical chance of survival after the negligent treatment, times the value of the lost life, we can imagine the bewildering sets of numbers with which the jury

> will be confronted, as well as the difficulties juries will have in assessing the comparative reliability of the divergent statistical evidence offered by each side.
>
> If the patient had a 51% chance of dying from an injury or disease and was negligently treated and died, it was probably the pre-existing medical condition, not the negligence, that killed the patient. Damages must be proven by a preponderance of the evidence. Damages are not proven when it is more likely than not that death was caused by the antecedent disease or injury rather than the negligence of the physician.

Fennell, supra, at p. 214.

A number of other courts have rejected the loss of chance rule for other and different reasons. See e.g., Connecticut, *LaBieniec v. Baker,* 11 Conn.App. 199, 526 A.2d 1341 (1987); Florida, *Gooding v. University Hosp. Bldg. Inc.,* 445 So.2d 1015 (Fla. 1984); Indiana, *Watson v. Medical Emergency Services,* 532 N.E.2d 1191 (Ind.Ct.App. 1989); Maine, *Phillips v. Eastern Maine Medical Center,* 565 A.2d 306 (Me. 1989); New Hampshire, *Pillsbury-Flood v. Portsmouth Hospital,* 128 N.H. 299, 512 A.2d 1126 (1986); New Mexico, *Alfonso v. Lund,* 783 F.2d 958 (10th Cir. 1986); and Ohio, *Cooper v. Sisters of Charity of Cincinnati, Inc.,* 27 Ohio St.2d 242, 272 N.E.2d 97 (1971).

The court in *Dumas v. Cooney,* 1 Cal.Rptr.2d 584 (Cal. App. 6th Dist. 1991), stated:

> Imperfect as it may be, our legal system attempts to ascertain facts to arrive at the truth. To protect the integrity of that goal, there must be some degree of certainty regarding causation before a jury may determine as fact that a medical defendant did cause the plaintiff's injury and should therefore compensate the plaintiff in damages. To dispense with this requirement is to abandon the truth seeking function of the law. Prof. King is willing to do so in his attempt to compensate for the precise magnitude of any lost chance. Prof. King's criticism of the more likely than not standard for causation, like the lost chance theory itself, is based on the erroneous premise that it is the purpose of tort law to compensate for lost chances. But tort law should not operate by the same principles that govern lotteries.

Nor can it. Prof. King, in developing his loss of chance theory to cancer cases, reasons from the analogy of a lottery wheel which gives the players 10 chances of winning and 9 chances of losing. The plaintiff is tortiously prevented from placing a bet. Since the defendant's conduct deprived the plaintiff of a probable win, the traditional rule would award the plaintiff the entire jackpot. If the plaintiff had 50/50 odds, however, i.e., 10 chances of winning and 10 chances of losing, the plaintiff would recover zero. King proposed that a better method of valuation would measure a compensable chance as a percentage probability by which the defendant's tortious conduct diminished the likelihood of achieving some more favorable outcome. King *Causation, Valuation and Chance in Personal Injury Torts Involving Pre-Existing Conditions and Future Consequences,* 90 Yale L.J. 1353 (1981).

Professor King's gambling scenario points up, albeit inadvertently, the infirmity of the loss of chance doctrine. Prof. King, assuming one game of chance, postulates 10 chances of winning and 9 chances of losing, or 10 chances of winning and 10 chances of losing. Unless Prof. King is omniscient, these are assumptions. He made them up.

By the same token, any expert witness addressing himself or herself to one particular patient claiming that a year's delay in diagnosis, for example, reduced plaintiff's chances of a better result by a certain percentage is not talking about probabilities, but upon assumptions that are really no more valid than the assumptions made by Prof. King. (See §§ 11.05 and 18.06).

Cancer is a cruel disease and the efforts of other courts to help ''innocent'' plaintiffs is understandable. Yet the generally accepted rule on causation is no more harsh when applied to cancer medical malpractice cases than it is to any other form of tort action. As one court observed:

> If lost chance is just in the context of a medical malpractice action, it would be equally just and applicable in such actions involving other professions, including the legal profession. For example, if a disgruntled or unsuccessful litigant loses a case and it could be shown through expert testimony that there was a 40% chance of winning the case, that the lawyer's negligent efforts reduced the chances of winning by some degree, the litigant would be able to pursue an action based upon the loss of chance doctrine. The injury would be the loss of chance as opposed to the unfavorable verdict.

Perez v. Las Vegas Medical Center, 805 P.2d 599, footnote 3 (Dis. Opn. of Steffen, J.)

As stated in *Dumas,* supra, the loss of chance theory transforms tort law from a compensatory system to a payout scheme on the basis of a statistical chance that the defendant caused the plaintiff's death.

The old saying that hard cases make bad law is truly applicable in cancer malpractice cases.

Obviously criticisms of the ''substantial possibility'' and ''loss of chance'' theories will have little, if any, effect on courts that have firmly embraced these concepts. However, not all courts have done so and in these courts the unfairness of the less than probable causation requirements can be forcibly addressed. It would appear that the following jurisdictions have not clearly recognized the doctrine:

See e.g., Colorado, *Mays v. United States,* 608 F.Supp. 1476 (D.Colo. 1985); but see *Kaiser Foundation Health Plan v. Sharp,* 7841 P.2d 714 (Colo. 1987); Illinois, *Chambers v. Rush-Pres.-St. Luke's Med. Ctr.,* 155 Ill.App.3d 458, 108 Ill.Dec. 265, 508 N.E.2d 426 (1987); but see *Curry v. Summer,* 136 Ill.App.3d 468, 91 Ill.Dec. 365, 483 N.E.2d 711 (1985) and *Hare v. Foster G. McGaw Hosp.,* 192 Ill.App.3d 1031, 140 Ill.Dec. 127, 549 N.E.2d 778 (1989); Louisiana, *Smith v. State Through Dept. HHR,* 523 So.2d 815 (La. 1988); *Bourne v. Seventh Ward General Hosp.,* 546 So.2d 197 (La.Ct.App. 1989) and *Hastings v. Baton Rouge Gen. Hosp,* 498 So.2d 713 (La. 1986), but see *Bartley v. Pailet,* 527 So.2d 430 (La.Ct.App. 1988) and *Pierre v. Lallie Kemp Charity Hospl,* 515 So.2d 614 (La.Ct.App. 1987).

In all cases a forcible attack can be made to the jury. It bears repeating that in any case involving failure to diagnose or treat, plaintiff brings the cancer to the defendant, the defendant does not create it. As set out in the medical part of this book, there is no way that any expert can say with any degree of reasonable certainty when a particular cancer metastasized. (Chapter 10). The overwhelming odds are that in any given case the cancer metastasized before it could be discovered by any known method. Any expert opinion that some particular delay resulted in a loss of a chance of recovery or extended survival is total speculation. To hold a defendant liable on the basis of possibilities only is unfair. It is unfair from a legal standpoint, and as shown by the medical portion of this book, unfair from the standpoint of the nature of the disease being dealt with.

CHAPTER 2: PREPARING YOUR DEFENSE

CHAPTER 2

PREPARING YOUR DEFENSE

§2.01 PRELIMINARY

As stated in the section on How to Use This Book, page 1, the purpose of the first five chapters is to help counsel in understanding and using the medical section of the book commencing with Chapter 6. While, as stated, it is not intended to be a primer on trial tactics, it must be kept in mind that the defenses available must be made aggressively.

Many defense counsels consider their role to be just that: to defend, to concede the momentum to the plaintiff, sit back and try to counter plaintiff's moves.

We have an adversary system for the trial of lawsuits. A trial is combat. It is combat within the ethics of the profession and within the atmosphere of professionalism. But it is combat, nonetheless.

It is said that when Franklin D. Roosevelt was elected president, he paid a visit to Justice Oliver Wendell Holmes, and stated: "Mr. Justice, you have lived many years, had many experiences and seen many things. What advice do you have for me?" To which Justice Holmes replied: "Mr. President, you are in a war. In a war, one marshals his forces and carries the fight to the enemy."

A lawyer should fight the war as a warrior and not as an assassin, but fight a war, nevertheless. The plaintiff's enemy is cancer, not the physician. The defense should commence when the client first appears and move quickly on the date counsel enters an appearance and files an answer. Preparation should always be on the basis of combat, not with the thought of settlement. Settlements come, of course, during the pendency of the action, but easier when one is prepared to try the lawsuit.

§2.02 LEARN ABOUT BREAST CANCER

In defending a breast cancer malpractice case defense counsel has many issues to face. Did the physician actually violate the standards of care? If so, how much time was actually lost? Lastly, if earlier diagnosis should have been made, was there causation—did the delay actually cause any harm?

To defend against a charge of failure to timely diagnose cancer, one must have a knowledge of the biology and natural history of cancer. To prepare this defense, to ask good questions, and to handle the expert witnesses the defense lawyer must learn about the disease process. Dr. Watts has spent a lifetime in practice and in research and the results of his study are set out in the medical section of this book at Chapter 6, et seq. A synopsis of these chapters, with appropriate references is as follows:

[a] What is a Cancer?

[1] Generally (Chapter 10) A cancer can be defined as a cellular tumor, the natural course of which is usually fatal. It is called cancer, which is a Latin word for crab, because of the crab-like extensions of cancer cells which invade into the adjacent normal tissues. It will be easier to understand cancer if we become familiar with the normal behavior of the cells that line the ducts and glands of the breast.

Normal breast cells cannot wander through the breast. The normal breast cells which form the lining of the duct and milk glands are firmly anchored to a structure (basement membrane) upon which they rest. They cannot move.

The growth of normal breast cells is controlled by certain genes. These genes direct the production of proteins which regulate the growth of the cell and tell the cell when to grow and when to stop growing. The growth regulatory process of a normal cell has well defined start and stop signals.

Breast cancers arise from a single breast duct cell when the genes controlling the growth of the cell are altered or damaged by a series of unknown events. When the growth regulatory genes of the breast duct cell are altered or damaged, the genes can no longer control or modulate growth. They are unable to tell the cell when to stop growing. The stop signal of the regulatory growth process has been lost. A cancer cell has been created. The cancer cell can now grow endlessly without aging.

Genes can be altered in a number of ways. Genes that suppress cell growth may be "turned off" and uncontrolled cell growth results. Genes that are associated with cell growth may be "turned on," thus stimulating the growth and metastasis of the cell.

The genes are the driving force which determine the behavior of the cancer. Some tumors can invade locally only and others can invade locally and also metastasize to distant sites as well.

Dr. Lance A. Liotta (1), Chief of the Laboratory of Pathology for the National Cancer Institute, had this to say about cancer: ". . . contrary to some early assumptions, metastasis is an active process and not an accidental consequence of tumor growth." He is saying that metastasis is not merely a time related, haphazard, accidental or passive event. It is an active process which is driven by the altered genes of the tumor cell. The altered genes direct the tumor cell to manufacture and secrete proteins (adhesion molecules, destructive enzymes and angiogenic factors, etc.). The adhesion molecules enable the tumor cell to attach to structures which they then will destroy with their powerful enzymes. This enables the cells to move through the adjacent tissue (invasion) and also enables the tumor cells to penetrate the walls of lymphatics and blood capillaries (metastasis). The angiogenic factors stimulate neighboring blood vessels to invade the tumor which increases its blood supply and helps it grow.

Thus, cancer cells differ from normal cells in several ways:

1. The cancer cells have acquired abnormal uncontrolled growth. This is the first step. (See above).
2. The cancer cells have acquired the ability to invade normal tissues (invasion). This occurs as the next step.
3. Some cancer cells, in addition to the power to invade, acquire the ability to metastasize (the final step). Not all acquire the ability to metastasize or at least the ability to establish a viable metastasis.

[2] Invasion (Chapter 10) Normal breast ducts are firmly anchored to the basement membrane of the duct or gland wall. However, when the duct cell acquires the ability to grow endlessly without control, the genes of the tumor cell are also altered in such a manner that:

1. The cancer cells have become more motile (have acquired a greater ability to move).
2. The cancer cells produce powerful enzymes (proteases) that break up proteins into small pieces. This enables these cells to free themselves from the basement membrane to which they are anchored and to invade the surrounding normal tissue by breaking down connective tissue fibers (proteins) which normally would obstruct their passage.

The composition of the tissue that lies between the milk ducts and the blood capillaries (extra cellular or interstitial space) consists of connective tissue, plasma proteins, fibrin-gel, inflammatory cells, etc. These tissues can be compared to a dense jungle through which ordinary cells and tumor cells cannot pass without breaking up some of the fibers with their powerful enzymes. Thus, the cancer cells that secrete powerful enzymes can now invade through this ''dense jungle'' and replace the normal breast tissue which surrounds the tumor.

[3] Metastasis (See Chapter 10) This is not a passive process which occurs as the tumor enlarges. It is an active process in which the tumor cell is an active participant. During the transition of a normal cell to a cancer cell, all acquire the ability to grow endlessly without aging and to invade the tissues locally. However, in some tumor cells the genes may be further altered in such a manner that the cells are now able to increase the production of:

1. Enzymes (proteases) which break down proteins of the basement membrane and the proteins of the connective tissue of normal breast tissue. This enables the tumor cells to invade the normal breast tissues adjacent to the tumor;
2. Angiogenic factors (angiogenic, fibroblast growth factors, etc). These proteins stimulate small capillaries to invade the tumor and furnish it with a greater blood supply. The improved blood supply helps the tumor grow; and
3. Adhesion molecules. In order for the tumor cell to accomplish anything, it must first adhere to the structure it wishes to destroy or alter. Thus adhesion molecules are important. Tumor cells that do not possess adhesion molecules will be unable to metastasize distant sites. Tumor cells produce and insert certain proteins (adhesion molecules) into their surface which adhere to adhesion molecules on the outer

surface of the capillaries or on the surface of the endothelial cells lining the blood capillaries. If the tumor cell is able to adhere to a blood vessel, it is usually able to penetrate the wall of the capillary and enter the blood stream where it is swept away in the blood or lymph (embolization) to distant sites. A tumor weighing one gram (¼ of a teaspoon) may shed 3-4 million cancer cells into the venous blood within a 24 hour period. At the distant sites, the adhesion molecules also help the cancer cell adhere to the capillary walls and then gain entry to the lung, liver, etc. Most of these shed cells are destroyed by the immune system and other factors. However, less than 1 in 10,000 survive and produce a distant metastasis or lymph node metastases. If appropriate growth factors are present at the distant site and if the tumor cell is not destroyed by the immune system, a viable metastasis will result. The foregoing matters are without dispute in the literature. Admission by plaintiff's experts can be important and valuable in connection with demonstrating that cancer is a very complex disease, that no cancers are alike, that contrary to some assumptions, metastasis is an active process and not an accidental consequence of tumor growth. (See §5.04 and Chapter 10).

[b] Different Types of Cancer

There are many different types of cancers. Each tends to have a certain pattern of behavior:

1. **Basal cell carcinoma of the skin** grows slowly, is locally invasive, lacks the ability to metastasize and is easily cured by simple excision.
2. **Carcinoma of the uterine cervix** has a long pre-cancerous phase, remains local for a considerable period of time. The Papanicolaou test (Pap smear) is an excellent screening tool while surgery and radiation are effective treatments. The mortality rate for this type of cancer has decreased dramatically during the past 30 years. (Chapter 7).
3. **Small cell cancer of the lung** metastasizes very early in its life cycle. In the vast majority of cases, distant metastases are present before the cancer can be detected by chest x-ray and

periodic chest x-ray screening has not helped. It is rare that surgery cures this type of cancer and it responds to chemotherapy for just a few months. The 10-year survival rate is less than 4%.

4. **Breast cancer.** Some breast cancers, like small cell cancer of the lung, metastasize very early in the life cycle of the tumor. Some, like cancer of the uterine cervix, spread later in the life cycle of the tumor and may not be detectable until too late due to tumor camouflaging. Some have a limited, or no capacity to metastasize or the ability to establish viable metastases because of an effective host immune response. Periodic mammographic screening of asymptomatic women improves survival, but altering the time of diagnosis after these lesions become symptomatic will not improve survival.

Conclusion: Cancers differ because their genes differ. The behavior of a cancer is determined by the extent and nature of the alteration of the genes of the cancer cell. This is something beyond the control of the clinician or the patient, and this truth must be repeatedly emphasized to the jury and at all phases of trial.

[c] Breast Cancers are not all Alike

Some breast cancers, even though quite large, do quite well following excision and remain recurrent-free for many years. Some small breast cancers recur soon after surgery and the patient quickly dies of systemic breast cancer. Two women, both aged 40, may have identical family histories, the same family doctor, the same surgeon, and their breast cancers appear to be identical:

2 cm in diameter	same histology
node status = 0	same prognostic factors.

Thus, even though the TNM Stages[1] are identical, one woman dies quickly and the other has a longtime favorable outcome.

1. Clinical staging—nomenclature developed by American Joint Commission on Cancer Staging. *Manual for Staging Cancer* (3rd Ed. 1989): T = tumor, N = nodes, M = metastases. (See Chapter 18).

Conclusion: The behavior of each breast cancer is dependent upon the extent and nature of the alteration of the genes of the cancer cell. The behavior (lethal potential) is something that is entirely beyond the control of the patient and/or the physician. Identical breast cancers treated by the same physician may behave quite differently in different individuals.

[d] Tumor Camouflaging

Tumor camouflaging, rather than the skill of the physician, usually determines the size at which it is possible to detect a breast cancer. (Chapter 14). Some breast cancers can be detected by mammography when the tumor is only 3 to 4 mm in diameter. Some cannot be detected by mammography even though the cancer is clearly palpable. (18% in one series (2)). Some breast cancers can be easily discovered by palpation when the tumor is only 1 cm in diameter and some cannot be detected by palpation until they attain diameters of 2, 3 or even 4 cm.

Tumor camouflaging defined: the presence of some tumors is hidden or masked within the breast tissue in such a fashion that the tumor must grow longer and attain a larger diameter before it can be detected by mammography or palpation. In some cases the tumor must attain a diameter of 3 or 4 cm before it can be identified.

Common causes of tumor camouflaging are dense breast, vague tumor border, absence of tumor specific microcalcifications, density of breast and tumor are similar and a unique pattern of tumor invasion. (Chapter 14).

Threshold size is the smallest size at which it is possible to detect a tumor by palpation and/or mammography. Camouflaged tumors, of course, have a much larger threshold size than tumors which are not camouflaged.

The breast itself contributes to the problem of tumor camouflaging. The density and consistency of the breast, unlike most other solid organs in healthy individuals, varies from woman to woman. Factors that contribute to this variation include, for example: High fat content (in older women): the breast is soft with low density and is uniform in consistency; high glandular and fibrous tissue content (in younger women): the breast is dense, firm and rubbery; irregular overgrowth of glandular, and/or fibrous tissue, and/or cyst formation: the breast is diffusely or asymmetrically nodular.

The detectability of breast cancers varies from relatively easy (the low density fatty breast) to exceedingly difficult (the high density, nodular breast, and/or cystic breast.)

Tumor cells are 70% water and have the consistency of a soft gel. When we diagnose a breast cancer, we usually are not detecting the collection of soft tumor cells, but rather the firm tumor-generated stroma (the tumor's support structure) within and sometimes surrounding the breast cancer.

The benign stromal elements of the tumor are generated by the tumor. Tumor cells secrete powerful proteins (vascular permeability factors, angiogenic factors, chemoattractants, growth factors, etc.). These proteins initiate a complex process which stimulates adjacent stromal elements (blood vessels, collagenous tissue, fibrous tissue, inflammatory cells, etc.) to invade the tumor and establish a stroma for the tumor. As the tumor grows, more and more stroma is created to provide scaffolding for the tumor and carry nutrition to and waste from the cancer cells (3). Without this supporting structure (stroma) the tumor could not survive and grow.

The progeny of a tumor generates a stroma which tends to be identical to the parent tumor because the generation of the tumor stroma is genetically controlled by the nature of the proteins secreted by the tumor cells (3).

Although the stroma of all breast cancers contains the same building blocks, some of the building blocks (usually connective tissue) can comprise as much as 90% or as little as 10% of the tumor. Since the concentration of connective tissue determines the density of the tumor, some breast cancers possess a chameleon-like ability to mimic the density of almost any normal breast tissue (3). Thus, the degree to which a tumor is camouflaged is genetically controlled by the genes of the tumor itself.

The degree of tumor camouflaging, of course, determines the size at which it is possible to detect the cancer (threshold size). Therefore, the size at which a tumor can be detected is determined by the genes of the cancer itself, and the density of the surrounding breast. Both the degree of alteration of the genes of the cancer cell and the density of the breast are beyond the control of the physician. Unfortunately, the phenomenon of tumor camouflaging is a serious and common problem for those responsible for the screening and diagnosis of breast cancer.

[e] Some Breast Cancers Metastasize Early

Prevascular phase: At the outset the cancer exists in the extracellular space (between and outside the blood vessels). It grows slowly because it contains no blood vessels and must obtain its nutrition by osmosis from the surrounding extracellular fluids. During this phase of tumor growth, metastases cannot occur because the tumor contains no blood vessels. The growth of a tumor that fails to generate a tumor stroma is arrested due to lack of nutrition when the tumor attains a diameter of about 1-2 mm. (Chapter 10).

Vascular phase: When the small cluster of cancer cells attains a diameter of .3 mm to 1 mm (¼ to ⅓ of the diameter of the common household pin), some of the genes of the cancer cells are activated or "switched on." Some think they are "switched on" because of the low oxygen tension within these tumors containing no blood vessels. The "switched on" cancer cells differ from the nonactivated cancer cells within the tumor in several respects. First, the "switched on" cancer cells secrete powerful proteins (angiogenic factors and other growth factors) which stimulate the neighboring blood vessels, fibrous tissue and inflammatory cells to aggressively invade the small tumor, thus furnishing it with a functioning system of new blood vessels.

Secondly, these "switched on" cancer cells can also secrete powerful proteolytic enzymes which enable them to invade the surrounding tissues. Unfortunately, the hastily formed new blood vessels are quite leaky and the "switched on" cancer cells, employing their powerful proteolytic enzymes, have no difficulty penetrating the walls of these leaky, poorly formed new capillaries and thus escaping into the blood stream. When the cancer is only ¼ the diameter of a common household pin, metastases can and do occur. A cancer which weighs only one gram (¼ of a teaspoon) sheds[2] 3-4 million cancer cells into the blood each 24 hours. Of course, all of these shed cells do not survive, but some do.

2. The term shed or shedding refers to the escape of cancer cells into the venous blood of the tumor. Most believe that the tumor cells actively penetrate the walls of the postcapillary venule. (Chapter 10).

[f] Cancer Cell Shedding Continues Throughout Life of the Tumor

About 50% of breast cancers do not possess the ability to metastasize or at least do not have the ability to establish viable distant metastases because of an effective host immune system. Many authorities are of the opinion that those cells that do possess the ability to metastasize do so at the first opportunity and do so in increasing numbers as the number of cancer cells in the tumor increases and the surface area of endothelial cells of the leaky vessels expands.

Most of these cells that escape into the blood do not survive due to trauma, immune cells, high concentration of plasma, etc., but unfortunately, some survive. The fact that the age-adjusted mortality rate of breast cancer has not improved since 1930 is stark proof of this fact. Forty-six thousand women died this year because distant metastases occurred before it was possible to detect these tumors.

How do we know these things? Experimental animal models help us study the growth characteristics of early breast cancer. Cancers can be transplanted to the:

1. *Vitreous (eye) of the rabbit.* The growth of the cancer can be visually monitored by the ophthalmic instruments;
2. *Ovary of the rat.* The venous blood returning from the cancer-containing ovary can be examined immunohistochemically and the number of breast cancer cells escaping into the blood can be determined; or
3. *Thigh of the mouse or rat.* Amputation of the cancer-containing thigh at periodic intervals following tumor implantation reveals the rate at which distant metastases occur. In some animal models 50% of the animals develop lung metastases within 9 to 10 days following implantation of the tumors into the thigh.

[g] Symptomatic Breast Cancers are Biologically Old Tumors

A symptomatic breast cancer is one that has grown large enough to produce symptoms that prompt a woman to consult her physician.

It is generally agreed that virtually all breast cancers are clinically undetectable by palpation until they attain a diameter of about 1 cm. Thus 75% of the life cycle of the tumor has elapsed before it can be detected by palpation. Many breast cancers cannot be palpated until they reach diameters of 2, 3 or 4 cm or even larger. These cancers are clinically undetectable during the first 80 to 90% of their life cycle. These symptomatic cancers are biologically old tumors that have entered the terminal stages of their existence.

Fisher, et al., National Surgical Adjuvant Breast Protocol, B-04, 1977 (4) observed that increasing the duration of symptoms (delay in diagnosis) of 9 months or more prior to treatment did not alter the disease-free survival rate. They concluded that this was secondary to the early metastases of these breast cancers.

In a 1977 test on 1,539 patients conducted by Fisher, et al., (4) it was determined that the relation of duration of symptoms of breast cancer and treatment failure was as follows:

Duration of Symptoms	Treatment Failure Rate
0 to 1 month	25.2%
1.1 to 3 months	27.3%
3.1 to 9 months	29.2%
longer than 9 months	19.5%.

(Reprinted courtesy of Fisher et al. (4). Cancer 40: 3160-3167, 1977 Table 1, page 3163).

These studies demonstrate breast cancers that have the ability to metastasize do so prior to the time the breast cancer becomes large enough to produce symptoms. Thus decreasing the durations of symptoms (delay in diagnosis) will not alter the survival. (See Chapters 10 and 11).

[h] Mortality Rate of Breast Cancer has Remained Stable Since 1930

We can learn much from these mortality data. The age-adjusted mortality data since 1930 have identified a unique group of breast cancers. All produced systemic disease before these lesions could be detected. Incredibly, the size of this group of tumors has remained constant at 27-28 deaths per 100,000 female population for the past 63 years in spite of a dramatic increase in the incidence of breast cancer. (Chapter 6).

From 1930 to 1960 diagnostic and screening mammography were not available. Therefore, these cancers were symptomatic breast cancers. That is, they grew unmolested within the breast until they produced symptoms that prompted the patient to consult her physician. Palpation and open biopsy then confirmed the diagnosis. We know that these symptomatic breast cancers are biologically old tumors that have entered the terminal stages of their life cycle.

The best efforts of the entire medical community, molecular biologists, oncologists and the American Cancer Society have failed to lower the age adjusted mortality rate of this hard core group of biologically old symptomatic tumors. This is stark proof that tumors with genetic instability undergo neoplastic progression and metastasis prior to the time these lesions become symptomatic. Thus, reducing the durations of symptoms by early diagnosis will not alter survival in this group of symptomatic cancers.

[i] Definitions

The following are definitions of key concepts necessary to a sound understanding of the issues surrounding breast cancer:

Cancer Control Window: This is that period of time from the moment the tumor reaches threshold size until metastasis occurs and the tumor becomes incurable. Several factors tend to shorten this window: 1) A large threshold size secondary to dense breast or pattern of tumor invasion which will shorten the window; and 2) metastasis of the cancer early in the life cycle of the tumor which will shorten the window. (Chapter 16).

Threshold Size: The threshold size of a breast cancer is defined as the smallest size at which it is possible to detect the breast cancer by mammogram or palpation. (Chapter 15). Tumor camouflaging refers to any process which effectively conceals or masks the presence of a carcinoma within the breast from the x-ray beam or palpation of the breast. (Chapter 14).

Lead Time Bias: While it is true that early diagnosis of tumors with systemic disease prolongs the interval between diagnosis and death, this reflects only the fact that the time of diagnosis was advanced and not that death was delayed. Conversely, in patients with systemic disease, survival from the date of diagnosis will appear shorter for those patients with a delayed diagnosis, a phenomenon described as lead time bias. (Chapter 22).

Patterns of Behavior: Different types of cancers have different patterns of behavior. Basal cell carcinoma of the skin, for example, grows slowly, is locally invasive, lacks the ability to metastasize, and is easily cured by simple excision. Carcinoma of the uterine cervix has a long pre-cancerous phase, and remains local for a considerable period of time. The Pap smear test is an excellent screening tool. For this type of cancer, surgery and radiation are effective treatments, and the mortality rate has decreased dramatically during the past 30 years (Chapter 6, Fig. 1).

Small cell cancer of the lung, however, is entirely different. It metastasizes very early in its life cycle and distant metastases are present before the cancer can be detected by chest x-rays in the vast majority of cases. Periodic screening with chest x-ray does not help, surgery fails to cure, it responds to chemotherapy for just a few months and the ten-year survival rate is less than 4%.

References

1. Liotta, Lance A. *Cancer Cell Invasion and Metasasis,* Scientific American, Feb. 1992, Vol. 266, No. 6, Feb. 1992.
2. Donegan, W. L. *Evaluation of a Palpable Breast Mass,* N. Eng. J. Med. 327(13):937-942, 1992.
3. Dvorak, Harold F. *Tumors: Wounds That do not Heal: Similarities Between Tumor Stroma Generation and Wound Healing,* N. Eng. J. Med. 315:1650-1659, Dec. 1986.
4. Fisher, E. R., et al. *A Perspective Concerning the Relation of Durations of Symptoms to Treatment Failure in Patients with Breast Cancer,* Cancer 40:3160-3167, 1977.

§2.03 STANDARD OF CARE

As set out in Chapter 1, there are two parts to any negligence action—whether the defendant violated the accepted standards of care and whether or not the deviation was a proximate cause of the injury—negligence and causation.

From a legal standpoint, the burden is upon the plaintiff to establish both items. From a practical standpoint, this may not be the case. When a jury views a woman with cancer of the breast diagnosed as terminal or views the family of a woman who just died of cancer, any instruction on burden of proof may be academic only.

If then, defense counsel has the burden of disproving negligence and causation, then let counsel assume the burden aggressively and not just defensively.

The first question is whether to attack the negligence assertion or the causation assertion or both. It is possible, of course, to confess the negligence and attack causation. No matter how strong the defense is on the issue of causation, this is risky. A confession that the defendant has violated the standard of care can either serve to inflame the jury or to otherwise make it blind and deaf to any argument on causation. Moreover, it is seldom, if ever, necessary. There are rogue physicians, to be sure, as well as incompetent ones. However, there are not very many and these seldom appear in a courtroom setting. The vast majority of accused physicians are caring and conscientious professionals, trying to deal with a vicious disease of which really little is known. And there are few black letter rules on standards of care.

Duties vary from one specialty to another and they are obviously not the same for primary care physicians and OB/GYN specialists as opposed to radiologists, surgeons, pathologists, and other like specialists. In each case, equally competent physicians provide contrary opinions on the same question.

[a] Radiologists

Historically the role of the radiologist is diagnostic and is created by the referral of a patient from a primary care physician who requests an imaging procedure, generally a mammogram.

In general, it is the duty of the radiologist to produce a reasonable mammographic image and offer a reasonable interpretation. Quality control standards to assure reliability in the production of images, proper breast positioning, compression and analysis have been developed, some even by statute, by way of congressional legislation which prescribed various parameters which in turn were adopted by the American College of Radiology in its accrediting process. (*The Breast Cancer Detection Demonstration Project: End Result;* Cancer, 37:5, 1987, *The Mammography Quality Standards Act of 1992,* P.L. 102539).

But, these standards and the criteria regarding mammography have been directed more toward image quality than interpretation. However, reasonable images and reasonable interpretations depend upon many factors and there are both medical and legal notions of each. Experts can and do disagree as to whether vague shadows on the screen are produced by malignancy. It is usually easy to detect a breast cancer in retrospect. When a radiologist knows the precise location of a cancer, it is simple to review previous mammograms and say "Ah, yes, here it is." However, in many cases these shadows on previous films are vague and nebulous.

Experts differ as to how long a delay between mammogram examinations is clinically significant. There is no persuasive evidence that mammograms done more often than 12 months are of value. (Chapter 21). There is also the fact that no matter how qualified the radiologist, early cancers can be missed. A tumor that is 100% camouflaged cannot be seen by x-ray. A tumor that is 50% to 80% camouflaged may be so vague and indistinct that it will be detected only in retrospect. The genes of cancer cells determine how dense the tumor will be and, therefore, when it can be detected. Sometimes the examiner is unable to initially recognize certain small abnormalities which do become recognizable when a more advanced lesion becomes present. (Chapter 14).

Many mammographic findings are equivocal and the interpretation is influenced by the clinical circumstances in which they are seen. The mammographer may interpret an otherwise borderline mammographic finding as suspicious depending upon whether the patient has exhibited symptoms or other clinical findings. The reasonableness of any interpretation in any particular case always involves the clinical context in which it is seen.

In the case of screening mammograms, experts do not agree on screening guideline interpretations and no agreed upon standards of care can be found for the ordering of periodic mammograms. (Brenner, infra.)

Standards of reasonable interpretation are difficult to define. As Dr. Brenner has pointed out, in a case subject to legal redress, experts are likely to be found to either corroborate or deny the reasonableness of mammographic interpretation. (Brenner, R. J. *Medicolegal Aspects of Screening Mammography* AJR Am. J. Roentgenol. 153:53 (1989)).

Moreover the interpretation of a diagnostic mammogram is different than the interpretation of a screening mammogram. Screening is an effort to detect mammographic abnormalities in an otherwise normal population. The instances of abnormalities in this group are low. Diagnostic imaging is usually the result of a clinical symptom of potential breast cancer and the incidence of cancer in this group is obviously higher.

Dr. Brenner (R. J. *Medicolegal Implications of Breast Imaging,* Surg. Oncol. Clinic N.A. Vol. 3:1, p. 75, Jan., 1994) points out that the primary mammographic signs of malignancy are all subject to differential diagnosis. Dr. Kopans points out the limitations of mammographic accuracy. Kopans, D.B. *The Positive Predictive Value of Mammograms,* AJR, Am. J. Roentgenol. 158:521 (1992).

For articles pointing out the various problems concerning diagnostic and screening mammography, see Brenner, R. J. *Evolving Medical-Legal Concepts for Clinicians and Imagers in Evaluation of Breast Cancer;* Cancer (Suppl.) 69:1950-1992; Brenner, R. J. *Medical-Legal Aspects of Breast Imaging; Variable Standards of Care Relating to Different Types of Practice*; AJR Am. J. Roentgenol. 156:719-723 1991; Hendrick, R. E. *Quality Assurance in Mammography*; Radiol. Clin. N. Am. 30:243-255 1992. As Dr. Spratt has stated, detection methods and rules are imprecise and at times paradoxic. (Spratt, J.S., *Realities of Breast Cancer Control, Public Expectations and the Law,* Surg. Oncol. Clin. North Am. 3:25-34, 1994). (See Chapter 21, and §§21.02 and 22.03, et seq.).

[b] Pathologists

Pathologists rarely appear as defendants in the malpractice setting. A review of claims arising from an alleged delay in diagnosis of breast cancer made by the Physicians Insurers Association of America (1990) listed only six claims against pathologists out of a total of 273. Cases in which experts disagree as to whether transformation to malignancy has occurred do happen, but most of these are borderline situations not normally considered a failure to diagnose and, in any event, if it is a failure to diagnose, causation is evident. Probably the more prevalent type of litigation involving pathologists relates to a claim of mistaken reports of malignancy. And neither fall within the concepts developed in this book. For the role of the pathologist, however, see Hutter, R. V. P., *The Role of the Pathologist in the Management of Breast Cancer,* Ca. 1991; 41:283.

[c] Primary Care and OB/GYN Specialists

By far the greatest number of malpractice cases involve the family practitioner, the internist and the OB/GYN specialist. While opinions may be offered freely in any given lawsuit, the standards of care as to such physicians are unclear in most situations. Obviously an appropriate medical history should be taken and an appropriate breast examination should be performed. But what constitutes an appropriate standard of care for this individual patient? The recommendation of mammography, needle biopsy, open biopsy or consultation depends upon the condition of the patient at the time of the examination. To set out in retrospect some set of guidelines that assume a set of symptoms that might or might not have been present and ignore the item of clinical judgment is faulty. Nor can any guideline insure the curability of an incurable disease.

Primary care physicians and OB/GYN specialists see many patients, but not many cancers, actually not more than one or two breast cancer cases per year. Dr. Murray Seltzer, Clinical Professor of Surgery of New Jersey College of Medicine, who confines his practice to breast diagnosis and surgery states that only 8% of the patients presented to him with a lump had breast cancer and he observes:

> The treating physician must first be sure that the suspected abnormality is real and not a transient finding.

(Remarks at ABA meeting August 3, 1993.)

Certainly if a patient presents herself with a 3-dimensional lump, it should be promptly investigated, at least by needle aspiration and probably by surgical biopsy if the mass does not disappear or recurs. Parenthetically, by the time tumors become symptomatic, those that possess the ability to metastasize will have done so, which of course, relates to causation and not to standard of care. (See Chapter 10, Metastasis: When Does it Occur).

However, most lumps are not discrete or 3-dimensional at the time they are first presented to the physician and commonly no lump or mass of any kind will be found. As pointed out by Strax, P. (General Motors Cancer Research Foundation Prize Winner Laureates, Lecturer Jack Massur, Auditorium National Institutes of Health, Bethesda, Maryland, 1988):

> The usual breast symptom of a lump or lumps, diffuse or localized, pain or nipple discharge, which would classify a woman as "symptomatic" are present to some degree in all women. The distinction between "symptomatic" and "asymptomatic" is quite blurred. Does a woman with the usual lumpiness, with perhaps one or more lumps which stand out qualify as "symptomatic?" Is a woman with premenstrual swelling or pain of varying degree "asymptomatic?" In truth, every woman has breast symptoms or signs of varying severity.

A frequent comment by plaintiff's counsel is that all lumps belong in bottles. If the statement is addressed to 3-dimensional lumps, it has a measure of truth. As to all lumps, this is an obvious absurdity—there aren't that many bottles.

A lump is defined in the dictionary as a piece or mass of indefinite or irregular shape, protuberance, a cluster, swelling or a growth. The word indefinite is defined as not definite, indeterminate, vague, immeasurable, or having boundaries that are unknown or only approximately known. The greatest problem in the clinical diagnosis of breast cancer lies in the differentiation of malignant tumors from benign lumps. (Scanlon, *The Early Diagnosis of Breast Cancer,* 48 Cancer 523 (1981)). A number of benign lesions may simulate carcinoma. These include a low grade abscess, traumatic fat necrosis, duct ectasis and adenosis. (Haagensen, Bodian and Haagenson, *Breast Cancinoma Risk and Detection,* W. B. Saunders Co. (1981)). Other diseases which may simulate metastasis to axillary nodes are heterotopic apocrine cysts in axillary nodes, adventitious prepectoral lymph nodes, primary carcinoma in axillary prolongation of the breast, hemorrhage produced by trauma, obscuring cancer of the breast, painful costochondral swelling and metastatic tumors of the breast. (Haagensen, supra). The accuracy and diagnosis of breast cancer on physical examination is only 70% even with the most experienced hands. (McWhirter, *Some Factors Influencing Prognosis in Breast Cancer,* 8 J.Fac.Radiol. 220-234). In general, various microscopic combinations of separate pathologic entities cannot be diagnosed by clinicians' physical examination. (Scanlon, supra). (See also Foster, *Limitations of Physical Examination in Early Diagnosis of Breast Cancer,* Surg. Oncol. Clinics of N.A., Vol. 3, No. 1, p. 55 (1994)).

It is important to understand the breast. (See §14.4). Adult women's organs such as the liver, kidney and pancreas may vary in size, but the texture, consistency and density is, for example, much the same in each case. However, the consistency, texture and density of the normal female breast varies markedly. Some are soft, low density with uniform texture because they have a high fat content. Other breasts have a low fat content with a high content of fibrous and/or glandular tissue. These breasts tend to be dense and rubbery in texture. Other breasts are also riddled with cysts or lumpy areas of fibrosis or overgrowth of normal glandular tissue. Some women complain of a lump and yet careful physical examination of the breast completely negates or limits this to a thickening, vague and indistinct. In fact, many examinations reveal only what appears to be ''normal'' breast tissue. These lumps are not discrete nor are they 3-dimensional.

Many sizeable tumors are not discovered because they are camouflaged, masked by such factors as a dense breast, tumor density similar to breast density, vague tumor borders, failure of tumor to form a distinct mass, lack of tumor specific microcalcifications and patterns of tumor invasion. (Chapter 14).

''Experts'' may appear at trial and recite certain standards of care as to what a primary care physician or OB/GYN specialist should do upon being presented with a ''lump.'' The question is how such recitals have any relevance to the case on trial without knowing what kind of a claimed ''lump'' the defendant physician was dealing with. In this connection, some experts have seized upon evidence of the size of the tumor at the time of the surgery and then attempted to reason backwards. For example, if the tumor at the time of surgery was 2.0 cm, the speculation will be that the tumor size 12 months before surgery was 1.0 cm. Statistics will then be introduced in an attempt to demonstrate that increasing tumor size correlates with the decrease in survival. Thus, the conclusion that delay in diagnosis results in a larger tumor and a decrease in survival and loss of chance for cure.

This line of reasoning ignores the fact that even as to the stage of the tumor at the time of surgery, there is disagreement concerning tumor size; surgeons and pathologists agree on only 54% of the cases and surgeons and radiologists agree on only 39% of the cases. As to the status of axillary lymph nodes, clinical evaluations said to be negative are wrong in 42% of cases and clinically said to be positive are wrong in 30% of the cases. (§18.02). The following are strong arguments supporting the notion that not every lump needs to be biopsied and that it is sometimes difficult to detect cancers even under the best of circumstances.

1. If no one can accurately determine the pathological stage several days before surgery, it is difficult for anyone to fairly contend the pathological stage can be determined 12 months prior to the surgery.
2. Retrospective estimations of tumor stage are subject to all the errors and limitations of the so-called doubling time defense. (Chapter 19).

3. Some tumors grow and become huge and still do not metastasize. In this situation, obviously, tumor size is meaningless.
4. Some tumors metastasize when they are about the size of the head of a common household pin. Again, tumor size is meaningless since the tumor has already metastasized.
5. Some tumors are unable to metastasize or establish a viable metastasis. Again, the size is meaningless.

[d] Diagnostic Mammograms

The standard of care for the 3-D mass would usually include a diagnostic mammogram. There can be exceptions. A negative mammogram may lead to a delay in operating and in some cases a mammogram can yield nothing except increased expense. In any event, what about the ''normal'' breast? What about a woman with an alleged lump, but the doctor finds her breast ''normal?'' Should every woman who comes to the doctor with breast symptoms have a diagnostic mammogram? As in so many cases, it becomes a judgment call. In a malpractice setting, such mammograms have missed from 37.5% to 80% of breast cancers (Chapter 14). False negative readings are something on the order of 15% to 20% and the younger a woman is, the higher this incidence of false negatives. For women in their 20's, mammograms are false negative 80% of the time. Kern, 127 *American Surgeon,* May 1992; see also Kern, *Historical Trends in Breast Cancer Litigation: A Clinician's Perspective,* Surg. Oncol. Clin. North Am. 3:1-24, 1994.

Moreover, it is impossible to detect tumors that are 100% camouflaged, and probably impossible to detect tumors that are 50% to 80% camouflaged. (Chapter 14).

The diagnostic mammogram is useful but has limitations. It is difficult to establish the standard of care in retrospect as to someone whose breasts have not been examined or whose breasts may well have been within the limits of normal at that time. For an extensive discussion of the medical/legal implications of screening and diagnosis of breast cancers and imaging, see Brenner, R. J., *Surgical Oncology Clinics of North America,* Vol. III, No. 1, January 1994.

[e] Screening Mammography

Screening mammograms are a valuable tool for screening asymptomatic women for possible abnormalities. But current emphasis on early diagnosis by screening mammography is subject to considerable debate. Not every patient, for example, should be submitted to screening mammography. Fisher, 40 *Cancer,* 3166 (1977). Its usefulness has been questioned, and at best it has its limitations. Eddy, *Screening for Breast Cancer,* 111 Annals of Internal Med. 389 (1989). It is very expensive, and in a health insurance plan (HIP) study, 40% of breast cancers were missed by screening mammography. Spratt, *Legal Perspectives on Mammography and Self-Referral,* 69, *Cancer* 599 (1985).

Spratt mentions that significant medical legal problems arise from the promoted position that breast cancer can be controlled by screening.

> The biology of breast cancer itself more frequently determines the proximate course of the outcome, regardless of the screening. This fact has not been recognized or appreciated by those who strongly promote screening mammograms for the control of breast cancer. Recommendations for screening mammography also differ. The National Cancer Institute advises against screening for women under the age of 50, with which position the American College of Radiology disagrees. Screening mammography will yield an increase in the detection of in situ cancers, small, indolent lesions that may never become clinically evident during the lifetime of the patient. These then are unnecessarily subjected to surgical biopsy.

Spratt, *Cancer,* supra at 600, asserts that:

> The latest studies available have again failed to show any reduction in mortality from breast cancer attributable to the screening of women 40 to 49 years of age. Between 50 and 59 years of age, the contribution of mammography to the reduction in mortality is equivocal. The most effective time interval between screening mammograms has not been well defined. The age of the women and the biologic activity of various breast cancers as a result of the enormous variance and growth rates, make the currently recommended time intervals for the various stages educated guesses at best. Thus, even if screening mammograms are beneficial, we do not know how best to use them. (Spratt, supra)

> Full implementation of current mammographic screening recommendations would necessitate the equivalent of every radiologist in the country interpreting ten examinations per working day, an obvious impossibility. Even those relatively few radiologists and surgeons who do interpret mammograms have rarely had formal training or extensive experience with this relatively imaging modality. (Hall, F.M., *Screening Mammography: Potential Problems on the Horizon,* 314 New England Journal of Medicine 53-55 (1986).

Current opinion agrees with Spratt that screening mammography will not lower the mortality rate of women under age 50, but holds that it will reduce the mortality rate above that age. It must be remembered that this involves only asymptomatic women. And there is no responsible dispute with Spratt's observation that in all cases the biology of breast cancer itself more frequently determines the proximate cause of the outcome, regardless of screening. (Tabar, L., Fagerburg C. & Day, N. E., *Breast Cancer & Natural History: New Insights From Results of Screening,* The Lancet, Vol. 339; 412-414; Feb. 14, 1992). See also Spratt, *Realities of Breast Cancer Control, Public Expectation and the Law,* Surg. Oncol. Clin. North Am. 3:25-34, 1994. (Chapter 22).

[f] Staging

Articles in plaintiff's trial magazines designed for the plaintiff's malpractice attorney have postulated that:

> The only scientifically accepted means of determining prognosis (damages) is tumor staging.

The suggestion is made that the TNM[3] staging system of breast cancer can be employed to prove that a delay in diagnosis results in progression of the disease and loss of chance for a cure. The postulate will be that the patient involved 12 months prior to diagnosis had a tumor at a stage of T1NOMO[4] and had an excellent chance of cure. At the time of surgery the time was stage T2N2MO[5] and the patient had a chance of cure of only 30%, thus suffering a 70% loss of chance. (Chapters 13 and 18).

The contention is ingenious, but demonstrably false. In the first place, classification by staging is usually based on anatomic features rather than microscopic physiologic features. Prognosis of breast cancer is based upon both anatomic and physiological features. Chareson & Feinstein, *A Critique of Existing Systems of Breast Cancer,* 73 Surgery (1973). Secondly, there are two types of staging, clinical (C) and

---

3. Tumor, nodes, metastasis, a staging system which measures tumor size, node status and distant metastases.
4. Tumor diameter less than 2.0 cm, nodes negative for metastases, no distinct metastases.
5. Tumor greater than 2 cm and less than 5 cm in diameter, two nodes contain metastases, no distant metastases.

pathologic (P). cTNM is staging performed before surgery. pTNM is staging after surgery from examination of the tumor, x-rays, and scans, together with lymph node resection. Even this staging is wrong about 30% of the time. (See §18.02).

cTNM staging performed just a few days before surgery is even less accurate and speculation about the (P) stage 12 months prior to surgery is equivalent in accuracy to the toss of a coin. Perhaps less. (Chapter 18).

> Plaintiff's attorneys invoke the loss of chance doctrine, stating that any patient who presents with breast cancer at the TNM Stages II through III has a loss of chance for survival to TNM Stage I. In the present study, no correlation could be demonstrated between the length of delay in diagnosis and the TNM stage of breast cancer or between the tumor size (diameter) and the length of the diagnostic delay.

Kern, *Causes of Breast Cancer Malpractice Litigation,* 127 Archives of Surgery 542 (1992).

> The legal dilemma is that the (case) law cannot alter the underlying biologic variables that are the proximate cause of outcome in breast cancer. The effects of these biologic variables are always operative and are independent of any alleged delay in diagnosis. Spratt, supra. (Chapter 20).

At best, clinical staging without analysis of tumor characteristics is an oversimplification. pTNM, node status and tumor size are predictors of prognosis. However, pTNM plus histologic type, tumor grading, information concerning invasion of lymphatics and blood capillaries, ER/PgR, and S-phrase add much more to the predictive power as to the lethal potential of the tumor. (Chapter 22).

[g] Biopsy

Certainly in the presence of a definite 3-dimensional mass a biopsy should be performed, but the idea that every breast complaint should be biopsied is dangerous. Blind biopsies are especially dangerous since a negative report provides only a false sense of security. Should a 2-D lump be biopsied? What about the breast that in the doctor's judgment is "normal?" Should a biopsy be performed when in all honesty there is nothing that can be accurately located? What about the PPV (positive predictive value)? If a doctor does 100 biopsies and finds one cancer, it results in a PPV of 1%. Is this unnecessary surgery? The same would hold if the PPV is 10 to 15%. Every biopsy creates some scarring, and sometimes a lot, especially if it is an open biopsy or if there is a complication such as hemorrhage or infection. Scarring makes future breast examinations more difficult; in fact, many unnecessary biopsies have been performed. Focal pain or tenderness is not an indication for biopsy. Over-reading of x-rays is a common practice by radiologists and often results in unnecessary biopsy. Again, the decision to biopsy is a judgment call, based upon what a reasonably careful physician would elect to do under all of the circumstances apparent at the time.

§2.04 CAUSATION

Few experts on the current scene will deny that in many cases breast cancer is not curable. A significant number say that it is not curable in any case.

> The evidence that breast cancer is incurable is overwhelming.

Skrabanek, *Screening for Disease: False Premises and False Promises of Breast Cancer Screening,* The Lancet 316, August 10, 1985. (Chapter 9).

In all events, the belief that early diagnosis and treatment can eliminate the symptomatic primary tumor before metastasis occurs goes entirely against all scientific evidence. It is simply not possible to demonstrate a relationship between the duration of symptoms and curability. The survival rate of the majority of women with breast cancer depends upon the biology of the cancer and not the time of diagnosis. The literature supports this concept. (Chapter 9).

Consequently, it is not sufficient for a plaintiff merely to offer expert testimony as to when a tumor should have been diagnosed, coupled with an unfortunate result. "Expert" evidence that a tumor did not metastasize early, without being based upon the biology of the tumor, is scientifically meaningless. (See §11.05). Except in some asymptomatic tumors detected by screening mammography, survivability does not depend upon time, but on kind. There is no relationship between the duration of symptomatic tumors and survival (Chapters 6, 10 and 11), and a failure by plaintiff to introduce any evidence as to the biology of the tumor should logically result in a dismissal. (See §3.06). Unfortunately, most courts will hold that failure to introduce evidence as to the biology of the tumor goes to the credibility of the expert witnesses and is a question for the jury and not the court to decide.

It then becomes incumbent upon defense counsel to study and produce the biological parameters of the tumor and use the medical literature to show how these parameters affect survival.

The key question is when did the breast cancer metastasize in *this particular patient*? This particular patient saw the defendant doctor because of symptoms related to the breast. We are then talking about a symptomatic breast cancer. Being symptomatic, the cancer is biologically very old and has entered into the terminal phase of its life cycle. If it had the ability to metastasize, it would have done so before it entered this phase. (Chapter 10). About 60% of breast cancers have a favorable outcome because a) the cancer is not able to metastasize; b) the cancer is unable to establish a viable metastasis because of a powerful host immune system; and c) the tumor had a prolonged doubling time of a year or more. Some of these tumors may not recur for 10, 20 or 30 years. In such cases a physician involved will not be drawn into malpractice litigation.

It is the 40% of tumors with unfavorable outcomes that may arrive in the courtroom. (Chapters 10 and 11). The majority of these can be classified as symptomatic breast cancer. That is, the cancer produced symptoms which prompted the patient to consult her physician and then a diagnosis of the cancer was established. About two-thirds of these cancers will have metastasized early in the life cycle (Chapter 10). However, virtually all of these cancers that have the ability to establish viable metastasis will have done so prior to the time these tumors enter the final phase of their life cycle. In obtaining evidence as to the biology of the tumor, defense counsel must do more than just read through the pathology report at the time of surgery. In some cases an examination of the pathology report, primary tumor and molecular factors will not prove helpful. In such cases, reliance will have to be made on the clinical history (before and after surgery) for proof of the aggressiveness of the tumor.

In many situations, careful examination of the gross microscopic and molecular features of the primary tumor will yield strong evidence of its lethal potential. Histologic type of the tumor must be considered. Some tumor types are much more aggressive than others. Tumor size, in some cases, may relate to prognosis. Did the plaintiff's cancer metastasize to the axillary lymph nodes? It is proof, of course, that the tumor did possess the power to metastasize. Gross examination of the tumor will reveal evidence that might suggest a camouflaged tumor or more invasive tumor.

Microscopic examination of the tumor is also important. Tumor grade, histologic grade, nuclear grade or mitotic grade may suggest that this was a more aggressive tumor. Microscopic evidence of lymphatic or vascular invasion will suggest a greater risk of recurrence. If no evidence of lympho-vascular invasion was found, special stains may be used to identify small capillaries and lymph channels. The presence of foci of tumor necrosis might suggest a rapidly growing tumor that was outgrowing its blood supply.

Molecular immunohistochemical studies should also be considered. The absences of estrogen and progesterone receptors will suggest that the tumor will be more rapidly growing. The high S-phase fraction (DNA flow cytometry) indicates a more rapidly growing and aggressive tumor. HER-2/neu protein over expression and/or gene amplification also may identify some more aggressive tumors. Recently it has become apparent that an increase in the number of microscopic vessels within the tumor is an ominous sign. (Chapter 23).

There are new tests such as epidermal growth factor—cathepsin-D and accumulations of a mutant P53 protein that can also be used.

To recapitulate several important points:

1. Cancers differ because their genes differ. The behavior of a cancer is determined by the extent and nature of the alteration of the genes of the cancer cell. This is something beyond the control of the clinician or the patient.
2. Breast cancers are not all alike. Identical breast cancers treated by the same physician may behave quite differently.
3. Tumor camouflaging rather than the skill of the physician determines the size at which it is possible to detect a breast cancer.
4. Some breast cancers metastasize early. A cancer which weighs only 1 gm (¼ of a teaspoon) sheds 3 to 4 million cancer cells into the blood each 24 hours. Some do not survive, but some do. The shedding of cancer cells continues through the life of the tumor.
5. Some breast cancers do not possess the ability to establish a viable metastasis because of an effective host immune sys-

tem. The cells that do possess the ability to metastasize do so at the first opportunity and do so in increasing numbers.

6. The age-adjusted mortality rate of breast cancer has not improved since 1930. 46,000 women will die this year because distant metastasis occurred before it was possible to detect these tumors.
7. Symptomatic breast cancers are biologically old tumors. On average, it requires a tumor about 8 to 10 years to grow to a size that can be detected by palpation.
8. The belief that early diagnosis and treatment can eliminate the primary tumor before the tumor metastasizes in all cases is the result of propaganda and has never been scientifically confirmed.

To properly obtain and present the prognostic factors as suggested, the help of a pathologist is required. Questions for the pathologist are suggested in 5.01[d], infra. See also Chapter 23.

CHAPTER 3: MOTIONS

CHAPTER 3

MOTIONS

§3.01 IN GENERAL

There are many motions available to litigants under the Federal Rules of Civil Procedure and under the Rules of Civil Procedure in most jurisdictions, and motion practice is virtually an art in itself. It is used for a variety of strategic purposes, to shape the issues, to dispose of unmeritorious claims, to restrict the introduction of irrelevant and prejudicial evidence, possibly to educate the court beforehand as to the position of the movant on the facts and the issues. Motions under Rule 12(b)(6) Fed. R. Civ. P. to dismiss for failure to state a claim upon which any relief can be granted are often used for this purpose.

There are motions available to attack service of process, to attack the form of the pleadings, to attack amendments, to attack jurisdiction, to transfer venue, to add or delete parties, to dismiss for nonjoinder, and to dismiss for nonsuit, for summary judgment, or for pretrial evidence rulings. Any of them might well be appropriate in a defense of a medical malpractice case, but to assume a factual situation for each motion is beyond the scope of this book.

In connection with the use of motion practice, it is suggested that motions should be used sparingly and only when clearly warranted. Most rules of civil procedure, including the federal rules, indicate necessary restraint in overuse of motions.

If the complaint or petition fails to state a claim upon which any relief can be granted, it is, of course, subject to a motion to dismiss (Fed. R. Civ. P. 12(b)(6)). This is in effect the ancient demurrer, and in view of modern rules on notice pleading, has limited success, with accent on the limited. It does not foreclose another try by plaintiff's counsel to plead adequate factual matters and other than to attempt to educate the court early on, it is not a very valuable tool.

§3.02 DISCOVERY MOTIONS

In connection with the discovery process (Chapter 4), motions may on occasion become important. Discovery includes locating and obtaining medical, employment and personal records of the plaintiff encompassing prior injuries, prior sicknesses, prior hospitalizations, prior surgery, prior medical care, hospital, radiology and pathology reports, as well as present medical records if plaintiff is living. All records should be made available without court involvement, but unfortunately this is not always the case, in which event motions requesting orders compelling discovery must be utilized.

Depositions and discovery rules are set forth in Federal Rules of Civil Procedure 26, et seq. Rule 34 provides for production of documents and things and Rule 35 provides for physical and mental examinations. As a general rule discovery requests are handled informally between counsel. In the event this is not possible, a motion for a discovery conference may be requested under Rule 26(f) which directs the court to hold a conference if one is requested. While generally used as a timetable, the conference is valuable in determining what is discoverable and what is not.

In the event discovery cannot be had by accommodation, motions for orders compelling discovery are available under Federal Rule of Civil Procedure 37(b) which also provides in Rule 37(b)(2) for the imposition of sanctions.

If physician and hospital records cannot be obtained from plaintiff or plaintiff's counsel once their location is determined by informal disclosure or by written interrogatories, a subpoena duces tecum is available under Federal Rule of Civil Procedure 45(d) which is designed not only to compel a non-party's attendance at a deposition, but to compel the witness to produce and permit inspection and copying of documents and tangible things.

Motions for sanctions under federal rules and under local rules are also available. They are an unfortunate part of current trial practice and are not relevant to or addressed by this book.

§3.03 LIMITATIONS

Motions for summary judgment based upon the question as to whether or not the cause of action is barred by the statute of limitations are very often in the picture. No fixed rule can be set out; views of the courts in different jurisdictions vary in their holdings as to the form of the action brought, contract or tort or a hybrid form. Different limitation periods are prescribed by statutes of the various states. In general, see 4 Am. Jur. Trials *Solving Statutes of Limitation Problems,* 441; Annotation, *Statute of Limitations Applicable to Malpractice Action Against Physician, Surgeon, Dentist, or other Practitioner,* 80 A.L.R. 2d 320 (1961).

Of growing significance is the adoption by the courts of the discovery rule, to the effect that the limitation period commences to run from the time that the act of malpractice with resulting injury is, or by reasonable diligence should be, discovered. See 61 Am. Jur. 2d *Physicians, Surgeons and Other Healers* §321, (1981); Annotation, *Medical Malpractice: Statute of Limitations in Wrongful Death Action Based on Medical Malpractice,* 70 A.L.R. 4th 535 (1989).

In breast cancer cases, it is increasingly held that the statute of limitations is governed by the discovery rule which is interpreted to mean the time that the cancer has metastasized and not at the time the alleged negligence became apparent. For a leading case discussing the problem see *Colbert v. Georgetown University,* 623 A.2d 1244 (D.C. App. 1993); see also *Bradley v. Ragheb,* 633 A.2d 192 (Pa. Sup. Ct. 1993).

§3.04 MOTION FOR SUMMARY JUDGMENT

Experienced counsel will promptly conduct discovery and attack, if indicated, by motion for summary judgment. If the answers to interrogatories, requests to admit and depositions make it uncertain that the defendant did anything to change the outcome, a motion for summary judgment seeking a ruling as a matter of law that the plaintiff's proof of causation is insufficient should then be considered. The standard for granting or denying is set out by Federal Rule of Civil Procedure 56(c).

> "(the judgment) shall bc rendered forthwith if the pleadings, depositions, answers to interrogatories and admissions on file, together with the affidavits, if any, show that there is no genuine issue as to any material fact and that the moving party is entitled to judgment as a matter of law."

This rule provides also for partial summary judgments in that the motion may go to any part of a claim and will permit judgment to be entered on liability alone. A court may also determine that some material facts are not in dispute and enter an order establishing those facts, removing them from the trial.

Another similar motion is that for a nonsuit. *Horn v. National Hospital Association,* 131 P.2d 455 (Or. 1942).

In jurisdictions in which there have been no prior rulings on issues of loss of chance, counsel should not overlook the possibility of obtaining a ruling requiring the plaintiff to establish a probability of better results absent malpractice.

In jurisdictions permitting reliance on increased risk, the plaintiff should be required to show not only that the malpractice increased the risk to the patient, but also that the harm thus risked actually occurred and that the increased risk was a substantial factor in bringing about the harm. The defense motion asking for a ruling that the plaintiff failed as a matter of law to show that the defendant's conduct was a substantial factor in bringing about any harm suffered should, after proper discovery, be considered. *Kimball v. Scors,* 399 N.Y.S.2d 350 (1977); *Hamil,* 392 A.2d 1280. Such matters can be, of course, raised under the summary judgment provision of the Federal Rules and, in addition, some state courts, such as Iowa, have special rules relating to separate adjudication of law points.

> "The court may in its discretion and must on application of either party, made after issues joined and before trial, separately hear and determine any point of law raised in any pleading which goes to the whole or any material part of the case. It shall enter an appropriate final order before trial of the remaining issues, adjudicating the point so

determined which shall not be questioned on the trial of any part of the case of which it is not disposed. If such ruling does not dispose of the whole case, it should be deemed interlocutory for purposes of appeal.'' Iowa R. Civ. P. 105.

§3.05 IN LIMINE

Motions in limine should always be considered. They grew out of the criminal law as a means of suppressing illegally obtained evidence. Annotation, *Modern Status of Rules as to Use of Motion in Limine or Similar Preliminary Motion to Secure Exclusion of Prejudicial Evidence or Reference to Prejudicial Matters,* 63 A.L.R. 3d 311 (1975). Their use is growing and has a positive role in bringing the factual issues to the judge in order to curtail inadmissible evidence that might be inadvertently admitted and to make the entire trial more predictable. The motion will raise questions about the admissibility of certain evidence and request an order directing counsel not to refer to it, as well as to instruct his or her witnesses not to mention the evidence thus declared to be inadmissible. There is no specific rule authorizing motions in limine under federal procedure, but it has been held that the court has inherent power. Federal Rule of Evidence 103(c) states:

> ''In jury cases proceedings shall be conducted to the extent practicable so as to prevent inadmissible evidence from being suggested to the jury by any means.''

Motions in limine are generally utilized more by plaintiffs than defendants. However, depending upon the circumstances, they may be valuable to the defendant as well. *Bruske v. Arnold,* 254 N.E.2d 453 (Ill. 1969). (Motion to suppress defendant's statement taken by plaintiff's investigator after defendant was represented of record by attorney, sustained as a sanction against unethical conduct of plaintiff's attorney and because pretrial discovery rules applied.) It is noted, of course, that when a motion in limine is overruled, the moving party is required to make proper objections at the proper time or the objections are waived. *Rush v. Sioux City,* 240 N.W.2d 431, 438 (Iowa 1976).

§3.06 FOR JUDGMENT AS A MATTER OF LAW (DIRECTED VERDICT)

In jurisdictions holding that proof of probable better results with proper treatment is necessary for recovery and plaintiff's proof does not reach that level, or, in jurisdictions recognizing loss of chance where plaintiff has not offered competent, credible evidence that the loss of chance was occasioned by the negligence of the defendant or in any other respect where plaintiff's proof has fallen legally short, a motion for directed verdict should, of course, be made.

1. If during a trial by jury, a party has been fully heard with respect to an issue and there is no legally sufficient evidentiary basis for a reasonable jury to have found for that party with respect to that issue, the court may grant a motion for judgment as a matter of law against that party on any claim, counterclaim, cross claim or third party claim that cannot under the controlling law be maintained without a favorable finding on that issue.
2. Motions for judgment as a matter of law may be made at any time before submission of the case to the jury. Such a motion shall specify the judgment sought and the law and the facts on which the moving party is entitled to the judgment.

(Fed. R. Civ. P. 50(a)(2).

Even in cases that do not require the alleged negligence to have "probably" or "more likely than not" caused the subsequent disability, there is still a causation issue, and plaintiff has the burden to establish by a preponderance of the evidence that the tortious aspect of the defendant's conduct is a "substantial possibility" to have produced the injury or created a "loss of chance." *Herskovits v. Group Health Cooperative,* 99 Wash.2d 609, 664 P.2d 474; *Waffen v. U.S. Department of Health and Human Services,* 799 F.2d 911 (4th Cir. 1986). In actions of this kind statistical evidence will be presented and in many cases there is a question as to whether the statistical evidence introduced is sufficient to sustain the burden. Does the evidence amount to sufficient proof, rising above speculation, that the physician's conduct was a proximate cause of the patient's death?

This question is not of fact alone, but it is also one of law. Statistics alone are not sufficient to prove proximate cause. They may create injuries, but whether they are substantial and more than pure speculation are matters for the court to consider before they are submitted to the jury. See Restatement (Second) of Torts, pgh. 434 (1965); *Scott v. Rainbow Ambulance Service, Inc.*, 75 Wash.2d 494, 452 P.2d 220 (1969).

Counsel will also recognize that when a motion for directed verdict is denied, the court is deemed to have submitted the action to the jury subject to a later determination of the legal questions raised by the motion. Known as a judgment notwithstanding the verdict, the same must be filed not later than ten days after entry of judgment and may be joined by a motion for a new trial under Federal Rule of Civil Procedure 59. Counsel will also recall that a motion for directed verdict having been made and overruled at the close of plaintiff's testimony must be renewed at the close of all the evidence or a motion for judgment notwithstanding the verdict will not lie.

§3.07 MOTION AS TO "EXPERTS"

Courts have always taken the position that in most malpractice cases expert testimony is necessary and that if medical experts cannot agree, it then falls to a judge or jury to decide the matter based upon what available medical facts are introduced. Breast cancer malpractice litigation will continue as long as experts testify to the harmful effects of delayed diagnosis regardless of the biology of the tumor.

Experts, of course, abound in all fields from polygraph operators to hypnotists to toxic substance research to handwriting and to the interpretation of dreams. In the medical field, experts are readily available to testify on any side of an issue. Some of them are "off the wall" theorists and with the modern judicial "liberal" tendency to admit "junk science," they are not unknown.

The problem was mentioned by Dr. Murray Seltzer at the Section of Tort and Insurance Practice of the American Bar Association, August 9, 1993 as follows:

> Lastly, there is concern in the medical community as to who represents an expert. The judicial system allows wide latitude, thus diminishing respect for the tort system to some degree by physicians. One certainly

wants to believe that plaintiff's expert possesses more knowledge and experience than oneself to qualify as an expert. There should be some criteria for designating a physician as an expert mutually agreed upon by medical and legal organizations.

This is discussed at greater length by Rovit and Hauber, *The Expert Witness: Some Observations and Response,* 74 Bulletin of the American College of Surgeons, 10-16 (1989). See generally Green, *Expert Witnesses and Sufficiency of Evidence in Toxic Substances Litigation: The Legacy of Agent Orange and Bendectin Litigation;* 86 NW. U.L. Rev. 643 (1992); and Foster, *When the Experts Can't Agree: What Determines the Admissibility of Scientific Testimony in Federal Trials?* American Bar Assn. Preview of U.S. Supreme Court Cases (March 1993) (Lexis, Gen. Fed. Library, U.S. Plus File).

Although there was not universal consistency among the states and the different federal circuits, the common law rule was that expert testimony to be admissible, must be deduced from a recognized scientific principle and must be established by general acceptance in the particular field in which it belongs. The standard was enunciated by the District of Columbia Court of Appeals in the criminal case of *Frye v. United States,* 293 F. 1013 (D.C. App. 1923). There the court declared that expert opinion based upon a methodology which diverges "significantly" from the procedures accepted by recognized authorities in the field cannot be shown to be "generally accepted as a reliable technique." This general acceptance standard in *Frye* originally applied to testimony based on a scientific device. But thereafter it was extended to scientific evidence in general.

An interesting book by Peter W. Huber, a Senior Fellow of the Manhattan Institute, is entitled *Galileo's Revenge, Junk Science in the Courthouse* 43 (1991), wherein he states, "The best test of certainty you have is good science—the science of publication, replication and verifications, the science of consensus and peer review."

While the *Frye* case was generally accepted, there was no consensus among federal appellate judges as to its applicability and the problem remained in every case of experts testifying on the basis of so-called scientific evidence was whether or not it needed "general acceptance" to be admissible at trial.

By reason of the divisions among the courts, the United States Supreme Court granted certiorari in the case of *Daubert v. Merrell Dow Pharmaceuticals, Inc.,* 509 U.S. ______, 113 S. Ct. 2786 (1993). This decision to grant certiorari was anticipated to have a major effect on future medical malpractice litigation. Marwick, Co., *What Constitutes an Expert Witness?* 269 JAMA 2057 (1993).

The court clearly overruled the common law *Frye* doctrine, but the answer as to "What is the standard for admitting expert scientific testimony at trial?" may, like beauty, lie only in the eye of the beholder. The court held that the common law rule remains as a source of guidance in interpreting the federal rules, but the rules may supersede a particular common law doctrine which they do not specifically incorporate. Thus, in the case of the *Frye* ruling, the court stated that *Federal Rule of Evidence 702* specifically addresses the issue. This rule states:

> If scientific, technical or other specialized knowledge will assist the trier of fact to understand the evidence or to determine a fact in issue, a witness qualified as an expert by knowledge, skill, experience, training or education may testify thereto in the form of an opinion or otherwise.

A generally accepted standard does not appear in the rules and such a standard would be in conflict with the rules' generally permissive, liberal approach. Thus, the general acceptance *exclusive* test in *Frye* for admitting some expert scientific testimony was incompatible with the Federal Rules of Evidence.

However, there is considerable question as to whether or not courts which had historically applied the *Frye* test will reach any different decisions on admissibility after *Daubert* than they would have before. (See summary of post-*Daubert* cases in Bert Black, *The Judicial Reaction to Daubert,* Shepard's Expert and Sci. Evid. Q319 (fall 1993)).

It would appear that *Daubert* actually requires trial judges to analyze and state their determinations in a more careful manner. While stating that "nothing in the text of this rule (F.R.D. 702) establishes general acceptance as an absolute prerequisite to admissibility," *Daubert,* 2794, in many cases it can be. (*Porter v. Whitehall Labs, Inc.*, 9 F.3d. 607 (7th Cir. 1993)).

Daubert interpreted Rule 702 to impose two requirements in the case of scientific expert evidence. One, the evidence must be reliable, that is, the underlying methodology from which the evidence is derived must be based on "scientific knowledge" and, two, the evidence must be relevant. This judgment must be made before the evidence is admitted by the judge acting as a "gate keeper" under Federal Rule of Evidence 104(a) (*Daubert,* 2796).

Chief Justice Rehnquist and Justice Stevens dissented in part, primarily because the construction of Rules 702 and 703 were very much in the abstract and so were the court's general observations regarding the judicial role to be performed by the trial judge.

Justice Blackmun listed four factors that would be useful: 1) whether the theory or technique can be and has been tested; 2) whether the theory or technique has been subjected to peer review and publication; 3) the known or potential rate of error or the existence of standards; and 4) whether the theory or technique used has been generally accepted. *Id.* at 2796-97. The court indicated that whether the theory or technique has been tested is a "key question." *Id.* at 2796. While it would appear that "general acceptance" may no longer be the standard of admissibility, it remains a part of the analysis.

The concept of relevancy invokes Federal Rules of Evidence 401 and 402, Rule 401 defining relevant evidence as that evidence which has "any tendency to make the existence of any fact that is of consequence to the determination of the action more probable or less probable than it would be without the evidence." The court in *Daubert* also referred to Rule 401(a) which instructs the judge to determine "preliminary questions" concerning an expert's qualifications and the "admissibility of evidence." Rule 104(b) further instructs the judge to keep track of and insist upon the need for each piece of evidence to be connected up to other evidence so as to insure the "foundation evidence is sufficient." The court also referred to Rule 706 which allows a trial judge to call an expert of the judge's own choosing and Rule 703 which permits an expert to base an opinion on facts or data that would not themselves be admissible, but only if they are "of the type reasonably relied upon by experts in the particular field in forming opinions or inferences upon the subject." *Daubert* at 2797. Finally, the court observed that Rule 403 provides a basis for excluding expert evidence the probitive value of which is "substantially outweighed by the danger of unfair prejudice, confusion of the issues, or misleading the jury." *Id.* at 2798.

From the lawyer's standpoint, the *Daubert* opinion suggests the importance of a pretrial procedure by which the trial judge gathers the necessary information and evaluates both the reliability of the underlying principles and methodology employed by the proposed expert witness and the potential relevance of the proposed evidence.

At the request of Frank C. Jones, President of the American College of Trial Lawyers, and his predecessor, Bill Haight, an ad hoc committee composed of Chairman Michael A. Cooper of New York, David J. Beck of Houston, Gregory P. Joseph of New York, James F. Stapleton of Stamford, Connecticut, and Fletcher L. Yarbrough of Dallas, analyzed the *Daubert* decision and prepared and circulated to Fellows of the College and members of the federal and state judiciaries a most impressive report. That portion of the report dealing with suggestions for prehearing procedures is as follows:*

> 1. Pre-Hearing Procedures
>
> *Suggestions for Trial Courts.* In jurisdictions subject to the recently adopted amendments to Rule 26(a)(3) of the Federal Rules of Civil Procedure, parties must now make a disclosure of information related to expert witnesses, including "a complete statement of all opinions to be expressed and the basis and reasons therefor."[6] It would clearly be appropriate to order, either by local rule or by special order in a particular case, that "the basis and reasons" for an expert's opinions, required to be disclosed by this Rule, include the factors which the expert (and the proponent of the testimony) claim support the validity of the methodology employed. Although the Rule does not explicitly provide that these disclosures be filed with the court, in any case in which expert testimony is to play a substantial role, the trial judge should order that a copy of the disclosure document be filed.
>
> In jurisdictions in which the recent expert disclosure amendments to Rule 26(a)(2) have not become operative,[7]

---

*Reprinted with permission of the American College of Trial Lawyers and its Federal Rules of Evidence Committee.

6. Fed. R. Civ. P. 26(a)(2)(B); see also *Robinson v. Missouri Pac. R.R.,* Nos. 92-6099 92-6112, 1994 WL 48505, at *5 (10th Cir. Feb. 15, 1994), (Rule 26(a)(2)B) "will permit an early and full evaluation of [the] evidentiary problems [posed by scientific expert opinions and films or animations illustrative of such opinions]").

7. A recent study conducted by Alfred W. Cortese, Jr., Esq. of Washington, D.C., indicates that the following twenty-two federal district courts have opted out of or modified some or all of the provisions of Fed.R.Civ.P. 26(a)(2), as applied to most or all civil cases: N.D., Ala., C.D. Cal., E.D. Cal., S.D. Cal., D. Conn., D. Haw., D. Idaho, N.D. Iowa, S.D. Iowa, E.D. La, M.D. La., E.D. Mich., W.D. Mich., D.N.H., N.D.N.Y., S.D.N.Y., W.D.N.Y, E.D. Okla., N.D. Tex., D. Vt. W.D. Wash., E.D. Wis. In addition, the following eight federal district courts have opted out of Fed.R.Civ.P. 26(a)(2) in certain limited categories of cases such as prisoner petitions, bankruptcy matters and social security appeals: E.D. Ark., N.D. Cal., C.D. Ill., W.D. Ky., D.N.J., D.N.M., E.D.N.C., N.D.W. Va. *Cf. Donna Steinstra, Implementation of Disclosure in Federal District Courts, With Specific Attention to Courts Responses to Selected Amendments to Federal Rule of Civil Procedure 26* (Fed.Jud.Ctr. Mar. 1, 1994).

we suggest that trial courts, in going about the task of gathering information necessary to make an admissibility evaluation, employ a questionnaire or disclosure requirement as part of a standard pretrial order. The questionnaire or pretrial order would require the litigants, with respect to each expert designated, to address the four factors listed in *Daubert,* if the proposed evidence is ''scientific'' in nature. If, however, the subject matter of the testimony relates to another field of specialized knowledge, the proponent would be required to state the principles on which it relies in asserting that the expert's methodology is sound. Counsel for other parties should be permitted to submit comments with respect to the proponent's submissions made pursuant to the questionnaire or pretrial order. These filings would identify points of contention to be addressed by the court in a pretrial conference or at a more formal Rule 104 hearing concerning the admissibility of the expert testimony. An inadequate response to the questionnaire or pretrial order would result in failure to qualify the witness.

Timing is an important consideration in these matters. If disclosures are made very late in a case (say, not later than 90 days before trial, which is the requirement of Rule 26(a)(2) in the absence of other direction from the court), there may not be enough time for the parties to do the work necessary to present the admissibility issue in an understandable fashion or for the court to make an informed judgment about the matter, particularly if complex scientific testimony is involved. The Rule provides that disclosures concerning expert testimony ''shall be made at the time and in the sequence directed by the court.''[8] Trial courts should make ample use of this authority when scheduling orders are entered in ''expert heavy'' cases, after conferring with counsel about what is appropriate in the particular case.

Responsibilities of Counsel. Counsel can greatly assist the trial court in gathering the necessary information for an

8. Fed.R.Civ.P. 26(a)(2)(C).

admissibility determination. It is plainly counsel's responsibility to bring to the attention of the trial judge at an early time the need for the court to pay special attention to the issue of expert evidence in a particular case. Given the condition of the dockets of trial courts, and the fact that Rule 26(a)(2) does not require the disclosures to be filed with the court, a trial judge may very well not learn about the need for special treatment with respect to expert evidence until it is too late to be meaningful without postponement of the trial. This notice function which trial counsel must perform can be carried out in any one of a number of ways, including a request for a scheduling conference, submission of a proposed scheduling order that deals with the timing and sequence of Rule 27(a) disclosures and expert discovery, and the presentation of motions to compel if the adverse party is not forthcoming with respect to discovery requests concerning expert evidence.

It is clearly the responsibility of counsel to carry out in a timely fashion the available discovery techniques with respect to expert evidence. For example, whether or not the necessary information is disclosed pursuant to Rule 26(a)(2), counsel should timely depose the opposing expert to obtain information relevant to the validity of methodologies employed, including the four enumerated *Daubert* factors.

If the substance of Rule 26 disclosures and expert deposition testimony is such that there appears to be a genuine issue as to the admissibility of the evidence, counsel should bring the matter to the attention of the trial court as soon as possible. A prctrial conference to discuss the issue[9] or a request for a Rule 104 hearing are the obvious vehicles; which is the better course will depend on whether there is an applicable local rule or individual judge's rule and, in the absence of such a rule, counsel's assessment of the preference of the particular trial judge. Counsel should file with the trial judge (and deliver to

9. Amended Rule 16, Fed.R.Civ.P., includes as a pretrial conference subject "the possibility of obtaining . . . advance rulings from the court on the admissibility of evidence." See *Robinson,* 1994 WL 48504, at *10 n. 6.

any court-appointed expert) all the information produced in conformance with Rule 26 and in response to any trial court questionnaire or pretrial order, and any relevant discovery materials, before a Rule 104 hearing, in order to give the court and any court-appointed expert a chance to review the information in advance.

2. The Rule 104(a) Hearing

Daubert mandates that ''[f]aced with a proffer of expert scientific testimony, then, the trial judge must determine at the outset, pursuant to Rule 104(a), whether the expert is proposing to testify to (1) scientific knowledge that (2) will assist the trier of fact to understand or determine a fact in issue.''[10] Rule 104(a) provides, in part, that ''[p]reliminary questions concerning . . . the admissibility of evidence shall be determined by the court . . .'' As Justice Blackmun pointed out in *Daubert,* the trial court's conclusion ''should be established by a preponderance of proof.''[11] Thus, the proponent of admissibility must establish by a preponderance of proof that the proffered evidence meets both the reliability and the relevance prongs of the *Daubert* case.

In many cases, it will be difficult for the court to evaluate the evidence presented at a Rule 104(a) hearing. Chief Justice Rehnquist, in his separate opinion in *Daubert,* saw in the majority's approach a danger that federal judges would attempt to become ''amateur scientists'' in an effort to perform this part of their gatekeeping responsibilities.[12] Clearly many judges and trial attorneys lack the background and training necessary to evaluate complex scientific issues.[13] This has always been one reason for the appeal of the *Frye* ''general acceptance'' test, and probably accounts for its survival as one of the four factors enumerated in *Daubert* as bearing on reliability.

---

10. *Daubert,* 113 S.Ct. at 2796.
11. *Id.* at 2796 n. 10.
12. *Id.* at 2800.
13. See Jack Weinstein & Margaret Berger *Weinstein's Evidence* ¶702[03], at 702-35 (1993).

Use of Court-Appointed Experts. One solution to this problem in appropriate cases is for trial courts to exercise more frequently their power under Rule 706 to appoint experts to help them assess the quality of the scientific expert evidence.[14] Although trial judges have been reluctant to use their power under Rule 706 to appoint independent experts to be substantive witnesses at trials, they should be more receptive to using experts in the more limited role of assisting in the evaluation of proffered scientific expert evidence at a Rule 104(a) hearing. Thus, a court can undertake the difficult task of comprehending and evaluating methodologies underlying proffered scientific expert evidence with the assistance of competent, independent expert testimony. The appointed expert's testimony should be limited to the appropriateness of the witness's reasoning and methodology and not extend to the validity of the witness's conclusions.

In rare cases, and despite the expense, it may be useful to appoint a Rule 706 "expert expert panel" and permit the panel to be questioned and cross-examined at a court-supervised pretrial hearing. That would eliminate duplicative discovery and minimize the burden on the appointed experts.[15] Thus, as Judge Weinstein has pointed out, where the court-appointed expert does not testify at trial, the expert's role can be characterized as that of "technical advisor" to the court, and depositions of such experts may not be required.[16]

Judicial Notice. Trial judges have an additional mechanism for effectively exercising their responsibility to evaluate the reliability of proffered scientific expert evidence: They can take judicial notice of other courts' opinions. The Eighth

14. See generally *Memorandum and Order on Motion to Quash Notice of Subpoena* in *In re Joint E. & S. Dist. Asbestos Litig. (In re Johns-Manville Corp.)*, 151 F.R.D. 540 (E. & S.D.N.Y. 1993) (hereafter "*Johns-Manville*"); Joe S. Cecil & Thomas E. Willging, *Court Appointed Experts: Defining the Role of Experts Appointed under Federal Rule of Evidence 706,* at 88-95 (Fed. Jud. Ctr. 1993).

15. *Johns-Manville*, 151 F.R.D. at 544-46.

16. *Id.* at 544; see also *Reilly v. United States,* 863 F.2d 149, 157 (1st Cir. 1988).

Circuit did just that in *United States v. Martinez.*[17] In that case, the Eighth Circuit affirmed the lower court's admission of DNA profiling evidence in a prosecution charging aggravated sexual abuse of a minor. The *Martinez* court observed that the Second Circuit had recently examined the general theory underlying DNA fingerprinting, as well as the specific techniques used by the FBI, and had concluded "that in the future courts could take judicial notice of their reliability."[18] Because the Second Circuit's reliability approach was similar to that taken in *Daubert*, the Eighth Circuit panel adopted the Second Circuit's conclusions and held that the general theory and techniques of DNA profiling are valid under the holding in *Daubert.*[19] In individual cases, factual questions will remain concerning, *inter alia*, whether the techniques were performed appropriately and under appropriate circumstances.

3. Summary Judgment

In *Daubert*, Justice Blackmun responded to concerns that abandonment of the *Frye* test would lead to a "free-for-all" in which befuddled juries are confounded by absurd and irrational pseudoscientific assertions."[20] Among the points he made was the observation that if the trial court concludes that "the scintilla of evidence presented supporting a position is insufficient to allow a reasonable juror to conclude that the position more likely than not was true," the court may grant summary judgment before trial or direct a judgment as a matter of law under Rule 50(a) during trial.[21]

Trial courts ought to make full use of these powers. The benefits are obvious of avoiding entirely or shortening a lengthy and complex jury trial, or even a complicated claim or defense, when the court concludes that there is no genuinely

17. 3 F.3d 1191, 1197 (8th Cir. 1993), cert. denied, 114 S.Ct. 734 (1994).
18. *Id.*
19. *Id.* (citing *United States v. Jakobetz,* 955 F.2d 786, 799-800 (2d Cir.), cert denied, 113 S.Ct. 104 (1992)).
20. 113 S.Ct. at 1798.
21. *Id.*

disputed issue of material fact. Of course, in such a case it is always better, if possible, to grant summary judgment before trial than to direct a judgment during trial, simply to conserve the resources of the court and the parties.

If the ground upon which summary judgment is sought is that an essential element of a claim (such as causation) depends entirely on expert testimony which is attacked as inadmissible, the determination of admissibility under Rule 104(a) must precede, or be resolved contemporaneously with, the motion for summary judgment. A side benefit of an antecedent Rule 104(a) hearing is that the court can gain a much better understanding of the issues in the case and how the proposed expert evidence relates to those issues, and thus be in a better position to make an informed decision about a later motion for summary judgment. Indeed the resolution of the prior Rule 104(a) hearing may obviate the need for, or dictate the result of, the later summary judgment motion.

If, on the other hand, the issue is not the admissibility of the expert evidence but, rather, its sufficiency to raise a genuinely disputed issue of material fact, no antecedent evidentiary hearing is required. The court simply judges the sufficiency on the basis of the summary judgment materials properly before it. It should be observed, however, that if the scientific issues are not easily understood, it will be much easier for the court to rule on the sufficiency point if there has been a prior admissibility hearing under Rule 104(a). In that circumstance, even though the court has ruled the evidence to be admissible under the *Daubert* standard, as both reliable and relevant, the knowledge gained in that hearing will almost certainly enhance the judge's familiarity with the issues and facilitate resolution of the sufficiency question on a summary judgment motion. Moreover, absent a Rule 104(a) hearing, trial courts are more likely to permit the proponent to introduce admissible, though possibly insufficient, evidence at trial, at least until the court has heard enough to be comfortable with a decision that the evidence is insufficient for a reasonable juror to find for that party. In many cases this approach may, in the long run, actually save resources by avoiding reversals on appeal from grants of summary judgment.

Issues During Trial

If the trial court and trial counsel have discharged their respective responsibilities before trial, the court should not have to rule on admissibility of scientific or other complicated expert evidence during trial, except in simple cases or in dealing with "surprise" evidence (which usually will be excluded, in any event, for failure to comply with pretrial orders). To the extent that the issue arises during trial, under *Daubert* the burden remains on the proponent to demonstrate by a preponderance of proof the reliability and relevance of the proffered evidence.

The principal issue for the judge at trial, therefore, is likely to be how to conduct the trial in order to maximize the jury's ability to understand the expert evidence. Justice Blackmun's answer in *Daubert* was the right one: No one should be "overly pessimistic about the capabilities of the jury, and of the adversary system generally. Vigorous cross-examination, presentation of contrary evidence, and careful instruction on the burden of proof are the traditional and appropriate means of attacking shaky but admissible evidence."[22] Thus, once the court has ruled that expert evidence is admissible, and assuming its sufficiency, a large part of the responsibility for making it understandable to the jury passes to the trial lawyers.

The trial court should make certain that those lawyers have the tools to carry out this responsibility. The court should consider, particularly in complex cases, such devices as an expanded *voir dire* in which counsel can discuss the expected expert testimony in the context of potential juror biases, the opportunity for counsel to make "mini-arguments" about the expert evidence both before and after its presentation (rather than having to defer that discus-

---

22. 113 S.Ct. at 2798.

sion to closing argument), and thc right of counsel to have the assistance of their own experts while conducting cross-examination.[23]

Conclusion:

Before the Supreme Court's June 1994 *Daubert* decision, lower federal courts disagreed as to the proper standard for determining the admissibility of scientific expert evidence. In *Daubert,* the Supreme Court not only resolved that disagreement, but in doing so proposed an analytical framework that will lead to sounder and more consistent rulings on the admissibility of not only scientific, but also non-scientific, expert evidence. As this report has shown, trial lawyers and trial judges have numerous tools at their disposal under the Federal Rules of Civil Procedure and the Federal Rules of Evidence to crystallize and resolve issues of the admissibility of expert evidence at the earliest practicable time in a litigation. April, 1994.

23. Fed. R. Evid. 615(3).

CHAPTER 4: DISCOVERY

CHAPTER 4

DISCOVERY

Experienced defense counsel are well aware not only of the necessity of proper discovery, but of the necessity of commencing it promptly. It is always a question whether to commence discovery by the taking of the oral deposition of the plaintiff or by filing interrogatories. In the event the plaintiff is in a terminal condition, the question may be academic for the first thing plaintiff's counsel will request is a videotaped deposition. *The Use of Videotape in Civil Trial Preparation and Discovery,* 23 AmJur Trials 95 (1976); *Annotation Use of Videotape to Take Depositions for Presentation in Civil Trials in State Court,* 66 ALR3rd 637 (1975).

If the patient is deceased, obviously the question is also academic. In the event, however, that the patient is living and in apparent good health, taking the patient's oral deposition prior to filing writing interrogatories should be considered. Oral depositions are much more productive with respect to detail, with respect to symptoms, thoughts and experiences than are written interrogatories. Answers to written interrogatories usually come back carefully framed by plaintiff's counsel. At the same time, physician and hospital records covering the claimed malpractice are necessary for a complete oral examination and these usually must be located by written interrogatories.

Medical records, the original pathology slides, tissue blocks and diagnostic reports in respect to the various surgeries undergone by the plaintiff should be obtained as well as any reports from any treating or examining physician. The records obviously should contain nursing notes, as well as all past hospitalization and all of plaintiff's past medical history.

Written interrogatories also have the value in inquiring as to plaintiff's legal theories. Sample interrogatories are as follows:

§4.01 WRITTEN INTERROGATORIES

1. With respect to the plaintiff (or plaintiff's decedent), please state:
   a. Age, marital status including number of marriages, number and age of children.
   b. Places of employment and types of businesses in which plaintiff was employed.
   c. Medical history including all surgeries, hospitalizations and all prescription drugs taken or prescribed.
   d. Names of parents and siblings, conditions of their health and present ages or, if any have not survived, age at time of death and the cause.
   e. Have either of plaintiff's parents or any of plaintiff's siblings ever suffered from breast cancer?
   f. If the answer to the foregoing is yes, please state in detail the first discovery of the breast cancer and ultimate result.
2. Please state when the plaintiff (or plaintiff's decedent) first consulted the defendant about her breast cancer or any condition ultimately involving the same.
3. Please state in detail how and in what manner plaintiff claims the defendant was negligent in not discovering or not properly treating plaintiff's breast cancer and how any alleged lack of discovery or treatment caused or contributed to plaintiff's death or present condition.
4. Please state whether or not plaintiff claims that but for defendant's alleged negligence plaintiff would probably have survived or her present condition probably would have been avoided.
5. Please state whether plaintiff's cause of action is based upon any other theory and, if so, specify the same.
6. State the name and address of each person whom you intend to call as an expert witness at trial and, as to each such expert, please state:
   a. The subject matter or area on which such expert is to testify.

b. Said expert's qualifications to testify as an expert on said subject.
c. The mental impressions and opinions held by said expert and the facts known to the expert (regardless of when the factual information was acquired) which relate to, or form the basis of, the mental impressions and opinions held by the expert.
d. A summary of the grounds for each opinion of such expert.
e. A complete bibliography of books, treatises, articles and other works which such expert regards as authorization on the subject on which the expert will testify.
f. The manner in which such expert became familiar with the facts of this case.
g. The educational background of the expert.
h. The expert's familiarity with similar medical occurrences.

§4.02 ORAL DEPOSITION OF PLAINTIFF

The circumstances of plaintiff's relationship with the defendant physician are too varied to pose specific questions. However, on oral deposition, detailed examination should be made of plaintiff's medical history, whether her parents or siblings ever had breast cancer, what she knew about breast cancer, what she had studied about breast cancer, what she knew about self-examination, whether she had conducted routine self-examinations, what she found as far as any thickening or lump is concerned, when she sought medical advice, what she advised the physician about her self-examination, what his examination consisted of, what he told her, whether he suggested a mammogram or whether she suggested it, whether one was taken, whether the results were explained to her, whether her relationship with the defendant physician was good, whether he appeared to be knowledgeable and conscientious, what her own fears and expectations were as far as the lump was concerned, whether she noticed any growth in the lump and over what period of time, and what her present health is. Not that the answers will all be favorable as far as a claim of negligence against the defendant is concerned, but they must be asked. And in the event that despite contending the defendant was negligent, the plaintiff will concede that he or she was kind, conscientious and concerned, this is a plus that may aid the defense.

§4.03 ORAL DEPOSITION OF PLAINTIFF'S EXPERT

It goes without saying that depositions, particularly of experts, should not be done in a slipshod or casual fashion. Total preparation is mandatory, and counsel should review the medical records and other information concerning the case, as well as be fully conversant with the literature on the subject. It is often advisable to prepare a checklist prior to the deposition of such expert to insure that all points are covered. It is suggested that depositions are not the time for cross-examination, but a time for exploration to determine the qualifications and standing the expert has in the profession, how he or she got into the case, if he or she has ever made a physical examination of the plaintiff, his or her knowledge of the standards of care, the medical theory of the expert, and his or her knowledge of the literature as it bears upon the defense of causation.

It is suggested that leading questions *generally* should be avoided, even though they are permissible. What the examiner wants to do is have the expert say in his or her own words what his or her own opinion is and what it is based upon. One not only gets more information by letting the expert testify in his or her own words, but there is the added advantage that if upon trial it becomes necessary to impeach the witness by a contradictory statement in the deposition, he or she can be confronted with his or her own words and deprived of the claim of being misunderstood.

Caveat: It is wise to include in the notice of deposition of plaintiff's trial expert a request for his or her records. It sometimes happens that the expert will have (conveniently) left his or her review notes at home or does not bring any records relating to research, etc.

As will be discussed under Chapter 5.04[b] use of medical literature in cancer cases is highly important. To use it, a foundation must be laid and the most effective foundation can be that of the adverse expert. Consequently, the examination of the witness in this respect should be addressed in the first part of counsel's deposition examination.

[a] Laying a Foundation—Sample Questions

Doctor, your specialty is in what branch?

How long have you specialized in that branch?

Would you say you are considered as an authority in this field?

Do you belong to the various societies and associations in your specialty?

Do these memberships entitle you to receive their official publications?

Do you also attend and participate in the conventions, the annual meetings and the various seminars conducted in this field?

Have you attended these conventions and meetings throughout the years?

Do you receive the official publications of these societies and associations?

You are also on the mailing list of the leading medical book publishers?

Have you purchased any books in your field of practice within the past _____ years related to this subject?

Do all of these publications help keep you abreast of all developments in the field of breast cancer?

Would you please name some text or literature in the field of breast cancer that you have read over the past 15 years?

Have you found these to be informative?

Are there any of them that you do not consider to be authoritative?

Are there any of them with which you disagree?

Are you acquainted with Dr. J. R. Harris? Harris, *Biology and Breast Diseases,* Second Edition, at 165-181.

Are you acquainted with Dr. Plotkin? Plotkin, *Cancer Management Controversy: Breast Cancer: Breast Cancer—Biology and Malpractice,* 14 Am. J. Clin. Oncol. 254 (1991).

Are you acquainted with Dr. Brinkley? Brinkley, *Long Term Survival Women with Breast Cancer,* 1 Lancet 1118 (May 1984).

Are you acquainted with Dr. Hibberd? Hibberd, *Long Term Prognosis of Women with Breast Cancer in New Zealand: Study of Survival to 30 Years,* 286 Brit. Med. Journal, 1777 (1983).

Are you acquainted with Dr. Rutqvist? Rutqvist, *Long Term Survival of 458 Young Breast Cancer Patients,* 55 Cancer 658 (1985).

Are you acquainted with Dr. J. B. Buchanan? Buchanan, *Tumor Growth Doubling Times and Inability of the Radiologist to Diagnose Certain Breast Cancer* 21 Radiologic Clinics North America 115 (1983).

Are you acquainted with what is known as the Fisher Doctrine? Fisher, *The Impact of Pathology on the Biologic, Diagnostic, Prognostic and Therapeutic Considerations in Breast Cancer* 64 (6) Surgical Clinics of North America 1073 (1984).

Are you acquainted with Dr. Kenneth Kern? *Historical Trends in Breast Cancer Litigation,* Surgical Oncology Clinics of N.A., Vol. 3, No. 1, p. 1, Jan., 1994.

Are you acquainted with Dr. R. James Brenner? *Medicolegal Aspects of Screening Mammography,* A.J.R. Am. J. Roentgenol, Vol. 3, No. 1, p. 67, Jan. 1994.

Or with Dr. Blake Cady? *Tumor Biology in Causation and Risk Management Strategies,* Surgical Oncology Clinic of N.A., (Preface) 70(4) p. xi, Aug. 1990.

If you are acquainted with any of the foregoing, do you consider them to be authoritative?

Do you consider the National Center for Health Statistics and the U.S. Bureau of the Census to be reliable sources of information?

Would you agree that the age adjusted mortality rate of breast cancer has not decreased since records were first kept in 1930? (Chapter 6).

Do you agree that many breast cancers metastasize to distant sites during or shortly after the period of vascularization? At this time, are they large enough to detect by any known method including mammography? (Chapter 16).

Would you agree that breast cancer is a complex disease?

Do you agree that last year 27 to 28 women per 100,000 population died of breast cancer? This was true 60 years ago and will be true this year. This is true despite the enormous research and clinical effort made to understand the disease and modify treatment? (Chapter 6).

Dr. Fisher stated that all breast cancers have systemic disease at the time of diagnosis and excision. Do you agree or disagree with that statement? (§7.03).

Isn't it true that simple lumpectomy is as effective as the most radical surgery in most cases? (Chapter 21).

And isn't this because systemic disease is present in about half of the patients?

And the variations in local and regional treatment will not alter survival, will they?

Please describe a systemic disease.

What is meant by the word doubling? (When the net number of cells within the tumor has doubled, one net cell doubling has occurred).

How many doublings does a cancer undergo during its life cycle and until the death of the host occurs? (40).

How large is a cancer after 20 doublings? (1 mm in diameter).

How large would a cancer be after 30 doublings? (10 mm or 1 cm in diameter) (Chapter 19).

Do you agree that most cancers cannot be detected by palpation until they have reached a diameter of 1 cm? (Chapter 20).

Do you agree that many cancers cannot be detected by palpation until they have obtained a diameter of 2 to 3 cm or even larger? (Chapter 20).

Do you agree that most breast cancers will obtain a blood supply when they are about 0.3 mm to 1.0 mm in diameter, that is, when the tumor is about 1/4 to 3/4 the diameter of the head of a common household pin? At that time they have the opportunity to spread to distant sites via the bloodstream. And they have the ability to metastasize? And yet, at 1.2 mm in diameter, the tumor is not discoverable by any means, including mammography? Some tumors metastasize and others don't, isn't this true? (§20.02).

Can you give us any estimate of the number of breast lumps that you have found either by palpation or mammography?

Can you tell us, at least as a percentage, how many have been benign as opposed to cancerous?

Can you give us some number as to breast cancers that you have found and treated?

Doctor, did any of these patients die of breast cancer?

Was this in spite of the time of diagnosis and quality of treatment?

Have you had patients with breast cancer that you were unable to save, and also patients with the same size of cancer, same age, that were saved?

Was this because the cancers were different in each woman?

In other words, it was the biology of the cancer that determined the outcome?

Are you familiar with the concept known as a cancer control window? Please describe it. (Chapter 16).

Are you familiar with what is referred to as the camouflaged tumor? Describe this. (Chapter 14).

What was the Halstead Doctrine? (That breast cancer spreads via the lymphathics and then to distant sites via the perivascular lymphathics, seldom if ever through the blood stream). (Chapter 7).

At this time Halstead and a Dr. Meyer popularized the radical removal of the breast, the underlying muscles and the regional lymph nodes known as the radical mastectomy.

Isn't it true that today the Halstead Doctrine is deemed to be incorrect, and it is accepted that breast cancer metastasizes both through lymphatics and through the blood stream? It is also accepted that lumpectomy has proved to be as effective as radical mastectomy, is it not? (Chapter 7; §21.04[b]).

Isn't it true that no patient chooses the type of tumor that she will have? And no physician has control over the lethal potential of the tumor he or she is treating?

Isn't it true that genetic alteration of the breast cancer is something entirely beyond the control of the patient and the clinician? If the breast cancer happens to be fully malignant at the time of vascularization and spreads to distant sites when the tumor is only 1 to 3 mm in diameter, there is nothing anyone can do about it, is there? (Chapter 10).

In this particular case, did you examine both the clinical history and the pathology of this cancer? Did you examine microscopic slides of the plaintiff's tumor?

What does the pathology report tell us about the histology, the tumor grading, microscopic features, flow cytometry, estrogen receptor, progesterone receptor?

Was there any immunohistochemical staining of the tumor tissue performed? What did it reveal?

Did you review the mammogram films?

How long was it after the surgery that the first symptoms of distant metastasis appeared?

Does this suggest that it was a highly lethal tumor that metastasized early in its life cycle?

Doctor, tell us how and in what manner and by whom you were contacted to become an expert witness in this case.

What material or other information were you furnished to study in connection with this matter?

Have you been an expert witness before in medical malpractice cases? What kind of cases? How many? Where have they been pending?

What do you charge for your services as a witness? Is that what you are charging in this case? When did you agree to take the case?

CHAPTER 5: TRIAL STRATEGY

CHAPTER 5

TRIAL STRATEGY

§5.01 PREPARING YOUR WITNESSES

[a] Preparing Your Defendant

Experienced defense counsel will agree that the defendant is his or her most important witness. Before a lawyer can sell the client's story, he or she must first sell the client.

Despite angry assertions at medical meetings, juries do not dislike doctors. Moreover, in most cases, they try very hard to be fair to them. They may be wrong, but wrong because they have misjudged the facts and the law, not because of any built-in hostility toward physicians.

As with all of us, juries evaluate people on the basis of ''partial assertions'' and ''total assertions.'' A person may have many faults and many character flaws, but if in total sum he or she comes across as an attractive, likeable and caring person, the faults and flaws are forgiven. In contrast, a person may be a saint in personal habits and character, but come across as one who is simply not likeable as a total person. Consequently, a little grooming of the defendant may be indicated. Personality, of course, is hard to change and advice is not always taken, but the defendant should be advised that the more he or she appears to the jury as a warm, concerned person, the more likely the jury will be to believe his or her story and consider the defense. For an excellent analysis of jury behavior and attitudes as well as how to take advantage of these at trial, see D. Vinson, *Jury Persuasion: Psychological Strategies and Trial Techniques* (Prentice Hall Law & Business, 1993).

The defendant should also be prepared for the probability that plaintiff's counsel may call him or her as a first witness. (See e.g. Fed. R. Evid. 611(e)). It is a common procedure, and in many instances, quite effective. It can also be a two-way street. The law of primacy tells us that juries are most impressed by what they hear first and what they hear last. If the defendant physician comes across as a likeable person, totally concerned about the patient and demonstrably touched by the adverse result, the defense will have set the stage for a sympathetic consideration of the defense.

The defendant should also be advised to respect the skill and medical knowledge of plaintiff's counsel. Physicians sometimes forget that lawyers can read medical literature and, as to any given medical problem, may be surprisingly knowledgeable. True, the defendant physician will have the advantage by reason of education, training and experience, but should not assume that this advantage carries over without timely and thorough preparation.

Defendant should also be cautioned to be totally professional in attitude, avoiding anger. This is sometimes difficult, given the average physician's antipathy to court procedure. Not unreasonably, the physician does not like to be accused of harming a patient or causing her death. The adversary process is foreign to the nature of most physicians and to be placed upon the witness stand and assaulted, either on the basis of lack of medical skill and knowledge, or on the basis of patient neglect, is traumatic. But, it has to be faced and anger will not help the cause.

Defendant physician should be subjected to cross-examination, not once but several times prior to trial. A sample of this cross-examination is included in Appendix 5-3 (at Chapter's end). Unlike the expert witnesses, the defendant physician will very likely not have had experience in testifying and must be made aware of the meaning of the phrase "standard of care" which in legal parlance may mean there was malpractice, but in medical terminology, may refer to the medical propriety of certain procedures. Defendant should be made aware of the possible usage of other phrases, such as ordinary care, standard of practice, good practice, avoidable result. He or she must be made aware that he or she will be examined on the basis of professional writings and avoid placing any blanket stamp of approval on any given book unless fully familiar with it and agrees with it.

Defendant must, however, be prepared to demonstrate that he or she was familiar with modern procedures for diagnosing breast cancer and be prepared to offer reasons why the lump was not discovered or, having been discovered, the reasons for any apparent delay in treatment. Insist that the defendant read and understand Chapter 14 on camouflaged tumors. Determine whether the defendant's findings of the breast examination were compatible with the camouflaged tumor. Did the physician find:

a) a dominant mass;
b) no definite mass;
c) an area of induration only;
  1) definite borders;
  2) vague, indistinct borders;
  3) soft, uniform induration;
  4) nodular induration?

Defendant should also be prepared to defend his/her decision not to order diagnostic modalities such as mammogram, needle aspiration or surgical biopsy as not indicated, or under the circumstances, appeared to do more harm than good. In short, the defendant physician should be prepared to negate the fact that hc or she was unconcerned or careless, but instead, considered carefully the examinations and findings that were prepared to him or her and that a considered clinical judgment was made.

As a tactical matter, upon the defendant being called as plaintiff's first witness, defense counsel has a judgment call. Should the defendant be cross-examined following the direct examination of the plaintiff, or should defense counsel wait until he or she puts on the defendant's case? There are valid arguments both ways. Plaintiff will, of course, have defendant's cross-examination transcribed and submitted to his or her experts prior to their testifying. However, the law of primacy is very real and given proper preparation of the defendant and his or her skills in defending themselves, the author is inclined to favor immediate cross-examination.

[b] Preparing Your Expert Witnesses

Obviously, no matter how well prepared defense counsel is on all aspects of breast cancer, he or she can only outline his or her theory to the jury. It must be supported by expert testimony. On this subject, more than most, the expert must be carefully selected, not only as to his or her background, education and stature, but also as to how well he or she comes across in communicating. The expert is going to have to convince the jury that what the jury may believe about cancer may not be true. As with the defendant physician, the personality of the expert is very important, as well as his or her thorough understanding of the particular case being tried, the literature in the field and, of course, the expert's full and complete agreement with the principles laid out in the medical section. In a case based upon failure to make a timely diagnosis of breast cancer, plaintiff's attorney will claim, for example, that if the plaintiff's breast cancer had been detected 6 to 12 months earlier, the tumor would have been confined to the breast and the patient would have had an excellent chance of cure. (§§7.05 and 10.11 and Visual Aid Appendix, Chapter 10). The allegation raises the following matters that should be discussed with and by the defense expert.

A. Reasons why the breast cancer was not detected 6-12 months earlier. (Chapters 14, 15, 17 and 20)
B. In the event of a delay in diagnosis of 12 months, for example, during which the tumor diameter increased from 1 cm to 2 cm, and the number of tumor cells increased from 1 billion to 8 billion, is this really critical? (Chapters 7.05, 10.11 and visual aids appendix, Chapter 10). Does this loss of time necessarily destroy the patient's chance of "cure?" (Chapters 7.05, 10.11 and Visual Aids, Chapter 10).
C. Is breast cancer really curable? (Chapter 9 and Appendix Chapters 9 and 10).
D. Does a diagnosis of breast cancer 6-12 months earlier guarantee a "cure?" (Chapters 9 and 10 and visual aids Chapters 6, 9 and 10).
E. When considering the possibility of "cure," which is the most important factor, the time of diagnosis or the inherent biology of the cancer? (Chapters 8, 9 and 10).

The authors of the literature referred to in Part II, the medical section, may make excellent witnesses, as will many physicians found in teaching hospitals. A caveat: once the experts are selected, counsel should not merely send the case to them with the request to give counsel a summary opinion. The experts should be sought out and the case discussed extensively. It should not be necessary to remind experienced defense counsel that the expert should not have his or her testimony presented on trial by way of deposition, but should be called personally or at least by video.

Preparing for possible cross examination, see Appendix 5-3.

[c] Preparing Your Radiologist

Schedule a meeting with your radiologist at his or her office for the purpose of reviewing the plaintiff's mammograms. Insist that your radiologist read the chapter "The Camouflaged Tumor" (Chapter 14) in this book. Ask your radiologist to consider the following factors: Could they or did they increase the threshold of the plaintiff's breast cancer?

CHECKLIST
(Chapter 23)

A. Density of the breast
B. Dysplasia of the breast
C. Density of the tumor
   1. Similar to the breast tissue
   2. Less than the density of the breast tissue
D. Absence of or minimal evidence of a central tumor mass
E. Vague and indistinct tumor borders
F. Lack of tumor-specific microcalcifications
G. Size of the breast
H. Location of the tumor within the breast
I. Did the tumor mimic a benign tumor?
J. No evidence of architectural distortion of the normal breast tissue
K. Minimal desmoplasia
L. Other factors which would have increased the threshold size of the plaintiff's breast cancer.

Does your radiologist agree that there were camouflaging factors involved in the plaintiff's breast cancer and/or breast tissue? Did these factors increase the threshold size of the plaintiff's breast cancer? Would this increase in the threshold size have resulted in a longer sojourn time of the plaintiff's breast cancer? Would this longer sojourn time have increased the likelihood of a systemic breast cancer? Does your radiologist have an opinion as to the age of the tumor? Is your radiologist confident of his or her opinions and will he or she be willing to testify?

[d] Preparing Your Pathologist

A meticulous examination of the plaintiff's breast cancer will often reveal prognostic factors not mentioned in the operative report that may provide significant information about prognosis. It is important, therefore, to meet immediately with your pathologist, and review the pathology report and the microscopic slides of the plaintiff's breast cancer. Ask your pathologist to read Chapter 23 on identifying the early metastasizing breast cancer. Ask if factors were found that could have helped camouflage the plaintiff's breast cancer and if there are any findings that might shed light upon tumor aggressiveness and lethal potential. Review with the pathologist the items on the following checklist, and if some of these have not been performed, discuss the feasibility of performing them with the pathologist and your expert medical witness. Schedule a meeting with the pathologist for the purpose of reviewing the microscopic slides of the plaintiff's breast cancer. Ask the pathologist to read the chapter "The Camouflaged Tumor" (Chapter 14). Ask the pathologist to consider the following factors: Could anything have helped camouflage the plaintiff's breast cancer?

CHECKLIST
(Chapter 23)

A. Cross-examination regarding the plaintiff's breast cancer:
   1. Was the tumor softer than the average invasive duct cell carcinoma and difficult to palpate?
   2. Was the tumor more of an area of induration rather than a discrete firm mass?
   3. Were the tumor borders poorly defined?
   4. Was it difficult to detect the tumor by gross examination?

B. Microscopic examination of the tumor:
   1. Was the lesion an invasive lobular carcinoma? (These lesions are not uncommonly present as camouflaged tumors).
   2. Was the pattern of tumor invasion similar to that of the invasive lobular carcinomas? This unique pattern of tumor invasion often results in a tumor with vague and indistinct borders or a vague area of soft swelling without a definite central tumor mass.
   3. Was the lesion an invasive duct cell carcinoma with a large component of intraductal carcinoma? The intraductal portion of this tumor is confined to the ductal system and therefore stimu-

lates little or no desmoplasia (increased production of excess fibrous tissue). Therefore, these lesions are difficult or impossible to detect by palpation.

4. Was there an absence of specific tumor microcalciflcations?
5. Can this pathologist testify that camouflaging factors were present in the plaintiff's breast cancer and/or the plaintiff's breast tissue that would have increased the threshold size of the plaintiff's breast cancer?
6. Does the pathologist agree with the findings in the medical section and will he or she testify and educate the jury as to the nature of cancer, the definition of metastasis, the variation in the lethal potential of breast cancers, net cell doubling time, vascularization and its clinical significance, and tumor cell shedding?
7. Will the pathologist be in a position to testify that the particular cancer of the patient involved became incurable before it was possible to be detected by mammography because it was either a camouflaged tumor or an aggressive early metastasizing breast cancer?

C. Metastasis and other factors:
1. Does the pathologist agree that there are three types of breast cancer: *non-metastasizing, early metastasizing,* and *late metastasizing?*
2. Ask if some tumors are unable to metastasize because they lack certain "tools" such as adhesion molecules, enzymes, and certain other factors that enable them to successfully metastasize. Doesn't host immunity also play an important role? Isn't it true that metastasis is not just a time-related, random event? Is it not true that whether or not that a cancer metastasizes is determined by the fact that some cancers possess the "tools" necessary to spread to lymph nodes and to distant sites?
3. Is it true that some breast cancers never metastasize? These, of course, would have little or no lethal potential.
4. Did not the plaintiff's breast cancer metastasize? If it did, it certainly could not be classified as a non-metastasizing breast cancer. Therefore, did not the plaintiff's breast cancer possess greater lethal potential than a non-metastasizing breast cancer?
5. *Infiltrating duct cell* and *atypical medullary* and *invasive lobular cell* are among the most aggressive breast cancers (excluding the uncommon inflammatory carcinoma). About 15 percent of breast

cancers have a much better prognosis and include tubular, papillary, adenoid cystic, and colloid carcinomas. We must stress that the plaintiff's breast cancer was one of the most aggressive histologic types of breast cancer.

6. What was the size of the tumor? Isn't it true that large tumor size is often secondary to a rapid growth of an aggressive tumor?
7. Lymph node status. Ask that the pathologist review Chapter 13. Some experts describe cancers as burglars. For example, to break into a building, the burglar needs certain tools. If he has the tools, break-in is simple. If he lacks the tools, he will be unable to break into the bank. Some cancers also possess the "tools" necessary to metastasize. The tools we are talking about are adhesion molecules, the ability to secrete certain proteolytic enzymes, motility factors, growth factors, etc. If the cancer lacks these "tools," it will be unable to metastasize successfully to the regional lymph nodes and/or distant sites via the blood stream. Tumors that lack or do not acquire these tools cannot metastasize and are called the non-metastasizing breast cancer. The plaintiff's breast cancer, therefore, possessed the tools necessary to metastasize the lymph nodes to distant sites. Thus axillary metastases indicate several things:
   a. The tumor was aggressive and possessed the tools necessary to successfully metastasize to the lymph nodes;
   b. Seventy percent of these women will die from the breast cancer within 10 years.
8. Microscopic examination of the plaintiff's cancer may reveal powerful evidence that the tumor was quite aggressive. See Prognostic Factors. (Chapter 23).
   a. Tumor grade correlates well with prognosis and should be determined. If the pathologist is unwilling to grade the tumor, ask that sections be sent to a medical center or a reference laboratory. Specifically request that the pathologist determine the *histologic grade, nuclear grade,* and *mitotic index.* The mitotic index is often falsely low (see Prognostic Factors), if this is the case use the S-phase from the DNA Flow Cytometry. If the mitotic index is low and the S-Phase is high, use the S-Phase as it is more reliable.
   b. Were foci of necrosis present within the tumor? These foci of necrosis may indicate a rapid rate of growth.

c. Vascular and/or lymphatic invasion (Chapter 23). Vascular and lymphatic invasion are both indications that the tumor is quite aggressive and has an increased risk of recurrence. If no evidence of vascular or lymphatic invasion was found, ask that special stains be employed to search for evidence of invasion. *Elastic stains* to identify blood vessel walls and *Immunohistochemical stains* to identify the endothelial cells of small capillaries and lymphatic capillaries.

d. Ask about the possibility of sending sections to a reference laboratory to determine the number of microvessels in the tissue with the use of Factor 8 immunohistochemical stains. Increasing evidence suggests that there is a powerful correlation of the frequency of microvessels within the tumor and prognosis. When checking for the frequency of microvessels, the pathologist should scan the section for the area containing the highest concentration of microvessels. This "hot spot" will yield the best prognostic information. (Chapter 23).

e. Finally ask that the following be determined: ER/PgR, DNA Flow Cytometry, and HER-2/neu amplification and overexpression. (Chapter 23).

Conclusion:

If the tumor contains a number of unfavorable prognostic factors but also several good prognostic factors, ask this question: Are not all breast cancers heterogeneous? That is, they may contain clones and/or areas containing good prognostic factors and in addition areas that contain unfavorable factors. The good prognostic factors are of no clinical significance; the clinical behavior of the cancer will be determined by the most aggressive cells and the cells with the greatest malignant potential.

§5.02 VOIR DIRE—EDUCATE THE JURORS

The defense lawyer must start as early as possible to educate the jury. In jurisdictions which permit counsel to conduct their own voir dire, the questions should be carefully framed to suggest the oncoming defense.

Jury selection is of the utmost importance; it can and it does make or break a case. Obviously, in the current climate where early diagnosis is equated with cure, voir dire has great importance to the defense. Here is where one starts to educate the jury.

However, jury selection by counsel is becoming more difficult. According to a survey conducted by the Federal Judicial Center, 49% of federal judges conduct the entire voir dire examination and use all of their own questions. Another 19% conduct their own voir dire examination but ask some questions submitted by the parties. 16% of the judges conduct a preliminary examination and then allow the lawyers to examine. Only 5% of the federal judges polled permitted the lawyers to conduct the entire voir dire examination. The same practice is increasingly copied in state courts.

Proponents of judge-controlled voir dire argue that it is quicker and more efficient. Possibly, but it seems that in recent years trials have become strewn with devices to promote efficiency at the expense of justice. In no type of case is this more apparent than in defense of a breast cancer malpractice case wherein defense counsel has the practical burden of overcoming the prejudice created by the propaganda that early diagnosis means cure. The fact that this is not true, the fact that the biology of the cancer is more significant than the time of diagnosis and the fact that it is even inaccurate to talk of cure must be conveyed by defense counsel. Consequently, the selection of the individuals to sit on the panel is not the entire purpose of a voir dire; the main purpose is to advise a proposed juror of these truths in order to determine their own prejudices, their own beliefs, and their ability to set these beliefs aside, if convinced to the contrary.

A judge's question "Can you be fair and impartial?" is unlikely to uncover any pre-existing bias. Only the attorney is able to elicit candid answers and uncover pre-existing bias through direct and personal communication.

In restrictive jurisdictions, consideration should be given to making a motion for the right to examine the jury panel. Despite the high percentage of federal courts that conduct their own voir dire examinations, they have, as do most state courts, wide discretion in permitting counsel to conduct the examination. Fed. R. Civ. P. 47(a). The appropriate motion might well include a request for an expanded voir dire examination on such a matter concerning breast cancer diagnosis and treatment that has appeared in pretrial publicity.

Consideration should also be given to hiring special consultants for jury selection. The forensic psychologist or forensic juror consultant may be particularly helpful in developing "ideal juror profile" in breast cancer cases. For an excellent study of the psychology of jury selection and the use of jury consultants, see D. Vinson, *Jury Persuasion: Psychology in Strategies and Trial Techniques* (Prentice Hall Law & Business 1993).

But obviously, picking a jury is not an exact science. The approach and feelings of experienced counsel are often of greater benefit than professional jury consultants. Assuming that counsel is given the opportunity to conduct or join in the voir dire, the following questions might be included:

[a] Sample Voir Dire Questions

Have you or any member of your family ever suffered from cancer?

If you would rather not answer, I will certainly understand, but if you are willing, will you tell me something about your experience.

Have you had close friends who have suffered from cancer?

Were all the people in your family or close friends who have suffered from cancer given, as far as you know, the best medical and surgical help in treating the disease?

Did any of them die, in spite of the best medical treatment available?

From that, you know that despite the most prompt and best medical treatment that people die from cancer.

Do you understand that despite all of the studies cancer is still a completely mysterious thing to medical science?

Would it surprise you to know that the survival rate of women developing breast cancer, regardless of diagnosis and treatment, has not improved in the past 63 years?

Would it surprise you to learn that a breast cancer throws off cancer cells into the blood stream in some instances years before the cancer can be discovered in the breast by any method known to medical science?

Would it surprise you to know that the prognosis of any cancer depends primarily upon what kind of cancer it is, and that some cancers are aggressive and that some are indolent?

If you are selected to sit here as a juror, will you carefully listen to and evaluate the medical evidence that will be introduced on these points?

§5.03 OPENING STATEMENT

All experienced trial lawyers and judges agree that the opening statement is the most important speech a lawyer makes to the jury. Writers on the subject have estimated that in 80 percent of the cases the jury makes its decision on the basis of the opening statement. This seems a little high, but certainly without an effective opening statement, the defense counsel in a breast cancer case can make no headway in getting the defense theory thoroughly fixed in the jury's mind. In making the opening statement, counsel might consider asking permission to use the demonstrative aids suggested in 5.06 hereafter.

As with cross-examination, every lawyer chooses his own words. An opening statement could, however, be something along the lines of the sample opening statement provided in Appendix 5-1 to this chapter.

§5.04 CROSS-EXAMINATION

[a] Of Plaintiff

If Plaintiff is living and testifies, cross-examination should be approached very carefully. The jury will already be sympathetic to the plaintiff and any type of cross-examination that appears to be a personal attack on the plaintiff is dangerous. If used at all, cross-examination should usually be directed to the sympathy and compassion shown by defendant physician, if such has actually been the case. This, of course, can be determined by discovery before trial and if the rapport between the plaintiff and the defendant is good, can be explored on cross-examination.

[b] Of Plaintiff's Experts

Plaintiff's experts, depending upon the jurisdiction, are going to claim 1) that the failure to timely diagnose *probably* provided the cancer additional time during which it metastasized and became incurable; 2) that failure to timely diagnose was a *substantial possibility* in the fact that the cancer metastasized and killed the patient; or 3) that the failure to timely diagnose destroyed plaintiff or plaintiff's decedent's *loss of chance* to cure the cancer or substantially delay its progress.

The expert's opinion in this regard will have been discovered by deposition, and counsel must, of course, be thoroughly prepared to launch the attack.

Cross-examination of plaintiff's witnesses, particularly the experts, is mandatory. The old saw that a lawyer should not cross-examine an expert in an expert's own field simply isn't true, but counsel must be adequately prepared. (Famed cross-examiner Louis Nizer commented on the role of luck in his success in the courtroom:

> What about luck? Oh, absolutely. It always visits me when I'm in the library at 3 in the morning. It never visits me on the golf course.

Adequate preparation commences prior to the taking of the expert's deposition. Start with getting acquainted with the expert's background. Check the expert's prior publications by searching the literature with a medical computer (Medline). Check the dictionary of medical specialists to determine if the witness is board certified. If the witness has testified on prior occasions, contact the lawyers involved and get transcripts of the prior testimony.

The primary goal is to turn the witness so that he or she supports defendant's theory of the case, to extract every concession that can possibly advance defendant's theories. It must be kept in mind, however, that while plaintiff's experts may be entirely honorable and conscientious, they are always adverse. If they were not, they wouldn't be testifying. Many of them well understand the basic principle of economic loyalty. The more realistic goal then is to cross-examine the witness so that he or she partially supports the defendant's theory of the case. If neither is possible, then cross-examination becomes a matter of trying to destroy or neutralize the witness.

The latter effort should be approached with caution. Personal attacks are unwise and the old adage has it that "to cross-examine does not mean to examine crossly" *Deinhardt v. State,* 348 A.2d 286, 289 (Md. Ct.

Spec. App. 1976) (Citing Ballantine, W. *Some Experiences of a Barrister's Life* (2 Ed. 1882).

This does not mean, however, that defense counsel cannot impeach the expert witness on the basis of prior inconsistent statements. Federal Rule of Evidence 613 allows impeachment of the witness or introduction of prior inconsistent statements without laying a foundation for the statement or showing the statement to the witness. Federal Rules of Evidence 613 and 801(d)(1)A allow prior inconsistent statements made under oath in a deposition or other legal proceeding to be used substantively. Many plaintiff's experts have testified extensively and their prior testimony or prior deposition testimony should be obtained.

Keep in mind also 803(18) Federal Rules of Evidence which allows the use of medical books and articles to cross examine medical witnesses. This is particularly important in breast cancer cases. The propaganda that breast cancer can be easily found and can be cured if diagnosed timely is sharply disputed by the medical literature. This literature can be used as an effective cross-examination. Local law, however, must be carefully analyzed as to the foundation necessary. If the expert has referred in direct examination to certain literature or has published the same, the matter poses no problem.

In other cases, the literature must be established by some means, such as "other expert testimony or by judicial notice." Fed. R. Evid. 803(18).

In addition to the court taking judicial notice of the reliable authority of the literature, it may in some places be established by the testimony of a medical librarian, a medical school teacher or the cross examiner's own medical witness. (*McDaniel v. Merck Sharp & Dohme*, 533 A.2d 436 (Pa. Super. Ct. 1987)). See also *Meshino v. North American Drager, Inc.*, 841 F.2d 429 (1st Cir. 1988).

It is assumed that counsel will have obtained either the agreement or refusal of the expert to agree on the authoritative aspect of the proposed literature in the discovery stage by way of deposition. This will enable counsel to prepare before trial on what is needed to establish the reliability of the literature intended to be used.

Cross-examination itself must be carefully prepared ahead of time and again, experienced counsel will have his or her own way of preparing, according to the facts and circumstances of the case. The following questions for use in cross-examination are suggestive, only:

Sample Cross-Examination Questions

Doctor, cancer is a very complex disease, is it not?

Medical science has been studying it for many, many years and still doesn't understand it.

And you don't purport to tell the jury that you do.

Doctor, it is true, is it not, that breast cancers, by and large, are different than other cancers?

For example, a basal cell carcinoma of the skin grows slowly and lacks the ability to metastasize, does it not?

Cancer of the uterus remains local for a long period of time and surgery and radiation are effective treatment. This is the type of cancer in which the mortality rate has decreased dramatically during the past 20 years. Consequently, early diagnosis in such cases is important and effective.

On the other hand, there are some tumors that are never curable from the day they can be diagnosed, isn't that correct?

For example, chronic lymphocytic leukemia. In such case, cure is never achieved no matter when the diagnosis is made, is that not true? Malignant brain tumors, in some cases where the cure rate is close to zero. Those things are true, are they not?

Dr. B. Cady stated "In no other human cancer (breast) has there been such enormous research and clinical efforts made to understand the disease and modify treatment according to current presentations and research findings." Would you agree with that statement? Blando and Cady, Breast Cancer Surg. Clinics N.A. (Aug. 1990).

Despite all of this effort and all this expense and despite newer methods of diagnosis and treatment, the age-adjusted survival rate of breast cancer has not decreased over the past 60 years, has it?

Since 1930 the death rate has remained at about 27 deaths per 100,000 women each year. (Chapter 6). Would you agree with those figures?

Do you anticipate that this ratio will be changed during this present year? If so, on what do you base it? (If the answer seeks to qualify these numbers by claiming the incidence of breast cancer has risen in recent years while the survival rate has held steady, see questions on Incidence Theory, next set out and Chapter 6).

Isn't it entirely possible that two women, for example, age 40 of identical family history, same family doctor, the same surgeon both have breast cancers which appear to be identical, same size in diameter, same histology, node status, same prognostic factors and yet one women dies quickly and the other has a long time favorable outcome? What is the reason for that, Doctor?

Isn't it true that one of them had a tumor with lethal potential that the other did not? Was this something that was within the control of the physician? It has to do with the biology of the tumor, does it not?

Isn't it true that some tumors may be diagnosed while still quite small and although promptly removed, the patient soon dies of breast cancer?

Isn't it also true that some tumors may not be diagnosed and removed until they are quite large and following removal, the patient does well for many years? (§8.02).

In your experience, have you seen this happen? Again, it has to do with the biology of the cancer, doesn't it?

At what size would you say a breast cancer can be detected by mammography? (The smallest size 2.1 mm, usually about 5 mm).

And at this time it is entirely possible that the cancer has been spilling cancer cells into the blood stream for a long period of time—for years. And all of these cells have the potential to metastasize, isn't that true? (Chapter 10).

And isn't it true that it only takes one cell to start the metastatic nodule? (§10.05[a]).

Isn't it true, Doctor, that a cancer usually must be at least 1 cm or larger to produce symptoms? In the case of a tumor 1 cm in diameter, would I be correct in saying that 75% of its life cycle has elapsed? Would I be correct in saying that from 2 to 3 cm in diameter 80 to 90% of a tumor's life cycle has elapsed? So, when we are talking about a tumor that is large enough to produce symptoms, we are talking about a biologically old tumor in the late stages of its life cycle, isn't that correct? (§7.05).

My point, Doctor, is that we get back to biology and not the time of diagnosis as a significant factor in these cases.

Do you consider the National Center for Health Statistics and the United States Bureau of Census to be reliable sources of information?

Are you acquainted with what is known as the Halstead doctrine? Was this the doctrine that breast cancer spread solely via the lympatics? (Chapter 7).

And if this was true, it was logical to conclude that early diagnosis and radical surgery would cure breast cancer. This is correct, is it not?

In support of this doctrine, Dr. Halstead and Dr. Meyer popularized the radical removal of the breast, the underlying muscles, and the regional lymph nodes and continuity. Yet this radical surgery failed to cure 50% of women with operable breast cancer.

After that clinical observations demonstrated that less aggressive procedures such as a simple local excision (lumpectomy) of the tumor with post operative radiation to the breast yielded as good results as the mutilating radical mastectomy. Is this not true? (§21.04).

In other words, stated more simple, the survival rate of simple lumpectomy is equal to that of the most radical surgery.

Was mammography was not generally accepted as a modality for the detection of breast cancer prior to 1962? And the concept of screening mammography was not commonly used until 1980, isn't that correct?

Now, since diagnostic mammography was not accepted as a diagnostic modality until 1962 and screening mammography was not widely used until 1980, the diagnosis of breast cancer from 1930 to 1980 had to be made on the basis of symptoms, physical findings and an open biopsy of the breast mass, is that not true?

Therefore, the cancers that were discovered between 1930 and 1980 were symptomatic cancers, were they not? The patient developed symptoms—went to the doctor—a mass was discovered—and a biopsy was performed. Mammographies were not commonly used during this period, were they?

And the bottom line is that the age adjusted mortality rate of breast cancer did not decrease during this time, isn't that correct?

Even after the introduction of diagnostic and screening mammography, the mortality rate of breast cancer did not improve. Still 27 to 28 women per 100,000 female population die each year of breast cancer. This was true back in the year 1933, was it not?

Are you acquainted with the studies of Bernard Fisher, known as the Fisher doctrine? This was a large study of the duration of symptoms and the disease-free survival of breast cancer, was it not? Fisher, *A Commentary on the Role of the Surgeon in Primary Breast Cancer.* Breast Cancer Research and Treatment 17 (1981); Fisher, supra.

Doesn't this study show that if a cancer does not have the ability to metastasize, it probably never will? And if it has the ability to metastasize, it will have already done so when first symptomatic?

Are you acquainted with Drs. Plotkin and Blankenberg? Plotkin, Breast Cancer Amer. Clinics Oncol. 14:254 1993.

These authors state "The preponderance of the available evidence leads us to conclude that cure of invasive breast cancer using current methods of treatment is not possible." Do you agree with this conclusion? Do you agree that these men are authorities in the field? Do you agree that they made this statement?

Does the American Cancer Society or the National Cancer Institute make the claim, either directly or by inference, that early diagnosis of a breast cancer means cure?

Are you acquainted with the studies of Dr. Greenberg, D.S., on *X-ray Mammography—Background to a Decision?* Dr. Greenberg quoted a Director of the National Cancer Institute by saying "Both the American Cancer Society and the National

Cancer Institute will gain a great deal of favorable publicity because they are bringing research findings to the public—this will assist in obtaining more research funds.'' Would you agree with this statement? Greenberg, *X-ray Mammography—Background to a Decision,* 295 New England Journal of Med. 739.

With respect to the National Cancer Institute claims of progress in curing breast cancer, are you aware that the General Accounting Office of the United States reported to the Congress that there was in fact no clear evidence that current diagnostic techniques and therapies had produced any impact on breast cancer survival? (General Accounting Office, *Cancer Patient Survival: What Progress Has Been Made?''* Pend. 87-13, March 1987) (Report to the Chairman, Subcommittee on Operations, House of Representatives).

Do you agree?

Even if you do not agree with this statement, is it your position that early diagnosis will always result in a cure?

Are you acquainted with the National Surgical Adjuvant Breast Project trials? (Chapters 10 and 11).

Would you agree that its studies show that no matter how radical the surgery when systemic metastasis is present, cure will not result?

Would you also agree that we can prove at least 25% of all women (node positive and node negative) with breast cancers with the diameter of 1 cm already have systemic disease? (Chapter 10). Would you also agree that in the malpractice setting this figure would be much higher? (Chapters 10 and 11).

And if metastasis is not present, radical surgery is not necessary, isn't that true? Simply local excision will effect a cure, correct? (§21.04).

On your direct examination you stated you had probably made a breast examination of ______ patients. Obviously in some of your examinations you found lumps. Have you also had patients in which no lumps were palpable, but you had positive findings on mammography? Did you biopsy all of these patients? Why not?

How many lumps that you detected would you say were cancerous as compared to being benign? Were there some cases in which you had a positive mammography or could palpate some kind of a lump in which you advised the patient to wait and observe and return to you at some future date? This is not an unusual occurrence as far as most experts are concerned, is it?

What is the definition of a camouflaging problem? (Chapter 14).

In some cases because of camouflaging, isn't it true that it isn't possible to detect many cancers until they reach the diameter of 2 or even 3 cm or larger?

Isn't it also true that 10-20% of breast cancers will never be visualized by mammography?

Is there such a thing as a cancer control window? How would you describe it? (The length of time between the moment the cancer becomes detectable and the time when it spreads systemically and becomes incurable.) (Chapter 16).

Is this cancer control window the same with every patient and in every circumstance? (No.)

Would the cancer control window be wider in a normal breast than in a dense breast? (Yes.) Why is this?

In the case of a rapidly growing aggressive cancer, does the window exist at all? (It may not.)

By the way, Doctor, do you treat all lymph node negative women with post-operative chemotherapy? If not, how do you decide which to treat, what prognostic factors do you use?

In making this determination, you are really attempting to determine the lethal potential of the tumor, are you not? And then you weigh the risk of recurrence, potential benefit of treatment and the risk of toxic reactions of adjuvant treatment?

And if chance of benefit is greater than the risk of toxicity, you will consider treating her, will you not?

Is it not also true that additional prognostic information could be obtained from such tests as HER-2/neu P53 and frequency of microvessels?

And if the lethal potential of the tumor is greater than the risk of severe toxic reactions from the post operative treatment, you will administer this adjuvant therapy?

Do you not agree that if you knew about the detection of distant metastasis, recurrence following surgery, and the post-operative clinical course of the plaintiff, would you not be able to give a more accurate opinion as to the aggressiveness and lethal potential of the tumor?

Have you ever had patients who complained of a lump that you could not find?

Have you ever found lumps that by feel you could tell were benign? What is your percentage of accuracy in this area?

Have you ever had a patient insist that at one time they had told you about a lump and they really hadn't?

Have you ever lost a patient to breast cancer?

Have you ever made what you thought to be an "early diagnosis" but in spite of this and your best management and prompt surgery your patient died of breast cancer? Was this your fault? Did it have anything to do with the inherent biology of the cancer?

In other words, some patients with an "early" clinical diagnosis will die because the tumor spread to distant sites before the tumor became clinically detectable, isn't that correct? Isn't it also true that by the time most tumors become clinically detectable (symptomatic), they are biologically old tumors and are in the terminal stages of their life cycle?

This being true, Doctor, is it accurate to say that breast cancer is ever detected early? In most cases, early is really biologically late, is it not?

In addition, Doctor, can we ever accurately use the term cure in relation to breast cancer?

Have you known women who have had a recurrence of breast cancer 25-35 years after their mastectomies? It isn't accurate then to talk about a five or 10 year cure. What we are talking about is a five or 10 year survival, isn't that true?

This again has to do with the biology of the cancer, isn't that true?

Do you believe that it is possible to determine the size of a tumor 12 months prior to the time of diagnosis and treatment?

Would a claim that one could so, be honest, in your judgment? (§11.05).

Have you testified before in breast cancer malpractice cases? In how many cases and on which side, the plaintiff or the defendant? Do you charge for your testimony? What is your charge?

When were you first contacted to testify for the plaintiff in this case and by whom? What records were you given to review? Is there anything that you have been furnished as far as the facts of this case are concerned that you think would help you in determining whether or not the cancer in this case was aggressive, of the early metastasizing type?

You have been advised, have you not, that the plaintiff in this case died within _____ months after her surgery? You have also been advised of the pathology of the tumor. Have you been advised of the histological type, tumor grade, the adverse microscopic risk factors such as vascular or lymphatic invasion, estrogen receptor assay, DNA flow cytometry, protein expression or amplification, tumor micro vessel counts or any other prognostic factor?

In this case, there isn't any question that the cancer did metastasize, is there? This is proof, is it not, that this tumor did have great invasive and lethal power?

This cancer could have spread to a distant site at the time or shortly after vascularization of the tumor, is that not true?

Isn't it also possible that it had metastasized before it reached the size that could be detected by mammography or any known means? Once it metastasized, it became incurable because the patient's immunity failed to control or destroy the metastasis?

You know from your experience and your reading that there is a certain subset of cancers that no matter how early the diagnosis, cure is not possible, isn't this true?

Whether or not you think it is probable, it is certainly possible that this is what occurred in this case.

When this cancer metastasized is something that you don't know, do you? All you can do is to speculate and you have chosen to speculate that the cancer had not already metastasized at the time it could first have been discovered.

It's just as easy, is it not, Doctor, knowing that this was an aggressive, early metastasizing tumor, to speculate that it had metastasized before it could have been observed and discovered?

In view of the fact that you know without question that it did metastasize, that it was a very fast growing tumor, that the pathology showed there was an invasion of vessels proving that the cancer had already spread throughout the body either by the venous channels or lymphatic channels, this speculation would probably be a little more honest, would it not?

[c] Incidence Theory

Plaintiff's experts sometimes seek to avoid the generally accepted fact that the age-adjusted survival rate of breast cancer hasn't improved since 1930 by claiming that the incidence of breast cancer has dramatically increased in recent years while the survival rate has held steady, the claim being that if 32.5 percent more women per 100,000 had breast cancer in 1987 as compared with 1980, greater numbers of women should be expected to die and don't.

A chart much like the following may be used:

A	B	C
1935—100,000 women 55 have breast cancer	1980—100,000 women 84.8 have breast cancer	1987—100,000 women 112.4 have breast cancer
# of deaths per 100,000 female population	# of deaths per 100,000 female population	# of deaths per 100,000 female population
28 died from breast cancer	28 died from breast cancer	28 died from breast cancer
Death rate for women who had breast cancer 51%	Death rate for women who had breast cancer 33%	Death rate for women who had breast cancer 25%

(Modified from Fox, Robert M., p. 437, Trial Lawyers Coop Publishing Co., Rochester, N.Y. 1993(6)).

Based on this chart, questions will be asked as to whether or not the same does not show that in 1935, 51 percent of women who had breast cancer died, in 1980, 33 percent and in 1987, 25 percent. This establishes, SOME plaintiff's counsel will claim, that early diagnosis and treatment has reduced the death rate among breast cancer patients.

The argument is ingenious, but a bit on the smoke and mirrors side. (See Chapter 6).

The rise in the "incidence" of breast cancer does not mean that 32.5 percent more women are developing cancer. It means that the screening of asymptomatic women with periodic mammograms has detected many cancers 1, 2, 3, or even 4 years before they ordinarily would have been detected by palpation. In addition, screening mammography has yielded an increase in the detection of in situ cancers, small and invasive cancers, and small, indolent lesions that microscopically resemble cancer. Some of these lesions might never become clinically evident during the lifetime of the patient. Additionally, about 25% of the increased incidence of breast cancer prior to 1982 can be attributed to improvements in the reporting of breast cancer. (Chapter 6). Thus, improved reporting of breast cancer and earlier diagnosis creates the *illusion* of an alarming increase in the incidence of breast cancer.

Thus we have a problem of lead-time bias. Screening mammography of asymptomatic women with periodic mammograms detect cancers one, two, three or even four years earlier than they would have been detected by palpation. This results in an apparent longer survival time, not because death is necessarily delayed, but because of earlier discovery. (Chapter 22).

Questions to Plaintiff's Expert Might Include:

Doctor, you make the assertion that in 1980, 84.8 women out of 100,000 had breast cancer and 28 died. That in 1987, 112.4 women out of 100,000 had breast cancer and still 28 died. (See Chapter 6).

Your claim is that more people had breast cancer in 1987 than they did in 1980 and yet the same number died. And to you this is evidence of the effectiveness of early diagnosis.

Do you really claim that more women got breast cancer in 1987 than they did in 1980? Or do you mean that more are being discovered by the use of screening mammography? (§6.03).

Doesn't this screen women who have no symptoms? Doesn't it pick up lesions exhibiting histological characteristics of cancer, but with benign biological properties, which may rarely or never metastasize? (Chapter 22).

Doesn't it also pick up in situ cancers? Doesn't it also pick up small and invasive cancers and some indolent lesions that only microscopically resemble cancer?

Isn't it true many of these lesions will never become clinically evident during the lifetime of the patient?

Isn't it true that epidemiologists who have studied the problem of the increased incidence of breast cancer conclude that 60-75% or more of the increased incidence of breast cancer is secondary to the earlier diagnosis of ordinary breast cancers? (Chapter 6).

So many of the increased incidence are not "extra" cancers, but the earlier diagnosis of ordinary cancers. (Chapter 6).

Isn't it true that the true increase in cancer of the breast is due to the following:

1. Improved reporting of breast cancers since 1982. (Prior to this time many breast cancers simply were not reported unless they died of breast cancer.) These women account for about 25% of the increase in the incidence of breast cancer. These are not extra cancers.
2. Lead time bias secondary to earlier diagnosis (these are not extra cancers).
3. Overdiagnosis—detection of small "look-like" cancers with little or no lethal potential (these are not extra cancers).
4. Women began to live longer (extra cancers).
5. Change of women's life style (extra cancers).
6. Unknown causes (extra cancers).
7. Many of these "extra cancers" were a more benign form of cancer. (See Chapter 6).

Isn't it true that there have been no significant improvements in the treatment of breast cancer since 1930?

Isn't it true that we know little or nothing about the biology of these "extra cancers'? (Chapter 6).

Many of these cancers could have less lethal potential? (See Chapter 6).

Isn't it also true that there is such a thing as lead time bias? This means, does it not, that patients diagnosed in an early stage of the disease may reflect only that the time of diagnosis was advanced and not that death was delayed? In other words, survival from the date of diagnosis will appear shorter for those patients with a delayed diagnosis. (Chapter 23).

Are you aware of the large study by Fisher, et al., that studied the relations of the duration of symptoms and the disease-free survival of breast cancer? Did they not find there was no significant difference in the disease-free survival of the following:

Duration of Symptoms	*Disease-Free Survival*
0-3 mos.	No Difference in Survival
3-6 mos.	No Difference in Survival
9+ mos.	No Difference in Survival

(Modified and reprinted courtesy of Fisher et al. Cancer 40: 3160-3167, 1977, Table 1, page 3163).

(See §10.11[c] and Visual Aids, Appendix 10-1)

Is it fair to say that by the time a cancer is large enough to produce symptoms, if it has the ability to metastasize, it will probably have done so? If it does not have such ability, it probably never will?

Would you agree that some breast cancers never metastasize even though they become huge in size?

Would you agree that some cancers, even if not diagnosed until they are quite large, following their removal, the patient does well for many years?

Would you also agree that many cancers diagnosed by early screening mammogram and promptly removed have already metastasized and the patient will eventually die of breast cancer?

Would it be fair to say then that survival rates, rather than being functions of the interval between onset of symptoms and treatment, depend upon the predetermined biology of the cancer? (Chapter 8).

And, despite any claim of therc being more women developing breast cancer, the fact remains that 28 out of 100,000 will die this year, no matter when diagnosed, and no matter what the treatment. (Chapter 6).

Again, Doctor, is it not true that no matter how and in what manner the tumor is discovered, it is the biology of the tumor that controls (Chapter 6).

Isn't it true that the only confirmed decrease in the mortality rate of breast cancer is limited to a very special group— a group of breast cancers discovered by the periodic screening with mammography of a group of self-selected, asymptomatic women? None in this group had breast lumps of any kind, did they? These are not the women who consult their family doctor concerning a breast lump or breast symptoms. (Chapter 6).

[d] Staging

Note: The TNM staging system does not consider the biology of the tumor, tumor type, histology—only size of tumor and whether or not the tumor metastasized to the nodes or distant sites.

In this connection, read and review Chapter 18 and consider asking the following questions of plaintiff's expert:

Doctor, isn't it true that the staging systems are a rather old form of describing the extent of breast cancers?

Isn't it true that the main value is in allowing one doctor to speak about a breast cancer as being a certain stage; he could then relay this information to another doctor by saying this is that stage of this stage?

When we speak of the staging systems, isn't it true that there are two staging systems, the clinical TNM and the pathologic TNM?

Is the clinical stage of any real importance? The clinical stage is what the lump feels like, what the surrounding tissue looks like, and what the armpit and the axilla feel like. This is only preliminary data, is it not?

Actually, trying to determine the size of the lesion by feeling it is most inexact because there is often dense breast tissue surrounding the cancer which makes it difficult to palpate the tumor.

And you would like to know what is actually in the lymph nodes in the armpit, and it is pretty inexact to try to determine that simply by feeling.

It's true, is it not, that any calculation of the node status by clinical TNM status will be wrong perhaps 30 to 40% of the time?

And in any event, you don't have very concise, uniform general boxes in which a group of patients can be deposited, do you?

For example, Stage II Breast Cancer may include patients with a 1 cm tumor with positive nodes and patients with 4 cm tumors with no lymph nodes. It may include patients with 2.1 cm tumors or 4.9 cm tumors.

It's kind of hard to put all of these different factors in one box and come up with the same outcome, is it not?

And average numbers are not meaningful without a specific patient in whom clear facts are known, isn't that true?

Now, the pathologic TNM staging permits you to know what the lesion looks like under the microscope. It permits you to know whether there is evidence of invasion of vessels that suggest that the cancer has already spread throughout the body, whether it be venous channels or lymphatic channels. It permits you to know whether or not there is necrosis which is the death of cancer cells.

Isn't it true that where there is necrosis this suggests that the cancer is growing so quickly that it is outgrowing its blood supply? It suggests a very aggressive cancer, does it not?

Can any of these things be determined by a clinical TNM staging?

One can determine the cTNM before surgery, but how often is it wrong? (At least 50% of the time).

Is it possible to determine the pTNM before surgery?

If there is any implication in this case that a pathologic TNM staging could have been done six or 12 months prior to the surgery, that is simply not true, is it?

Isn't it also true that even the pathologic TNM staging does not take into account any of the following:

a) Tumor type—some have a good prognosis and in some the prognosis is poor?

b) Tumor grading—histological grade, nuclear grade, mitotic index?

c) Microscopic features (all unfavorable), vascular invasion, lymphatic invasion, multiple foci of tumor necrosis, S-phase, ER and PgR and so on?

Is it not possible to have two breast cancer patients who are the same age, the same pathologic TNM stage and find that one does very well and the other does quite poorly?

This being true, Doctor, is it not fair to say that the pathologic TNM staging system does not take into account the aggressiveness of the tumor, the rate of growth, the histologic tumor type, or the clinical history?

Simply stated, it really is not as complete and accurate as one might be led to believe.

§5.05 FINAL ARGUMENT

A minister once observed that if he could not convert his congregation within the first 15 minutes, they were lost. The rule of primacy being what it is, most experienced trial lawyers agree that if the jury has not been converted by the time of the conclusion of the evidence, final argument may well not change the outcome. By the time the case reaches this point, it is felt that most of the jurors will have made up their minds.

Yet this is not always true. The opinions held may not be fixed. Even if it were true, it does not mean that final argument is of no value. Some jurors will favor the plaintiff and some the defendant. Ultimate persuasion, one way or the other, may well take place during jury deliberations and an effective argument will arm the advocates for defendant's cause in persuading the others.

As with other trial tactics, experienced counsel will have his or her own approach to final argument. However, a defense of breast cancer malpractice cases differs from other types of actions and consequently the generally accepted rules of final argument must be tailored.

For example, the issues are simple. Ordinarily, there will not be many witnesses and summing up by going over all the evidence in detail is not indicated. The dispute will revolve around the credibility of the expert witnesses. In this connection, the use of demonstrative aids must not be overlooked. Jurors have trouble with oral testimony, particularly scientific presentations. The more the testimony can be made visual, the better. (§5.06).

Argument should, of course, emphasize the court's instructions on burden of proof and the oath taken by the jurors to follow these instructions. An attempt must also be made to persuade the jury that plaintiff's obligation to prove the case is a heavy one. This must be done, even though realistically the legal burden of proof may not make much difference in the outcome of the case.

In closing argument counsel must assume the original recognition that he or she has the real burden. Consequently, closing argument should never be defensive. Preparation for it begins when counsel first gets the case and it is a continuation of the same theme emphasized in the opening statement. Counsel should not be defensive in the sense of laying back and fending off plaintiff's claim. Plaintiff's tragedy can be recognized and even emphasized, but it must be emphasized, too, that the tragedy was caused by a vicious disease which, in turn, swept up and embroiled the honor and reputation of a conscientious physician. A last suggestion: Ordinarily it is not wise to argue damages in defense of any case. It is particularly unwise to do so in this type of litigation. Arguing damages implies liability. Moreover, so very much of the defense of a breast cancer malpractice case is philosophical. Where does a jury—the conscience of the community—place the blame for a cruelty of nature? The following are comments that might be included in counsel's argument:

> Ladies and Gentlemen of the Jury:
>
> The play is about over. Very shortly the participants and the actors will depart, the curtain will be closed, and you will have the awesome responsibility of passing judgment.
>
> It is not an easy responsibility, but we have a system that believes that submitting our disputes and our problems to a jury of our peers is essential to our freedoms.
>
> As a jury, you go back almost 800 years in an unbroken line to a field called Runnymede in England where in the year 1215 King

John was forced to give to his people thc Magna Carta, which contained the right to trial by jury.

As jurors, you occupy a position of great power. You are not required to give reasons for your verdict and no one under the sun, including the judge, can force you to do anything you do not want to do.

Your only guideline is your conscience and this is the only force to which you must answer.

You have taken an oath that you will decide this case solely upon the evidence introduced, guided by the court's instructions, among which will be that in considering this case, you must not be influenced by emotion or sympathy or prejudice. It is obvious, I think, why I am also emphasizing that fact.

You will also be instructed that the burden of proving that Dr. Jones caused the death of Mrs. Smith is at all times on the plaintiff. And if the plaintiff does not meet the burden, no matter how much you naturally sympathize with the tragedy that has struck a lovely person and her family, you will rcturn a verdict for the defendant.

As I mentioned to you in opening statement and as I think has appeared forcibly from the evidence here, the villain in this scenario is cancer and its victims are both the plaintiff and the defendant. Every single minute in this world cancer finds a victim.

To try to place the blame for this dreadful disease and its outcome upon the physician who treats it is unfair. The cancer that destroyed the life of this plaintiff can also destroy the reputation and perhaps the professional life of Dr. Jones.

You know from the evidence that Dr. Jones was concerned and attentive from the very beginning. You have learned from the testimony that the threshold size of breast cancers, that is, the first time they may be detected, varies tremendously depending upon the consistency of the breast and the nature of the tumor. There are such things as camouflaged tumors. For someone who never examined the patient to state that at the time the plaintiff first came to Dr. Jones she had a "lump" of certain size, and that it should have been detected at any given time, is pure conjecture and a totally unfair conjecture.

To say further that this cancer did not metastasize until after the plaintiff saw Dr. Jones completely ignores the aggressiveness of this particular cancer and indulges in possibilities that are so strained as to approach the dishonest.

Mrs. Smith's cancer was what is known as systemic. Not days, not months, but years before her cancer could be detected by any known method, it was throwing off cancer cells into her blood stream. One or more of these cells metastasized and caused her death. To try to say with any degree of medical certainty that these cells did not metastasize until after Dr. Jones saw her, if it has any credence at all, is to offer the sheerest possibility.

And you are called upon to find that Dr. Jones caused the death of Mrs. Smith on the basis of the sheerest possibilities. There is no possible way for a physician to ascertain with any degree of certainty whether under any circumstances Mrs. Smith would have survived. Counsel has repeated to you the propaganda played up by the press, radio and television that early diagnosis means cure. But you know from the experts here that this simply is not true. All of them agree that the age adjusted survival rate of breast cancer has shown no improvement during the past 63 years no matter when the cancer was diagnosed.

The most that any plaintiff's expert has stated was that, based upon his opinion and conjecture, the plaintiff would have had a 25 percent better chance of a cure if the cancer had been diagnosed earlier. Even he, therefore, admits that there was a 75 percent chance that she would not have survived no matter when the diagnosis. Is it this easy for plaintiff to sustain his burden of proof? Is a verdict based upon a 25 percent versus 75 percent either logical or fair?

The thrust of plaintiff's case is not logic, but emotion. All of you, as with all of us, have an intuitive sense of humanity which mostly makes you want to compensate anyone for the loss of chance of survival regardless of how remote it is. But such a finding is so loose as to produce more injustice than justice. The guess of Dr. ________ on loss of chance is still a guess. Under your instructions you must find this as a certainty, and I don't think it has ever been expressed to you as a certainty.

When you ladies and gentlemen visited with me at the time you were being selected to sit on the jury, you promised me that you would decide the case solely upon the evidence, guided by the instructions that the court gave you, and that you would, one and all, lay aside any sympathy in arriving at your verdict.

This is what I ask you now.

§5.06 THE USE OF DEMONSTRATIVE AIDS IN CLOSING ARGUMENT

A verbal description of the problems involved in the diagnosis and treatment of breast cancer is frequently unsuccessful because the spoken words of the witnesses do not always strike home; the jurors may have failed to hear the testimony entirely or failed to understand the meaning of words. Closing argument becomes much more effective if the testimony can be made visual by the use of visual aids.

One of the best demonstrative aids for a defense attorney is two ordinary lead pencils, the first with a common household pin stuck into the eraser. The head of the pin is 1.2 mm in diameter. Tumors with a diameter of 1.2 mm have undergone 20 doublings. Their life cycle is 50 percent over, and they have already started shedding cancer cells into the blood. (Chapter 10).

The second is an ordinary lead pencil without the pin. The eraser measures 6 mm in diameter. Tumors with diameters of 6 mm have undergone 25 net cell doublings and 62 percent of their life cycle is over or has elapsed.

Demonstrative aids can also, of course, be done by pictures, by graphs and by the introduction of learned treatises and similar material.

Actually, counsel's entire argument may, if appropriate, be placed in writing for viewing on a flip chart. It has an advantage in that the jurors can both hear the attorney speak and read the shorthand version of it as presented on the chart.

Certainly in breast cancer cases the opportunity for visual aids is significant. The medical section of this book makes use of many graphs and illustrations. Any one or more of them should be considered by counsel as a visual aid in connection with closing argument. Consider the following:

Appendix Chapter 6
- Age-adjusted mortality rate of breast cancer: no change since 1930
- Effectiveness of early diagnosis dependant upon biology rather than physician skill
- Definition and significance of the term ''symptomatic breast cancer''

Appendix Chapter 9—In a strict sense breast cancer is not curable
- Limitations of 5 and 10 year survival data containing ''inflationary arithmetic''
- Definition of a cure
- Thirty year survival of breast cancer
- Doubling times of breast cancer, range of

Appendix Chapter 10—Metastasis occurs earlier than most physicians realize
- Historical
- Cure rate of radical mastectomyt vs. lumpectomy
- Breast cancer cannot be proven to be cured at 30 years
- Age adjusted mortality rate of breast cancer since 1930
- Delay in diagnosis of symptomatic breast cancers does not alter survival
- Animal studies demonstrate early metastasis of experimental cancers
- New tumor blood capillaries poorly constructed and quite leaky. Tumor cells easily gain entrance to blood stream
- Conclusion—Scientific evidence supports early metastasis of breast cancer

Appendix Chapter 10—Visual aids by Plotkin and Blankenberg: Is breast cancer curable?
- Range of breast cancer doubling times—261
- Breast cancer survival—262
- Diagnosis of primary and metastatic breast cancer—264
- Fusion of multifocal sites—266
- Major mammographic screening studies—268

Counsel can as well prepare his or her own visual aids to emphasize the testimony or to present any matter which he or she feels particularly important in the particular case being tried.

As an example, the camouflage defense is particularly important. Sometimes it is unsuccessful because the jury perceives it to be an alibi for the failure to make a timely diagnosis. Consequently, this misconception must be dispelled and in order to dispel it, a simple visual presentation of the problem caused by camouflaging may be made. (Chapter 14).

If tempted, suggestions are as follows:

A. Use a white or light gray 28 x 44 poster board
B. Paint tumors dark gray
C. Make suggested tumor sizes 0.3 mm to 3.5 cm
D. Use layers of white tissue paper to simulate breast density
E. Place the poster board on an easel 10-15 feet from the jury
F. In argument, ask the jurors to mentally identify the smallest tumor on the poster board 1) without the tissue paper; 2) with one layer of tissue paper in place; 3) with two layers of tissue paper in place; 4) with three layers of tissue paper in place
G. With three or four layers of tissue paper in place, the jurors should have difficulty identifying even the larger tumors.

The use of visual aids is usually discretionary with the trial judge. See Am. Jur. Trials 41; 5 Am. Jur. Trials 553, Introducing & Marking Exhibits (1966); Am. Jur. *Proof of Facts, Hospital Records* (1960); Annotation, *Admissibility in Evidence of Colored Photographs,* 53 A.L.R. 2d 1102 (1957); *Sheets v. Davenport,* 150 N.W.2d 224 (Neb. 1967); *State v. Blyth,* 226 N.W.2d 250 (Iowa 1975); *Goldstein v. Gontarz,* 309 N.E.2d 196 (Mass. 1974); *Campbell v. Menze Construction Co.,* 166 N.W.2d 624 (Mich. App. 1968); *Johnson v. Heintz,* 213 N.W.2d 85 (Wis. 1973); *Southern Cement Co. v. Patterson,* 122 So. 2d 386 (Ala. 1960). See also *Ga. Code Ann.* §§9-10-183.

§5.07 INSTRUCTIONS

Instructions in every aspect of the trial, from marshalling instructions to instructions on the substantive issues and damages, vary widely among the several jurisdictions. Some instructions, as stated, require causation based upon a showing that the injury was to a reasonable medical certainty due to the negligence of the defendant. (See cases cited in §1.01, supra). Other courts submit the "substantial possibility" test. (See §1.01[a]). Others the "loss of chance" theory (See §1.01[b]).

Not all of these instructions are uniform. Some instructions channel the jury's consideration of the measure of injury in terms of a ''good chance'' of ''greater recovery.'' Some permit recovery for loss of a ''reasonable possibility'' *Garder v. National Bulk Carriers, Inc.,* 310 F.2d 284 (4th Cir. 1962) or ''probability.'' *Harvey v. Silber,* 2 N.W.2d 43 (Mich. 1942) and *Clayton v. Thompson,* 475 So.2d 439 (Miss. 1985).

The instruction on ''substantial possibility'' is most commonly found in failure or delay in diagnosis. According to Rosati, *Causation in Medical Malpractice: A Modified Valuation Approach,* 50 Ohio State L.J. 469, this is the least stringent standard of the burden of proof, the complete opposite of ''reasonable medical certainty standard.''

''Substantial'' is defined by different instructions. In the case of *DeBurkarte v. Louvar,* 393 N.W.2d 131 (Iowa 1986), the court defined ''substantial'' as conduct that has such an effect in producing harm as to lead a reasonable person to regard it as a cause.

Other instructions coupling ''possibility'' with ''substantial'' permit a jury to compensate a plaintiff even when there is only a 10% chance of recovery. Christine A. Carolan, *Case Notes on Pre-Existing Condition,* 23 Rutgers L.Rev. 169 (1991). See also Miller, *Negligent Creation of a Substantial Risk of Injury is a Compensable Harm,* 9 U.Puget Sd.L.Rev. 251 (1985).

In Minnesota a jury instruction permitted both a ''but for'' and ''substantial factor'' causation test in a case where the hospital and physician presented a joint defense. *Fehling v. Levitan,* 382 N.W.2d 901 (Minn. App. 1986).

In *Scafidi v. Seiler,* 119 N.J. 93, the court emphasized that the ''increased risk of injury'' standard was limited to cases in which a defendant's negligence combined with a pre-existing condition to cause harm and presented to the jury a two pronged instruction:

(a) To determine whether there was a medical probability that the defendant's negligence increased the harm from the pre-existing condition.

(b) If the first question was answered affirmatively, the jury must then determine whether the increased risk was a substantial factor in producing the ultimate harm.

The American Medical Association once suggested a standard of causation: the plaintiff must prove that it is more likely than not that the physician's negligence was a contributing factor in causing the plaintiff's injury. If the physician's negligence was a contributing factor, his liability is limited solely to the extent of his responsibility for the injury. The physician will not be liable for the contributions of other individuals, including the patient or other factors such as the patient's pre-existing medical condition. This was an A.M.A. Specialty Society Medical Liability Project: *A Proposed Alternative to the Civil Justice System for Resolving Medical Liability Disputes.* An unpublished manuscript is on file at Ohio State Law Journal. (See Vol. 50 at p. 485). No cases have been found where this instruction was requested and why it was not published is not known.

As previously stated in Section 1.03, some courts submit instructions permitting plaintiff to recover all damages resulting from an injury for which the defendant may be only partly responsible. (*Thompson v. Sun City Community Hospital,* 141 Ariz. 598, 688 P.2d 605 (1984). Other courts instruct that recovery can be had only for the lost chance of survival. *DeBurkarte,* supra. In some cases the instructions spell out how the damages should be computed. *Mays v. United States,* 608 F.Supp. 1476 (D. Colo. 1985). And of course, as also set out in 1.03, supra, *Scafidi,* supra, instructed that where the damages are apportionable between the pre-existing condition and the defendant's negligence, the defendant has the burden of proving what part of the harm is not attributable to his negligence.

Of interest is the growing use of pattern or uniform approved jury instructions, in many cases mandatory. A sample of such pattern instructions are the Illinois Pattern Jury Instructions 1 and 2 which in general conform to those adopted by most states, with one caveat. With some equivocation (*Purtill v. Hess,* 111 Ill.2d 229, 489 N.E.2d 867 (1986)), Illinois continues to adhere to the locality rule. Most states presently do not. (See Appendix 5-2).

The movement for the adoption of standard pattern instructions is active and has been spreading. In some cases these instructions are recommendations only, which the court is not required to use. *Ellis v. DiChiara* 38 App.Div.2d 780, 328 N.Y.S.2d 36. In other cases the pattern instructions are mandatory and failure to give the same is considered prejudicial error. *Brown v. St. Louis Public Service Company,* 421 S.W.2d 255 (Mo. 1967). For a complete discussion of uniform jury instructions, see 49 ALR3d 128.

Counsel will not overlook the necessity of drafting and submitting requested jury instructions. See Rule 51, F.R.C.P. and related rules of the several states.

Neither the "substantial possibility" or the "loss of chance" rule removes the issue of causation from the case. The jury should be instructed that the plaintiff has the burden of proving by a preponderance of the evidence that the loss of chance was occasioned by the negligence of the defendant or that proper treatment would with a reasonable probability have produced a better result. *Waffen v. U.S. Department of Health and Human Services,* 799 F.2d 911 (4th Cir. 1986); *Harvey v. Silber,* 2 N.W.2d 43 (Mich. 1942); *Clayton v. Thompson,* 475 So.2d 439 (Miss. 1985); *Allesio v. Crook,* 633 S.W.2d 770 (1982); *Sherer v. James,* 334 S.E.2d 283 (S.C. App. 1985); *Connellan v. Coffey,* 187 A. 901 (1936).

The Restatement (Second) of Torts, pgh. 432(1), (1965), provides:

> One's negligent conduct is not a substantial factor in bringing about the harm to another if the harm would have been sustained even if the actor had not been negligent.

As pointed out in §1.03, most courts have limited damages to the patient's lost chance of survival. But an instruction should be requested clearly emphasizing this rule.

The right to request instructions is established by Federal Rule of Civil Procedure 51 and by procedural rules, statutes or case law in the various jurisdictions. They are for the purpose of insuring that the court completely instructs the jury on all significant legal issues and also to preserve these issues for appeal. Although Federal Rule of Civil Procedure 51 refers to filing a written request, an oral request made on the record may also be sufficient. See *Dunn v. United States,* 318 F.2d 89 (5th Cir. 1963). But obviously the requests are more effective if made in writing.

Notice should always be taken that objections to the instructions must be made on the record prior to the time the jury retires and the objections must be made clear and understandable.

In connection with limiting damages to the patient's possibility of survival, and in connection with statistical evidence regarding plaintiff's loss of chance, consideration should be given to requesting special verdicts and interrogatories. Federal Rule of Civil Procedure 49 describes the appropriate situations for the use of special verdicts and general verdicts accompanied by answers to interrogatories. Applicable rules, statutes and case law will determine the scope and applicability of these requests.

APPENDIX 5-1—
SAMPLE OPENING STATEMENT

Ladies and gentlemen of the jury:

Shakespeare observed that all the world is a stage in which we make our exits and our entrances. It seems to me that this is true and if it is true, a courtroom is a stage within a stage in which the citizens of a free society play out before a jury of their peers their problems and their grievances.

Seldom on this stage do we play comedies. Almost always we who are lawyers come before a jury to play out a tragedy.

Plaintiff's counsel has stated to you most eloquently a part of that tragedy. It involves the tragic death (or other occurrence) of someone that was a good wife, a devoted mother, altogether a lovely person. Her death is a complete tragedy.

She died of cancer, a disease process that goes back to the beginning of life itself, and its study goes back several thousand years. It was Hippocrates who first used the term carcinoma and defined its grave prognosis.

What plaintiff's counsel has not stated to you and which I do now is that there is presented here on this stage another tragedy, arising out of the same circumstances. Dr. Jones is a physician, well educated and well trained, of impeccable credentials and of impeccable integrity. He/she has practiced medicine for ____ years. In that time he/she has religiously taken care of the sick and the hurt, dried many tears, held many hands and saved many lives.

But after ____ years of serving the community, Dr. Jones stands before you accused of the worst transgression that a physician can commit—of causing the death of a patient.

Make no mistake about it, stripped of all the legal language and polite euphemisms, this is the charge.

So this tragedy being presented to you is twofold. Both Mrs. Smith and Dr. Jones are victims. The villain is cancer. It is cancer that killed Mrs. Smith and it is cancer that brings Dr. Jones before you as the accused.

You should not misunderstand this, ladies and gentlemen. You are being asked to find by your verdict that Dr. Jones by reason of negligence or omission caused the death of Mrs. Smith by delay in diagnosis. Again, I say to you that this is the issue.

When we were visiting during jury selection, you will recall that I stated I was not asking you not to have complete and absolute sympathy for the tragedy that befell this fine lady. But that I did ask you to give me your promise that in deciding the guilt or innocence of Dr. Jones you would lay aside sympathy and emotion and decide this case solely upon the evidence presented to you guided by the court's instructions. You will recall that, I am sure.

In this connection, I want to say to you now that the instructions of the court will advise you that when you consider this case you must keep in mind that the plaintiff has the burden of proof—of proving to you by a preponderance of the competent, credible evidence that Dr. Jones caused or contributed to this lady's death.

To do this, plaintiff's counsel, as he/she has already indicated, will remind you of current propaganda to the effect that early cancer diagnosis means cure. And there will be experts called to tell you they know the answer, not of cancers in general, but about this particular cancer. And in every case, they will be talking in retrospect and on the basis of guesswork. None of these experts will have ever seen this particular lump, will not have examined the plaintiff, and will base their opinions upon speculation only. And bluntly, they will be trying to convince you that they know something that they don't know.

Consider this first. All of you know people who have had cancer—either friends or perhaps in your own families. Perhaps you have had cancer yourself. You know of your own knowledge that some people contract cancer and live for many years, some see it cured, and others die of it. In some cases, very quickly. And you know of your own knowledge that some people die of cancer no matter how much medical and surgical attention they get or how soon. So, you know beforehand that there are many different kinds of cancers. And you know, too, that the propaganda that early diagnosis means cure is not true as to every cancer.

The reason? Not all cancers are alike. Some, such as basal cell carcinoma of the skin, grow slowly and lack the ability to metastasize. Cancer of the uterus remains local for a long period of time and surgery and radiation are effective treatment. Small cell cancer of the lung, however, metastasizes very early in its life cycle—before the cancer can be detected by x-rays in the vast majority of cases. This is also true of many types of breast cancers. Since 1930, 27 to 28 women per 100,000 female population have died of breast cancer each year. The same number will die this year. And the next.

Why? Not because of any fault on the part of the women or their physicians, but because of factors beyond their control. It is because of the type of breast cancer it is, it is because of the biology of the cancer, a biology that has as of now defied modern medical research and surgery.

Again, ladies and gentlemen, this lady died of cancer. In order to determine if Dr. Jones is guilty of doing something or not doing something that caused or contributed to this lady's death, you must learn something about cancer. Possibly more than you really want to know.

In simple terms, a cancer cell is biological insanity. A normal cell contains growth regulatory genes that tell it when to grow and when to stop growing. All normal cells have a stop signal.

The cancer cell is a cell in which the mechanism that regulates growth has been damaged by some method and it has no stop signal. It has the ability to divide endlessly, without aging.

The endlessly growing cancer cell secretes powerful proteins which enable it to invade adjacent normal tissues. The cells are what is called motile, that is, they can crawl and wiggle through small crevices and openings. Once they gain entry to the lymph or blood, they are swept away to distant sites such as the lungs, liver, bone, etc., and have the ability to metastasize, invade these parts and eventually cause death.

That is exactly what happened to Mrs. Smith. The cancer originated in her breast, got into the blood stream, metastasized, and caused her death.

The trouble with much of the propaganda and the trouble with this present indictment of Dr. Jones is that it implies that all breast cancers are alike. Not true. They differ. There is the non-metastasizing breast cancer which grows very slowly and seldom spreads. Some of them demonstrate sizeable lumps which remain without spreading for 30 or 35 years or more. There is also what is known as a late metastasizing breast cancer which initially has little or no capacity to metastasize and does so only after a considerable age. What is important to us here is that there is also an early metastasizing cancer. And this is what we are dealing with in this case.

An early metastasizing breast cancer becomes fully malignant at the time of inception or very early in its life cycle. Before it reaches the size that it can be detected by any known means, tumor cells will have invaded the blood stream in quantity up to a million or more cancer cells each day. Most of these cells will be destroyed by the immune system. Some, however, survive, metastasize and kill the patient.

It is estimated that in the case of a tumor 2.7 mm in diameter, it will have been shedding cancer cells into the blood for about two years. A tumor 1 cm in diameter has been shedding cancer cells into the blood for four or five years. You will keep in mind that a tumor 2.7 mm is about twice the diameter of the head of a common pin. If a tumor 1 cm in diameter which has been shedding cancer cells into the blood for four or five years was surgically removed a day following its discovery by the patient, it would already have metastasized.

We know in this particular case that this lady died within ____ months after surgery. From this we know without question that it was a lethal, early metastasizing cancer. We know that it was systemic, that is, it spread through the blood stream and did, in fact, establish a viable metastasis. If it had been a non-metastasizing breast cancer or a cancer with a prolonged doubling time, this lady would be alive today.

This type of cancer is entirely beyond the control of any physician. The outcome didn't have anything to do with the diagnosis, but had everything to do with the biology of the tumor. To say, as the plaintiff does here, that the cancer did not metastasize until after it was discoverable is something that no honest expert can tell you and I don't believe any honest expert will try.

What they will try to do is speculate. They will talk about loss of chance. To attempt to sustain plaintiff's burden of proving that there is a causation connection between what Dr. Jones did or did not do and the death of this lady, plaintiff's witnesses will not talk to you about probabilities. They will only talk of possibilities, and ask you to find Dr. Jones guilty of this charge on the basis of speculation and conjecture.

In the ordinary case, ladies and gentleman, a plaintiff would not ask a jury to convict someone of malpractice on the basis of speculation and conjecture. However, the thing we have to deal with, from a defense standpoint, is that this case involves cancer, a subject which is surrounded by myth and propaganda.

For example, when a relative or one of our close friends dies of cancer, most of us have the immediate reaction that "they didn't catch it soon enough." But unless we assume that every physician who has ever lost a patient to cancer has been negligent, we know this isn't true.

In this case, we will show you, through expert testimony, why it isn't. We will discuss with you the nature of the cancer cell, the different kinds and types of breast cancers, how they spread and metastasize. We will discuss with you what is known as a cancer control window, what is known as tumor camouflaging, how detection is determined by the threshold size of the tumor and composition of breast tissue, the size at which different breast cancers can be determined by palpation or by mammography, what has happened by the time breast cancer has become symptomatic and, all in all, ladies and gentlemen, we will show you in this case how wrong it would be to convict this man on the basis of sheer speculation.

APPENDIX 5-2— PATTERN JURY INSTRUCTIONS

1. 105.1 In providing professional services to (patient/client's name), a (insert appropriate professional person) must possess and apply the knowledge and use the skill and care ordinarily used by a reasonably well qualified (insert appropriate professional person) [practicing in the same or similar localities] under the circumstances similar to those shown by the evidence. A failure to do so is professional negligence.

2. 105.2 A (insert appropriate professional person) who holds himself out as a specialist and provides service in his specialty must possess and apply the knowledge and use the skill and care ordinarily used by a reasonably well-qualified specialist [practicing in the same or similar localities] under circumstances similar to those shown by the evidence. A failure to do so is professional negligence. [The only way in which you may decide whether (a) (any) defendant possessed and applied the knowledge and used the skill and care which the law required of him is from (expert testimony) (and) (or) (evidence of professional standards or conduct) presented in the trial. You must not attempt to determine this question from any personal knowledge you have.]

APPENDIX 5-3— QUESTIONS OFTEN PROPOUNDED TO DEFENDANT AND DEFENDANT'S EXPERTS, WITH SUGGESTED ANSWERS

1. Q. Assuming that at the time a cancerous lump was discovered it had spread to five axillary nodes. Do you claim that the cancer has so spread before it was found?
   A. Yes.
2. Q. Assuming a one-year delay from the time it should have been found and the time it actually was found, do you contend that this one-year delay did not affect either the morbidity or mortality?
   A. That is correct.
3. Q. Is it your opinion since the spread had already occurred to the five axillary nodes by the time the lump was discovered the additional one-year delay during which nothing was done would make no difference in the final result?
   A. That is correct.
4. Q. During that year delay, wasn't the primary cancer seeding cancer cells out to the axillary nodes?
   A. Yes, during that time the primary cancer was also shedding cancer cells into the blood stream.
5. Q. Assuming the breast cancer lump was the primary cancer, the cancer cells that were found in the axillary nodes could not have originated from anywhere except the primary cancer, isn't that true?
   A. Yes, in all probability the cancer cells in the axillary lymph nodes originated in the primary tumor.
6. Q. Assuming you are correct in your opinion that the axillary nodal metastasis had already occurred when the primary cancer was first discovered, do you know whether the cancer was still confined to the area of the nodes and the axilla at that time?
   A. At the time the plaintiff first developed symptoms (12 months before the diagnosis was made) the tumor was

already a biologically old tumor. 75 to 80% of its life cycle had elapsed. Those tumors with the ability to metastasize had already done so. The prognosis was either bad or good, but it had been determined. In this case the cancer had already spread to distant sites via the blood as well as to regional lymph nodes. At this late stage neither patient nor physician delay will alter the outcome. (Chapter 10).

7. Q. A year later at the time of surgery, can you guarantee medically that the cancer still had not spread beyond the axillary nodes?
   A. A year later the patient still had systemic disease, that is, metastases to distant sites.

8. Q. The cancer had an entire year to break out of those axillary nodes and send cancer cells to other areas of the body, isn't that true?
   A. Yes, during that year the primary tumor continued to shed tumor cells into the blood. Most died, of course, but even if some did survive, it does not alter the outcome. Metastasis to distant sites in women who already have distant metastases is interesting, but again, it does not alter the outcome. (Chapter 10).

9. Q. And you can't tell really whether cancer cells will metastasize to the liver or the lungs unless there were overwhelming numbers of them, isn't that true?
   A. No, we cannot detect micrometastases until they attain a diameter of 5-10 mm.

10. Q. Very early metastasis to bones, lungs and liver may not show up on any scan or other test, isn't that correct?
    A. Yes, although sometimes small metastases can be detected by such things as bone scans.

11. Q. But if the five axillary nodes that had cancer in them were cut out before they sent out cancer cells elsewhere in the body, this would have reduced tumor burden on the patient, isn't that correct?
    A. Removal of the five axillary lymph nodes (assuming they did contain metastatic breast cancer) would not alter the final

outcome. The plaintiff had systemic breast cancer prior to the time the lesion became large enough to produce symptoms. Removing those five nodes would not have made one bit of difference. (§7.03[g]).

12. Q. Metastasis to the axillary nodes is called regional metastasis and to the lung, liver or to the bone is called distant metastasis, isn't that correct?

    A. Yes, axillary metastasis is classified as regional disease while spread to the lung, bone and liver is classified as distant metastasis.

13. Q. Wouldn't it have been far better for the patient to have had the cancer eliminated while it was still only regionally metastasized in the area of the axilla?

    A. Yes, it would be nice to cure the patient by eliminating the cancer while it was still confined to the regional nodes. Halsted taught this was true back in 1905, but sadly it is not true. Breast cancer does not spread in an orderly, time related fashion as Halsted taught. It does not spread first through the breast, then via the lymphatics to the axillary lymph nodes where if it is not promptly removed it will spread to distant sites. Halsted taught that early diagnosis with radical removal of the breast and axillary lymph nodes would cure the patient. It did not. More radical surgery did not. The addition of x-ray did not. Our attempts to diagnose earlier did not. In fact, there has been no improvement in the age adjusted survival since 1930 when records were first recorded. (Chapter 7).

14. Q. And the one-year delay in diagnosis and treatment in a patient like this does increase the risk of distant metastasis, isn't that right?

    A. The one year delay in diagnosis did not and will not alter the outcome. As a matter of fact, it is a well known fact that patients with long delays in diagnosis do much better than those with a one month delay in diagnosis. The answer is in the biology of the cancer. Slow growing indolent cancers often tend to be less lethal. Even though rapidly growing lethal cancers are detected promptly, they have distant metastasis and the outcome is poor. (Chapter 10).

15. Q. And if there is distant metastasis instead of only regional metastasis, the tumor burden on the body is much greater, isn't that true?
    A. There is no IF they have distant disease. Symptomatic breast cancers all develop distant metastases prior to the time they develop symptoms. Decreasing the duration of symptomatic cancers will not alter the outcome.

16. Q. So if during the year of delay cancer cells did leave the axillary node area and travel to the lungs or liver, then the delay could be significant, isn't that right?
    A. No, the metastases occurred prior to the time the breast cancer produced symptoms that led to its detection.

17. Q. And the reason for the delay in diagnosis and treatment could be significant is because the delay exposes the patient to the risk of distant instead of regional metastasis, isn't that true?
    A. No, the delay in treatment was not significant.

18. Q. And if a woman has distant metastatic spread, she is usually not curable, isn't that right?
    A. True, a woman with distant metastases is usually not curable. Life can be prolonged with appropriate adjuvant therapy, but cure seldom occurs. Some may live for years if the tumor has a prolonged doubling time or a powerful immune system.

19. Q. During the year of delay, wasn't the patient exposed to the risk of cancer cells being spread throughout her body by circulation in the lymphatic drainage system?
    A. During the year of delay, shedding of cancer cells continued to occur and embolization into the lymphatic system probably also occurred. You must remember that the vast majority of those shed do not survive, they die as a result of: 1) trauma of the rough and tumble world in the blood stream; 2) some destroyed by the immune system; 3) many cannot survive in high concentration of plasma pro-

teins; 4) some are dead when they were shed; or 5) some lack adhesion molecules and cannot escape from the blood stream. A few may survive, but will not alter the outcome.

20. Q. And the lymphatic system is a fluid circulation system that goes throughout the entire body. One of the ways that breast cancer can metastasize is to travel by using the lymphatic system, isn't that correct?
    A. Yes.

21. Q. And if nothing is done to stop it, the primary breast tumor is capable of seeding cells into the system.
    A. Yes, but again this will not alter the outcome.

22. Q. Where there is metastatic spread from the upper outer quadrant of the breast—like in the 1 o'clock position— it is usually to the axillary nodes, isn't that right?
    A. Yes, tumor in the upper outer quadrant tend to metastasize to the axillary nodes. Inner quadrant lesions also spread to the mediastinal nodes.

23. Q. These are the nodes that are under the arm in the armpit area.
    A. Yes, the axillary nodes are under the arm, armpit or axilla.

24. Q. But, can breast cancer also metastasize from the upper outer quadrant to nodes such as the central pectoral nodes?
    A. Yes, breast cancer can also metastasize to the central pectoral nodes.

25. Q. Can it also metastasize to the internal mammary chain of nodes?
    A. Yes, breast cancer can also metastasize to the internal mammary nodes.

26. Q. With patients whose cancers do metastasize to the internal mammary chain, these cancers can either remain there and grow or continue spreading elsewhere in the lymphatic system, isn't that correct?

A. To repeat, it would be nice to cure the patient by eliminating the cancer while it was still confined to the breast or the regional nodes. But as stated, breast cancer does not spread in an orderly, time related fashion as Halsted taught. (Chapter 7).

In spite of all our efforts, we have been unable to lower the age adjusted mortality rate of breast cancer since we first started keeping records in 1930. The reason is because the outcome of breast cancers is secondary to the biology of the cancer. Some cancers do very well because they: 1) lack the ability to metastasize; 2) lack the ability to establish a viable metastasis; or 3) the tumor had a prolonged doubling time. Tumors with doubling time of a year or more may survive for 20, 30 or even 40 years even though they have distant metastasis. Other cancers spread to distant sites before they can be detected by mammography (2.1 mm). Still others spread to distant sites before these tumors produce symptoms that lead to their detection. It is the biology that determines the outcome. Tumors with relatively unstable DNA will metastasize early, certainly before the lesion is clinically detectable in these biologically old tumors. Tumors with relatively stable DNA and/or prolonged doublings will outlive their tumor and have a favorable outcome. The appendix of Chapters 6, 9 and 10 contain visual aids that will bring these points across to the jury. (Chapter 6).

27. Q. Isn't it true that delay in diagnosis and treatment for a year gives the primary cancer an additional opportunity to seed cancer cells into the internal mammary chain?

A. To repeat, yes, it would be nice to cure the patient by eliminating the cancer while it was still confined to the breast or the regional nodes. If we could. (Chapters 6 and 7).

28. Q. And there may not be any evidence of spread into the internal mammary chain for a number of years until the spread goes on to more distant sites, causing distant rather than regional metastasis, that can happen, can't it?

A. To repeat, yes, it would be nice to cure the patient by eliminating the cancer while it was still confined to the breast or the regional nodes. (See answer to Q. 26, Chapter 7).

29. Q. Isn't it medically logical that it is easier for the doctors to treat breast cancer while it is still confined to the breast and near the breast in the axilla?

A. To repeat, yes, it would be nice to cure the patient by eliminating the cancer while it was still confined to the breast or the regional nodes. (See prior answer, Q. 26, Chapter 7).

Staging:

30. Q. Isn't staging used to determine how far advanced breast cancer is?

A. Yes, staging determines how advanced the cancer is. The plaintiff may prefer the Columbia Clinical Staging System because he/she can compare the clinical stage of axilla 12 months prior to and at the time of surgery. There is no pathological stage, just clinical.

31. Q. Is it true that physicians put breast cancer patients into stages to help determine what treatment to give?

A. Yes, staging helps determine the types of treatment.

32. Q. Don't some physicians use staging to help them arrive at an opinion on life expectancy?

A. Yes, some use staging to predict survival.

33. Q. There are many physicians who believe in the value of staging cancer patients, isn't that true?

A. Yes, many physicians believe all patients should be staged.

34. Q. Columbia University uses the A,B,C,D clinical classification stages, does it not?

A. The Columbia staging system classifies the patients A, B, C or D. The Columbia Clinical staging system was designed during the days of the radical mastectomy and was used to identify cases that were not operable. The TNM staging system is now considered the standard.

35. Q. In Stage A the doctor cannot feel any axillary nodes, isn't that right?
    A. Yes, in Stage A the nodes are not palpable.
36. Q. The patient in this case, according to the record, had no clinically palpable axillary nodes, did she?
    A. That is correct. Our patient did not have palpable nodes.
37. Q. Does this mean that when the lump was first discovered, the doctor could not feel any lymph nodes when he examined the area?
    A. Yes, at the time the alleged lump was discovered by the patient, examination of the axilla by the doctor revealed no evidence of axillary metastases.
38. Q. So, she would have been in Stage A according to the Columbia staging system, isn't that true?
    A. Yes, she would have been a Stage A.
39. Q. About a year after the lump was discovered and the clinical examination was first made, the patient was again examined just before surgery. And at this preoperative examination, the doctor found two clinically palpable nodes in the axilla. So, this means that just before surgery and before she was opened up, two of the lymph nodes could be actually felt, isn't that true?
    A. Yes, one year after the lump was discovered, clinical examination of the axilla revealed two suspicious nodes.
40. Q. And according to the Columbia classification system that placed the patient in Stage B?
    A. Yes, according to the Columbia system that placed the patient in Stage B.
41. Q. Please explain how doctors use staging.
    A. TNM and the Columbia staging is used to: 1) determine whether or not a patient is operable; 2) inoperable patients might be treated with chemotherapy and radiation and become operable; 3) select patients who might benefit from postoperative adjuvant therapy; or 4) select patients who do not need postoperative adjuvant therapy.

42. Q. Isn't staging used to help determine if the patient is operable?
    A. Yes, it helps to determine if a patient is operable. However, common sense can do the same thing without staging.
43. Q. If the patient is in Stage D, that means it is a much more advanced breast carcinoma than for Stage A, isn't that true?
    A. Yes, patients with Stage D disease have advanced breast cancer.
44. Q. And some physicians would consider not operating at all if the patient was in Stage D, isn't that correct?
    A. Yes, many of these Stage D patients would be treated with chemotherapy, radiation and hormones.
45. Q. But if the patient has moved from Stage A to Stage B, she would still be in a situation where an operation might help, isn't that right?
    A. Yes, patients who moved from Stage A to B would still be operable.
46. Q. Getting back to the patient in this case, if the one-year delay caused plaintiff to move from a Stage A to Stage B, and using this Columbia clinical chart for classification purposes, she has obviously moved to a less favorable stage, hasn't she?
    A. Yes, according to the Columbia clinical staging system during the one year the patient moved from Stage A to Stage B. However, you must remember that the Columbia staging system is a *clinical staging system.* When the axilla is said to be clinically normal, it actually contains axillary node metastases in 42% of the cases (§18.02[a]). Therefore, it is quite possible or even probable that the patient was a Stage B 12 months prior to surgery.
47. Q. When a patient using the Columbia system of staging moves from Stage A to Stage B, do you have an opinion as to whether or not this would affect how long she would have to live?

A. When evaluating symptomatic breast cancers, no one has ever proven that decreasing the durations of symptoms will alter the survival of breast cancers. Fisher, et al, in an NSABP prospective trial, evaluated 1535 women and found that neither physician nor patient delays of 3 to more than 9 months altered the disease free survival. A number of studies during the 1940's, 1950's, 1960's and 1970's have come to the same conclusion. Once a breast cancer becomes symptomatic, it doesn't make any difference whether it is a Stage A or Stage B. The outcome will be the same. (See visual aids for Chapters 6, 9 and 10).

48\. Q. Are you acquainted with the studies that have been done to predict survival odds based on staging?

A. Yes, I am acquainted with survival studies based on staging.

49\. Q. At the clinical Stage A, according to the chart, a patient has an 81% chance of surviving 10 years. Does this mean that for patients' studies, 81% of them were still alive at the end of 10 years?

A. According to your figures clinical Stage A cancers had a 10 year survival of 81% and this would indicate that 81% would be alive but some would have evidence of recurrence. However, you must remember that studies with fixed periods of 5 and 10 years are subject to many biases, such as: 1) selection bias (exclusion of unfavorable cases); 2) fixed end-point studies such as this are subject to serious lead time bias; 3) inadequate numbers of patients; 4) whether there was a control group; 5) the mix of patients including histologic types of cancers (%), histologic grade, nuclear grade, mitotic grade, molecular prognostic indicators. I would not accept your figures. (Chapter 18 TNM Staging System).

50\. Q. Looking at the 10 year survival rate for clinical Stage B, these patients had only 36% alive after 10 years.

A. Once again you are asking about a clinical stage, this time a clinical Stage B tumor. It is well known that when it is said that the axillary lymph nodes are clinical positive the examiner is wrong in 30% of the cases (§18.02[a]). About 70% of patients with pathologically proven axillary lymph node metastases will be dead within 10 years.

51. Q. Would the plaintiff, Mrs. B, if we apply this clinical staging to her and use this charge, doesn't this show that her life expectancy has dropped from 81% to 36%?
    A. No, using a clinical staging system it would be inaccurate to state that node negative women would have a 10 year survival of 81% and node positive women would have a survival of 36%. A clinical staging system cannot tell you what the actual pathology is or was. Secondly, your survival data are subject to many biases. Third, you have not considered: 1) tumor type; 2) microscopic appearance of the tumor including histologic grade, nuclear grade, mitotic index or adverse microscopic features including vascular invasion, lymphatic invasion or foci of tumor necrosis; and 3) molecular prognostic factors including ER/PgR, HER 2-neu oncogene and microvessel count.

52. Q. When the lump was first found in the breast, she had no clinically palpable nodes, did she?
    A. That is correct.

53. Q. A year later, just before surgery, she had two clinically palpable nodes. So, according to the chart, she would be in Stage A when first examined and Stage B just before surgery, isn't that correct?
    A. That is correct.

54. Q. Isn't a drop from 81% to 36% significant?
    A. No, as I stated before, using a clinical staging system would be inaccurate to state that node negative women would have a 10 year survival of 81% and node positive women would have a survival of 36%. A clinical staging system cannot tell you what the actual pathology is or was. Secondly, your survival data are subject to many biases. Third, you have not considered: 1) tumor type; 2) microscopic appearance of the tumor including histologic grade, nuclear grade, mitotic index or adverse microscopic features including vascular invasion, lymphatic invasion or foci

of tumor necrosis; and 3) molecular prognostic factors including ER/PgR, HER 2-neu oncogene and microvessel count.

55. Q. So, her odds of living 10 years, according to the staging chart statistics, dropped from 81% to 36% and she had a loss of life expectancy of approximately 55%, isn't that true?
A. No, using a clinical staging statistics, that would be inaccurate statement.

56. Q. Doesn't this mean that in a group of 100 women in Stage A, 81 will survive at the end of 10 years?
A. No, once again I must state that using a clinical staging system would be inaccurate to state that node negative women would have a 10 year survival of 81% and node positive women would have a survival of 36%. A clinical staging system cannot tell you what the actual pathology is or was. Secondly, your survival data are subject to many biases. Third, you have not considered: 1) tumor type; 2) microscopic appearance of the tumor including histologic grade, nuclear grade, mitotic index or adverse microscopic features including vascular invasion, lymphatic invasion or foci of tumor necrosis; and 3) molecular prognostic factors including ER/PgR, HER 2-neu oncogene and microvessel count.

57. Q. And doesn't this mean that in a second group of 100 women in Stage B, only 36 of them will survive at the end of 10 years, isn't that correct?
A. No, using a clinical staging system would be inaccurate to state that node negative women would have a 10 year survival of 81% and node positive women would have a survival of 36%. A clinical staging system cannot tell you what the actual pathology is or was.

58. Q. Are there physicians who believe that early diagnosis and treatment do not help?
A. We do not state that early diagnosis and treatment will not help. Early diagnosis is an excellent goal and will always be something toward which we should strive. We do agree that

early diagnosis is quite effective for some cancers such as cancer of the uterus in which the cancer spreads to distant sites at a later time in the life cycle of the tumor. In other cancers such as small cell cancer of the lung, early diagnosis has failed because this tumor spreads to distant sites long before it is possible to detect this cancer. Thus, the effectiveness of early diagnosis depends upon the biology of the cancer.

We do say that thus far our efforts to lower the age adjusted mortality of breast cancer since records were first recorded in 1930 have failed. The cancers diagnosed in the 1930's and 1940's were truly symptomatic cancers. Diagnostic mammograms were seldom used and screening mammography had not yet been introduced. These women developed symptoms, consulted the doctor, and diagnosis was made by palpation and open biopsy. The death rate then was 27-28 women per 100,000 female population and has remained stable since then. No one has ever proven that decreasing the duration of symptoms (earlier diagnosis) will alter the survival of these women.

The fact that lumpectomy is as effective as the most radical operation proves that 40 to 50% of these women have systemic breast cancer at the time of surgery. Therefore, no matter how radical the surgery, it will not increase the cure rate. We must learn to accept this and concentrate on developing more effective adjuvant therapies.

59. Q. Yet, they go ahead and cut off women's breasts or give radiation or chemotherapy when they really don't think it helps.

A. Even though we know we cannot cure these symptomatic breast cancers, we still treat them for the following reasons: 1) dying from chest wall recurrence is a miserable way to die; therefore, we remove the primary tumor and use radiation as necessary; 2) lumpectomy gives good cosmetic results and takes care of the primary; 3) some may need radiation to the axilla; 4) some will have a longer survival with adjuvant therapy; and 5) some will have a long survival because of a prolonged doubling time.

COMMENT

The foregoing questions and suggested answers indicate that cross-examination by plaintiff's counsel will likely include an attempt to demonstrate the statistics that increasing tumor size (delay) means decrease in survival and loss of chance. The claim may be that 12 months prior to surgery the tumor stage was low, but increased during the alleged 12 month delay.

The answer is that the plaintiff had systemic disease when the symptoms first were noted, 12 months prior to the surgery. Earlier diagnosis (smaller tumor size) in a woman with systemic disease indicates she would seem to live longer, but will still die from the cancer at the time determined by the biology of the tumor.

To the assertion that the nodes were negative 12 months prior to the surgery, but at the time of surgery, the nodes were positive, the answer is that this proves only that this was an aggressive cancer that had the ability to metastasize. Not all tumors have this ability. It proves that the woman did indeed have systemic cancer prior to the time the lesion developed symptoms. The probability is that she had axillary metastases 12 months prior to the surgery.

To the question as to whether it is not true that this particular lesion was shedding cancer cells into the system for 12 months prior to the surgery, the answer is found in Chapter 10.

Pre-vascular growth phase; §10.02

Angiogenesis; §10.03

Tumors (one gram) shed 3,000,000 to 4,000,000 cancer cells into the blood each day; §10.03[b]

Experimental animal models—50% of the animals have lung metastases by the fifth day after the onset of angiogenesis; §10.08

Tumor cells are stimulated to become more aggressive and lethal by the a) invading endothelial cell; b) tissue damage by the invading tumor cells; c) by the growth factors released by the wound healing response triggered by the damage created by the invading tumor cells and the invading endothelial cells §10.06[c].

Dr. Plotkin, Skrabanek, Spratt, ER Fisher, and many others are convinced that cancers have the ability to metastasize between the 14th to 20th doubling time of the tumor and we think they may be correct. We can prove, however, that breast cancers that have the ability metastsize prior to the time the tumor reaches the terminal stage of its life cycle (75% to 80%) has elapsed and becomes large enough to produce symptoms. (Chapter 10).

Note: The visual aids for Chapters, 6, 9 and 10 are helpful in establishing that breast cancers that have the ability to metastasize will do so prior to the time these symptoms are large enough produce symptoms.

The questions propounded in Appendix 3 are taken or suggested in the article by Robert M. Fox, *Countering the Standard Defenses in a Breast Cancer Malpractice Case,* 30 AmJur Trials 437, and are being used or adapted with the permission of the publisher, Lawyers Cooperative Publishing, a Division of Thomson Legal Publishing, Inc.

AUTHOR'S OBSERVATION

Cancer litigation has been around for more than 100 years. The first case, according to medical literature, was a purported traumatic cancer erupting in a soldier's chest wound. (Stole, H, Crissey, J. T. *Epithelioma From Single Trauma,* N.Y. State J. Med. 15-496 (1962)). With the development of the worker's compensation laws not only in the United States, but throughout Europe, claims were made that trauma was the cause of many cancers, including breast cancer. Knox, L. C., *Trauma and Malignant Tumors,* Am.J.Surg. 26:66-73, 1934. These claims were supported solidly by American doctors. Traumatic cancer was explained by a "parasite theory" of cancer induction, ascribing malignant "neoplasia" to a universal infection in humans. The role of biology in the cancers was limited or non-existent and the theory that trauma was the sole cause of breast cancer was generally accepted. (*Menarde v. Philadelphia Transport Company,* 103 A.2d 681 (Penn. 1954)).

With study and particularly the research by James Ewing (Ewing, J. *The Relation of Trauma to Malignant Tumors,* Am.J.Surg. 40:30-36 (1926)) medical opinion changed and in 1955 the forensic pathologist Huper (*Section on Environmental Cancer,* NIH circa 1950) stated that "It seems that the time has come when the concept of a primary traumatic causation of cancer should permanently be laid to rest by the medical and legal professions, and should no longer form a subject of litigation before courts and compensation boards." (Huper, W. C. *Medical Legal Aspects of Cancer,* Am.J.Clin. Pathol. 25:116-125, 1955). As Dr. Spratt has pointed out, whenever any disease control system is over-promoted as to its efficacy, false expectations are created in the mind of the public. With the constant publicity that breast cancer can be controlled or cured by early diagnosis, the victim of a disease blames the system and medical malpractice cases arise. (Spratt, *Surgical Oncology Clinics of North America,* Vol. 3, No. 1, Jan. 1994).

The conflicting testimony from medical experts must in some way be resolved by some method of establishing medical/legal guidelines for breast cancer litigation such as those suggested by Kern (*Historical Trends in Breast Cancer Litigation,* Vol. III, No. 1, Jan.

1994) and hopefully will be developed by scientific research rather than political pronouncements of the National Cancer Institute sponsored "consensus." As Spratt has also pointed out, scientific evidence must override empiricism, entrepreneurship and even the biases inherent in the consensus process. As he states, few epidemics are ever controlled before a cause is identified and prevented. (Spratt, supra).

Rovit, M.D. and Hauber, J.D., writing in the *American College of Surgeons Bulletin,* Vol. 74, No. 7, state the situation most succinctly:

> Similar to post mortem examinations, the litigation takes place after the fact and is separated by time, additional data and irreversible changes. Surgeons are well aware of the clarity of retrospective vision. Likewise, the expert witness, often imported from academic ivory towers, must appreciate the complexities of a developing and unstable situation in which decisions are made with no knowledge of future consequences. *

---

* Professional medical organizations can help curb some of the abuses inherent in the present expert witness system. Two primary objectives might be attempted. The first deals with promulgating and gaining legislative approval of acceptable professional qualifications for an expert witness. The second is concerned with developing methods of insuring that expert medical testimony is indeed expert, fair and accurate.

Other professional organizations are in the process of constructing similar minimum goals. One would expect that someone who proposes to provide expert medical testimony in a professional liability case be at least Board certified in the same specialty as the litigant, be actively practicing within that specialty and be able to demonstrate by practice characteristics, publications, and other criteria, special knowledge of the matter under dispute. It is paradoxical that some of the same groups who actively promote standards for professional qualifications in medical care are loath to insist on similar expertise for medical testimony in court.

It would seem too, that our courts must increasingly exercise the authority given under Rule 702 of the Federal Rules of Evidence and comparable state rules and become more actively involved in considering what makes science scientific, to the end that an expert's testimony rests on a reliable foundation. (See Ayala, F. J., Black, B. *Science and the Courts,* American Scientist 81:193 (1988). See also §3.07 Motion as to Experts.

None of this means, as far as the authors are concerned, that a disposition of disputes, including medical malpractice claims, should be taken from the courts. There are physicians who are incompetent. There are also physicians, both competent and professional, who unfortunately, are sometimes negligent. A patient injured thereby should be reasonably compensated and should be compensated within the framework, we believe, of the judicial system. Solutions to revise the tort system should be approached with caution. The no fault compensation program, for example, by eliminating any determination of fault, runs contrary to society's ancient beliefs and to attempt to compensate everyone for every injury would result in an enormous increase in costs. Arbitration raises more problems than it solves. The tort concept, and the judicial system, including the jury system, are part of our political inheritance and essential to our liberties. Yet we must also insure that breast cancer cases, particularly those involving an alleged delay in diagnosis, do not become a form of sickness insurance against natural occurrences.

PART II

MEDICAL SECTION

Campbell F. Watts, M.D.

CHAPTER 6: MORTALITY AND INCIDENCE RATES OF BREAST CANCER: A 63-YEAR OLD ENIGMA

CHAPTER 6

MORTALITY AND INCIDENCE RATES OF BREAST CANCER: A 63-YEAR OLD ENIGMA

§6.01 NO IMPROVEMENT IN AGE-ADJUSTED SURVIVAL OF BREAST CANCER SINCE 1930

The age-adjusted mortality rate of breast cancer has remained stable since 1930 (1). "Age-standardization is a method used to make valid comparisons among rates by assuming the same age distributions occurs among the different groups being compared" (1). The death rate has remained at about 27-28 deaths per 100,000 female population each year. It is estimated that 182,000 women will be diagnosed with breast cancer in 1994 and that 46,000 women will die (2).

The failure of the age-adjusted mortality rate of breast cancer to improve since 1930 is especially discouraging since:

> "In no other human cancer has there been such enormous research and clinical effort made to understand the disease and modify treatment according to current clinical presentations and research findings (3)."

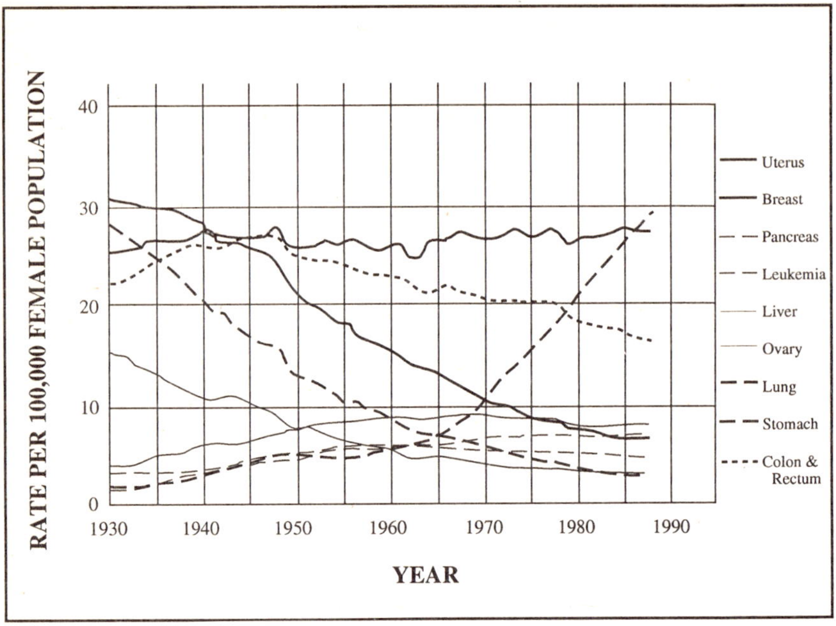

Figure 6-1. Age-Adjusted Cancer Death Rates for Selected Sites, Females, United States, 1930-1988. Boring CC, Squires TS, and Tong T. Cancer Statistics-1993, Ca-A Cancer Journal for Clinicians, 43(1):7-26, Jan-Feb, 1993, page 16. Sources: National Cancer Center for Health Statistics and US Bureau of the Census. Reprinted courtesy authors and publishers.

These efforts have included:

Patient education

The American Cancer Society has conducted massive educational programs concerning the benefits of monthly breast self examinations, mammography and early diagnosis and treatment.

Physician education

The quality of medical education has steadily improved since 1930.

Molecular biology

During the past 20 years there has been an explosion in our knowledge of the molecular biology of the cancer cell.

Mammography

The widespread use of mammography has resulted in a 24-32% increase in the detection of breast cancers.

New diagnostic modalities

The CT scan, MRI, and ultrasound have proven of great value for many cancers but are not as accurate as mammography for breast cancer.

These cancers, especially those between 1930-1970, were truly symptomatic breast cancers, that is, they were diagnosed solely on the basis of symptoms, palpation, and biopsy. During 1990, 44,000 women died because their breast cancers metastasized to distant sites before the cancers became symptomatic and could be detected by palpation or by mammography. But why, have we been unable to detect and remove the breast cancers from these 44,000 women before they became incurable with systemic disease? For several reasons:

1. Many cancers are so genetically unstable that neoplastic progression (the ability to metastasize) occurs before these lesions become symptomatic or detectable. (See also Chapter 10).
2. Some tumors are camouflaged, that is, the presence of the tumor within the breast is hidden or masked by such factors as a dense breast, tumor density similar to breast density, vague tumor borders, failure of tumor to form a distinct mass, lack of tumor specific microcalcifications, and pattern of tumor invasion. (See also Chapter 14).These tumors must grow longer (increased sojourn time) and attain a larger size (larger threshold size) before it will be possible to detect them by mammography and/or palpation. (See also Chapter 15).

§6.02 A STEADY RISE IN THE INCIDENCE OF BREAST CANCER SINCE 1930

Throughout this same period of time (1930-1987), during which the age-adjusted mortality of breast cancer has remained relatively stable, there has been a dramatic increase in the incidence of breast cancer. From 1940 to 1980 the incidence of breast cancer increased at a rate of 1% each year. Since 1980 the incidence of breast cancer has been rising at the rate of 3% per annum (4). Garfinkel (5) and Boring, et al. (1) summarized the phenomenon of the increasing incidence of breast cancer in a recent publication of the American Cancer Society:

Increasing Incidence of Breast Cancer
An increase of 32.5% between 1980 and 1987

Year	Incidence of breast cancer per 100,000 female population
1935	55
1980	84.8
1987	112.4

Modified from Boring, et al. (1) and Garfinkel (5).

It is interesting that this long–term increase in the incidence of breast cancer also has been observed in industrialized and developing countries throughout the world (6).

§6.03 HOW CAN WE EXPLAIN THE PHENOMENA OF A STABLE AGE–ADJUSTED MORTALITY RATE IN THE PRESENCE OF A SHARP RISE IN INCIDENCE AND AN APPARENT INCREASE IN THE OVERALL SURVIVAL OF BREAST CANCER? (See Figure 6-2).

The phenomenon of a stable mortality rate and a dramatic increase in the incidence of breast cancer is perplexing. However, Harris, Lippman, Veronesi, and Willet (6) in their excellent three part review of breast cancer conclude that all of the following factors appear to be contributing to the divergence of the mortality and incidence rates of breast cancer (6):

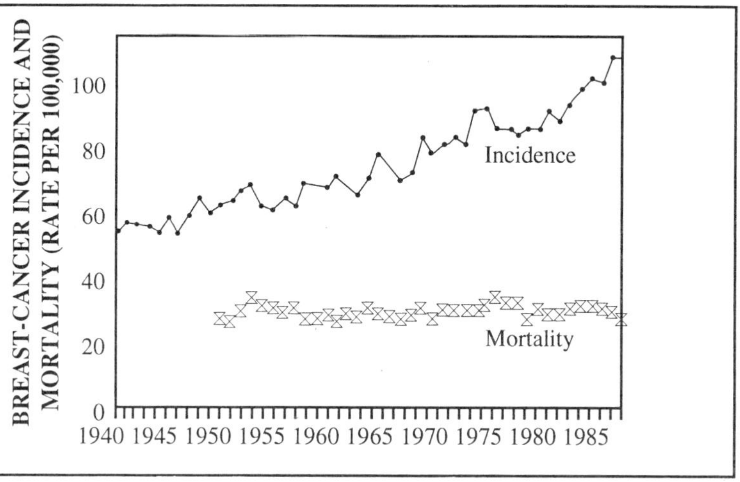

Figure 6-2. Age-Standardized Incidence of Breast Cancer and Mortality Rates in Connecticut from 1940 to 1988. Data from the Surveillance, Epidemiology, and End-Results Program. Harris JR, Lippman ME, Veronesi U, and Willett W. Medical Progress-Breast Cancer, Part 1. New Eng J Med 327(5):319-328,1992, Figure 1 page 320. Reprinted courtesy of authors and publisher.

---

1. A more complete reporting of breast cancer cases.
2. Earlier detection of breast cancer.
3. Increased overall survival secondary to adjuvant therapy.
4. A more benign form of breast cancer.

We will summarize Harris et al.'s (6) discussion of these four factors and add a few comments of our own in the following sections.

[a] The Reporting of Breast Cancer Was Not Thorough Until the Mid 1970's (6)

It has been estimated that about 25% of the increased incidence of breast cancer prior to 1982 can be attributed to improvements in the reporting of breast cancer (6). Prior to 1982, many breast cancers with good outcomes were not reported. The additional increase is thought to be secondary lead time bias (earlier detection), over-diagnosis bias, and a true increase in incidence secondary to changes in life style.

[b] Increase in the Incidence of Breast Cancer Secondary to the Widespread Use of Screening Mammography

[1] Glossary

A. Screening Mammography—

The screening of large numbers of asymptomatic women to identify a small group with mammographic abnormalities that require further evaluation.

B. Diagnostic Mammography—

This is a diagnostic test which evaluates the abnormalities discovered by screening mammograms and women with breast symptoms or physical findings.

[2] Screening Mammography Seldom Used Prior to 1970 and Not Commonly Used Prior to 1980

The use of diagnositic mammography began in 1913. However, it was not until the improved techniques developed by Egan became available in 1960 that mammography was widely accepted as a modality for the detection of breast cancer (7). In 1963 the concept of mass screening of asymptomatic women with mammography was introduced by Shapiro and Strax (8). In the 1970's the American Cancer Society and the National Institute of Health sponsored large mass screening programs for 250,000 asymptomatic women with periodic mammograms (7).

The initiation of screening programs with mammography will temporarily increase the incidence by advancing the time of diagnosis. "If regular screening is continued . . . a new steady-state incidence will be achieved at a rate close to that which will occur without screening (6)". Tabar (9) has reported that mass screening of asymptomatic women with periodic mammograms results in a 30% reduction in mortality for those who are 50 years or older at 7 and 11 years. However, in 1984 the number of women receiving annual screening did not exceed 15% (10). In an HMO in Oregon in 1985 only 9% of breast cancers had been initially detected by screening (11) and it was estimated that screening could account for no more than 5% of incident cases. Harris, et al. (6) concluded that *since screening causes only a transient increase in incidence and was not used widely until the 1980's it can explain little of the long-term increase in the incidence of breast cancer* (emphasis is ours).

The screening of women in the 1980's did result in an increase in detection of lesions smaller than 2.0 cm, in-situ carcinomas, and localized cancers. This may eventually result in a decrease in the number of deaths from breast cancer. Some predict that when all adult women are periodically screened with mammograms there will be a 25% reduction in the mortality rate of breast cancer.

[c] Increased Overall Survival Secondary to Improvements in Treatment?

Surgery—Modifications of breast cancer surgery have reduced the need for total and radical mastectomy and improved cosmetic results but there has been no improvements in survival secondary to these changes.

Adjuvant therapy—Although improvements in adjuvant therapy have produced modest increases in survival of small subsets of breast cancers it is important to remember that ". . . on an absolute scale the survival benefits of these therapies are small (12)". The numbers of patients in these small subsets are not large enough to significantly impact the age-adjusted mortality rate of breast cancer.

Contrary to what we read in the mass media there have been no dramatic improvements in our management of breast cancer. Walt (13) in a lecture presented at the Mayo Clinic in 1991 stated:

> "These are the facts: 170,000 new cases will be reported in 1991. Approximately 48,000 patients will die. Although the incidence is increasing, cure as yet is not . . . Sadly, despite our best efforts, we have not as yet produced data to show that we have improved the overall mortality rate [of breast cancer]. This may come later as smaller lesions are discovered; but, there is much about the biology of breast cancer that we do not understand and we should be cautious about projections. Currently our muted triumphs lie mainly in the area of extended palliation and in the avoidance of unnecessarily destructive surgery".

[d] A More Benign Form of Breast Cancer Since 1930

Miller (14) concluded that an increasing incidence and stable mortality rate with no improvements in the results of treatment suggests a major change in our methods of detection and diagnosis of breast cancer. Miller (14) has also stated that "if there was no improvement in the results of treatment, then only about one in ten of the 'excess' cancers, compared with the beginning of the 1950's, was lethal. This would strongly suggest that there has been a major change in the diagnosis and detection of breast cancer". Miller (14) continued, "... it seems likely that they [the excess cancers] can be attributed to greater care in the diagnosis and detection of breast abnormalities with more surgical biopsies performed and more extensive pathological examination of resected material. However, it would seem that these extra cancers do not have the same biologic potential to cause death" since:

It would appear that the increasing incidence of breast cancer is secondary to:

- Better reporting of cases with a good outcome. In the past there was better reporting of cancer deaths than those with a good outcome.
- Perhaps 5 to 10% +/− of the long-term increase in incidence is secondary to earlier detection. Screening mammography was not widely used prior to 1980.
- Major changes in our methods of detecting and diagnosing breast cancer which detect many small lesions with no or low lethal potential.
- Changes in life style and the fact that women simply live longer.

There has been little improvement in survival secondary to treatment except for modest increases in small subsets of women secondary to adjuvant therapy. Therefore, the phenomena of a stable age-adjusted mortality rate and a rising incidence rate suggests we are dealing with increasing numbers of a more benign form of breast cancer.

Practice Note

The statistics on the rise of the incidence of breast cancer provided above could be used to counter plaintiff's arguments which rely on the incidence theory. See §6.03 supra.

§6.04 RATIONALE FOR THE APPEARANCE OF A MORE BENIGN FORM OF BREAST CANCER SINCE 1930

a. Between 1930 and 1970 there was an estimated 1% annual increase in the incidence of breast cancer (40 × 1% = 40% estimated increase in incidence).

b. During this same period 1930-1970 there was:

[1] No increase in survival secondary to improvements in surgical management.
[2] No mammography screening available, therefore, no earlier diagnosis secondary to screening.
[3] No increase in survival secondary to adjuvant therapy prior to 1970.

c. Therefore, the age-adjusted mortality rate of breast cancer remained stable, in part, because of the detection of a more benign form of breast cancer.

d. This trend has continued to the present time.

Thus, as suggested by Harris et al. (6), a number of factors are involved in balancing the mortality and incidence rates of breast cancer while maintaining a stable mortality rate. However, we suspect that the emergence of a more benign form of breast cancer plays a larger role than most realize.

§6.05 CONCLUSION

However, regardless of how we interpret the increasing incidence and stable age-adjusted mortality rates the fact remains that there is a significant group of breast cancers that we have been unable to detect prior to the time viable distant metastases occur.

- These are the cancers of the women who will die each year because we have been unable to solve the problems presented by:
  a) early metastasis, see Chapter 10;
  b) tumor camouflaging, see Chapter 14.
- These are the symptomatic cancers that have resisted the best efforts of the medical community since 1930.
- These are the breast cancers of the 46,000 women who will die of breast cancer in 1994.
- These are the women who have been dying of breast cancer at the rate of 27-28 per 100,000 female population for the past 63 years.
- These are the symptomatic cancers we will generally encounter in the malpractice arena.
- These are the cancers whose genes have sustained a series of sequential alterations resulting in tumors with great metastatic potential.
- Finally, these are the cancers which we primarily, address in this book. The public must understand that the unfavorable outcome of most breast cancers is secondary to the biologic aggressiveness of tumors that have overpowered the immunity of the host.

It is recognized that the longevity of humans is secondary to the inheritance of "good" genes. Many do not realize that, to a large extent, our success in treating cancer is dependent upon the degree to which the genes of the cancer cell have been altered. Cancer cells with less damaged genes are easier to cure since they are:

- less invasive
- metastasize less often or not at all.

Unfortunately we must continue to cope with this hard-core group of symptomatic breast cancers until their numbers are depleted by one or more of the following:

1. The periodic screening of the majority of asymptomatic adult (over the age of 40) women with mammograms.

2. More effective postoperative adjuvant therapy programs [with chemicals or biologicals] for the women who harbor microscopic foci of distant metastases.
3. Understanding those biologic factors which predispose to the development of breast cancer.
4. Effective breast cancer prevention programs.

Practice Note

The defense can use graphs such as figures 6-1 and 6-2 to provide demonstrable evidence regarding the significance of the term ''symptomatic'' breast cancer, our failure to improve the survival rate of ''symptomatic'' breast cancers since 1930, and evidence to prove the appearance of a more benign form of breast cancer during the past 60 years. See APPENDIX 6-1—VISUAL AIDS

References

1. Boring CC, Squires TS, and Tong T. Cancer Statistics-1993, Ca-A Cancer Journal for Clinicians, Jan.-Feb, 43(1):7-26, 1993.
2. Garfinkel, L. Cancer Statistics and Trends. *Clinical Oncology,* Holleb, Fink, and Murphy, eds. American Cancer Society, 1991, Figure 1.1, page 2. Sources: National Cancer Center for Health Statistics and US Bureau of the Census.
3. Bland I and Cady B. Preface. Surg Clin N Am 70(4):page xi, August 1990.
4. Reynolds Tom. News, News. J Natl Cancer Instit 82(12): 264-265, 1991.
5. Garfinkel L. Current Trends in Breast Cancer. Ca-A Cancer Journal for Clinicians 43(1):5-6, Jan-Feb, 1993.
6. Harris JR, Lippman ME, Veronesi U, and Willett W. Medical Progress - Breast Cancer, Part 1. New Eng J Med 327(5):319-328, 1992.
7. Kinne DW and Kopans DB. Physical Examination and Mammography in the Diagnosis of Breast Disease in

Breast Diseases, Harris, Hellman, Henderson, and Kinne, eds, pages 81-106, JB Lippincott, 1991.

8. Forrest AP. Screening and Breast Cancer Incidence. J Natl Cancer Instit 82(19):1525-1526, 1990.
9. Tabar L, Fagerberg G, Day NE., et al. Breast Cancer Treatment and Natural History: New Insights from Results of Screening. The Lancet 339:412-414, Feb 15, 1992.
10. Howard J. Using Mammography for Cancer Control: An Unrealized Potential. CA Cancer J Clin 37:-48,1987.
11. Glass AG, Hoover RN. Rising Incidence of Breast Cancer: Relationship to Stage and Receptor Status. J Natl Cancer Inst 82:693-596,1990.
12. Harris JR, Lippman ME, Veronesi U, Willet W. Medical Progress, Breast Cancer (third of three parts). N Engl J Med 327(7):473-480, 1992.
13. Walt, Alexander. Breast Cancer: Totems, Taboos, Torts, and Tomorrow. Mayo Alumni, Mayo Foundation, Spring 1992, pages 12-10.
14. Miller AB. Causes of Breast Cancer and High Risk Groups in *Breast Diseases,* Harris, Hellman, Henderson, and Kinne, eds. JB Lippincott, 1991, pages 119-126.

APPENDIX 6-1—VISUAL AIDS

[a] No Reduction in the Age-Adjusted Mortality Rate of Breast Cancer Since 1930

Defense counsel can use the graph presented below as a visual aid in the courtroom to prove to the jury that the rate of breast cancer mortality has remained stable. (See Figure 6-3). The following points should be made to the jury during counsel's argument:

Narration

[1] Do you consider the National Center for Health Statistics a reliable government agency?

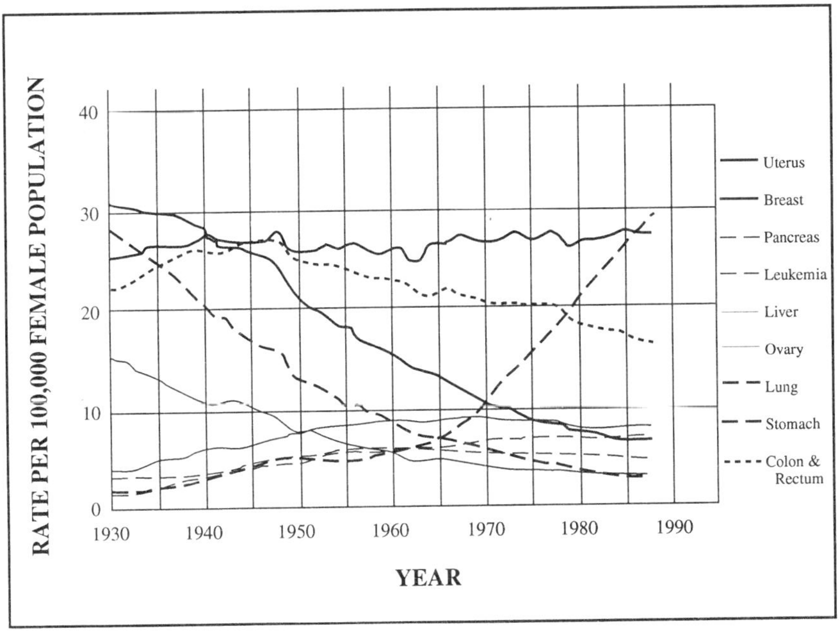

Figure 6-3. (Repeat of Figure 6-1). Age-Adjusted Cancer Death Rates for Selected Sites, Females, United States, 1930-1988. Boring CC, Squires TS, and Tong T. Cancer Statistics-1993, Ca-A Cancer Journal for Clinicians, 43(1):7-26, Jan-Feb, 1993, page 16. Sources: National Cancer Center for Health Statistics and US Bureau of the Census. Reprinted courtesy authors and publisher (1).

[2] Do you consider the US Bureau of the Census to be a reliable government agency?
[3] Is it not true that there has been no improvement in the age-adjusted mortality rate of breast cancers since records were first recorded in 1930?
[4] Have not 27-28 women per 100,000 female population died of breast cancer each year since 1930?
[5] And that's in spite of the best efforts of the medical community, is it not?

[b] The Effectiveness of Early Diagnosis is Dependant Upon the Biology of the Cancer Rather Than Physician Skill

Note - This graph is identical to the graph in [a], above, except that all data have been removed except for cancers of the uterus, lung and breast. (See Figure 6-4).

Defense counsel can use this graph as a visual aid in the courtroom to prove that the survival rate of breast cancer is secondary to the biology of the cancer rather than physician skill or lack of skill. The following points should be made to the jury during counsel's argument.

Narration

[1] Is the mortality rate of cancer of the lung increasing because of poor physician care?
[2] Is the mortality rate of cancer of the uterus decreasing because of better physician care?
[3] Is the mortality rate of cancer of the breast unchanged since 1930 because of negligent physicians?
[4] Is not the true culprit the biology of the cancers?
   A. Cancer of the uterus spreads late in its life cycle and, therefore, early diagnosis is quite effective. The routine Pap smear has been quite helpful. Is not this correct?
   B. Small cell cancer of the lung, on the other hand, spreads so early in its life cycle that early diagnosis is ineffective. In the best of hands the 10 year survival is less than 4%, long term survival is less than 1%. (2). Isn't this true?

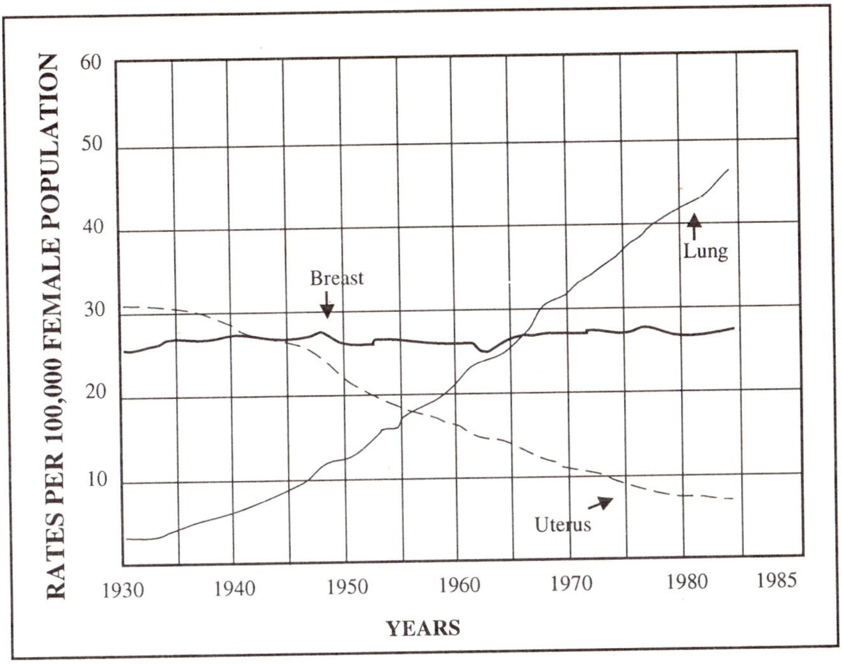

Figure 6-4. (Modified from Figure 6-1). Age-Adjusted Cancer Death Rates for Selected Sites, Females, United States, 1930-1988. Boring CC, Squires TS, and Tong T. Cancer Statistics-1993, Ca-A Cancer Journal for Clinicians, 43(1):7-26, Jan-Feb, 1993, page 16. Sources: National Cancer Center for Health Statistics and US Bureau of the Census. Reprinted courtesy authors and publisher.

C. Cancer of the breast:

1. Many (40% +/−) spread to distant sites before the tumors become large enough to produce symptoms. Although early diagnosis by screening mammography may be effective for some of these women, it will not help all women since many cancers spread before they can be detected by mammograpy. Unfortunately, the tumors with significant genetic instability will undergo neoplastic progression and metastasis before they become large enough to produce symptoms. Neither patient or physician delay will alter the outcome of symptomatiic breast cancers.

2. About 60% +/- of breast cancers have relatively stable DNA and do not undergo neoplastic progression (metastasis) or do well because of a favorable host-tumor relationship and/or a prolonged tumor doubling time.
3. Thus the mortatity rate of breast cancer has remained stable.

[5] Does not the above suggest that the biology of the cancers, not variations in standard of care, is responsible for the disparate outcomes of these cancers?

[6] Repeat the following to the jury as frequently as possible:

- The age adjusted mortality rates of cancers of the uterus have decreased 78% since 1930 (3, 4).
- The age adjusted mortality rate of cancer of the breast has not changed since 1930.
- In fact, the age adjusted mortality rate of cancer has not decreased following the introduction of screening mammography (3).
- "Between 1982 and 1989 the incidence of regional and distant disease in American women older than 49 has decreased only 8 and 10%, respectively, while the corresponding incidence of local disease increased 52%" (4, 5).
- Thus, is it not true that United States national health statistics reveal that widespread screening programs... "have yet to show any savings in lives and show only a slight reduction of regional or advanced disease at the time of diagnosis (4)"?
- Is not this explained by the differences in the biology of cancers of the uterus and breast?

References

1. Boring CC, Squires TS, Tong T, Montgomery S. Cancer Statistics-1993. Ca-A Cancer J for Clin 44:7-26, 1993.
2. Mountain CF. Clinical Biology of Small Cell Carcinoma: Relationship to Surgical Therapy. Semin Oncol 5:272-279, 1978.

3. Boring CC, Squires TS, Tong T, Montgomery S. Cancer Statistics-1994. Ca-A Cancer J for Clin 44:7-26, 1994.
4. Dupont WD. Evidence of efficacy of mammographic screening for women in their forties. Cancer 74(4):1204-1206, 1994.
5. Miller BA, Feuer EJ, Hankey BF. Breast cancer [letter] N Engl J Med 327:1756-1757, 1992.

[c] Definition and Significance of the Term Symptomatic Breast Cancer (See Figure 6-5).

Defense counsel can use the following graph to define and explain to the jury the significance of the term symptomatic breast cancer.

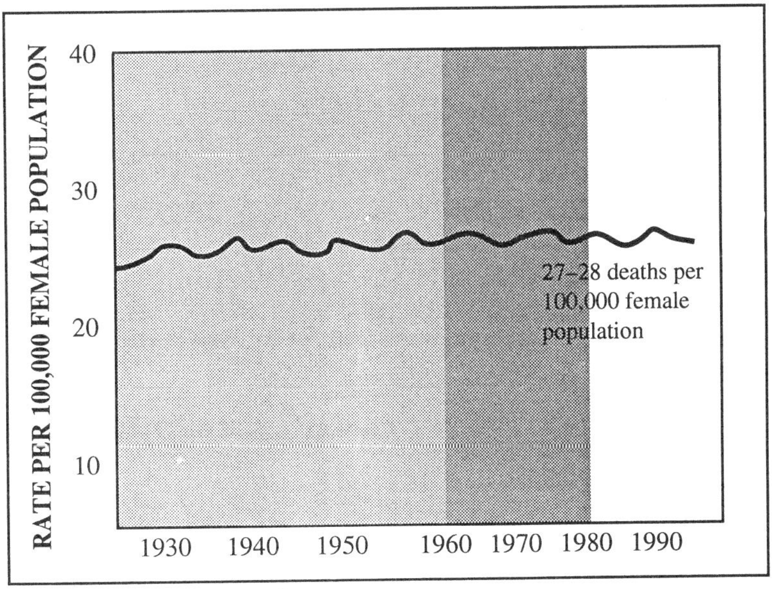

Figure 6-5. (Modified from Figure 6-1). Age-Adjusted Cancer Death Rates for Selected Sites, Females, United States, 1930-1988. Boring CC, Squires TS, and Tong T. Cancer Statistics-1993, Ca-A Cancer Journal for Clinicians, 43(1):7-26, Jan-Feb, 1993, page 16. Sources: National Cancer Center for Health Statistics and US Bureau of the Census. Reprinted courtesy authors and publisher.

Narration

[1] Again, the age-adjusted mortality breast cancer has not changed since 1930. Isn't that true?

[2] What type of breast cancers were detected between 1930 and 1970?

A. Diagnostic mammography was seldom employed before 1960 because of technical difficulties (light shading).

B. The concept of screening mammography was not introduced until about 1963, and was not widely used until in the 1980's (dark shading).

C. These were depression years and money was scarce.

D. During the depression years women did not consult their physicians unless they had symptoms.

[3] Thus, during the 1930's (1930-1935):

A. Breast cancers grew within the breast until they became large enough to produce symptoms.

B. Symptoms prompted the women to consult their family doctor.

C. Palpation of the breast by their doctor confirmed the presence of a mass and open biopsy confirmed the diagnosis.

[4] Were not these truly symptomatic breast cancers that were diagnosed only after symptoms of the cancer focused the patient's attention upon her breast?

[5] Even after the introduction of diagnostic and screening mammography the age-adjusted mortality of breast cancer remained unchanged, did it not?

[6] Conclusion: Unfortunateley, breast cancers with genetic instability undergo neoplastic progression (metastasis) prior to the time these cancers become large enough to produce symptoms. Cancers with stable DNA are unlikely to metastasize during the life span of the tumor. Thus, neither patient or physician delay in the diagnosis of symptomatic breast cancers will alter the outcome. This is the major reason for our failure to lower the age-adjusted mortality rate of breast cancer for over 60 years (§10.11).

CHAPTER 7: THE EVOLUTION OF OUR PRESENT DAY CONCEPT OF THE NATURAL HISTORY OF BREAST CANCER

CHAPTER 7

THE EVOLUTION OF OUR PRESENT DAY CONCEPT OF THE NATURAL HISTORY OF BREAST CANCER

§7.01 INTRODUCTION

The "dark ages" of breast cancer lasted 5,000 years. During this time there was no effective local, regional or systemic treatment of any kind. The dawn of the evolution of the surgical management of breast cancer arrived sometime between 1890 and 1910, when the concept that breast cancer spread solely via the lymphatics became widely accepted. William Halsted, agreeing with Samson Handley, stated (1):

> "Breast cancer spreads centrifugally and in continuity via the lymphatics through the breast and tissue planes to the regional lymph nodes and then to distant sites via the perivascular lymphatics" [Spread through the blood stream was thought to occur rarely, if ever].

It was logical to conclude, therefore, that early diagnosis and radical surgery would cure breast cancer. This concept became known as the Halsted Doctrine.

§7.02 THE HALSTED DOCTRINE

William Halsted and Willie Meyer popularized the radical removal of the breast, the underlying muscles, and the regional lymph nodes in continuity. Radical surgery did result in a dramatic reduction in the frequency of local recurrences of the tumor but failed to cure 50% of women with operable breast cancer. Even the addition of postoperative radiation and removal of the supraclavicular nodes (lower neck) and mediastinal nodes (in the chest) failed to improve the survival rate of breast cancer. Although the radical mastectomy remained the gold standard of breast surgery for many years, eventually the consistent failure of the operation to help 50% of the women with operable breast cancer led some to question the validity of the Halsted Doctrine. Then, there was the problem of women who refused to accept the mutilating radical mastectomy. Vera Peters tells us about this problem (2):

> ''Patients who refused mastectomy were the true pioneers of conservative treatment of early breast cancer. Our apprehension about their outlook soon changed to interest, and later to conviction on observing that the majority were free from disease 10 to 20 years later. Conservative treatment for early breast cancer was overwhelmingly opposed until the recent change in concept of the mode of spread of the disease.''

Harris and Hellman (8) have summarized the Halsted, Fisher and Intermediate Doctrines in the following table.

Halsted	*Fisher*	*Intermediate*
Tumor spreads in an orderly manner based on mechanical considerations.	There is no orderly pattern of tumor cell dissemination.	In most patients, axillary nodal involvement precedes distant metastases.
The positive lymph node is an indicator of tumor spread and is the instigator of distant metastases.	The positive lymph node is an indicator of a host–tumor relationship that permits development of metastases, rather than the instigator of distant metastases.	The positive lymph node is an indicator of a host–tumor relationship that is correlated with the subsequent appearance of distant disease.
Regional lymph nodes (RLN) are barriers to passage of tumor cells.	RLN are ineffective as barriers to tumor cell spread	RLN are ineffective as barriers to tumor spread, but involvement of RLN is not always associated with distant metastases.

Halsted	*Fisher*	*Intermediate*
The bloodstream is of little significance as a route of tumor dissemination.	The bloodstream is of considerable importance in tumor dissemination.	The bloodstream is of considerable importance in tumor dissemination.
Operable breast cancer is a local–regional disease.	Operable breast cancer is a systemic disease.	Operable breast cancer is a systemic disease in many, but not all, cases.
The extent and nuances of the operation are the dominant factors influencing a patient's outcome.	Variations in local–regional therapy are unlikely to affect survival.	Variations in local–regional therapy are unlikely to have a major influence on survival, but are of significance in some patients.

Reprinted courtesy of Harris JR and Hellman S. Biology-Natural History of Breast Cancer. Chapter 9, pages 165-214, *Breast Diseases*. Harris, Hellman, Henderson, and Kinne, eds, JB Lippincott, 1991, page 177.

§7.03 THE FISHER DOCTRINE

[a] The Pieces of the Puzzle Begin to Fall in Place

The few brave heretics who dared question the Halsted doctrine as early as the 1920's-1930's were finally joined by other dissenters throughout Europe and the United States in the 1960's. Examination of surgical specimens failed to reveal the consistent involvement of the lymphatic channels with cancer that one would expect of a tumor that spread in continuity through the lymphatics (3). It became evident that 20 to 30% of women with no involvement of the axillary lymph nodes develop distant metastases (3). Certainly, in these women, the spread of the cancer to distant sites did not occur via the lymphatics.

And finally, clinical observations demonstrated that less aggressive procedures such as a simple local excision of the tumor with postoperative radiation to the breast with or without axillary sampling gave results equal to those of the mutilating radical mastectomy (2,3,4,5,6,).

The Halsted doctrine was so entrenched in the minds of surgeons that it was difficult for them to accept that Halsted was wrong and that during the past 75 years thousands of women with early breast cancer had been unnecessarily mutilated by the radical mastectomy. Gradually, however, it became apparent that breast cancer frequently spread via the blood stream. Bernard Fisher (3,5) best articulated this new hypothesis and it has been called the Fisher Doctrine. It states that there are two types of breast cancer:

1. Cancers that tend to remain local and rarely establish viable metastases at regional or distant sites. For these cancers only minimal surgery is required. Local recurrence can be effectively treated by further excision or mastectomy.
2. Cancers that spread systemically before a clinical diagnosis can be established. Although the primary tumors are operable, distant metastases are present. No matter how radical the surgery, these patients will not be cured. For these cancers, minimal surgery is also sufficient. Hopefully, improvements in postoperative adjuvant chemotherapy will "cure" some of these women.

[b] The Puzzle is Solved

The spread of cancer of the breast to the regional nodes occurs by a process of embolization of individual cells and clumps of cells through the lymphatic channels rather than by direct extension through the lymphatics. Distant spread also occurs through the bloodstream but does not occur in a two-step process, first to the lymph node and then to distant sites (3,4,5,6,7,8).

The presence of cancer in the regional lymph nodes is not an instigator of distant disease, but rather it is an indication that the cancer has the lethal potential to metastasize via the lymphatic capillaries and via the blood. It also indicates that the immune system has failed to control the growth of metastases in the lymph nodes and perhaps distant sites as well (6).

[c] Factors Supporting the Fisher Doctrine

[1] Tumors That Have the Ability to Metastasize Do So at the First Opportunity The first opportunity occurs during the period of vascularization when the tumor is less than the diameter of the head of a common household pin (6). Thus many women with breast cancers measuring 1 cm already have systemic breast cancer (6).

[2] An NSABP Study Confirmed That Many Breast Cancers Metastasize Quite Early The National Surgical Adjuvant Breast Protocol (NSABP-1977) has refuted the significance of delays in diagnosis and treatment of symptomatic breast cancers (6). This was thought to be because of the early metatasis of breast cancer.

[3] Host Immunity They remind us of the important role host immunity plays in breast cancer. Prospective randomized trials of women with clinically negative axillae were conducted by the NSABP (National Surgical Adjuvant Breast Protocol). In the radical mastectomy arm, 40% of the women with clinically negative axillae were found to have axillary metastases. Interestingly, only 16% of the women who had total mastectomy with only observation of the axilla developed clinical evidence of axillary metastases within 10 years (9). The survival of these two groups was identical. This suggests that host immunity controlled the axillary metastases in 60% of these women treated with total mastectomy only. It also has been demonstrated that patients with axillary micrometastases less than 1.3 mm in diameter do as well as those women with negative lymph nodes (10).

§7.04 THE INTERMEDIATE DOCTRINE (7)

[a] Introduction

Others still cling to the notion that nodal metastasis precedes distant metastasis and state that in addtion to Fisher's two groups of cancers there is a third group that may metastasize after the tumors become large enough to produce symptoms. This concept has been called the Intermediate Doctrine (7). It states that there are three types of cancers (7):

1. *Non-metastasizing cancers* (as in the Fisher Doctrine). These tumors have relatively stable DNA and seldom undergo neoplastic progression (acquire the ability to metastasize).
2. *Early metastasizing cancers* that spread to distant sites before it is possible to detect them by currently available diagnostic modalities (as in the Fisher Doctrine). These tumors have great genetic instability and undergo neoplastic progression soon after vascularization of the tumor. Most metastasize before the tumors can be detected by mammography.
3. *An intermediate group of late metastasizing cancers.* These cancers have less genetic instability than the early metastasizing cancers and proponents state that some will undergo

neoplastic progression and metastasize even after they become symptomatic.

[b] Factors Supporting the Intermediate Doctrine

The most powerful evidence supporting the intermediate thesis is the 30% reduction in mortality for asymptomatic postmenopausal women whose breast cancers were discovered by mass screening programs with mammography (3,11). This is good news but it does not necessarily prove the Fisher Doctrine to be incorrect. When interpreting this data we must consider the following biases:

[1] Lead Time Bias (See Chapter 22).

[2] Overdiagnosis Bias

Some of the extra cancers diagnosed since 1930 may have less lethal potential than those detected in the 1930's and 1950's (see Chapter 6).

[3] Host Immunity Must Be Considered

a) NSABP studies (9) have demonstrated that following the removal of the primary tumor almost two thirds of the expected axillary metastases (in the women with observation only of the axilla) did not become clinically evident within 10 years.

b) Additionally, following removal of the primary tumor women with axillary metastases less than 1.3 mm in diameter do as well as those with negative axillary nodes (10). Thus it is possible that following removal of a small breast cancer detected by screening asymptomatic women, the immune system either destroys or controls the distant micrometastases in some cases. All too often we ignore the role of host immunity in those with favorable outcomes.

[c] Conclusion

It would appear that some of the increased survival may be real and that the periodic screening of asymptomatic women may eventually lower the age- adjusted mortality rate of breast cancer. However, we have found no convincing evidence that reducing the durations of symptoms of symptomatic breast cancers will alter survival.

§7.05 CONCLUSION—FISHER AND INTERMEDIATE DOCTRINES ARE PARTIALLY CORRECT

A ten year study of the Halsted doctrine, Fisher doctrine, the Intermediate doctrine and the phenomena of the stable age-adjusted mortality rates and rising incidence rates (presented in Chapter 6) has led us to conclude the following: Both the Fisher and Intermediate doctrines have merit. We agree that many breast cancers metastasize before they can be detected by mammography and that some cancers never acquire the ability to metastasize or at least are unable to establish a viable metastasis because of an effective immune system. We also agree that some tumors may undergo neoplastic progression (metastasis) after they become detectable by mammography. Certainly the detection of small cancers by the periodic screening of postmenopausal asymptomatic women with mammograms appears to have improved survival of this small subset of patients. However, we will not know how much of this increase in survival is secondary to lead time and overdiagnosis bias for at least 10 to 20 years. Unfortunately, most cancers remain clinically undetectable (subthreshold in size) during the first 75% of their life cycle. Many breast cancers remain undetectable until 80% to 95% of their life cycle has elapsed. Sadly, by the time these tumors become symptomatic, the tumors with genetic instability will have undergone neoplastic progression and metastasis. Reducing the duration of symptoms (delay in diagnosis) of these biologically old symptomatic tumors will not alter the survival rate. As Spratt (12) has so aptly stated ". . . The biologic lethality of a breast cancer is determined before the cancer is large enough to produce symptoms". Thus Spratt is saying that by the time a breast cancer is large enough to produce symptoms ". . . The prognosis may be good or bad but it is determined". Furthermore, our failure to lower the age-adjusted mortality rate of breast cancer since 1930 is because of this same group of biologically old symptomatic tumors. Additional evidence to support our conclusions will be presented in Chapters 8, 9 and 10.

References

1. Halsted, William. Original Memoirs: The Results of Radical Operations for the Cure of Carcinoma of the Breast. Ann Surg XLVI (1);1-20, July 1907.

2. Peters MV. ''Local'' Treatment of Early Breast Cancer. Surg Clin N Am 60(6),1151-1154, December 1984.
3. Harris, Jay R and Hellman, Samuel. Etiology: Natural History of Breast Cancer. *Breast Diseases,* 2nd ed, Harris, Hellman, Henderson, and Kinne, eds. JB Lippincott, 1991, pp 165-181.
4. Crile, George Jr. Breast Cancer: a Personal Perspective. Surg Clin N Am 64(6):1145-1149,1984.
5. Fisher, Bernard. A Commentary on the Role of the Surgeon in Primary Breast Cancer. Breast Cancer Research and Treatment. 1:17-26, 1981.
6. Fisher E. The Impact of Pathology on the Biologic, Diagnostic, Prognostic, and Therapeutic Considerations in Breast Cancer. Surg Clin N Am. 64(6):1073-1093, 1984.
7. Hellman, Samuel. Concluding Remarks, Primary Treatment Breast Cancer. *Breast Diseases,* 2nd ed, Harris, Hellman, Henderson, and Kinne, eds. JB Lippincott, 1991, pp 420-425.
8. Harris JR and Hellman S. Biology-Natural History of Breast Cancer. Chapter 9, pages 165-214, Breast Diseases Harris, Hellman, Henderson, and Kinne, eds. JB Lippincott, 1991 (figure page 177).
9. Fisher ER, Gregorio R and Fisher B. The Pathology of Invasive Breast Cancer. A syllabus derived from the findings of the National Surgical Adjuvant Breast Project (Protocol 4) Cancer 36:1-86, 1975.
10. Fisher ER, Palekar AS, Rockette H, et al. Pathologic Findings from the National Surgical Adjuvant Breast Project (Protocol 4), Significance of Axillary Nodal Micro and Macrometastases. Cancer 42:2032-2038,1978.
11. Tabar L, Fagerberg G and Day NE, et al. Breast Cancer and Natural History: New Insights from Results of Screening. The Lancet vol 339:412-414, Feb 15, 1992.
12. Spratt, John S, Realities of Breast Cancer Control, Public Expectations, and the Law. Surgical Oncology Clinics of North America. 3(1):25-34, January 1994.

CHAPTER 8: NATURAL HISTORY OF BREAST CANCER

CHAPTER 8

NATURAL HISTORY OF BREAST CANCER

§8.01 CELL KINETICS OF BREAST CANCER

[a] Growth Fraction

Well developed breast cancers contain millions of cancer cells that are nourished by a delicate system of blood vessels. Approximately 5 % of the cancer cells are situated close to the blood vessels and are adequately supplied with nourishment and oxygen. These cells are very active and are constantly growing and dividing to form new cancer cells. They are collectively referred to as the *growth fraction* of the tumor. Approximately ninety-five percent of the cancer cells are located too far from the blood vessels to obtain adequate nutrition and as a result are inactive and do not replicate and produce new cancer cells. (Other complex factors may be involved.)

[b] Cell Cycle Time

The time required for a cancer cell to complete the process of cell division is about 36 to 48 hours. The cells in the growth fraction are dividing constantly, and millions of new cancer cells are created in just a few days. However, about 75% of these new cells perish (cell loss factor) secondary to necrosis of clusters of cells, single cells, and by shedding cancer cells into the blood and lymph. When the total number of cells in the cancer has doubled *one net cell generation (one net cell doubling)* is said to have occurred.

[c] Net Cell Generation or Net Cell Doubling Time

When the total number of cancer cells within the tumor has doubled, one net cell generation has occurred. We use the prefix net to remind us that we are talking about the *total new cell production minus the cell loss factor.* For example:

Net Cell Generation

# Net Cell Generations	Total Number of Cells in the Tumor
0	1
1	2
2	4
3	8
4	16
5	32
10	1,000 (numbers rounded)
20	1,000,000 " "
30	1 billion " "
40	one trillion. The human body contains about 11 trillion cells. Death usually results when 10% of the body is replaced by cancer cells.

[1] Clinical Doubling Time (Diameter)

When the diameter of a tumor has doubled, its mass will have increased eightfold. An eightfold increase in mass requires three net cell generations or doublings. For example: If we start with a tumor containing 1,000 cells, then:

NET CELL GENERATIONS

One net cell doubling------2,000 cancer cells
Two net cell doublings-----4,000 cancer cells
Three net cell doublings----8,000 cancer cells or an 8× increase in the mass of the tumor. The diameter of the tumor will have doubled.

[2] Net Cell Doubling Time of Breast Cancer Varies

The time required for the number of cells in a breast cancer to double varies from 9 to over 900 days (average between 100 to 185 days). Spratt and Spratt report doubling times of 32 breast cancers calculated from serial mammograms vary from 109 days to 944 days. The median doubling time was 324 days (1). Some have even reported doubling times as long as five years.

RELATIONSHIP BETWEEN THE NET CELL DOUBLING, NUMBER OF CANCER CELLS, AND THE DIAMETER OF THE TUMOR

# NET CELL DOUBLINGS	CELLS IN TUMOR	APPROXIMATE DIAMETER mm	EVENTS IN LIFE CYCLE OF TUMOR*
0	1		
9.97	1,000	0.12mm	
13.3	10,000	0.3 mm -------	Vascularization tumor
19.9	1,000,000	1.2 mm	
23.3	10,000,000	2.7 mm -------	Occasionally seen in the mammogram
25	100,000,000	5.8 mm -------	difficulty detecting lesions smaller than 5 mm
29.9	1 billion	12.4 mm -------	Often palpable but not always
33.2	10 billion	26.7 mm -------	Common size at time of clinical diagnosis
36	100 billion	56.6 mm	
39.9	1 trillion	124 mm -------	Death of host

* As interpreted by the author.

Notes:

diameter of the head of a common household pin = 1.2 mm
diameter of the eraser on a lead pencil = 6 mm
cm − centimeter (one centimeter = 10 millimeters)
mm = millimeter (10 millimeters = one centimeter)
1 inch = 2.5 cm or 25 mm
1 billion = 1,000 million
1 trillion = 1,000 billion
Number of cells in the human body—about 11 trillion. When the number of cancer cells within the body approaches 10% of the total number of cells in the body death usually results.

Source: Modified from Spratt JS, et al Geometry, growth rates, and duration of cancer and carcinoma in situ of the breast before detection by screening.
Cancer Research 46:970,1986 (2). Also page 278 of Donegan and Spratt's Cancer of the Breast, 3rd ed., WB Saunders, 1988 (3)

[d] Growth Rates

Spratt and Spratt have written an excellent chapter on the growth rate of breast cancer which appears in *Cancer of the Breast,* 3rd ed by Donegan and Spratt (1). Readers interested in this subject should consult this chapter. The following are the different types of growth patterns seen in breast cancers:

[1] Linear (1)

At first the small cluster of cancer cells is thought to increase its mass by a specific amount each day regardless of the size of the tumor. This type of growth is thought to occur when cell division is largely limited to the periphery of the tumor. (See §10.02 [b]).

[2] Exponential (1)

When the tumor develops a blood supply most cells become well nourished and oxygenated. More cells now participate in cell division and there is a sudden and temporary spurt in the growth of the tumor which is geometric in nature. For example, when the number of cells in a tumor increases from 10,000 to 20,000, to 40,000, to 80,000 etc. growth is said to be geometric or exponential. (See §10.3 [a]).

[3] Deceleratory (Gompertzian) (1)

Few cells can maintain geometric growth for long. As the tumor increases in size the growth rate gradually slows (constantly decelerates). The reason for this is not clear but such factors as growth inhibitory feedback may be one of the factors.

[4] Growth Spurts (1,4)

Temporary growth spurts may be secondary to loss of inhibitory feedback or other poorly understood factors.

[5] Irregular Growth (Plateaus of Slow or No Growth) (1,4)

Plateaus of no growth or slow growth interspersed with periods of Gompertzian growth are not uncommon and may persist for months. The cause is uncertain but may be secondary to episodes of necrosis, spontaneous regression, errors of measurement of the tumor or other unknown factors.

[6] The Preclinical Growth Phase

The average tumor requires 8 to 10 years to grow from one

cell (inception) to a diameter of one centimeter (clinical detection). However, this will vary according to the doubling time of the tumor and the pattern of growth as described above.

References—Cell Kinetics

1. Spratt JS and Spratt JA. Growth Rates in *Cancer of the Breast*, 3rd ed, Donegan and Spratt. WB Saunders, 1988, pp 270-302.
2. Spratt JS, et al. Geometry, Growth Rates, and Duration of Cancer and Carcinoma in Situ of the Breast Before Detection by Screening. Cancer Research 46:970-974,1986.
3. Spratt JS and Spratt JA. Growth Rates in *Cancer of the Breast,* 3rd ed, Donegan and Spratt, WB Saunders. 1988, figure 10-2, page 278.
4. Retsky, Michael, et al. Is Gompertzian or Exponential Kinetics a Valid Description of Individual Human Cancer Growth? Medical Hypothesis 33(2):95-106, 1990.

§8.02 THE NATURAL HISTORY OF UNTREATED BREAST CANCER

The clinical behavior of breast cancer is so unpredictable that an examination of the history of untreated breast cancer is helpful. Bloom et al (1) reported on the records of 250 untreated breast cancer patients that were admitted to the Middlesex Hospital in England between 1850 and 1933. The majority of these patients had far advanced disease (74% were Stage IV and 23% were Stage III). Although 25% of these patients died annually it is interesting that 18% survived for five years and 4% survived for 10 years. This suggests that the natural history of breast cancer covers a span of 20 to 30 years and that the survival can be lengthy even without treatment. This is convincing evidence that there was a group of indolent slow growing cancers in this group of aggressive cancers that were dying at the rate of 25% each year.

Fox (2) examined the records of a large group of treated breast cancer patients for the Biometry Branch of the National Cancer Institute.

Analysis of the survival data suggested that these patients could be divided into two large subsets.

- In 60% of the patients the cancer had an indolent course, and only 2.5% died each year for a period of 20 years.
- In 40% of the patients the cancers were aggressive and the patients died at the rate of 25% annually with or without treatment. Most were dead within five years.

Fox's study provides additional support for the accuracy of our clinical observation that some cancers are indolent and slow growing while others are aggressive and highly lethal.

§8.03 BREAST CANCERS ARE NOT ALL ALIKE (1-6)

The public generally accepts the "conventional wisdom" that holds that all breast cancers are alike and that the only factor of importance in deciding outcome is the time of diagnosis. They are unaware that some breast cancers grow for years and never establish a viable metastasis while others metastasize before they can be detected by the most astute mammographer. Experienced observers of breast cancer are well aware that there are extreme variations in the clinical behavior of breast cancer. These differences in the biologic behavior of breast cancer have been described as (3):

1. Non-metastasizing breast cancers
2. Late metastasizing breast cancers
3. Early metastasizing breast cancers. (Other examples of early metastasizing cancers would include small cell cancer of the lung, and nodular melanoma.)

Now the molecular biologists are beginning to explain why this tremendous variation in the lethal potential of breast cancer occurs. It is generally agreed that a breast cancer arises when the genes of a normal duct cell sustain a series of alterations. Neoplastic progression (acquiring the ability to metastasize) is thought to occur when the genes of the cancer cell suffer a number of additional and sequential alterations. These sequential alterations may occur very early in the life of the cancer

(Fisher Doctrine) or at any time throughout the life cycle of the tumor (Intermediate Doctrine). (See Chapter 7).

[a] Non-Metastasizing Breast Cancers (1,3,4)

In some cancers the alteration of genes may be largely limited to the genes coding for the proteins that modulate and control the rate of cell division (3). These cancers will grow and invade the local tissues but possess no or limited capacity to metastasize even though the primary tumor may become quite huge.

[b] Late Metastasizing Breast Cancers (1,4,5)

When, in addition to genes involving the control of cell growth, another set of genes is damaged there may be a problem of mutations. If the DNA of genes which are involved in DNA repair, DNA synthesis, integrity of the mitotic spindle, and other DNA related functions are altered, genetic instability may result. That is, alteration of this set of genes increases the frequency of errors of cell division (mutation), which often result in the creation of highly lethal and/or drug resistant clones of tumor cells (4). Thus genetic instability frequently contributes to the neoplastic progression by creating mutant lethal clones of tumor cells (3).

The longer the period of time between inception of the tumor and surgical removal (sojourn time) the greater the number of cell divisions the tumor will undergo. The greater the number of cell divisions, the greater the likelihood that the genetically unstable tumor cell will suffer an error of cell division that will produce a highly lethal drug-resistant clone of tumor cells that can easily metastasize. These highly lethal clones of tumor cells are responsible for the progression of the tumor from an indolent breast tumor to an aggressive lethal cancer. These tumors tend to metastasize as the tumors increase in size. A few *might* have a phase beyond threshold size that could be called early (3). There is controversy regarding the size of this group, and in fact, a number of investigators (7,8) are of the opinion that cancers with significant genetic instability will undergo neoplastic progression and metastases prior to the time these lesions become large enough to produce symptoms. Those that do not metastasize prior to this time have relatively stable DNA and will not undergo neoplastic progression during the life of the tumor.

[c] Early Metastasizing Breast Cancers (4,6,9)

Other cancers become fully malignant when, in addition to the alteration of the genes controlling cell division and cell stability, an entirely different set of genes is altered. This third set of genes is involved with the production of angiogenic factors, proteases, and adhesion molecules discussed below (4). Some breast cancers become fully malignant at the time of inception or very early in the life cycle of the tumor. That is, before they reach the size that they can be detected by mammography. These fully malignant tumors have the ability to aggressively invade and to successfully metastasize to distant sites because they are able to produce:

[1] Angiogenic Factors

As we have seen angiogenic factors produced by tumor cells stimulate blood vessels to grow toward and aggressively invade the tumor and establish a functional set of blood vessels. Some have observed that tumors that have the greatest number of capillaries and microcapillaries have the highest metastatic potential (10).

[2] Proteases

Powerful proteolytic enzymes are secreted into the tissues surrounding the cancer cell which enables it to gain entrance into the capillary lumen by degrading the protein wall (basement membrane) which surrounds the endothelial cells of the capillary (9).

[3] Adhesion Molecules (11)

Only a rare cancer cell (1/100,000 to 1/1,000,000) that gains entry into the blood stream will survive. The vast majority will be destroyed by the immune system. Only that exceptional cancer cell that possesses an adhesion molecule receptor on its surface will be able to adhere to the adhesion molecule on the surface of an endothelial cell in the capillary wall at a distant site. However, once fixed to the endothelial cell the enzymes from the cancer cell destroy the basement membrane of the capillary wall and the cancer gains entrance into the interior of the distant organ where it will grow and form a metastasis if appropriate growth factors are present in the parenchyma of the distant organ.

Small clusters of cells (emboli) passively trapped at a distant site rarely form metastases (11). The cells usually break up and pass into the venous system where they are eventually destroyed by the immune system. Only the rare cell that displays an adhesion molecule receptor will be able to adhere to an endothelial cell and be able to escape from the blood stream into the surrounding tissues.

§8.04 BIOLOGIC PREDETERMINATION

Originally the term biologic predetermination referred to the concept that breast cancers acquire or do not acquire full malignant potential at the very moment the cancer arises. Thus, the outcome was thought to be predetermined at the very outset. Today most agree that that full malignant potential is acquired when the DNA of the tumor cell sustains an additional and sequential series of alterations. This can occur at any time during the life of the breast cancer. Nevertheless, some breast cancers undergo neoplastic progression (acquire the ability to metastasize) as the result of a series of sequential alterations of its DNA prior to the time it is possible to detect the tumor by mammography. These cancers are called the early metastasizing tumors, and of course, will have an unfavorable outcome. In a sense, the outcome of this subset of tumors is predestined by the fact that the tumor cells have great genetic instability and neoplastic progression occurs very early in the life cycle of the tumor.

§8.05 CONCLUSION

We must dispel the notion that all breast cancers are alike. The clinical behavior of breast cancer depends upon the nature and degree of the alteration of the DNA of the individual tumor cell. As a result, the doubling time, pattern of tumor growth, and lethal potential will vary from tumor to tumor. Some breast cancers will grow extremely slowly (a few may require several years or more to double in diameter). Some will never metastasize. For some cancers no matter how early the diagnosis cure is not possible. Others will acquire the ability to metastasize later in their life cycle. During the past 63 years there have been dramatic improvements in patient education, physician skills, and the technique of mammography, yet the age-adjusted mortality rate has not improved because many breast cancers metastasize before detection is possible. (See Chapter 6).

References

1. Harris JR, and Henderson IC. Natural History and Staging of Breast Cancer. *Breast Diseases,* Harris, Hellman, Henderson, and Kinne, eds. JB Lippincott, 1987 pp 233-258.
2. Fox MS. On the Diagnosis and Treatment of Breast Cancer. JAMA 241:489-494, 1979.
3. Spratt JS, Donegan WL, and Greenberg R. Screening and Follow-Up. *Cancer of the Breast,* 3rd ed, Donegan and Spratt, WB Saunders, 1988, pp 558-590.
4. Nowell, Peter C. Commentary—How Many Human Cancer Genes? Journal National Cancer Institute. 83(15):1061-1064, 1991.
5. Fisher B and Fisher ER. Experimental Studies of Factors Influencing Hepatic Metastases. I: The Effect of Number of Tumor Cells Injected and Time of Growth. Cancer 12:926-941, 1959.
6. Brylawski, Robert. Study Links Microvessel Counts in Breast Tumors to Metastasis Risk. (An interview of Judah Folkman by Robert Brylawski) Oncology Times, May 1991, pp 50-53.
7. Fisher ER, et al. A Perspective Concerning the Relation of Durations of Symptoms to Treatment Failure in Patients with Breast Cancer. Cancer 40:3160-3167,1977.
8. Spratt, John S, Realities of Breast Cancer Control, Public Expectations, and the Law. Surgical Oncology Clinics of North America. 3(1):25-34, January 1994.
9. Marx, Jean L. How Cancer Cells Spread in the Body. Science News 244:147-148, April 1989.
10. Weidner N, Semple JP, Welch WR, and Folkman J. Tumor Angiogenesis and Metastasis—Correlation in Invasive Breast Carcinoma. N Engl J M 324-1-8, 1991.
11. Zetter, Bruce R. The Cellular Basis of Site-Specific Tumor Metastasis. New England Journal of Medicine 322(9):605-612,1990.

CHAPTER 9: CAN BREAST CANCER BE CURED?

CHAPTER 9

CAN BREAST CANCER BE CURED?

§9.01 WHAT DO STATISTICS TELL US ABOUT THE CURABILITY OF BREAST CANCER?

Before we discuss the curability of breast cancer we must define the word "cure". When the word cure is used most people are talking about survival for a 5 or 10 year period of time. When we speak of "cure" we are talking about:

[a] Personal Cure (1)

When a woman dies of an intervening illness or old age and the cancer has been in remission without evidence of recurrence of the breast cancer she is said to have had a personal cure.

[b] Clinical Cure (1)

Clinical cure refers to the complete eradication of the disease. If a long follow-up of the causes of deaths (from death certificates) reveals that the risk of dying of breast cancer is the same for the woman in the breast cancer group as the control population a clinical cure is said to have been attained. Unfortunately this technique is not reliable since the information from death certificates is often inaccurate.

[c] Statistical Cure (2)

Statistics provide the most convincing evidence that in a strict sense breast cancer is not curable.

[1] Calculation of the Relative Survival Rate (2)

The relative survival rate is an epidemiologic tool used to calculate the true survival rate of breast cancer. The relative survival rate tells us the percentage of women who have been cured of breast cancer. To determine the relative survival rate we must have the following information:

A. *The expected survival rate* of an unselected control population of women over a certain period of time. This information can be obtained from the United States Bureau of the Census and the National Center for Health Statistics.

B. *The observed survival rate* of a group of women who have been treated for operable breast cancer over the same period of time.

C. *Calculation of the relative survial rate*—we must divide the observed survival rate by the expected survival rate and multiply by 100 = the relative survival rate (%). (See Figure 9-1).

A relative survival rate of 100% indicates that the women in the breast cancer group have a hazard for death that is precisely the same as the women in the unselected control population and can be said to have been cured. If the relative survival curve has a downward slope (less than 100%) we know the women in the breast cancer group are dying of breast cancer at a rate greater than the women in the control population and that all of the breast cancers have not been cured (2).

§9.02 LONG–TERM SURVIVAL STUDIES FAIL TO PROVE THAT IN A STRICT SENSE BREAST CANCER IS CURABLE

The vast majority of long–term studies have revealed persistently negative relative survival curves indicating that not all of the women in the breast cancer group have been cured. Brinkley and Haybittle (3) followed 704 breast cancer patients for 31 years. (See Figure 9-2). The number of deaths from cancer of the breast after 25 years was still 15

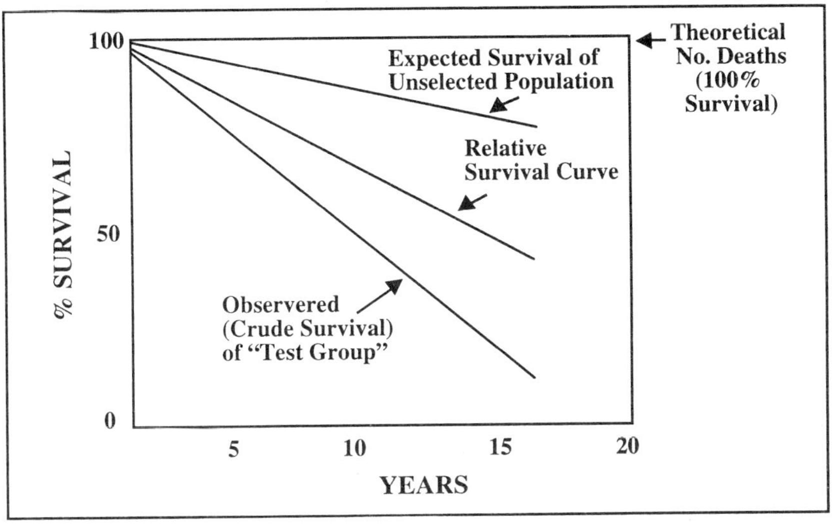

Figure 9-1. Idealized Relative Survival Graphic. Plotkin D and Blankenberg F. Cancer Management Controversy: Breast Cancer—Biology and Malpractice. Am. J. Clin. Oncol. 14(3):254-266, 1991. Figure 1, page 256. Reprinted courtesy of authors and publisher.

The relative survival curve is determined by dividing the observed survival rate of the study group by the expected survival of the control population and multiplying by 100. A relative survival curve with a persistently negative slope (less than 100%) indicates the study group cannot be said to have been cured.

---

times greater in the breast cancer group than in the unselected general population. Thus a long–term follow-up of 31 years reveals that a statistical cure for breast cancer cannot be demonstrated. Nevertheless, 26% of the women died of intervening illnesses without evidence of recurrent breast cancer and therefore obtained what is called a "personal cure". Hibberd et al. (4) followed a large group of women for 30 years and observed an excess of observed deaths over expected deaths between the 25th and 30th years of follow-up. Rutqvist and Wallgren (5) followed 458 patients aged 40 or less at diagnosis and noted an excess mortality from breast cancer to still persist at 40 years.

The relative survival method (2) remains the most accurate method for determining the curability of breast cancer. Long–term studies using this method tell us that women with breast cancer are dying 40 years later at rates in excess of that in a control population. As yet, breast cancer has not been proven to be curable. Thus, relative survival data provide

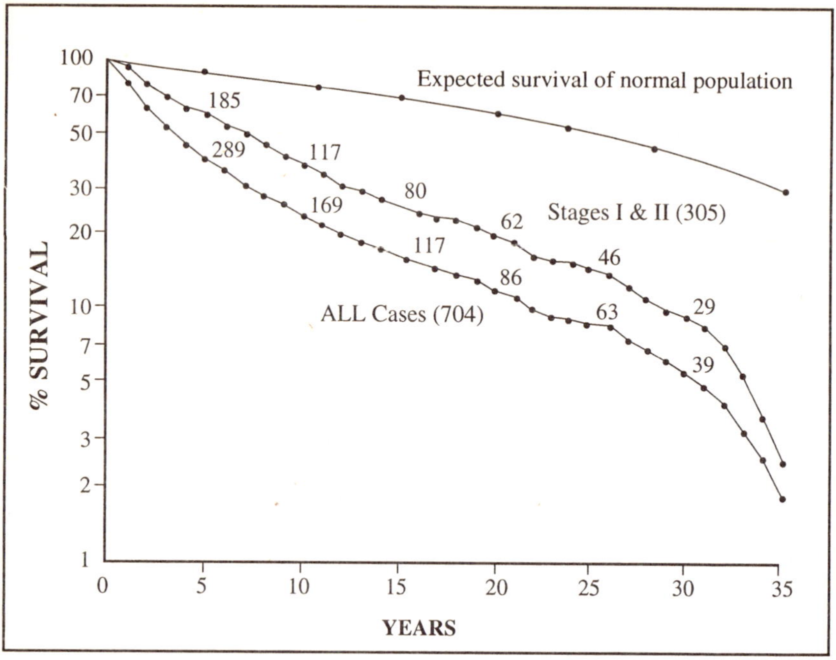

Figure 9-2. Observed Survival Curves of a Group of Stage I and II Breast Cancer Patients and the Expected Survival Curves from a Normal Population of the Same Age Distribution. Brinkley D and Haybittle JL. Long–term survival of women with breast cancer. The Lancet, May 19, 1984. Figure 1, page 1118. Reprinted courtesy of authors and publisher.

Note that the observed survival of the study group and the expected survival of the control population never become parallel. Thus, the breast cancers in the study group cannot be said to have been cured.

---

convincing evidence that breast cancer is a systemic disease at the time of diagnosis and treatment.

§9.03 THE AGE-ADJUSTED MORTALITY RATE OF BREAST CANCER

[a] Mortality Rate Stable Since 1930

In previous chapters we have discussed our failure to improve the age-adjusted survival rate of breast cancer during the past 63 years (See

Figure 9.3). This also is convincing evidence of the incurability of breast cancer in spite of:

- Improved public education
- Improved physician training
- Tremendous advances in molecular biology
- Widespread increase in the use of mammography

[b] Some Claim That the Mortality Rate of Breast Cancer Has Decreased From 50% to 25% Since 1930

This is not true. When we state that there has been no improvement in the age-adjusted mortality of breast cancer since 1930, doubters will quickly remind us of the dramatic increase in the incidence of breast

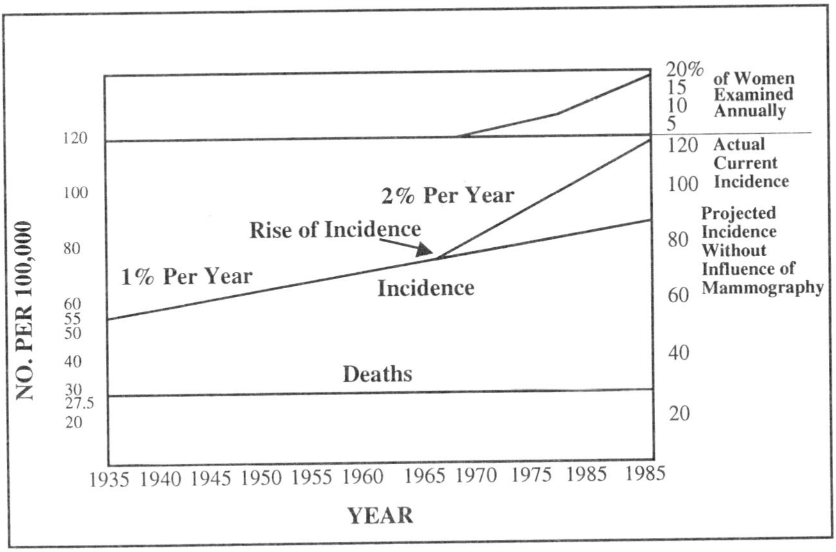

Figure 9-3. Annual Age-Adjusted Mortality, Incidence, and Percentage of Women Undergoing Mammography. Plotkin D and Blankenberg F. Cancer Management Controversy: Breast Cancer—Biology and Malpractice. Am. J. Clin. Oncol. 14(3):254-266, 1991. Figure 2, page 256. Reprinted courtesy of authors and publisher.

Note that the age-adjusted mortality of breast cancer has remained stable at 28-29 deaths per 100,000 female population since 1930. Also note the increasing incidence of breast cancer and the increasing use of mammography.

cancer during the past 30 years. Some will allege that the combination of a remarkable increase in incidence in the presence of a stable age-adjusted mortality rate indicates that the mortality rate of breast cancer has fallen from approximately 50% to 25% since 1930. Epidemiologists, however, report that the increase in the incidence of breast cancer is secondary to more complete reporting of breast cancer, an increase in a more benign form of breast cancer, earlier detection, and only modest improvements in survival secondary to treatment (see Chapter 6).

[c] Only Modest Improvements in Survival of Small Subsets of Patients Secondary to Improvements in Treatment Since 1975

The only significant increase in the survival of breast cancer has been secondary to the early detection of breast cancers by the periodic screening of self-selected asymptomatic women with mammography. Sadly, our improvements in the treatment of symptomatic breast cancer have been limited to the use of conservative breast surgery (lumpectomy) and the prolonged palliation of recurrent breast cancer. Recently some have reported modest improvements of survival in small subsets of patients treated with adjuvant therapy but these involve small numbers of patients.

[d] Considerations When Evaluating Claims of Increase in Survival of Asymptomatic Cancers Detected by Screening Mammography

[1] Overdiagnosis Bias

- Some of these breast cancers may have no lethal potential, they may only be "look like" cancers (6).
- Some may have low lethal potential.

[2] Lead Time Bias

(See Chapter 22).

[3] Prolonged Doubling Times (see Figure 9-4).

a. Fournier (7) has reported doubling times of 44 days to 5 years. In another series he reported doubling times of 0.2-11 years.

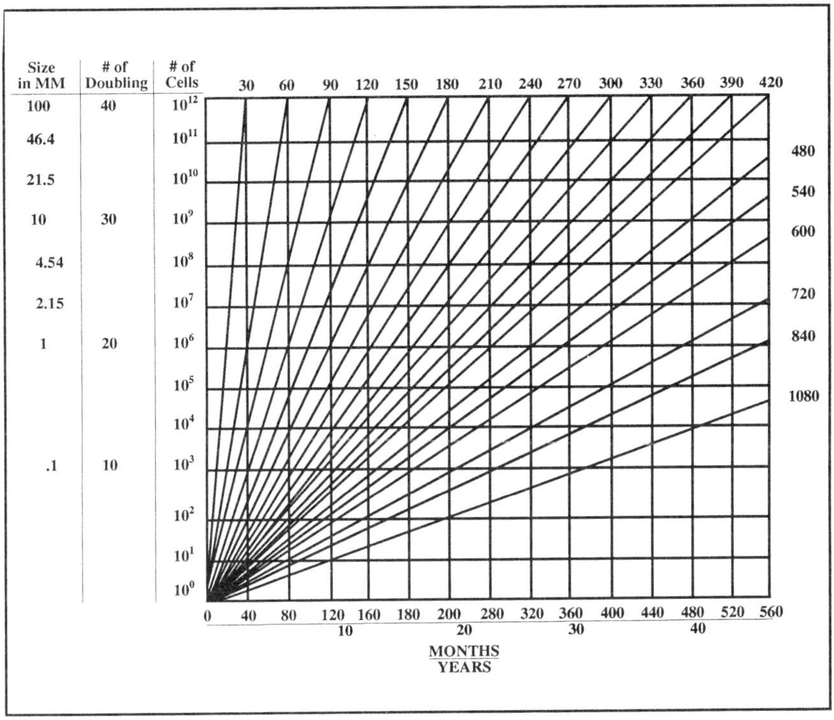

Figure 9-4. Range of Doubling Times and Corresponding Growth Slopes Seen in Breast Cancer. Plotkin D and Blankenberg F. Cancer Management Controversy: Breast Cancer—Biology and Malpractice. Am. J. Clin. Oncol. 14(3):254-266, 1991. Figure 4, page 260. Reprinted courtesy of authors and publisher.

The range of doubling times of breast cancer from 30 to 1080 days indicates that the life cycle of breast cancer will vary from several years to well over 40 years.

---

b. The slowest doubling time reported by Buchanan (8) was 944 days.

c. Arnerlov et al. (9) calculated the doubling times of 158 breast cancers from serial mammograms and also found a great variation of the doubling times.

Doubling Times of 158 Breast Cancers

(Calculated from measurements of serial mammograms)

Months	%
0-3	13.9
3-6	19.6

Months	%
6-9	16.5
9-12	10.8
12-18	15.8
18-24	10.8
24-48	4.4
48-72	1.3
72-96	0.0
too slow to measure	7.0

Reprinted courtesy of Arnerlov C, et al. Cancer 70:1829-1934, 1992, Figure 1, page 1930, reference (9).

It is interesting that 40% of these breast cancers had doubling times of 12 months or more while 33.5% had doubling times of 6 months or less.

d. Skrabanek (10) stated that an unrecognized microscopic metastases from a tumor below 1 cm in diameter will on average become detectable about 10 years later. Foci of micrometastases with extemely long doubling times might not become clinically detectable for many years, sometimes as long as 30 or 40 years.

§9.04 IS FISHER'S CONTENTION THAT OPERABLE BREAST CANCER IS A SYSTEMIC DISEASE COMPATIBLE WITH THE CLINICAL BEHAVIOR OF BREAST CANCER? (11,12)

Statisticians tell us that long–term relative survival data (30-40 years) reveal that, in a strict sense, breast cancer cannot be proven to be curable (2,3,4,5). Thus relative survival studies support Fisher's (11) contention that all operable breast cancers have systemic disease. But doesn't this conflict with the classification of breast cancers into non-metastasizing, late metastasizing and early metastasizing cancers? Not really, since Fisher does not imply that all women harboring systemic breast cancer will die of their disease. In fact, he provides convincing evidence that many survive for years because of a favorable host–tumor relationship. Fisher's data (11,12) suggest that:

[a] Regional Lymph Nodes Can Destroy Cancer Cells

Regional lymph nodes possess the power to destroy small clusters of metastatic breast cancer. For example, women whose regional lymph nodes contain metastatic foci of cancer smaller than 1.3 mm. have the same survival rate as women whose lymph nodes are negative (12).

[b] NSABP Studies Confirm That Lymph Nodes Can Destroy or Control Foci of Breast Cancer

A prospective randomized study (NSABP) of a large group of women with operable breast cancer and no clinical evidence of axillary metastases compared the effectiveness of axillary node dissection, radiation to the axilla, and simple observation of the axilla with excision of axillary disease when it became apparent. Two important observations were made (11):

- The survival rates of the three groups were nearly identical.
- Axillary node dissection identified cancer in the lymph nodes in about 40% of the women, yet in the observation group only 16% developed clinical evidence of axillary metastasis within 10 years. This suggests that the immune system destroyed or contained the growth of the axillary metastases in 60% of these women in the observation group.

[c] Some Tumor Cells Remain Dormant for Long Periods of Time

Some cancer cells remain dormant until there is an impairment of the host immunity (11) or there is an oncogene activation secondary to such things as medications, infections, diet, or unknown factors.

[d] Some Tumors Have Prolonged Doubling Times (See Figure 9-4).

The vast differences in the clinical behavior of these three groups of breast cancers can be easily explained by the extreme variations in the doubling time of breast cancer (from a few days to several years) and/or the complex relationship of the lethal potential of the tumor and host immunity. Metastases with prolonged doubling times may not surface for 15, 20, 30 or 40 years.

§9.05 CONCLUSION–NO CONVINCING EVIDENCE IN THE STRICT SENSE THAT CANCER IS CURABLE

Plotkin and Blankenberg studied this problem of the curability of breast cancer and concluded that "The preponderance of the available evidence leads us to conclude that cure of invasive breast cancer (literally defined) using current methods of treatment is not possible" (2). There is hope, however, that mammographic detection of breast cancers in asymptomatic women will lower the age-adjusted mortality rate of breast cancer. Unfortunately, we will not have the final answer for 10-20 years.

Certainly Fisher's studies (11) and long–term relative survival data (2,3,4,5) for periods of 25 to 40 years support the concept that all breast cancers have systemic disease at the time of diagnosis and excision. All agree that current data fail to prove, that in a strict sense, breast cancer is curable. Plotkin and Blankenberg (2) have written an excellent article on this subject which should be read by those interested in this subject.

References

1. Harris JR and Hellman S. Biology: Natural History of Breast Cancer. *Breast Diseases,* 2nd edition Harris, Hellman, Henderson, and Kinne, eds. JB Lippincott, 1991, pages 165-181.
2. Plotkin D and Blankenberg F. Cancer Management Controversy. Breast Cancer—Biology and Malpractice. Am J Clin Oncol 14(3):254-266, 1991.
3. Brinkley, Diana and Haybittle JL. Long–Term Survival of Women With Breast Cancer. Letters to the editor. The Lancet, May 19, 1984, page 1118.
4. Hibberd AD, et al. Long–Term Prognosis of Women with Breast Cancer in New Zealand: a Study of Survival to 30 Years. Br Med J. 286:1777, 1983.

5. Rutqvist LE and Wallgren A. Long–Term Survival of 458 Young Breast Cancer Patients. Cancer 55:658-665, 1985.
6. Nielsen M, Jensen J, and Anderson J. Precancerous and Cancerous Lesions During Lifetime and at Autopsy. Cancer 54:612-615, 1984.
7. Fournier D vcn, et al. Growth Rate of 147 Primary Mammary Carcinomas. Cancer 45:2198-2207, 1980.
8. Buchanan JB, Spratt JS, and Heuser LS. Tumor Growth, Doubling Times, and the Inability of the Radiologist to Diagnose Certain Breast Cancers. Radiol Clin N Am 21:115-126, 1983.
9. Arnerlov C, Emdin SO, Lundgren B, et al. Breast Carcinoma Growth Rate Described by Mammographic Doubling Time and S-Phase Fraction. Cancer 70:1928-1934, 1992.
10. Skrabanek, Petr. False Premises and False Promises of Breast Cancer Screening. The Lancet, August 10, 1985 pages 316-319.
11. Fisher, Bernard. A Commentary on the Role of the Surgeon in Primary Breast Cancer. Breast Cancer Research and Treatment. 1:17-26, 1981.
12. Fisher E.R The Impact of Pathology on the Biologic, Diagnostic, Prognostic, and Therapeutic Considerations in Breast Cancer. Surg Clin N Am. 64(6):1073-1093, 1984.

APPENDIX 9-1— VISUAL AIDS

The defense can use the following tables and graphs in the courtroom to demonstrate to the jury the true facts concerning the death rate of breast cancer.

[a] Five and Ten Year Survival Data

In the courtroom in full view of the jury ask for a blackboard and do the following:

Sketch on a black board the five or ten year survival data presented by the plaintiff.

Narration

[1] Each year since 1930 there have been optimistic reports, such as the above, touting a decrease in the mortality rate of breast cancer. If these reports were true, there would be few deaths from breast cancer today. Unfortunately, the age-adjusted mortality rate of breast cancer has not changed since 1930. These fixed end-point survival studies as demonstrated by the plaintiff ignore several important truths:

A. The mortality rate of breast cancer does not stop at 5 or 10 years; it continues at a steady rate for 10, 15, 20, 25, 30, and even 35 years.

B. Since 1930 there have been no improvements in surgery or radiation that could possibly increase the survival rate of breast cancer. We have better cosmetic results, better control of regional disease, but no decrease in the mortality rate of breast cancer.

C. Adjuvant therapy (postoperative chemotherapy and hormonal therapy) have prolonged life for 1 to 2 years, but very few, if any, can be said to have been cured.

[2] These reports clearly illustrate that survival statistics of fixed end-point studies, such as the above, can be falsely improved in many ways:

A. By selecting more favorable groups of cancers.

B. By changing the starting time. Earlier diagnosis of women who have systemic disease will improve the five and ten year survival rate but will not alter the time of death of these women (lead time bias).

C. Over-diagnosis bias. Screening mammmography and improved biopsy techniques identify many small lesions that "look like" invasive breast cancers but have less or no lethal potential. Many would never have become clinically overt during the lifetime of the patient.This falsely improves the survival rate of breast cancer.

D. Adjuvant chemotherapy and hormonal therapy may postpone death for 1 to 2 years but thus far "cures", if any, have involved very few patients.

[3] C. Barber Mueller (1) labels these five year studies as "Inflationary Arithmetic" and to illustrate his point, made this statement. The following is paraphrased from Mueller's excellent article:

> The following statement (the numbers change each year) appears in almost every paper on breast cancer "120,000 women will be diagnosed with breast cancer this year and 40,000 will die of it", implying that 80,000 will not die of breast cancer. This incomplete statement carries a subtle message by omitting the fact that it uses 5-year survival data, not total death data. It should read: "120,000 women will be diagnosed with breast cancer and 40,000 will die from it within five years and breast cancer deaths will continue at a steady annual rate for at least 20 more years (actually, the force of mortality operates for at least 30 to 35 years).

[4] Survival statistics can be quite misleading, therefore, consider having a statistician examine the plaintiff's survival data. McGuire (1,2) commented on a NSABP B-14 trial that examined the benefits derived from treatment and reported a 6% difference in the absolute risk, a 26% reduction in treatment failure (relative risk), and a 75% greater chance of remaining disease free (relative odds ratio). He stated that all of these figures are correct and technically equivalent but are quite confusing to the casual reader. Also question whether logarithmic or arithmetic methods were used. Logarithmic ordinates create impressions of survivability. Arithmetic methods better express the true force of mortality (1).

References

1. C. Barber Mueller. Breast Cancer: Reporting with Inflationary Arithmetic. Cancer Management Controversy. Am J Clin Oncol (CCT) 17(1):86-92, 1994.
2. McGuire W. Adjuvant Therapy of Node-Negative Breast Cancer. N Engl J Med 320:525-527, 1989.

[b] Definition of a Cure (2), (See §9.01).

Definition of a Cure
When the hazard from death has been reduced to the same level as that in the general population.

Defense counsel can show the above to the jury in a table format to define the word "cure".

Narration

[1] A good example of a cure is pneumococcal pneumonia (1).

Death rates for a large group of pneuomonia patients successfully treated with antibiotics and the general population are the same at five and ten years. Therefore, pneumonia is a curable disease. The relative survival curves (§9.01[c]1) of both groups are the same. Therefore, pneumonia is a curable disease.

Reference

1. Plotkin D and Blankenberg F. Cancer Management Controversy. Breast Cancer—Biology and Malpractice. Am J Clin Oncol 14(3):254-266, 1991.

[c] Breast Cancer—Long-Term Survival Compared to the General Population (3)

Note that the observed survival curve of the study group and the expected survival curve of the control population never become parallel. Thus the breast cancers in the study group cannot be said to have been cured. (See Figure 9-5).

Narration

[1] Brinkley and Haybittle (1) followed 704 breast cancer patients for 31 years. The number of deaths in the breast cancer group at 25 years was still 15 times higher than in the general population. The

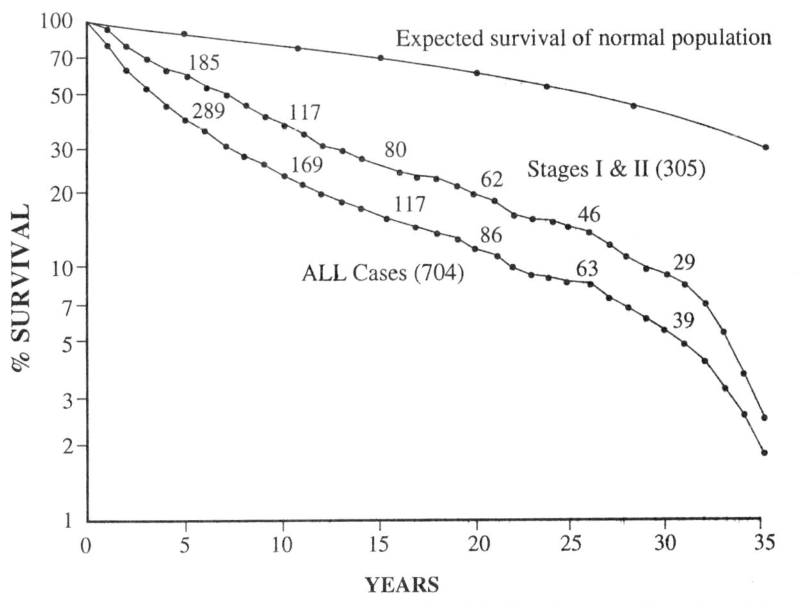

Figure 9-5. (Repeat of Figure 9-2). Observed Survival Curves of a Group of Stage I and II Breast Cancer Patients and the Expected Survival Curves from a Normal Population of the Same Age Distribution. Brinkley D and Haybittle JL. Long–term survival of women with breast cancer. The Lancet, May 19, 1984. Figure 1, page 1118. Reprinted courtesy of authors and publisher.

Defense counsel can use this graph to demonstrate to the jury that breast cancer is not a curable disease.

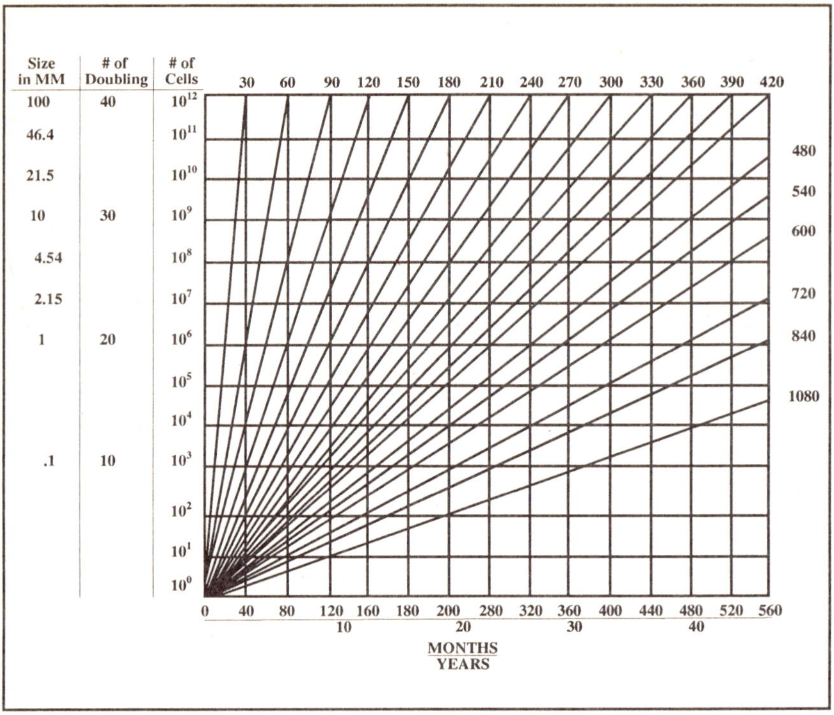

Figure 9-6. (Repeat of Figure 9-4). Range of Doubling Times and Corresponding Growth Slopes Seen in Breast Cancer. Plotkin D and Blankenberg F. Cancer Management Controversy: Breast Cancer - Biology and Malpractice. Am. J. Clin. Oncol. 14(3):254-266, 1991. Figure 4, page 260. Reprinted courtesy of authors and publisher.

The range of doubling times of breast cancer from 30 days to more than 1080 days indicates that the life cycle of breast cancer will vary from several years to well over 40 years.

---

survival curves (§9.01[c]1) are not the same. Therefore, at 25-30 years breast cancer cannot be said to be a curable disease.

[2] Hibbard et al. (2) reported an excess of observed deaths from breast cancer between the 25th and 30th year.

[3] Rutquist and Wallgren (3) followed 458 patients aged 40 years or less and found an excess mortality from breast cancer at 40 years.

[4] Thus long–term studies suggest that systemic disease at the time of diagnosis is far greater than many suspect, especially when

we consider that 26% of the women died of a competing illness before demonstrating gross evidence of recurrent breast cancer.

References

1. Brinkley, Diana and Haybittle JL. Long–Term Survival of Women with Breast Cancer. Letters to the editor. The Lancet, May 19, 1984, page 1118.
2. Hibberd AD, et al. Long–Term Prognosis of Women with Breast Cancer in New Zealand: A Study of Survival to 30 Years. Br Med J. 286:1777, 1983.
3. Rutqvist LE and Wallgren A. Long–Term Survival of 458 Young Breast Cancer Patients. Cancer 55:658-665, 1985.

[d] The Range of Doubling Times of Breast Cancer (2)

Narration

[1] Amerlov et al. (9) reported that about 40% of breast cancers have doubling times of one year or more. See §9.03 [d].

[2] Breast cancer metastases with doubling times of one year or more may not surface for 20, 30 or 40 years following surgery.

[3] Certainly metastases which surface within five years of surgery did not arise during the 12 month period prior to surgery (2). They arose during the first five years of the life of the breast cancer (2) well before the tumor became symptomatic.

CHAPTER 10: METASTASIS: WHEN DOES IT OCCUR?

CHAPTER 10

METASTASIS: WHEN DOES IT OCCUR?

§10.01 INTRODUCTION: SOME FACTS

When discussing the causes of treatment failure, we are primarily interested in how frequently breast cancer metastasizes before it can be detected by mammography or clinical examination. Many studies have reported that only about 10% of node-negative tumors less than 2.0 cm in diameter will recur within five years (1). Yet, when Rosen et al. (2) using the methods of Brinkley and Haybittle (3) to compare the observed survival with expected survival they found that 20% of node-negative patients with tumors 1 cm or smaller had tumor recurrence and died within 20 years after diagnosis and 30 % of patients with tumors in the 1-2 cm range had tumor recurrence and died within 20 years (1). This would indicate that at least 25% of all (node negative and positive) breast cancers have metastasized to distant sites prior to the time they attain a diameter of 1 cm.

Of course, the incidence of incurable disease is even greater in the node-positive breast cancers with diameters of one centimeter or less. Consider these facts:

> 16 to 22% of breast cancers with a diameter of only 1 mm have been found to have evidence of axillary lymph node metastasis (4,5).

When we consider *all* cases of breast cancer, both node negative and positive, we discover the incidence of incurable disease in breast cancers with diameters one centimeter or less to be at least 25%. All authorities will agree to this figure. We use the word incurable because we know that long-term studies have demonstrated that 25% of the women eventually died of breast cancer. It is entirely possible that many more women had systemic micrometastases at the time of surgery, but did well because the micrometastases were destroyed or controlled by an effective immune system or had tumors with prolonged doubling times. (See chapter 9).

§10.02 TERMINOLOGY

[a] Shedding

The term shedding refers to the continual escape of cancer cells into the venous blood draining from breast cancers. Many investigators have observed that millions of cancer cells are shed into the blood over a period of 24 hours from breast cancers with a diameter of only one centimeter. This sounds incredible, so let's examine how and why this happens.

[b] Prevascular Growth Phase

At the outset, the breast cancer exists as a tiny cluster of cells in the extravascular space. It grows slowly because it has no blood supply and must obtain its nourishment from the surrounding fluid by osmosis. Metastasis cannot occur because the tumor does not have a blood supply.

[c] How The Cancer Cell Spreads to Distant Sites

To metastasize, the cancer cell must gain access to the blood stream via a blood capillary or by entering the lymphatic capillary from where it is transported by the lymph to the blood stream via the thoracic duct. Additionally, cancer cells may gain access to the blood through numerous lympho-venous communications.

[d] The Normal Blood Capillary and Lymphatic Capillary

Since these structures play such a vital role in metastasis we will briefly consider their microscopic anatomy. (See Figure 10-1).

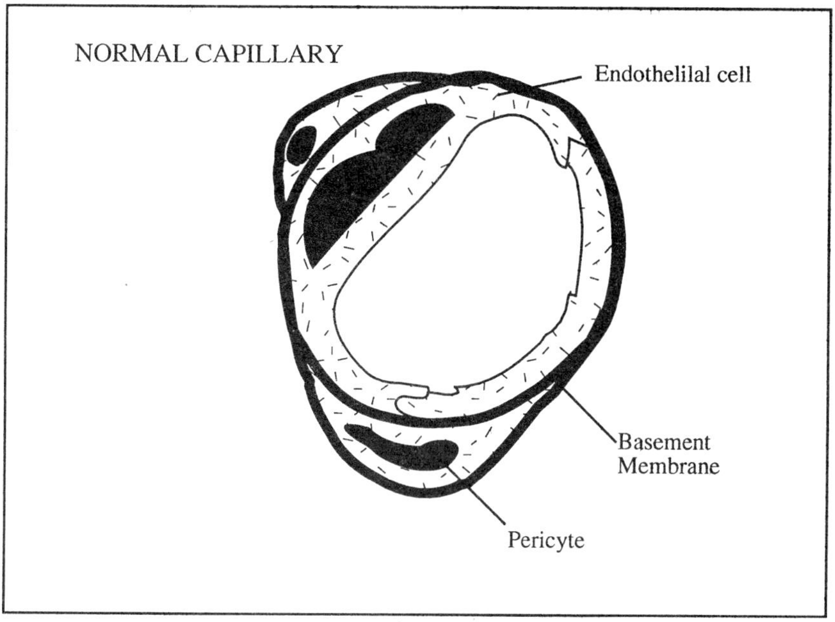

Figure 10-1. Normal Capillary. Modified from Ham, Arthur W. Histology, 7th edition, JB Lippincott Co, 1974, chapter 8 Connective Tissue, Figure 8-2, page 214. Reprinted courtesy of author and publisher.

---

1. *The blood capillary and postcapillary venule consist of (6):*

- An inner lining of a single layer of endothelial cells
- A sturdy basement membrane surrounds the tube of endothelial cells.
- A single layer of pericytes surrounding the basement membrane. The basement membrane splits to surround both the outer and inner surface of the pericytes.

2. *The lymphatic capillary has an entirely different structure (6):*

- A single layer of endothelial cells.
- A thin layer of connective tissue fibers.
- The lymphatic capillary has no basement membrane and no pericytes. It is designed to absorb excess fluid and large protein particles from the extracellular space and return them to the blood via the lymph stream.

Normal cells cannot gain entry or exit from the blood capillary except when the structures are altered by trauma or inflamation, or are attacked by "switched on" cells which we shall discuss below. Less is known regarding the precise process by which the cancer cell gains entry into the lymphatic capillary. We suspect, however, that "switched on" tumor cells need only to make contact with the wall of the lymphatic channel.

§10.03 VASCULARIZATION OF THE TUMOR

[a] Angiogenesis

The precise mechanism of tumor vascularization is poorly understood. However, it is thought that when the breast cancer reaches a diameter of **0.3 mm to 1.0 mm** the angiogenic genes of some of the cancer cells are genetically "switched on" to produce powerful proteins such as fibroblast growth factors, angiogenin, etc. (7,8,9). These powerful angiogenic factors stimulate the surrounding endothelial cells to behave not un-like cancer cells (9). The endothelial cells proliferate rapidly, and grow toward and aggressively invade the young breast cancer thus supplying it with a complete network of new blood vessels. Some have speculated that the "switch on" of the angiogenic genes of the cancer cells may have been triggered by the low oxygen tension of the prevascular tumor cells (9). Following vascularization the tumor, the cancer cells not only grow more rapidly (the cells are better oxygenated), but are said to grow exponentially or geometrically. That is, the tumor has a randomly steady increase in the number of cells. For example, an increase in the net number of cells from 1,000,000 to 2,000,000 to 4,000,000 to 8,000,000 would represent geometric or exponential growth (10). The tumor cells that have been genetically "switched on" to secrete these powerful angiogenic proteins can now invade the blood vessels and produce systemic disease (8). Some authors have stated that cancer cells that possess the metastatic phenotype metastasize at the first opportunity (7). The first opportunity is provided by the process of vascularization. Thus shortly before the tumor reaches the diameter of 0.5-1.0 mm it will be possible for the tumor cells to spread to distant sites via the blood and lymph vessels. Some researchers are of the opinion that those tumor cells that had a "switch on" of angiogenic genes are more capable of escaping into the blood stream than tumor cells that have not been "switched on" (8).

[b] How Many Cancer Cells are Shed into the Blood Stream Each 24 Hours?

Butler and Gullino (11) in 1975 transplanted mammary carcinomas to the rat ovary and analyzed the venous return from each tumor. Immunohistochemical studies with fluorescent dyes revealed that each gram of tumor shed three to four million cancer cells into the blood stream in a 24 hour period. The fact that three to four million cancer cells can escape (are shed) from one gram of breast cancer each day suggests that escape from the tumor must not be difficult for these cancer cells. **How can they escape into the blood stream so easily and in such great numbers?** There are a number of reasons. First, the hastily formed tumor capillaries are poorly constructed: (a) The outer layers of pericytes are absent, (b) The basement membranes are thin and fragmented, (c) There are fewer tight and gap junctions between the endothelial cells, (d) Substances secreted by tumor cells [Vascular Permeability Factor] also makes the tumor capillaries more leaky (12) (see tumor capillary Figure 10-2).

Second, 40 to 60% of the tumor cells genes are "switched on" to secrete angiogenic factors such as angiogenin which stimulates the growth of blood vessels into the tumor. These cancer cells with "switched on genes" are said to be more capable of penetrating the walls of tumor capillaries (8).

§10.04 THE LEUKOCYTE (6)—ANATOMY AND FUNCTION

The leukocyte is a cell that is normally not activated or "switched on". Non activated leukocytes cannot penetrate the wall of the post capillary venule and continue to circulate in the blood stream. However, when the leukocyte becomes activated its behavior closely resembles that of a cancer cell (13). Examination of the cancer-like behavior of the activated leukocyte will help us understand the behavior of the "switched on" cancer cells during and shortly after the vascularization the small breast cancer.

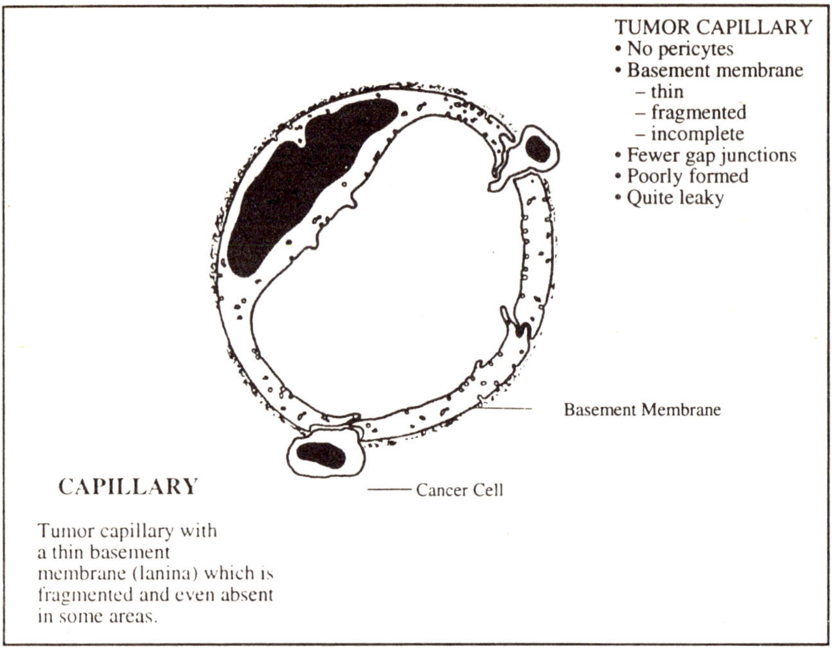

Figure 10-2. Tumor Capillary. Drawn from information obtained from: (a) Butler TP and Gullino P. Quantitation of cell shedding into efferent blood of mammary adenocarcinoma. Cancer Research 35:512-516, 1975 (b) Zetter, Bruce R. The cellular basis of site-specific tumor metastasis. N Eng J Med. 322(9):605-612, 1990: (c) Zetter, Bruce. Personal communication to the author (cfw) June 11, 1992.

---

[a] Characteristics

1. **Function**—to seek and destroy bacteria that threaten to infect the body.
2. **Motility**—have great ameboid activity, very motile.
3. **Cytoplasm**—contains 50-200 tiny granules which contain six or more powerful enzymes.

[b] Modus Operandi (6,13,14)

The modus operandi of the leukocyte has been used by the immune system for thousands of years. It is simple, yet sophisticated, and amazingly effective. When the alarm sounds warning of an invasion by bacteria, the following sequence of events occurs:

Leukocytes drifting along in venules near the site of infection respond to the alarm by becoming activated and inserting adhesion molecules into their outer cell membranes which adhere to endothelial cells of capillaries near the infection site. The endothelial cells retract (13) exposing the basement membrane. The exact mechanism by which the tumor cells gain access to the basement membrane is not known. One of the authors (CFW), however, has hypothesized that endothelial cells may contain allosteric proteins. Allosteric is a Greek word meaning *other shape* (15). It is possible that the attachment of the leukocyte to the endothelial cell triggers a transient chemical reaction within the cell which causes certain allosteric proteins to undergo a transitory conformational change. It is conceivable that the alteration of the shape of the allosteric proteins could produce a momentary retraction of the cell membrane, just long enough for the pseudopod of the leucocyte to attach to the exposed basement membrane (13,16).

The pseudopod of the leukocyte adheres to the basement membrane upon which the endothelial cells rest. The basement membrane is an efficient barrier against the passage of proteins and macromolecules but since it consists of proteins and carbohydrates it is no match for the proteolytic enzymes of the killer cell which easily destroys proteins (13). The leukocyte secretes its powerful enzymes which, like an acetylene torch, disintegrates the basement membrane creating a small defect in the membrane. The killer cell wriggles into the defect and pulls itself into the extracellular tissue. It then "cuts" its way through the connective tissue fibers of the extracellular space with its special enzymes until it locates the bacteria (13,14).

§10.05 THE BEHAVIOR OF THE ACTIVATED LEUKOCYTE AND THE CANCER CELL ARE QUITE SIMILAR

[a] In General

Our examination of the leukocyte's invasive and cancer-like behavior in the inflamatory response tells us that when a cell is activated (by bacteria in this situation) and has acquired the "tools of the trade" (adhesion molecules and powerful enzymes) it can easily and quickly penetrate the wall of the blood vessel. In fact, it can't help itself. When it is activated and has "the tools of the trade" the result is inevitable. It will rapidly penetrate the blood vessel wall (13). Cancer cells easily mimic the technique the leukocyte employs for escaping from the venule and skillfully reverse the technique to gain entry into the blood and lymph vessels (13). Cancers and leukocytes share these characteristics:

- The cancer cell is also motile and has pseudopods.
- The cancer cell can also "open the door" by adhering to the endothelial cell and causing it to retract.
- Cancer cells can also produce and secrete powerful enzymes capable of disintegrating the protein and carbohydrate molecules of the basement membrane.

[b] There is Nothing Novel About the Behavior of the Cancer Cell

Normal cells can do everything the cancer cell is able to do (13). The major difference is that the normal cell stops when its task is completed. The cancer cell does not stop until it has killed the host.To gain entrance into the venule, the cancer cell simply adheres to the basement membrane and destroys it from without—then adheres to the outer surface of the endothelial cell—the endothelial cell retracts and the cancer cell pulls itself between the endothelial cells and gains entrance into the blood stream.

When the cancer cells reach the capillary or venule at a distant site, those with adhesion molecules attach to the endothelial cells of the host's capillary and the cancer cell penetrates the capillary wall using the same technique used by the leukocyte when it responds to the threat of infection (13,16). It then enters the parenchyma and, if appropriate growth factors are available, the cancer cell will grow and establish a viable metastasis.

The lymphatic capillary is an "easy touch" for the cancer cell since it has no pericytes and no basement membrane. The precise method by which the tumor cell enters the lymphatic capillary is not known (12).

The cancer cells whose genes are "switched on" or activated to produce the powerful angiogenic factors that initiated the process of vascularization also produce adhesion molecules and powerful enzymes (8,16,17). We know this is true because these "tools" are needed to penetrate the venule wall and gain entrance into the blood. Indeed, the escape of three to four million cancer cells for each 24 hour period from a one gram tumor is proof enough. Like the leukocyte these activated cancer cells possess the "the tools of the trade" and need only to make physical contact with a venule to initiate the process of penetration of the vessel wall. Most of these shed cells are destroyed by the immune system but some survive. It has been estimated that less than .01% survive to produce a metastasis (18).

§10.06 FACTORS THAT FACILITATE METASTASIS DURING ANGIOGENESIS (VASCULARIZATION OF THE TUMOR)

[a] Tumor Blood Vessels are Abnormal (19,20) (See Figure 10-2).

The hastily constructed new tumor blood vessels are distinctly abnormal. The outer layer of pericytes is absent. The basement membrane is thin and fragmented. There is a reduced number of tight and gap junctions between the endothelial cells. Some vessels contain areas with no endothelial lining. The vascular architecture is poorly organized and chaotic. These new vessels are quite leaky and injected fluorescein dye rapidly escapes from these newly formed blood vessels. In many areas of the tumor, cancer cells can be seen within the lumen or traversing the walls of these vessels. In other areas, tumor cells lie in contact with the thin fragmented basement membrane. These vessels are easily penetrated by "switched on" cancer cells.

[b] The Solid Tumor Does Not Have an Anatomically Functioning Lymphatic System (19,20,21)

Less is known about lymphatic spread but investigators know that angiogenesis does enhance lymphatic metastases as well as spread through the blood stream. For some reason new lymph channels are not created during the process of angiogenesis and vascularization. As a result, the newly vascularized tumor contains no new lymphatics, just a few remnants of lymph channels from the invaded host breast tissue. The few lymph channels in the young tumor are unable to carry away the large amounts of fluid escaping from the leaky blood vessels. As a result, fluid accumulates in the center of the tumor and the increased hydraulic pressure literally forces fluid and tumor cells to the periphery of the tumor and into the low pressure of the lymphatics of the adjacent normal breast tissues of the host. The precise method by which the tumor cells gain entry into the lymphatic capillary is not known (20). This phenomenon explains why some breast cancers spread to the regional lymph nodes before the tumor reaches a diameter of one millimeter (4,5).

[c] Growth Rate, Motility, and Invasiveness of Tumor Cells are Increased During the Period of Vascularization (8,22,23,24)

The time during and shortly after the vascularizatioon of the breast cancer can only be described as a period of frenzied activity. The small cluster of breast cancers is being rapidly invaded by columns of endothelial cells whose aggressiveness is not unlike that of the cancer cell (9). The enzymes produced by the cells at the leading edges of the columns of endothelial cells not only destroy connective tissue to create a path for the advancing columns of endothelial cells but also stimulate the motility and invasiveness of the nearby cancer cells (9,22).

The tissue injury produced by the enzymes of the invading endothelial cells and the rapidly expanding, well-oxygenated tumor cells triggers a stereotyped response, that is, the normal wound healing response (23,24). Unfortunately the protein fragments that orchestrate the wound healing response also stimulate the tumor cells by enhancing their motility and invasive capabilities. Thus, a vicious cycle has been initiated. The tumor cells have usurped the signals for the wound healing response and as a result cause additional tissue damage which will again trigger the normal wound healing response (23).

The cluster of previously half-starved cancer cells now has an ample supply of oxygen and other nutrients. In the milieu of the above enzymes, growth factors, motility factors, chemoattractants, and other protein fragments the cancer cells began to grow rapidly in an exponential fashion.

§10.07 BREAST CANCERS HAVE A SPECIAL FRAGILITY (19)

For many years it has been well known that manipulation of tumors in experimental models (even palpation of the tumor) produce "showers" of tumor cells into the blood stream. This has been demonstrated in breast cancers as well (19).

§10.08 VASCULARIZATION AND TUMOR SHEDDING IN ANIMAL MODELS

Liotta, et al. (25) implanted fibrosarcoma T241 into the thighs of mice and found cancer cells in the venous blood draining the implanted tumors within a few hours after the onset of vascularization. In fact, cancer cells were being shed into the venous blood the very day that the first tiny capillary sprouts were seen in the periphery of the tumor.

Day 1--- Implantation of 40 mg fibrosarcoma T241 into thigh of mice.
Day 2--- No shed tumor cells.
Day 3--- No shed tumor cells.
Day 4--- A few small capillary structures found in peripheral regions of several tumors. **A few shed cancer cells** found in venous return.
Day 5--- All tumors contain small vascular sprouts in periphery of the tumors. **1400 cancer cells shed** in 24 hour period.
Day 10-- Thin walled vascular structures present throughout the tumor mass, but still with highest concentration in the periphery of the tumor. **38,000 cancer cells shed** per 24 hour period.
Day 15-- **150,000 cancer cells shed** in 24 hour period.
Days 4 to 9--A total of approximately 100,000 cancer cells were shed into the venous return from these implanted tumors (25).

Source: text from Liotta LA, Kleinerman J, and Saidel GM. Quantitative Relationships of Intravascular Tumor Cells, Tumor

Vessels, and Pulmonary Metatases Following Tumor Implantation. Cancer Research 34:997-1004,1974 reference # 25.

Koike (26) estimated that it requires 100,000 shed cells to establish pulmonary metastases with fibrosarcoma T241 in 50% of the mice. When the tumor bearing legs were amputated on Day #9 fifty percent of the mice developed pulmonary metastases (27). Thus 50% of the mice developed distant metastases during the first five days following the onset of vascularization (27). This is indeed startling since the process of vasculaization was not completed until several days after the amputation. We contend that the unfortunate outcome of many women with breast cancer is caused by a similar group of early metastasizing tumors.

§10.09 WHAT DO CLINICAL STUDIES TELL US ABOUT THE TIME OF METASTASIS?

Physicians intuitively recognize that many breast cancers metastasize early in their life cycle. It has been estimated that 50% of women with a breast cancer measuring 1 cm in diameter already have systemic disease (12). But, what proof do we have to substantiate this statement?

A. Christine Carter, et al. (28)— Studied the records of 24,740 breast cancer patients. They stated:

> "... because of our large sample size, we were able to identify a subset of small but highly virulent tumors that have metastasized to 4 or more nodes by the time of diagnosis. These cases have a survival rate of only 54 to 59% at five years. . . ."

The survival rate at ten years, of course, would be considerably less; therefore, it is likely that more than 50% of these small lesions had spread systemically before they could be detected.

B. Atkinson, Brown and Montague (29)— Measured the tumor diameter and time to distant metastasis in 2,663 breast cancers that were followed for a period of 20 years. Fifteen percent of these tumors were discovered by mammography before they could be palpated. They observed that:

> ". . . in the group with no known nodal involvement, even at the smallest size of detection 25% developed (distant) metastasis."

When 1-3 nodes were involved even at the smallest size of detection 40% developed distant metastasis. Of course, in the malpractice setting, in which all breast cancers with a favorable outcome have been excluded, the number of women with distant micrometastases at the time of diagnosis would be far greater.

The authors calculated the number of tumor cells in their tumors, and, using the number of patients who developed distant metastasis, computed the theoretical metastatic potential per tumor cell for each of the cancers. They found that the smallest tumors had the highest metastatic potential per tumor cell. This metastatic potential per tumor cell decreased rapidly as the tumors enlarged. Thus they concluded:

> "... another facet of the data shows quite clearly the extraordinary large contribution to metastasis of very small tumors."

C. Margolis DS (4) reviewed the Connecticut Tumor Registry for the years 1979 to 1986 and identified 137 invasive breast cancers 1 millimeter or less in diameter. These were incidental to the removal of benign lesions of the breast and 22 of these small cancers (16%) had already spread to the axillary lymph nodes. Margolis concluded that once these small lesions spread to the axilla they behave very aggressively. The fact that these tumors metastasized to the axilla when the tumor was less than 1 mm in diameter indicates that they were aggressive tumors. This study clearly demonstrates that even the smallest invasive breast cancers have the ability to metastasize to the regional lymph nodes. It is quite frightening to think that 16% of breast cancers had spread to the axillary lymph nodes even though they were smaller than the head of an ordinary pin, which is 1.2 mm in diameter.

D. Kopald, et al. (5) reviewed the records of 125 nonpalpable breast cancers. Nine of the 115 patients that had an axillary dissection had between one and ten involved axillary nodes. In two of these nine cases the primary tumors were microscopic in size! That is, the primary tumors in 22% of the patients with axillary metastases were invisible to the naked eye.

§10.10 CLINICAL SIGNIFICANCE OF TUMOR ANGIOGENESIS

Neoplastic progression (acquiring the ability to metastasize) occurs when the DNA of a breast cancer cell sustains an additional sequential series of genetic alterations. This can occur very early in the life of the tumor or at any time throughout its life cycle. The susceptibility of the tumor's DNA to sequential alterations and/or mutations varies. Thus tumors with considerable instability of their DNA might undergo genetic alteration early in the life cycle and have a poor prognosis while other tumors with more stable DNA would be less likely to undergo genetic alteration and therefore would be more likely to have a good outcome. Those with stable DNA might never metastasize.

Tumors do not develop a blood supply until the genes of some of the tumor cells are "switched on" or genetically altered to secrete powerful angiogenesis factors which stimulate neighboring blood vessels to grow into the tumor. Some of the tumor cells that are "switched on" to secrete these angiogenetic factors also acquire the ability to metastasize at this time (undergo neoplastic progression). Thus many of breast cancers metastasize during the period of angiogenesis or shortly thereafter.

Recent studies reveal that the early detection of asymptomatic breast cancers by screening mammography result in a 30% increase in the survival rate (30). This indicates that we may be detecting some small tumors whose DNA had not yet been "switched on" to provide the tumor cell the ability establish a viable metastasis.

All would also agree that the neoplastic progression secondary to the sequential genetic alteration of tumors with metastatic disease or of metastatic disease itself, although interesting, will not alter survival.

Practice Note

We conclude that tumors with significant genetic instability will have undergone neoplastic progression (metastasis) prior to the time these tumors have completed 75-90% of their life cycle. Tumors that have not undergone neoplastic progression by this time have relatively stable DNA and are not likely to do so during the remaining 10 to 20% of their life span. Symptomatic breast cancers (tumors that are large enough or growing fast enough to produce symptoms) are biologically old tumors that have completed 75-90% of their life cycle. They have entered the terminal phase of their life span. Decreasing the durations of symptoms of symptomatic breast cancers will not alter the outcome. See APPENDIX 10-1—VISUAL AIDS

§10.11 WHAT TYPE OF BREAST CANCER IS INVOLVED IN LITIGATION?

[a] The Majority Will Have Metastasized Early in Their Life Cycle

Twenty-five percent of ALL breast cancers (node negative and node positive) will have viable systemic metastases by the time they attain a diameter of 1 cm. (1,2,3).

Approximately sixty percent of all cancers have a favorable outcome as a result of one or more of the following:

1. The tumor does not have the ability to metastasize. The sequential genetic alterations necessary for the ability to metastasize were not completed.
2. The tumor does not have the ability to establish a viable metastasis because of powerful host immunity.
3. The tumor has the ability to establish viable metastases but has a prolonged doubling time (sometimes a year or more).

Since tumors with favorable outcomes are rarely involved in malpractice litigation we will eliminate cancers with a good outcome (100% − 60% = 40%). Forty percent of cancers with a poor outcome will remain and all will be candidates for litigation.

Since 25 of 100 cases metastasize by the time the tumor attains a diameter of 1 cm, we must divide 25 by 40 (the number of cancers with a poor outcome) to obtain the percentage of poor outcome cancers that metastasized early in their life cycle. Twenty-five divided by 40 equals .62 or 62%.

Thus, almost two thirds of the breast cancers we encounter in the courtroom will have metastasized early in their life cycle. We consider this estimate falsely low since long-term studies of breast cancer reveal an excess mortality from breast cancer for over 40 years.

[b] Tumors with Significant Instability of Their DNA That Metastasized Prior to the Time the Cancer Became Symptomatic

The tumors with significant instability of their DNA that did not metastasize early in their life cycle will have done so before these tumors become symptomatic. We define symptomatic breast cancers as those tumors large enough or which are growing fast enough, to produce symptoms sufficient to prompt the patient to consult her physician. Although some tumors produce symptoms when only 1 cm in diameter, others because of tumor camouflaging, may not produce symptoms until they attain diameters of 1.5, 2.0, 3.0 or even 4.0 cm. Tumors with significant genetic instability will have undergone sequential genetic alteration and neoplastic progression (metastasis) before these tumors enter the terminal phase of their life cycle and produce symptoms.

[c] NSABP Study Confirms That Neither Patient Nor Physician Delay of Diagnosis of Symptomatic Breast Cancers Alters the Outcome

Fisher et al. (31) studied the duration of clinical symptoms and the disease-free survival of 1,539 women.These authors (31) found that a delay of diagnosis and treatment (increasing the durations of symptoms) of 3, 6 or more than 9 months did not alter the disease-free survival rate. They concluded that this was secondary to the early metastases of these breast cancers.

[d] Spratt Confirms Results of NSABP Study

Spratt (32) states that "The biologic lethality of a breast cancer is determined before the cancer is large enough to produce symptoms. The result is that if prognosis is measured from the onset of symptoms, then neither physician delay nor patient delay alters prognosis. The prognosis may be good or bad bad, but it has been determined." The conclusions of Fisher et al. (31) and Spratt (32) are also supported by the work of Dennis et al (33), Skrabanek (34), and Plotkin and Blankenberg (35). The authors agree with Dennis, Fisher, Spratt, Skrabenek, and Plotkin and Blankenberg.

§10.12 CONCLUSION

And finally, to answer our question, what type of cancer will we encounter in the courtroom? We will encounter breast cancers that had significant genetic instability. Many will have undergone neoplastic progression (metastasis) very early in their life cycle while the remainder acquired the ability to metastasize prior to the time these tumors became symptomatic. Breast cancers with relatively stable DNA are not likely to be encountered in the courtroom. By the time a breast cancer becomes large enough to produce symptoms, all of the cancers with significant instability of their DNA will have metastasized. Neither patient nor physician delay in the diagnosis of symptomatic breast cancer will alter the outcome.

References

1. McGuire WL, et al. How to Use Prognostic Factors in Axillary Node-Negative Breast Cancer Patients. J Nat Cancer Instit 82(12):1006-1015, 1990.
2. Rosen PP, Groshen S, Saigo PE, et al. Pathologic Factors in Stage I (T1 N0 M0) and Stage II (T1N1M0) Breast Carcinoma: A Study of 644 Patients With a Median Follow-Up of 18 Years. J Clin Oncol 7:1239-1251, 1989.
3. Brinkley D and Haybittle JL. Long-Term Survival of Women With Breast Cancer. The Lancet 1:1118, May 19, 1984.
4. Margolis DS. Is Axillary Dissection Obligatory? Oncology Times 13(1):1-3, January 1991.
5. Kopald KH, et al. The Pathology of Nonpalpable Breast Cancer. The American Surgeon 56(12):782-787, 1990.
6. Ham, Arthur W. Histology, 7th edition. JP Lippincott Co, 1974, pages 559-592.
7. Fisher ER. The Impact of Pathology on the Biologic, Diagnostic, Prognostic, and Therapeutic Considerations in Breast Cancer. Surg Clin N Am. 64(6):1073-1093, 1984.
8. Folkman, Judah, quoted by Brylawski, Robert. Study Links Microvessel Counts in Breast Tumors to Metastasis Risk. Oncology Times, May 1991, page 50.
9. Presta M and Rifkin DB. New Aspects of Blood Vessel Growth: Tumor and Tissue Derived Angiogenesis Factors. Haemostasis 18:6-17, 1988.
10. Spratt JS and Spratt JA. Growth Rates in *Cancer of the Breast,* 3rd eds. Donegan and Spratt, WB Saunders, 1988, pages 270-302.

11. Butler TP and Gullino P. Quantitation of Cell Shedding into Efferent Blood of Mammary Adenocarcinoma. Cancer Research 35:512-516, 1975.
12. Zetter, Bruce R. Personal Communication, June 11, 1992.
13. Liotta, Lance A. Cancer Cell Invasion and Metastasis. Scientific American 266(2):54-63, Feb. 1992.
14. de Duve, Christian. A Guided Tour of the Living Cell. WH Freeman and Co Ltd. 1984 Volume I, page 36.
15. Albert A, et al. Molecular Biology of the Cell. Garland Publishing Co. 1983.
16. Zetter, Bruce R. The Cellular Basis of Site-Specific Tumor Metastasis. N Eng J Med. 322(9):605-612, 1990.
17. Nowell, Peter C. Commentary: How Many Cancer Genes? J National Cancer Institute 83(15):1061-1064, 1991.
18. Liotta, Lance. Personal Communication February 14, 1992.
19. Gullino, Pietro M. Natural History of Breast Cancer. Progression From Hyperplasia to Neoplasia as Predicted by Angiogenesis. Cancer 39:2697-2703, 1977.
20. Zetter Bruce C. Personal Communication February 26, 1992.
21. Butler TP, Grantham FH, and Gullino PM. Bulk Transfer of Fluid in the Interstitial Compartment of Human Tumors. Cancer Res 35:3084-3088, 1975.
22. Weidner N, Semple JP, Welch WR, and Folkman J. Tumor Angiogenesis and Metastasis—Correlation in Invasive Breast Carcinoma. N Engl J M 324-1-8, 1991.
23. Dvorak, Harold F. Tumors: Wounds That Do Not Heal. New Eng J Med 315:1650-1659, 1986.
24. Blood, Christine and Zetter, Bruce. Tumor Interaction With the Vasculature: Angiogenesis and Tumor Metastases. Biochemica et Biophysica Acta 1032:89-118, 1990.
25. Liotta LA, Kleinerman J, and Saidel GM. Quantitative Relationships of Intravascular Tumor Cells, Tumor Vessels, and Pulmonary Metatases Following Tumor Implantation. Cancer Research 34:997-1004, 1974.
26. Koike A. Mechanism of Blood-Borne Metastases-I. Some Factors Affecting Lodgement and Growth of Tumor Cells in the Lungs. Cancer 17:450-460, 1964.

27. Romsdahl MM, Chu EW, Hume R, and Smith RR. The Time of Metastases and Release of Circulating Tumor Cells as Determined in an Experimental System Cancer. Cancer 14:883-888, 1961.
28. Carter CL, Allen C, and Henson DE. Relation of Tumor Size, Lymph Node Status, and Survival in 24,740 Breast Cancer Cases. Cancer 63:181-187, 1989.
29. Atkinson EN, Brown BW, and Montague ED, Tumor Volume, Nodal Status, and Metastasis in Breast Cancer in Women. J National Cancer Institute 76:171-178, 1986.
30. Tabar L, Fagerberg G, Day NE., et al. Breast Cancer Treatment and Natural History: New Insights from Results of Screening. The Lancet 339:412-414, Feb 15, 1992.
31. Fisher ER, et al. A Perspective Concerning the Relation of Durations of Symptoms to Treatment Failure in Patients with Breast Cancer. Cancer 40:3160-3167, 1977.
32. Spratt, John S, Realities of Breast Cancer Control, Public Expectations, and the Law. Surgical Oncology Clinics of North America. 3(1):25-34, January 1994.
33. Dennis CR, Gardner B, Lim B. Analysis of Survival and Recurrence vs. Patient and Doctor Delay in Treatment of Breast Cancer. Cancer 35:714, 1975.
34. Skrabanek, Petr. False Premises and False Promises of Breast Cancer Screening. The Lancet, August 10, 1985 pages 316-319.
35. Plotkin D and Blankenberg F. Cancer Management Controversy. Breast Cancer—Biology and Malpractice. Am J Clin Oncol 14(3):254-266, 1991.

APPENDIX 10-1—
VISUAL AIDS

These graphs and tables are designed to demonstrate to the jury that breast cancers metastasize to distant sites prior to the time the tumor becomes large enough to produce symptoms. Defense counsel will find them to be more effective, if they have been introduced by the visual aids prepared for Chapters 6 and 9.

[a] Historical

[1] In the 1900's breast cancer was thought to spread by direct extension through the local tissues and via the lymphatics to the regional nodes and distant sites. Therefore, early diagnosis and radical surgery should have been curative. Is not that correct?

[2] And, radical surgery (radical mastectomy) did reduce the problem of local recurrence but consistently failed to cure 40-50% of the patients, is not that true?

[3] The addition of postoperative radiation and even more radical surgery failed to increase survival, did it not?

[4] Eventually a few brave pioneers (considered to be heretics by their peers) suggested that the mutilating radical mastectomy was not necessary, did they not?

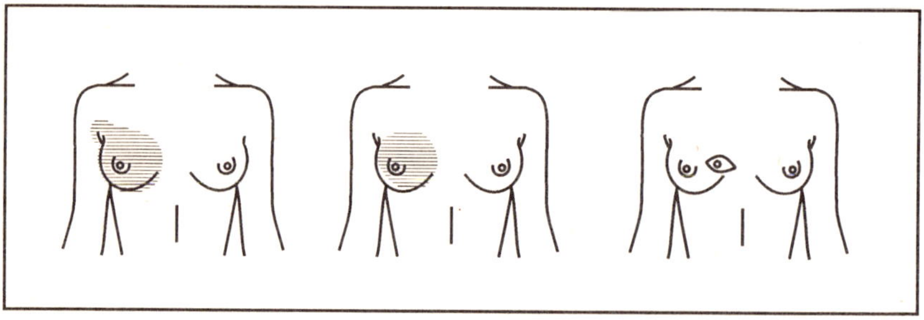

Figure 10-3. Radical Mastectomy, Total Mastectomy, and Lumpectomy. Comparison of extent of surgery.

[b] Radical Mastectomy Versus Conservative Breast Surgery

Narration

[1] Incredibly, did not the survival rate of simple lumpectomy equal that of the more radical and mutilating surgery?

[2] Does this suggest that large numbers of breast cancers have metastasized by the time clinical detection was possible?

[3] Thus, even the most radical local-regional treatment will not help women who have distant metastases at the time of surgery. Is not this correct?

[4] And when the disease is confined to the breast, conservative surgery will suffice, will it not?

[c] Eight-Year Survival Rate of Total Mastectomy and Lumpectomy With or Without Radiation

Narration

[1] Does not the fact that survival following simple lumpectomy, which removes only the cancer with the narrowest margin of

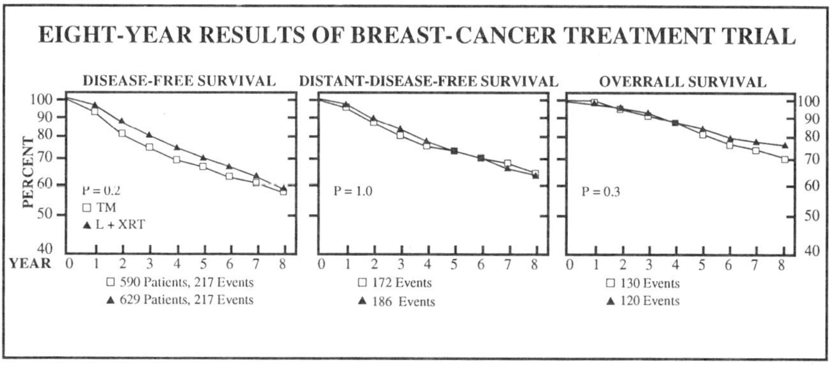

Figure 10-4. Life-Table Analysis Showing Rates of Disease-free Survival, Distant Disease-free Survival, and Overall Survival of Patients Treated With Total Mastectomy (TM) or Lumpectomy and Breast Irradiation (L + XRT). Fisher B. et al. Eight-Year Results of a Randomized Clinical Trial Comparing Total Mastectomy and Lumpectomy with or without Irradiation in the Treatment of Breast Cancer. N Eng J Med 320:822-828, March 20, 1989, Figure 3, page 825. Reprinted courtesy of authors and publisher.

normal tissue, equals that of the most radical surgery prove we have a serious problem?

[2] Is not the conclusion inescapable, 40% (+/−) of clinically detected breast cancers during the 1970-80's had distant metastases at the time of diagnosis and treatment?

[3] Is it not true that no matter how high the standard of care surgery fails to cure these women?

[d] Long-Term Studies of the Survival of Breast Cancer

Long-term studies suggest that the 40% incidence of systemic disease found at the time of surgery in the above studies is far too low (2).

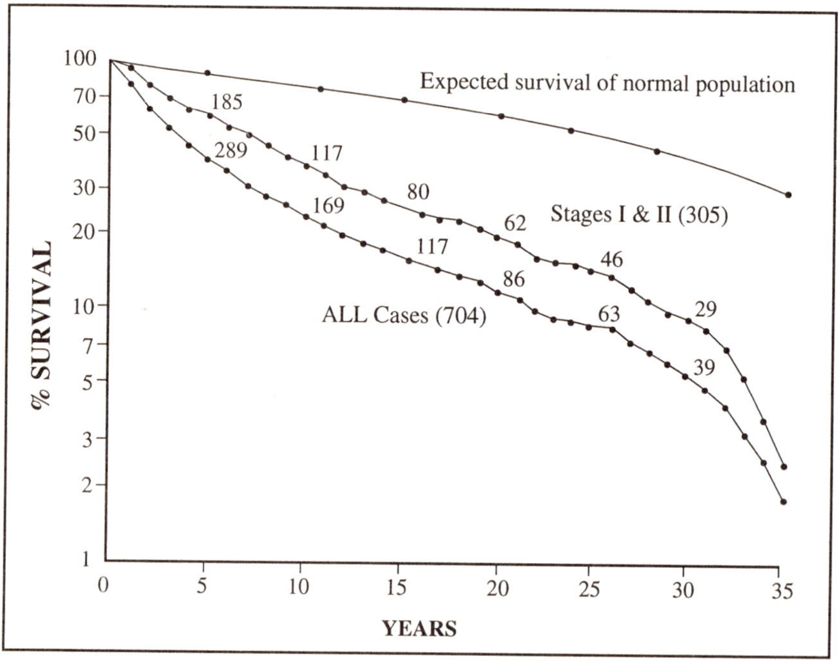

Figure 10-5. (Repeat of Figure 9-2). Observed Survival Curves of a Group of Stage I and II Breast Cancer Patients and the Expected Survival Curves from a Normal Population of the Same Age Distribution. Brinkley D and Haybittle JL. Long term survival of women with breast cancer. The Lancet, May 19, 1984. Figure 1, page 1118. Reprinted courtesy of authors and publisher.

Narration

[1] Brinkley and Haybittle (2) followed 704 patients for 31 years and found the number of breast cancer deaths to be 15 times greater in the breast cancer group than in the general population between the 25th and 30th year of follow-up.

[2] Other long-term studies (§9.02) have found an excess of breast cancer deaths to persist at 30 and 40 years.

[3] Doesn't this suggest that the incidence of distant disease at the time breast cancers become clinically detectable is significantly greater than 40%?

[e] The Age-Adjusted Mortality Rate of Breast Cancer

Narration

[1] Our failure to improve the mortality rate of breast cancer since 1930 provides additional proof that clinically detected breast

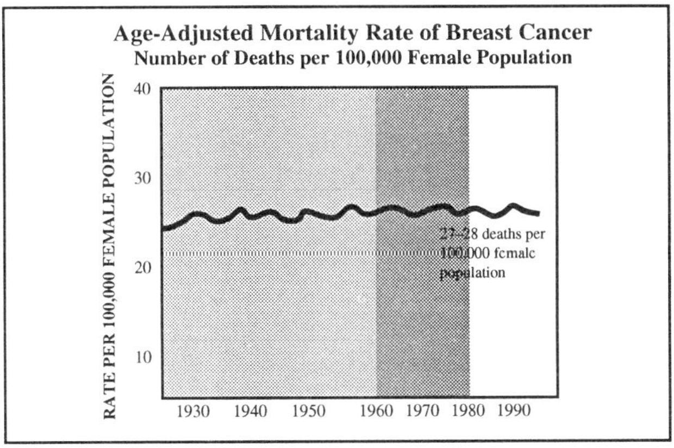

Figure 10-6. (Modified from Figure 6-1). Age-Adjusted Cancer Death Rates for Selected Sites, Females, United States, 1930-1988. Boring CC, Squires TS, and Tong T. Cancer Statistics-1993, Ca-A Cancer Journal for Clinicians, 43(1):7-26, Jan-Feb, 1993, page 16. Sources: National Cancer Center for Health Statistics and US Bureau of the Census. Reprinted courtesy authors and publisher.

cancers since 1930 have had a consistently high rate of systemic disease at the time of surgery, does it not?

[2] Doesn't this prove that more than 40% of women harbor distant metastases at the time of clinical diagnosis?

[3] Again, isn't it true that no matter how high the standard of care, these women will not be cured unless we improve adjuvant therapy?

[f] The Studies of Fisher et al. (4) and Dennis et al (5) Suggest That We Cannot Improve the Age-Adjusted Mortality Rate of Breast Cancer Because Cancers That Have the Ability to Metastasize Do So Prior to the Time These Cancers Become Large Enough to Produce Symptoms

Relation Durations of Symptoms and Treatment Failure in 1,539 Patients With Cinical Stage I and II Breast Cancer (4)

Durations of symptoms (months)	(%) treatment failures at 32 months
0-1.0 month	25.2%
1.1-3.0 months	27.3%
3.1-9.0 months	29.2%
> 9.0 months	19.5%

Reprinted courtesy of Fisher et al. (4). A Perspective Concerning the Relation of Durations of Symptoms to Treatment Failure in Patients With Breast Cancer. Cancer 40:3160-3167, 1977, Table 1, page 3163.

Narration

The study of Dennis et al. (5) also found that decreasing the durations of symptoms of breast cancers does not alter the outcome. Kern (6) reviewed breast cancer malpractice litigation in the US federal and civil court system over a period of 20 years and found no correlation between the length of delay in diagnosis and the TNM stage of breast cancer or between tumor diameter and the length of diagnostic delay. Delays in diagnosis of two to five years had no effect on survival from breast cancer. These reports support Spratt's (7) conclusions that by the time a breast cancer becomes large enough to produce symptoms, all of the cancers with genetic instability will have metastasized. Those with relatively stable DNA will not do so during the life of the cancer. By the time a breast cancer develops symptoms, it is a biologically old tumor and the prognosis has been determined. Neither patient nor physician delay will alter the outcome. See also Visual Aids Appendix 6-1[c]. Definition and Significance of the Symptomatic Breast Cancer.

[g] Animal Models Demonstrate Why Some Breast Cancers Metastasize So Early

Implantation Fibrosarcoma T241 Into The Thigh of Mice, Liotta et al. (8), Romsdahl, et al. (9)

Day 1--Implantation fibrosarcoma T241 into thigh of mice (8,9).

Day 5--Few capillaries invading periphery of tumor—1400 cancer cells shed into blood and numbers of shed cells increases exponentially during next 10 days (8).

Day 9--Although the tumor bearing thighs of mice were amputated on the 9th day, 50% of the animals developed lung metastases (9).

Table prepared from texts of:

Liotta LA, Kleinerman J, and Saidel GM. Quantitative relationships of intravascular tumor cells, tumor vessels, and pulmonary metatases following tumor implantation. Cancer Research 34:997-1004,1974

Romsdahl MM, Chu EW, Hume R, and Smith RR. The time of metastases and release of circulating tumor cells as determined in an experimental system cancer. Cancer 14:883-888,1961

Narration

a. Thus only four days after the onset of vascularization, 50% of the tumors had metastasized to the lung!
b. In the malpractice situation, all tumors with favorable outcomes (about 60%) will have been eliminated. Therefore, the number of tumors that metastasize during or shortly after the period of vascularization (prior to attaining a diameter of 1 cm) will be quite high (we estimate approximately two thirds).

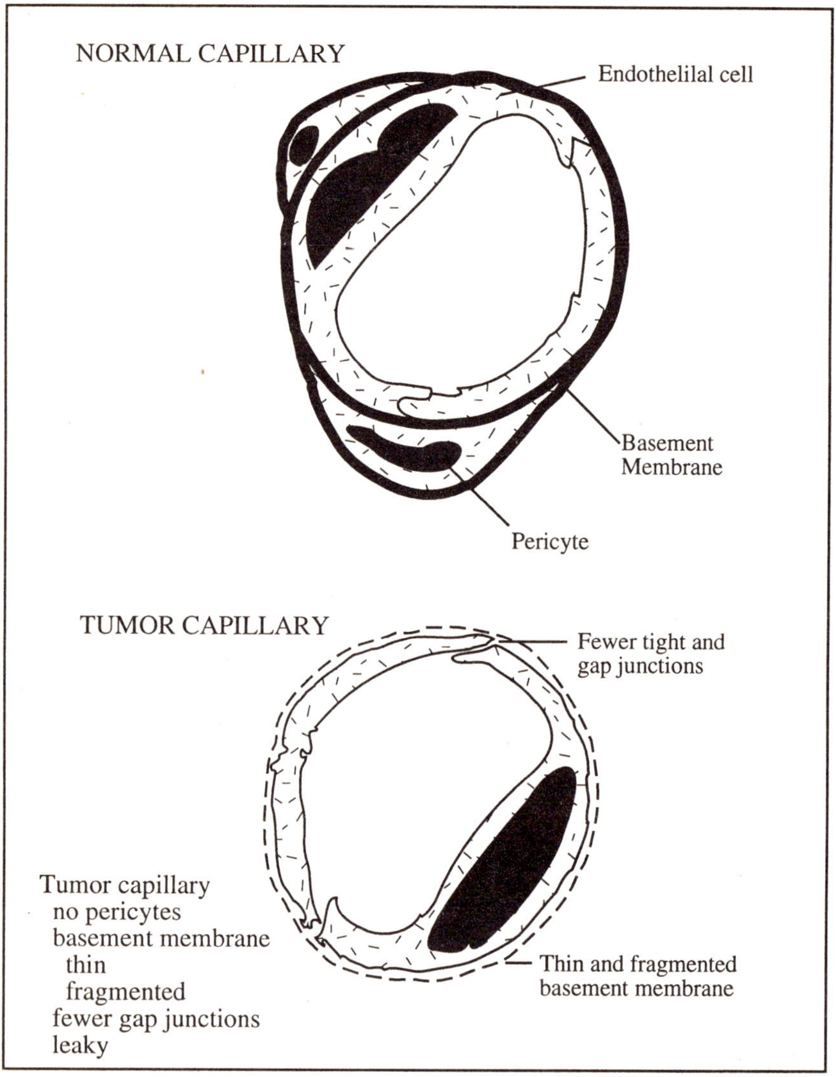

Figure 10-7. A Comparison of a Normal and a Tumor Capillary. Note the poor construction of the leaky tumor capillary. Normal capillary (a repeat of Figure 10-1. Ham, Arthur W. Histology, 7th edition, JB Lippincott Co, 1974, Figure 8-2, page 214. Reprinted courtesy author and publisher). Tumor capillary (Modified from Figure 10-2).

[h] Why Do So Many Cancers Metastasize During or Shortly After the Period of Vascularization?

Narration

[1] Normally it is not easy for cancer cells to gain entry into the blood stream.

[2] However, the blood capillaries that invade the tumor are hastily and poorly constructed: See Figure 10-7 and §10.02[d] and §10.06 [a], [b] and [c].

a. The outer layer (of pericytes) is absent.
b. The basement membrane (middle layer) is fragmented and in some areas completely absent.
c. The gap junctions between the lining endothelial cells (inner layer) are poorly constructed and/or absent.

[3] As a result the capillaries are quite "leaky" and cancer cells have no difficulty gaining entrance into the blood stream.

[4] Tumor cells are stimulated to be more invasive by the enzymes released by the invading endothelial cells.

[i] Conclusion

In the vast majority of cases our failure to cure breast cancer is secondary to the inherent biology of the breast cancer rather than physician error.

[1] By the time a breast cancer becomes large enough to produce symptoms, it is a biologically old tumor. Seventy-five to eighty-five percent of its life cyle has elapsed. Breast cancers with significant genetic instability will have undergone neoplastic progression and metastasis prior to the time these tumors enter the final stages of their life cycle. Those tumors with relatively stable DNA will not metastasize during the short time remaining in the life cycle of the tumor. Metastases of tumors with prolonged doubling times (360 days +/−) may not surface until 20, 30, or 40 years following surgery. We agree with Spratt's statement (7):

> "The biologic lethality of a breast cancer is determined before the cancer is large enough to produce symptoms. The result is that if prognosis is measured from the onset of symptoms, neither physi-

cian delay or patient delay alters prognosis. The prognosis may be good or bad but is has been determined."

a. Thus, simple lumpectomy is as curative as the most radical surgery.
b. Thus we have failed to improve the age-adjusted mortality rate for the past 63 years.
c. Thus, the inability of long-term survival studies to prove that breast cancer is curable.
d. Thus, the pattern of metastasis of many breast cancer resembles that which we encounter in experimental animal models.
e. Thus, the observations of Dennis et al. (5), Fisher et al. (4), and Spratt (6) that neither patient or physician delay of diagnosis of symptomatic breast cancers fails to alter survival are not fortuitous.
f. Thus, the observation that mammographic detection of asymptomatic breast cancer may increase survival.

[j] Once a Myth is Entrenched in the Minds of the Medical Community it is Difficult to Expel

As we study breast cancer we cannot help but remember a statement made by Will Rogers, "It ain't what we don't know that gets us into trouble, it's what we know for sure that's wrong." That is precisely the problem caused by myths regarding breast cancer. For example, between 1920 and 1950 a few astute physicians observed that conservative surgery with radiation was as effective as radical mastectomy. However, so entrenched was the Halsted doctrine that the medical community considered these reports to be heretical. Sadly, it was not until the 1970's that NSABP prospective randomized studies demonstrated conservative surgery and radiation to be as effective as the mutilating radical mastectomy. Thus, a period of 50 years elapsed before scientific facts could dispel the myths created by anecdotal retrospective studies.

Today, a similar situation exists regarding the value of early diagnosis of symptomatic breast cancers. In the 1940's, 1950's and 1960's a few discerning clinicians (11-16) observed that the delay of treatment following the onset of symptoms did not alter the survival of breast cancer. In this era, in which few dared to criticize the Halsted doctrine, some of these investigators attempted to prove their own data in error. Others were accused of falsifying their data. Recently reports of Dennis et al. (5), and ER Fisher et al. (4) support these observations. Today the truth of this seeming paradox is best articulated by Spratt (6), Skrabanek (17), and Plotkin and Blankenberg (18). However, some still cling to the last vestiges of the disproven Halsted doctrine. Once again, it may require more than 50 years to dispel a myth created by anecdotal retrospective studies.

References—Visual Aids, Chapter 10

1. Fisher, et al. (1) Eight-Year Results of a Randomized Clinical Trial Comparing Total Mastectomy and Lumpectomy With or Without Irradiation in the Treatment of Breast Cancer. Cancer 320:822-828, March 20, 1989. Figure 3, page 825.
2. Brinkley, Diana and Haybittle JL. (2) Long-Term Survival of Women With Breast Cancer. Letters to the editor. The Lancet, May 19, 1984, page 1118. Figure 1, page 1118.
3. Boring CC, Squires TS, and Tong T. (3) Cancer Statistics-1993, Ca-A Cancer Journal for Clinicians, 43(1):5-26, Jan-Feb, 1993 [Figure 1, page 16], Sources: National Cancer Center for Health Statistics and US Bureau of the Census.
4. Fisher ER, et al. A Perspective Concerning the Relation of Durations of Symptoms to Treatment Failure in Patients With Breast Cancer. Cancer 40:3160-3167, 1977.
5. Dennis CR, Gardner B, Lim B. Analysis of Survival and Recurrence vs. Patient and Doctor Delay in Treatment of Breast Cancer. Cancer 35:714, 1975.
6. Kern KA. Causes of Breast Cancer Malpractice Litigation—a 20 Year Civil Court Review. Arch Surg 127:542-547, 1992.
7. Spratt, John S, Realities of Breast Cancer Control, Public Expectations, and the Law. Surgical Oncology Clinics of North America. 3(1):25-34, January 1994.
8. Liotta LA, Kleinerman J, and Saidel GM. Quantitative Relationships of Intravascular Tumor Cells, Tumor Vessels, and

Pulmonary Metatases Following Tumor Implantation. Cancer Research 34:997-1004, 1974.

9. Romsdahl MM, Chu EW, Hume R, and Smith RR. The Time of Metastases and Release of Circulating Tumor Cells as Determined in an Experimental System Cancer. Cancer 14:883-888, 1961.
10. Ham, Arthur W. Histology, 7th edition. JP Lippincott Co, 1974, pages 559-592.
11. Bloom HJG. Further Studies on Prognosis of Breast Carcinoma. Br J Surg 4:347-367, 1950.
12. Bloom HJG. The Influence of Delay on the Natural History and Prognosis of Breast Cancer. Br J Can 19:228-262, 1965.
13. McKinnon NE. Canadian Med Assoc 73:614, 1955.
14. Park WW and Lees JC. Surg Gynecol Obstet 93:129, 1951.
15. Haagensen CD and Stout AP Ann Surg 134:151, 1951.
16. Delario AJ. Breast Cancer, Factors Modifying Prognosis. New York (Macmillan) 1960, page 123.
17. Skrabanek, Petr. False Premises and False Promises of Breast Cancer Screening. The Lancet, August 10, 1985 pages 316-319.
18. Plotkin D and Blankenberg F. Cancer Management Controversy. Breast Cancer—Biology and Malpractice. Am J Clin Oncol 14(3):254-266, 1991.

APPENDIX 10-2— THE CURABILITY OF INVASIVE BREAST CANCER

Commentary by:

David Plotkin, MD, Associate Clinical Professor of Medicine, UCLA Associate Clinical Professor of Medicine, USC Director, Memorial Cancer Research Foundation of Southern California, Los Angeles, California

Francis G. Blankenberg, MD, Acting Assistant Professor of Radiology, Stanford University, Palo Alto, California

I. ISSUES SURROUNDING CURE AND METASTASIS

This invited commentary will address three inter-related issues: 1) Is breast cancer curable? It is assumed that the breast cancer under discussion here is invasive, not in situ, an admittedly curable lesion in 75 to 80% of women so affected (1,2,3). 2) If invasive breast cancer is not curable, are we not obligated to conclude that the metastatic process occurs regularly *before* the time of clinical recognition and treatment. An extension of this question must focus on whether there is ever an interval of time *after* a breast malignancy goes from in situ to invasive, that still permits excision with cure. 3) Confounding many legal and medical professionals required to deal with this issue in medical malpractice actions, is the third question, i.e. when do metastases begin and its corollary, is there a reliable way to compute this? Since most cases of "failure to diagnose breast cancer in a timely manner" involve alleged delays in diagnosis of from three months to three years, the issue further narrows to whether or not metastases may take place *after a diagnosis becomes possible but was missed* (4). Put another way, is the allegation of plaintiff's counsel that a window of opportunity for cure closed because of an attending doctor's negligence? This is the basis for the loss of chance doctrine.

II. AN ACCURATE DEFINITION OF "CURE"

It must be obvious to professionals taking stands on both sides of this issue that how one defines cure is a crucial determinant of one's position. The term cure therefore demands the closest scrutiny.

One might think that cure, at least as it relates to the issue of health, is free of ambiguity. Alas, not so. The word is used in several ways, at times creating great confusion. The dictionary most commonly defines cure as a remedy that restores one to health (5). With this definition there is no comment as to the permanence of health. Unstated but acknowledged is ultimate mortality of any cohort for some reason. Implicit, and probably the crucial element in the definition, is freedom from recurrence of the treated disease that is total and for the individual's lifetime, thus eliminating death due to the disease under consideration. The permanent eradication of a disease that guarantees cure in its most pristine definition may be best termed actuarial cure (6,7). Simple examples of this unquestionably accurate definition of cure includes appendectomy for appendicitis, antibiotics for many infections, etc. In oncology, the successful use of chemotherapy in childhood acute leukemia, the use of radiation therapy in eliminating certain cancers of the uterine cervix, the surgical removal of a low-grade sarcoma are all cures in an unqualified sense. Beyond such examples, the definition of cure becomes less clear. Widely used is the expression five year cure, a potentially oxymoronic term that actually means "alive" five years after diagnosis of a cancer. The irony of death due to the cancer a year or two after the five year mark is reached is therefore made especially bitter. A far better and totally accurate expression is simply five year survival. Indeed, accurate notation of survival for any length of time after primary diagnosis and treatment 1, 3, 5, 10, 15, 20, 30, etc. is above any reproach.

[a] Personal Cure

An expression, "personal cure" appears frequently in the oncology literature emanating from the United Kingdom (8). It is defined as death following treatment for cancer that is totally unrelated to the cancer. Implicit in this definition is the fact that many cancer patients, especially the elderly, have other illnesses competing for their mortality. At times cancer death is simply avoided by an earlier death owing to, e.g., cardiovascular disease.

[b] Statistical Cure

The term statistical cure has also been used that clarifies little. In a real sense, all definitions of cure, even those lacking precision, are statistical, i.e., the assembly and classification of numeric data so as to present significant information. The problem, therefore, is in selecting the right definition of cure for making a valid point. If all patients treated for a particular cancer are totally and forever free of recurrence after a five year free interval, the term five year cure is quite accurate. Sadly, in the zeal to display good results, many authors and spokesmen, fail to acknowledge the limited value of our struggle with cancer by reporting the timed survival data that represent metaphorical "partial scores."

[c] Key Definition of "Cure"

In summary, the key definition of cure is the restoration of a cancer afflicted individual's life expectancy to the same level as a cohort of "normal," age and gender equivalent individuals, not so afflicted. Obliged to adhere to this concept, examination of the publications purporting to demonstrate cure of breast cancer must follow.

III. DO THE MAJOR MAMMOGRAPHIC SCREENING TRIALS SUPPORT BREAST CANCER CURABILITY?

[a] When Is Cure Possible?

Virtually no one maintains that cure of breast cancer is possible when it is diagnosed as stage III or IV disease, i.e., locally far advanced or frankly metastatic. No one disagrees, however, with the fact that some of these women, especially those with hormonally dependent tumors who are elderly and otherwise infirm, may achieve personal cure. Even patients with surgical stage II disease, i.e., not locally advanced and therefore routinely operable, but with regional axillary lymph node metastases, are usually considered incurable although the proportion of personal cures in this group is much higher than it is in stage III or IV. The controversy centers on the likelihood of stage I disease curability. Women with easily operable lesions, free of metastases to regional nodes as determined by routine pathology, are often felt to be cured. With the abundance of literature that correlates smaller tumor size and lesser to absent lymph node metastases with better prognosis, the rationale for earlier clinical diagnosis is clear (9,10,11,12,13). This has indeed been the basis for numerous mammography trials that led to earlier clinical diagnosis with unquestionably improved five year survival rates (14,15,16). What must be addressed then, is whether the improvement of survival in a test versus a control group in five year, even 10 year survival rates, is a reflection of actuarial cure. It is just such literature that reports the results of a number of mammography trials in which the concept of cure of invasive breast cancer is based.

[b] The Major Screen Trials Do Not Confirm a Decrease in Mortality

[1] Contradictory Results

Support for the cure of breast cancer has largely focused on the seven "randomized" mammographic screening trials as summarized in Table I (14). A randomized study by definition assigns every patient into a control group (no mammographic screening offered) or a study group (offered mammographic screening) in a blinded fashion without any bias. Each patient is then followed for a specific length of time using the same procedures such as periodic examinations, mailings and/or telephone calls. Implicit in all the randomized mammographic screening trials is the equivalent exclusion of women at time of initiation of the trial who had prior breast carcinoma in the study and control groups. If all the steps above are strictly adhered to then any decrease in breast cancer mortality in the study group as compared to the control group must be due to mammographic screening. Only two trials, however, the HIP and the Swedish W.E. studies, have demonstrated a significant decrease in breast cancer mortality (15,16). The most recent randomized trials, most notably the Canadian National Breast Screening Study, have failed to confirm the results of the HIP and Swedish studies (17,18).

These contradictory results can only be explained by failures in either the positive or negative trials to properly manage one or more of the following key issues: 1) the randomization of patients, 2) the exclusion of certain patients, 3) the follow-up of patients and 4) the quality of the performance and interpretation of mammograms. Currently the Canadian trial has come under heavy scrutiny and criticism particularly for allegedly poor mammographic quality control and interpretation (19,20,21,22). The arguments presented against the Canadian study appear to be spurious for several reasons. The first is that the sensitivity of the mammographic detection of breast carcinoma was greater than any previous trial, 75%, though when reference radiologists were consulted this rate increased to 89% (23). Furthermore, the Canadian study fulfilled all the latest guidelines for desirable results of screening mammography as proposed by Tabar with respect to tumor size, the percentage of women free of nodal metastases, and the detection rate at the first screening (24). Secondly, it seems implausible that the mammographic techniques and the medical record keeping of the late 1960's and 1970's could approach the mammography techniques, the national tumor registries, the methods of follow-up, and the general overall quality of medical care and record keeping of the 1980's. In the interest of fair play one is obligated to re-examine the HIP and Swedish studies.

[2] Re-evaluating the HIP Study

The maximal benefit of screening in the HIP trial was found after ten years of follow-up. At this time the difference in the size of the study (30,239) versus control (30,756) group was 517 and has been attributed to a greater number of exclusions in the study group owing to pregnant women and women with prior mastectomies, a difference considered to be slight by Shapiro, et al. (16). However, if a large contribution to the excluded women was because of prior mastectomy (which appears likely as the number of pregnant women aged between 40 to 64 years in the 1960's would be small) then the number of exclusions with respect to the total number of breast cancer diagnosed (1234; study: 617, control: 617) has potential significance.

The authors of the study noted that the status of the study group for pregnancy and prior mastectomy was "more completely ascertained" when compared to the control group (16). To this date the actual numbers of excluded women and their reason for exclusion from the study or control group have not been published. Clearly it would be simple to exclude from the study women who were pregnant or who had prior mastectomy when arriving for an initial mammogram, physical examination and medical history. But how precise was the ascertaining of pregnancy or prior mastectomy in the control women when that determination was made years later? What if only 10% of the 500 extra women in the control group slipped through the ascertaining process, by an error in placing the time of mastectomy after the institution of the trial especially if patient memory was the only source of this crucial bit of history? This would translate into at least 25 breast cancer deaths (using an optimistic overall ten year breast cancer survival rate of 50% for women who did not undergo mammographic screening). If 25 breast cancer deaths are removed from the total breast cancer deaths in the control group (193 deaths) then the reduction of breast cancer mortality in the screened group (147 deaths) would fall from 30% to below 20%, thus jeopardizing the statistical significance of the study. Another infrequently mentioned feature of the HIP study was the lower breast cancer mortality rate in the study women who refused mammographic screening as compared to the women who accepted screening (16). Therefore, the impact of the reports coming from the HIP study which correctly included all study women was enhanced, rather than diluted by the inclusion of women who were offered screening but refused it. Being offered breast cancer screening and refusing it could hardly be expected to lower mortality. Because of the unusual nature of the offered but refused group which had an extraordinary low mortality from breast cancer, the reported benefit from the HIP study is open to question.

[3] Re-evaluating the Swedish Study

The Swedish study only showed one-third the effect on breast cancer mortality as that purportedly shown by the HIP study (25). Furthermore the same problems in the exclusion of women that possibly occurred in the HIP study might have taken place in Sweden as well. Another totally different confounding factor, e.g., the use of tamoxifen in stage 2 breast cancer in Sweden during those years would have delayed mortality in the screened group (26). Lastly, it has been observed that overall mortality (from all causes) in the Swedish study group is slightly higher than the control group, thus making any benefit from screening seemingly insignificant (27).

IV. UNDERSTANDING THE TRUE DYNAMICS OF BREAST CANCER

There is the generally accepted notion that cancer should be diagnosed as early as clinically possible. The rationale for this is straightforward. Explicitly, the smaller a cancer is at diagnosis, the less mutilating the surgery needed to excise it. Implicitly, the removal of the cancer may be accomplished before it has metastasized. For most of this century, it has been assumed that the ability to remove all local evidence of cancer justifies optimism for the patient. Many disappointments ensued, however (28,29). Surgical pathology eventually came to be relied upon as a better barometer of outlook for patients with breast cancer. It became axiomatic that the larger the primary tumor, and/or the more lymph nodes were involved by metastatic disease, the worse the prognosis. Conversely, small tumors with no surgical pathology demonstrable lymph node involvement, had a good prognosis. There were still, however, frequent exceptions. Long before chemotherapy and antiestrogen therapy, experienced clinicians noted that some patients with ominous pathology lived for decades while other patients with small tumors, seemingly confined to the breast would develop clinical evidence of metastatic disease and rapidly succumb to it. What could account for this? Early on it was felt by pathologists and clinicians that the degree of tumor differentiation held the clue to prognosis. Moreover, tumor histology was often consistent with tumor size and regional lymph node involvement, but not always. Pathologists struggled to separate breast cancers into three groups, well differentiated, moderately differentiated and poorly differentiated (30). The classification helped to sort out some of the clinical paradoxes that befuddled us. The best effort of the most skillful pathologists still left the outcome of many cases unsatisfactorily explained. Added to this was the problem of inter-observer differences and probably most importantly, a limited ability to separate moderately differentiated from poorly differentiated, the two categories that account for probably 90% of the total (31). In short, routine, Virchowian histopathology has been a less–than–effective classification.

Because of the frustration in prognosticating using traditional, descriptive tools, focus began to shift to analyses of the dynamic aspects of cancer. Thymidine labelling index (TLI) was the first measure of tumor proliferative rate to be developed (32). It permitted the categorizing of breast cancers into three groups: one, a virulent type (fast proliferative rate), another an indolent tumor (slow proliferative rate) and a group of cancers between these extremes, remarkably still constituting at least 50% of the total, characterized by an average degree of clinical aggressiveness and with average proliferative rates. Even with the advent of TLI, a difficult essentially research laboratory procedure, there were still cases that did not fit the emerging model. Only in the last decade has flow cytometry (FCM) and image cytometry (IC) been developed, techniques that are clinically practical (33,34). With DNA histograms, usually more conveniently derived from FCM, estimates of tumor ploidy are now reliably computed as long as it is the tumor that is being tested and not non-neoplastic stroma. In short, all of this investigation strongly suggests that diploid (euploid) tumors are slower to invade than are aneuploid tumors. Not unexpectedly, correlation between diploid state and slow to average proliferative rate has been observed by most investigators. Similarly, correlation between aneuploidy and average to fast proliferative rate seems also to be a sound conclusion.

Lastly, in our slow grasp of the dynamics of breast cancer, a substantial number of investigators over the last several decades have measured tumor volume doubling time (35,36,37,38,39,40). This has been done more often in the clinical setting of advanced disease but more recently using tumor diameter measurements in serially obtained mammograms (41,42,43). To this body of information, the traditional and the dynamic data banks are in the process of being blended. The conclusions are best seen in graphic form (Figure 1). It is worth emphasizing that a new form of breast cancer is now identifiable. This more contemporary form of the disease is a particularly indolent, slow growing type that is typically discovered mammographically and now constitutes as much as 30% of all currently diagnosed breast cancers (44).

V. SURVIVAL CURVES DO NOT INDICATE BREAST CANCER IS ACTUARIALLY CURABLE

With all of the foregoing in mind, the survival curves of breast cancer published over the last half century begin to make more sense, especially the basis for the apparent improvement. The shape of a survival curve is mathematically dependent on the range and average of doubling times observed in a type of cancer.

Some confounding of this data is clearly related to the increased use of cytoreductive chemotherapy and/or endocrine manipulation in lengthening life after the diagnosis of metastatic disease. In earlier years this life extension owing to systemic treatment would have been even more modest than it is now, attributed only to oophorectomy, adrenalectomy, hypophysectomy and radiation therapy.

Even with the impact of modern therapy on breast cancer survival, is the invasive form of the disease truly curable? The answer has to be no. The negative slope of relative survival curves reflect the inexorable thrust of breast cancer mortality (4,45,46). Death due to breast cancer is obviously at times delayed for years by slow growth of metastases. Even without chemotherapy or tamoxifen, spontaneous menopause in women, pre-menopausal at time of diagnosis with an estrogen receptor positive, progesterone receptor positive tumor would serve to reduce tumor burden and lengthen life. Indeed, a one log drop in tumor cell number results in a prolongation of life that is 3.33 doubling times of the specific tumor. An example would be a two log drop (99% cytoreduction) of a tumor with a doubling time of 180 days; this would extend life as follows: $2 \times 3.33 = 6.67 \times$ six months $= 40$ months or 3 1/3 years.

It should be emphasized that an important role of chemotherapy in pre-menopausal women is the reduction in ovarian estrogen production. The separation of purely cytotoxic related diminution in metastatic tumor burden from the regression caused by clinical oophorectomy is not, however, easily computed. Inference drawn from the much reduced effect of chemotherapy in postmenopausal women is a probable important clue that the direct anti-tumor of chemotherapy is usually not great, estimated at no more than a 99% cell kill or 2 log drop on average (47,48,49).

VI. CONCLUSION

The conclusion that seems most appropriate is that invasive breast cancer is not curable in a strict actuarial sense. The survival of women after a diagnosis of breast cancer can be entirely accounted for by the growth rate of the metastatic process, the cytoreductive effect of systemic treatment, the age of the patient at diagnosis and presence or absence of competing illness (50,51,52). Added to this list must now be the inclusion of large numbers of women in the breast cancer data base who have tumors that are very slow growing. Follow up of breast cancer patients will now therefore produce survival curves that seem significantly improved over the past. In fact, we are fearfully measuring the rising incidence of breast cancer that is not being accompanied by a corresponding rise in mortality. We are in the midst of the evolution of an epidemic that has much less dire consequences than the term implies. Only through our failing to distinguish between "old and bad" versus "new and not so bad" breast cancer, even though we have the technological capability to do so, do we do a disservice to our patients and to professionals who have to deal with this issue in malpractice actions.

The range of tumor doubling times in breast cancer is seen in Figure 10-8. Computation of doubling time requires reasonably accurate serial measurements of tumor diameters with a minimum of one month between observations. Clearly more than one set of observations over longer intervals of time enhances accuracy. Prior to the advent of CT and MRI, the preponderance of cases found suitable for measurements relied on sequential chest x-rays. Mastectomy site recurrences, osteolytic bone metastases or easily palpable superficial lymph nodes were occasionally adequate. Determinations made from these sources produced the first data bank with a range of doubling times, 30 to 300 with a mean of 90 days. It must be emphasized that these figures were derived from cases with advanced disease (35,36,37,38). The addition of data from other

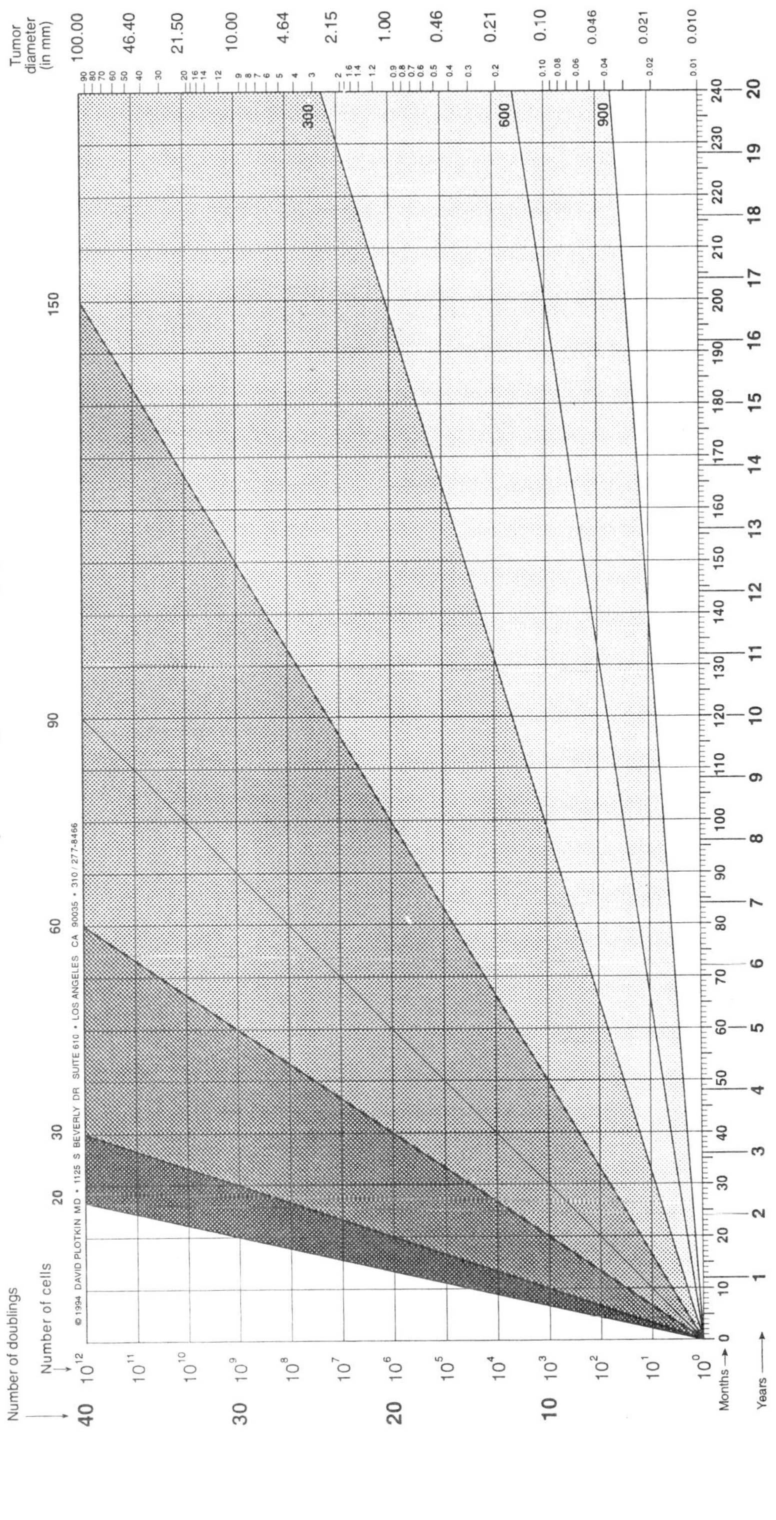

Figure 10-8. Range of Breast Cancer Doubling Times.

advanced cases in the last 10 years that included CT and/or MRI determinations did not significantly change the range or mean values (unpublished data).

In sharp contrast to breast cancer growth rate analysis from advanced disease are data computed from serial mammographic measurements. The number of publications in this area are fewer than the older reports of advanced disease but the numbers of patients per publication are generally quite a bit larger (41, 42,43,44). Of greatest importance is the fact that the range of doubling times has expanded, especially at the long doubling time end of the scale.

Based on mammography, the range of tumor doubling time has been reported as from 10 days to 5000 days, with a mean value of

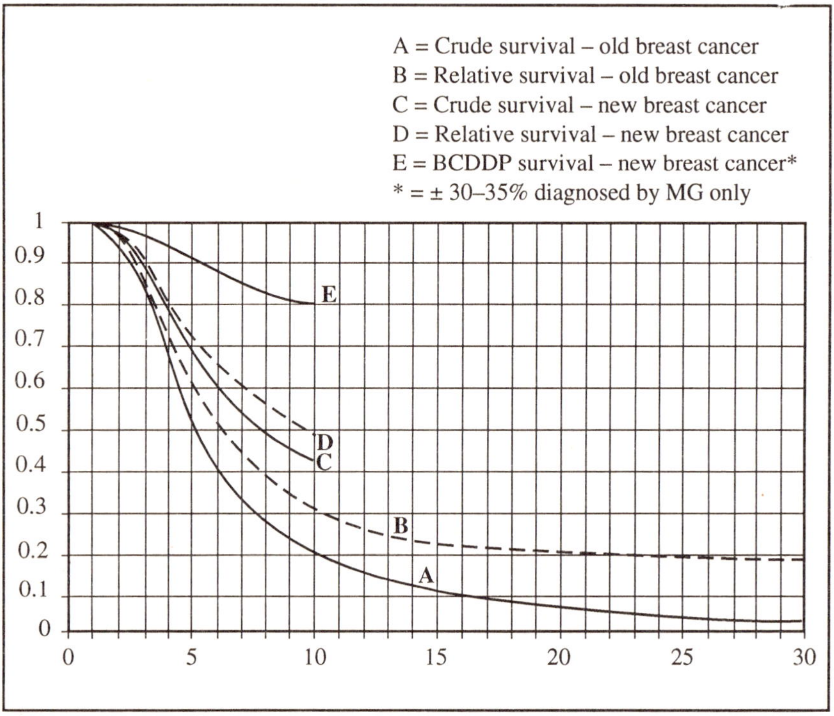

Figure 10-9. Breast Cancer Survival.

260 days. This required the addition of a new category of breast cancer growth rate, i.e., very indolent or very slow growing cancer.

With a distribution of doubling times that essentially adds a new compartment, i.e., very indolent or very slow growing disease, it is mathematically deducible that the shape of a survival curve including such cases must be different from a curve describing breast cancer survival derived from data of 25 to 50 years ago (6,7).

The difference in the slope of curves describing breast cancer survival of 50 to 25 years ago with studies of the last 25 years appears to be a function of the admixture of "old" breast cancer, diagnosed by palpation only, with "new" breast cancer in which about one-third of cases are diagnosed by mammography only, i.e., the tumor is non-palpable.

A rational basis for estimating the time at which the primary tumor invades lymphatics and/or capillaries requires acknowledgment that breast cancer of this type has progressed beyond the in situ phase of the disease and is frankly invasive. In most patients with surgical pathology stage 2 breast cancer, the diameter of metastatic deposits in regional axillary lymph nodes provides unequivocal evidence of this phenomenon. Such metastatic foci can be measured assuming that the microtome cut in the preparation of slides was at the center of the spheroidal deposit. The number of tumor cells in the metastasis, of average 10 micron diameter, can then be readily computed. If the microtome slices through the tumor nodule off to one side or the other of its center, the computation of tumor cell number based on a spuriously small diameter would be falsely low. Therefore, based only on what is actually seen and measurable in the metastatic deposit are computations made. We can then proceed with our graphic analysis but only after a crucial element of the calculation is accepted. The slope of the growth curve, whether of the primary or a metastasis, has to be placed into one of the four possible categories of growth rate from fast to very slow. This estimate of growth rate must be consistent with the observed degree of differentiation and one or another measure of proliferative rate, S-phase index, PCNA or Ki-67 (4). This then permits an extrapolation back to the horizontal baseline coordinate of a semi-log plot. If the primary tumor has been similarly plotted

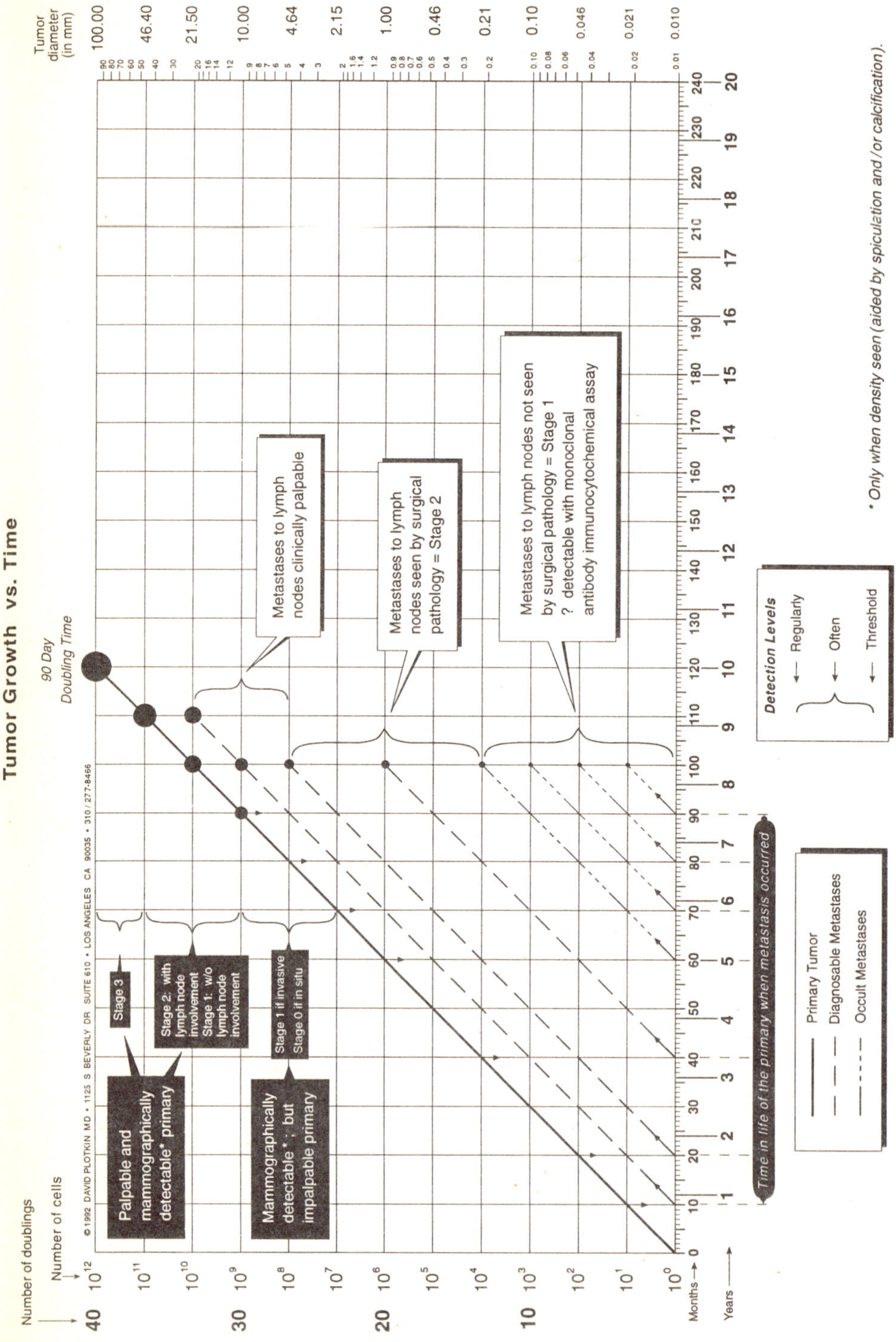

Figure 10-10. Diagnosis of Primary and Metastatic Breast Cancer.

from its origin as one cell to its size at time of excision, the interval of time between the beginning of the primary and the inception point of metastases can be measured. Moreover, the size of the primary at the time of metastases can be rationally estimated and a determination of its diagnosability can also be made. Clearly, if the metastatic process begins when the primary is less than 1 mm in diameter, one million cells, but rather typically when it is 0.1 mm in diameter or 1000 cells, well below even the most sensitive mammographic technique, then a subsequent delay, real or imagined, in diagnosing the tumor after it has reached a palpable level of 10 mm in diameter or one billion cells, becomes moot.

In the above figure, it can also be seen that our detection of lymph node metastases progresses from gross clinical to gross surgical pathology to microscopic pathology to finally the research method using immunocytochemical techniques requiring monoclonal antibodies (53,54). The key lesson here is that as our technology has improved, previously undetected metastatic disease has become demonstratable.

There has been much discussion of the consistency of tumor doubling time over time. A deceleration of growth rate, whether due to Gompertzian effect or some other alteration of unweighted exponential growth has been elegantly discussed by Spratt (55). It should be emphasized that the deceleration phenomenon seems only to apply in practical terms to tumors with slow to very slow growth rates. The tumors whose doubling times have been computed from advanced disease exhibit deceleration only as a terminal event, if at all. It appears that human tolerance of rapidly growing malignancies is so poor that death ensues before the cancer growth rate can be significantly affected.

One of the more puzzling aspects of primary breast cancer diagnosis is seen in Figure 10-11. A strikingly large tumor is suddenly discovered by a perfectly competent clinician who has repeatedly examined the patient for the preceding 12-24 months and has not recommended a biopsy. The startling "new" finding that finally evokes an invasive reponse suggests either a very rapidly growing cancer or negligence on the part of the attending physician for failure to recognize the presence of a slow or average growth rate

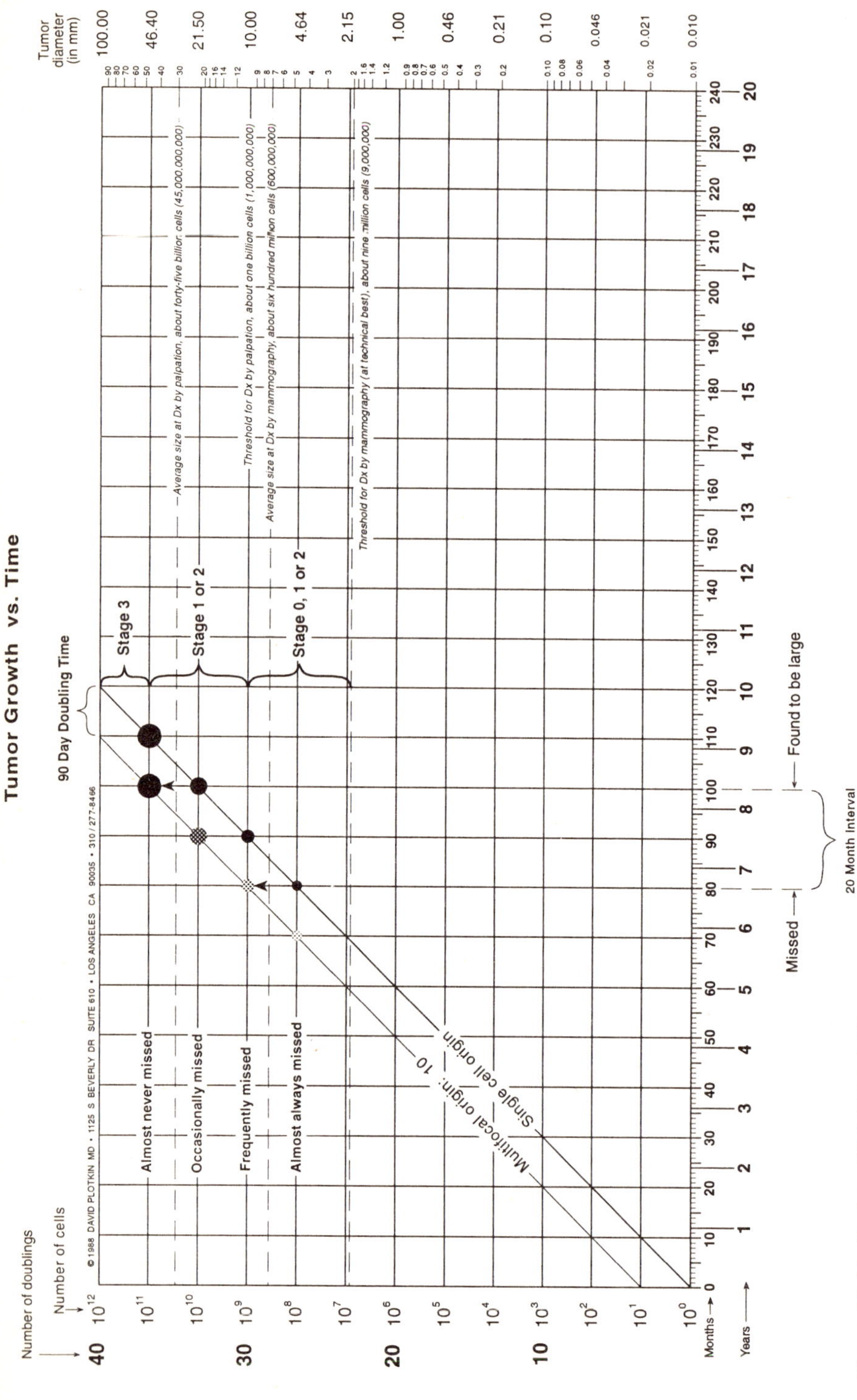

Figure 10-11. Fusion of Multifocal Sites.

tumor. An examination of the type of cancer and the patient's subsequent clinical course provide the explanation. Some cancers do grow very rapidly. They are uniformly poorly differentiated with a high mitotic count and numerous foci of necrosis. Their DNA histograms reveal high SPI's although when aneuploid, as they often are, rendering SPI measurement technically impossible, other estimates of proliferative rate like PCNA, or Ki-67 are employed to reveal their kinetic virulence. ER and PR are typically negative (56,57). The patient's subsequent rapid downhill course invariably confirms the inference drawn from the pathology, DNA and other studies.

On the other hand, and occurring far more frequently than the preceding example, the pathology, DNA examinations, ER and PR determinations and subsequent course of the patient are consistent with a relatively slow growing or at least average growth rate cancer with a correspondingly better prognosis than would be expected from the tumor size at time of diagnosis. The most plausible explanation of this phenomenon is seen in the figure by noting that when there are 10 multifocal, more or less simultaneous, origins of cancer, these initially separate lesions eventually fuse into a large one. No case will be made to insist on 10 multifocal points as a magic number opposed to 20, 40 or a 100. The graphic serves only to show how even 10 sites can, and probably do, contribute to confusion on the part of clinicians, patients, and atttorneys in attempting to understand how a large primary tumor could have been missed. This is confounded further by the demonstration of relatively lesser malevolent pathology, and a subsequent clinical course that fits the kinetics of the tumor but not its large size at diagnosis. The only rational explanation of this not infrequently observed phenomenon virtually requires a fusion of multicentric sites. The frequency of multifocality or multicentricity in breast cancer is well documented elsewhere (56).

Table 1 Major Mammographic Screening Studies

Randomized Studies	Dates of Enrollment	Ages	Study Group	Control Group	Mammographic Screening Interval	Follow-up Clinical Breast Exam (CBE)	Decrease in Breast Cancer Mortality	Comments
H.I.P	1963-1969	40-64	30,239	30,756	1 yr x 4 (2 views)	1 yr x 4	30% significant (p<0.05) after 5 years of F/U	#1
WE Trial	1977 -	40-74	78,085	56,782	2 - 3 yr x (3-4) (1 view)	none	31% significant (p<0.05) after 4 years of F/U	#2
Malmö	1977 -	45-69	21,088	21,195	1.5 - 2 yr x 5 (1 view)	none	20% age > 55 years not significant after 9 yrs of F/U	
Edinburgh	1979 -	45-65	23,226	21,904	1, 3, 5, 7 yrs (1 view)	1 yr x 7	20 % not significant after 7 years of F/U	
Canada	1980-1985	40-59	44,925	44,910	1 yr x 5 (2 views)	1 yr x 5	none after 7 years of F/U	
United Kingdom	1979 -	45-64	109,477	127,117	2 years (1 view)	1 exam/yr	none after 7 years of F/U	
Stockholm	1981 -	40-64	40,000	20,000	28 mos (1 view)	none	none after 7 years of F/U	

Comments:

#1 Study group deaths—147 versus control group deaths—193 after 10 years follow-up. Of the 147 study deaths, 100 occurred in the screene accepted group (20,200 women), 47 occurred in the screened-refused group (10,000 women).

#2 Three times the number of women screened to avoid one breast cancer death as compared to H.I.P.

References

1. Betsil WL Jr, Rosen PP, Lieberman PH, et al. Intraductal Carcinoma. Long-Term Follow-Up After Treatment by Biopsy Alone. JAMA 239:1863-1867, 1978.
2. Page DI, DuPont WD, Rogers LW, et al. Intraductal Carcinoma of the Breast: Follow-Up After Biopsy Only. Cancer 49:751-758, 1982.
3. Farrow JH. Current Concepts in the Detection and Treatment of the Earliest of the Early Breast Cancers. Cancer 25:468-477, 1970.
4. Plotkin D, Blankenberg FG. Breast Cancer—Biology and Malpractice. American Journal of Clinical Oncology 14(3):254-266, 1991.
5. Merriam Webster's Collegiate Dictionary, Tenth Edition. Merriam-Webster, Inc. Springfield, Massachusetts, 1994.
6. Cutler SJ. A Description of the Force of Mortality Associated With Cancer. In Denoix P, Rouquette C, eds. Symposium on the Prognosis of Malignant Tumors of the Breast. Hafner Publishing Co, New York 1963.
7. Berkson J, Harrington SW, Clagett OT, et al. Mortality and Survival in Surgically Treated Cancer of the Breast. A Statistical Summary of Some Experience of the Mayo Clinic. Proc. Staff Meet. Mayo Clinic 32:645, 1957.
8. Haybittle JL. Is Breast Cancer Ever Cured? Endocrine Related Cancer 14:13-18, 1983.
9. Adair F, Berg J, Joubert L, Robbins GF. Long-Term Follow-Up of Breast Cancer Patients: The 30-Year Report. Cancer 33:1145-50, 1974.
10. Koscielny S, Tubiana M, Le MG, et al. Breast Cancer: Relationship Between the Size of the Primary Tumor and the Probability of Metastatic Dissemination. British Journal of Cancer 49:709-715, 1984.
11. Donegan WL. Staging and Primary Treatment. In: Donegan WL, Spratt JS, eds. Cancer of the Breast, 3rd Ed. Philadelphia: W.B. Saunders, 1988:336-402.
12. Fisher B, Bauer M, Wickerham DL, Redmond CK, Fisher ER. Relation of Number of Positive Axillary Nodes to the Progno-

sis of Patients with Primary Breast Cancer: An NSABP Update. Cancer 52:1551-1557, 1983.

13. Carter CL, Allen C, Henson DE. Relation of Tumor Size, Lymph Node Status and Survival in 24,740 Breast Cancer Cases. Cancer 63:181-187, 1989.
14. Harris JR, Lippman ME, Veronesi V, Willett W. Breast Cancer (first of three parts). NEJM 375(5); 319-328, 1992.
15. Tabar L, Gad A, Holmberg LH. Reduction in Mortality From Breast Cancer After Mass Screening With Mammography. Lancet 1:829-32, 1985.
16. Shapiro S, Venet W, Strax P, Venet L. Selection, Follow-Up and Analysis in the Health Insurance Plan Study: A Randomized Trial With Breast Cancer Screening. In Garfinkel L, Ochs O, eds. Selection, follow-up and analysis in prospective studies: A workshop. NIH Publication 85-2713; National Cancer Institute Monograph 67. Washington, D.C.: Department of Health and Human Services, Public Health Service, 1985.
17. Miller AB, Baines CJ, To T, Wall C. Canadian National Breast Screening Study: 1. Breast Cancer Detection and Death Rates Among Women Aged 40 to 49 Years. Canadian Medical Association Journal 147(10); 1459-1476, 1992.
18. Miller AB, Baines CJ, To T, Wall C. Canadian National Breast Screening Study: 2. Breast Cancer Detection and Death Rates Among Women Aged 50 to 59 Years. Canadian Medical Association Journal 147(10); 1477-1488, 1992.
19. Baines CJ, Miller AB, Kopans DB, Moskowitz M, Sanders DE, Sickles EA, To T, Wall, C. Canadian National Breast Screening Study: Assessment of Technical Quality by External Review. AJR 155:743-747, 1990.
20. Kopans D. The Canadian Screening Program: A Different Perspective. AJR 155:748-750, 1990.
21. Miller AB, Baines CJ, Sickles EA. Canadian National Breast Screening Study. (Letter) AJR: 1133-1134, 1990.
22. Merz B. Author of Canadian Breast Cancer Study Retracts Warnings. JNCI 84:832-834, 1992.
23. Babinski ASH. The Canadian National Breast Screening Study: Opportunity for a Rethink. Canadian Medical Association Journal 147(10); 1431-1434, 1992.

24. Starreveld AA. The Canadian National Breast Screening Study: A Clinician's Perspective. Canadian Medical Association Journal 147(10); 1437-1439, 1992.
25. Wright CJ. Breast Cancer Screening: A Different Look at the Evidence. Surgery 100:594-598, 1986.
26. Early Breast Cancer Trialists' Collaborative Group. Systemic Treatment of Early Breast Cancer by Hormonal, Cytotoxic, or Immune Therapy. Lancet 339:1-15, 1992.
27. Skrabanek P. The Other Side of the Story. BMJ 297:971-972, 1988.
28. Bailar JC, Smith EM. Progress Against Cancer? NEJM 314:1226-1232, 1986.
29. Cairns J. The Treatment of Disease and the War Against Cancer. Scientific American 253(5):51-59, 1985.
30. Page DL, Anderson TJ. Diagnostic Histopathology of the Breast. Edinburgh: Churchill Livingstone, 1987.
31. Le Doussal V, Tubiana-Hulin M, Friedman S, Hacene K, Spyratos F, Brunet M. Prognostic Value of Histologic Grade Nuclear Components of Scarff-Bloom Richardson (SBR): An Improved Score Modification Based on Multivariate Analysis of 1262 Invasive Ductal Breast Carcinomas. Cancer 64:1914-1921, 1989.
32. Meyer JS, Hixon B. Advanced Stage and Early Relapse of Breast Carcinomas Associated With High Thymidine Labeling Indices. Cancer Research 39:4042-4047, 1979.
33. Coon JS, Landay AL, Weinstein RS. Biology of Disease: Advances in Flow Cytometry for Diagnostic Pathology. Laboratory Investigation 57(5):453-479, 1987.
34. Fallenius AG, Franzen SA, Auer GU. Predictive Value of Nuclear DNA Content in Breast Cancer in Relation to Clinical and Morphologic Factors. Cancer 62:521-530, 1988.
35. Lee YTN, Spratt JR. Rate of Growth of Soft Tissue Metastases of Breast Cancer. Cancer 29:344-348, 1972.
36. Kusama S, Spratt JS, Donegan WL, Watson FR, Cunningham C. The Gross Rates of Growth of Human Mammary Carcinoma. Cancer 30:594, 1972.
37. Perlman AW. Breast Cancer—Influence of Growth Rate on Prognosis and Treatment Evaluation. Cancer 38:1826-1833, 1976.

38. Spratt JS, Spratt JA. Growth rates. In: Donegan WL, Spratt JS, eds. Cancer of the Breast 3rd. ed. Philadelphia: W.B. Saunders, 1988;270-302.
39. Lundgren B. Observations on Growth Rates of Breast Carcinomas and its Possible Implications for Lead Time. Cancer 40:1722-1725, 1977.
40. Heuser L, Spratt JS, Polk HC. Growth Rates of Primary Breast Cancers. Cancer 43:1888-1894, 1979.
41. Fournier DV, Schiller U, Junkermann H, Legler H, Baur M. Natural Growth Rate in 300 Primary Breast Carcinomas and Correlation to Hormone Factors. Annals NY Academy of Science 464:563-565, 1986.
42. Spratt JS, Spratt JA. Growth Rates and the Cytokinetic Behavior of Breast Cancer. In: Kubli F, Fournier DV, et al. Breast diseases. Berlin: Springer-Verlag, 1989; 97-110.
43. Kuroishi T, Tominga S, Morimoto T, et al. Tumor Growth Rate and Prognosis of Breast Cancer Mainly Detected by Mass Screening. Jpn. J. Cancer Research 81(5):454-462, 1990.
44. Baker LH. Breast Cancer Detection Demonstration Project: Five-year Summary Report. Ca-A Cancer Journal for Clinicians 32(4), 1982.
45. Brinkley D, Haybittle JL. Long-Term Survival of Women With Breast Cancer. Lancet 1:1118, 1984.
46. Rutqvist LE, Wallgren A. Long-Term Survival of 458 Young Breast Cancer Patients. Cancer 55:658-65, 1985.
47. Henderson IC. Adjuvant Systemic Therapy of Early Breast Cancer. In: Harris JR, Hellman S, Henderson IC, Kinne DW, eds. Breast Diseases. Philadelphia: J.B. Lippincott, 1987; 428-79.
48. Henderson IC. Chemotherapy for Advanced Breast Disease. In: Harris JR, Hellman S, Henderson IC, Kinne DW, eds. Breast Diseases. Philadelphia: J.B. Lipppincott, 1987; 428-79.
49. Glick J. Commentary: Meeting Highlights: Adjuvant Therapy for Breast Cancer. JNCI 80:471-475, 1988.
50. Mueller CB, Ames F, Anderson GD. Breast Cancer in 3,558 Women: Age as a Significant Determination in the Rate of Dying and Causes of Death. Surgery 83:123-32, 1978.
51. Rutqvist LE, Wallgren A, Nilsson BO. Is Breast Cancer a Curable Disease? A Study of 14,731 Women with Breast

Cancer From the Cancer Registry of Norway. Cancer 53: 1793-1800, 1984.

52. Langlands AO, Pocock SJ, Kerr GR, Grove SM. Long-Term Survival of Patients With Breast Cancer: A Study of the Curability of the Disease. British Med J 2:1247-1251, 1979.
53. Trojani M, de Mascarel I, Bonichon F, Coindre JM, Dilsol G. Micrometastases to Axillary Lymph Nodes From Carcinoma of the Breast. Detection by Immunohistochemistry and Prognostic Influence. British Journal of Cancer 55:303-306, 1987.
54. International (Ludwig) Breast Cancer Study Group. Prognostic Importance of Occult Axillary Lymph Node Micrometastases From Breast Cancers. Lancet 335:1565-1568, 1990.
55. Spratt JS, von Fournier D, Spratt JA, Weber EE. Decelerating Growth and Human Breast Cancer. Cancer 71(6):2013-2019, 1993.
56. Mittra I, MacRae KD. A Meta-Analysis of Reported Correlations Between Prognostic Factors in Breast Cancer: Does Axillary Lymph Node Metastasis Represent Biology or Chronology? Eur J Cancer 27(12):1574-1583, 1991.
57. Jensen HM. Breast Pathology, Emphasizing Precancerous and Cancer-Associated Lesions. In: Bulbrook RD, Taylor DJ, eds. Commentaries on Research in Breast Disease Vol. 2. New York: Alan R. Liss, Inc., 1981.

CHAPTER 11: TUMOR SIZE

CHAPTER 11

TUMOR SIZE

§11.01 INTRODUCTION

The plaintiff will attempt to prove delay of diagnosis with loss of chance for cure by exhibiting statistics, charts, and graphs that demonstrate a correlation between tumor size and the frequency of axillary lymph node metastases and the survival rate of breast cancer. These data are misleading and there are many exceptions. When the plaintiff talks of survival he/she is usually considering a five year survival rather a 10, 15, 20 or 30 year survival.

§11.02 TUMOR SIZE DOES NOT ALWAYS CORRELATE WITH SURVIVAL

Tumor size does correlate with prognosis, but there are many exceptions. For example:

[a] Some of the largest tumors are slow growing (have prolonged doubling times) and are slow to metastasize. Some of these large tumors have an excellent survival. Some may never metastasize. For these cancers, tumor size is meaningless.

[b] Some breast cancers do not have the ability to metastasize or do not have the ability to establish a viable metastasis. For these cancers, tumor size is meaningless.

[c] Some breast cancers metastasize before it is possible to detect the tumor by mammography. Again, for these cancers tumor size is meaningless.

[d] The symptomatic breast cancer. See §11.03.

§11.03 THE SYMPTOMATIC BREAST CANCER: IS TUMOR SIZE RELEVANT?

As discussed in Chapters 6-10, when a breast cancer becomes large enough to produce symptoms, it is a biologically old tumor. By this time the tumor cells with genetic instability will have undergone neoplastic progression and metastasis. Tumor cells with relatively stable DNA will not have undergone neoplastic progression and are not likely to do so during the short period of the remaining life cycle. When survival is measured from the onset of symptoms no one has ever proven that patient or physician delay in diagnosis will alter the outcome. Spratt (1) succinctly stated that when a breast cancer develops symptoms "The prognosis is either good or bad but it has been determined." Thus, by the time a breast cancer becomes large enough to produce symptoms the die has been cast. Tumor size is irrelevant.

§11.04 LARGE TUMOR SIZE DOES NOT ALWAYS INDICATE A DELAY IN DIAGNOSIS

Many assume that large tumor size indicates a delay in diagnosis. In some cases this may be true but more commonly large tumor size is secondary to:

[a] A Camouflage Problem

[1] Palpation A serious camouflaging problem will increase the threshold size of the average breast cancer to diameters of 2.0, 3.0, or even 4.0 cm. This is by no means unusual.

[2] Mammography Ten to eighteen percent of breast cancers cannot be visualized by mammography (2). Some clearly palpable

tumors cannot be detected by mammography (3). Donegan (4) evaluated 205 palpable breast cancers and found that 18% could not be visualized by mammography. Spratt, et al (5) state that 10-30% of breast cancers are not detected on screening mammograms.

[b] Short Tumor Doubling Times

The diameter of a rapidly growing tumor may easily double two to three times within a 12 months screening interval. The diameter of a tumor with a net cell doubling time of 60 days will double its diameter twice within 12 months. A tumor with a net cell doubling time of 40 days will double its diameter three times within a period of 12 months. Arnelov et al (6) calculated the doubling times of 158 breast cancers from serial mammograms and found that approximately 14% (1 in 7) had doubling times of 90 days or less.

§11.05 IT IS IMPOSSIBLE TO DETERMINE TUMOR SIZE 12 MONTHS PRIOR TO SURGERY

It is impossible to determine the size of a tumor 12 months prior to the time of diagnosis and treatment.

1. The growth rate of breast cancer varies from very slow to very fast and has been described as linear, exponential, deceleratory, or erratic (with periods of no growth, very slow growth or periods of very rapid growth). An estimate of the growth rate would be nothing more than conjecture. See §8.01[d].
2. Tumor size determined by the surgeon several days prior to surgery and the pathologist after surgery agree only 54% of the time. Tumor size determined by the surgeon and the radiologist agree only 39% of the time. See §18.02.

Thus it is apparent that calculating tumor size 12 months prior to surgery would at best be sheer speculation. See §18.06.

One of the reasons why retrospective studies fail to demonstrate that early diagnosis improves the survival rate of breast cancer is because of the group of rapidly growing aggressive breast cancers. The vast majority of investigators recognize the existence of these rapidly growing tumors that metastasize to distant sites early in their life cycle. Early diagnosis with currently available diagnostic modalities fails to cure these tumors.

§11.06 CONCLUSION

When the plaintiff speaks of survival, he/she talks of a 5 year survival, long-term survival at 10, 15, 25 years is rarely, if ever considered. And, when the value of early diagnosis is promoted, the biology of the tumor is ignored. It is nice to know tumor size, but the biology of the tumor is far more imporant. Once a breast cancer has become large enough to produce symptoms, tumor size is not relevant. Neither patient nor physician delay will alter the outcome of symptomatic breast cancers when survival is measured from the onset of symptoms.

References

1. Spratt JS. Realities of Breast Cancer Control, Public Expectation, and the Law. Surg Oncol Clin N Am. 3(1): 25-34, 1994.
2. Bassett LW, Manjikian Viken III, and Gold R. Mammography and Breast Cancer Screening. Surg. Clin. N. Am. 70(4):775-800, 1990.
3. Mann BD, Guiliano AE, and Bassett LW, et al. Delayed Diagnosis of Breast Cancer as a Result of Normal Mammograms. Arch. Surg. 118:23, 1983.
4. Donegan WL. Current Concepts: Evaluation of a Palpable Breast Mass. New Eng J Med 327(13):937-942, 1992.
5. Spratt JA, Fournier D von, Spratt JS, and Weber EE. Mammographic Assessment of Human Breast Cancer Growth and Duration. Cancer 71:2020-2026, 1993.
6. Arnerlov C, Emdin SO, Lundgren B, et al. Breast Carcinoma Growth Rate Described by Mammographic Doubling Time and S-phase Fraction. Cancer 70:1928-1934, 1992.

CHAPTER 12: LYMPH NODE STATUS: CLINICAL SIGNIFICANCE

CHAPTER 12

LYMPH NODE STATUS: CLINICAL SIGNIFICANCE

§12.01 INTRODUCTION

The presence of axillary lymph node metastasis has important clinical and biologic significance. The absence of lymph node metastasis suggests that the tumor lacked the ability to metastasize (a few can bypass the axillary lymph nodes and metastasize to the mediastinal lymph node or via the blood to distant sites). Conversely, the presence of axillary lymph node metastasis proves that the plaintiff's breast cancer was aggressive and had acquired the ability to metastasize. It also tells us that the plaintiff also had distant metastases at the time of surgery. Most women (70%) with lymph node metastases will die within 10 years. Only those with a powerful immune system or a tumor with a long doubling time will have a prolonged survival. See below.

§12.02 THE LYMPHATIC AND VASCULAR SYSTEMS ARE INTERRELATED

The lymphatic system and the vascular system are so interrelated that they are essentially two parts of one system (1). The lymphatic system not only drains into the blood stream but there are numerous lymphovenous communications between the two systems. Tumor cells in the lymph can easily gain entrance into the blood stream and tumor cells from the blood can readily gain access to the lymphatic system. For example, the vast majority of women with axillary node metastases have systemic disease. Seventy percent of women with axillary nodal metastases will die of breast cancer within 10 years. Some are of the opinion that those who survive, do so because of an effective immune system.

§12.03 THE PRINCIPAL FUNCTON OF A LYMPH NODE IS BIOLOGICAL RATHER THAN MECHANICAL

Formerly it was thought that the lymph nodes primarily functioned as a mechanical barrier or filter for cancer cells escaping from the breast via the lymphatics. Now most agree that the principal function of the lymph node is biological (1). Experimental evidence suggests that immune factors (cytotoxic cells) within or generated by the lymph nodes can destroy cancer cells within the lymph node. For example: the National Surgical Adjuvant Breast Project (NSABP-04, 1971) conducted a prospective randomized study of over 1,700 women with primary breast cancer and with no clinical evidence of axillary metastases. The women were divided into three different treatment groups:

1. Radical mastectomy (axillary lymph nodes were removed)
2. Total mastectomy with irradiation to the axilla
3. Total mastectomy with no immediate treatment of the axilla. The axillary nodes were removed only if clinical metastases occurred.

Interestingly, survival of these three disparate treatment groups was not significantly different. We know, from the radical mastectomy group, that 40% of these 1700 women did have positive nodes. And since this was a prospective randomized study, we know that 40% of the women who had a total mastectomy without axillary dissection also had axillary metastases. However, only 16% of the women who had no treatment of any kind to the axilla developed evidence of axillary metastasis within 10 years. Thus 60% of the axillary metastases in the observed group must have been destroyed or controlled by the immune system. Other studies have demonstrated that women with axillary metastases less than 2 mm in diameter do as well as women with negative lymph nodes (2).

§12.04 CLINICAL SIGNIFICANCE OF A NEGATIVE AXILLARY LYMPH NODE

There are several possibilities that explain why an axillary lymph node would be negative.

a. The tumor did not have the ability to metastasize to the regional lymph nodes.
b. Fisher and his colleagues (1) have demonstsrated that tumor cells can easily pass unscathed through the lymph node and enter the efferent lymph channels. Once in the efferent lymph channels they can easily gain access to the blood stream via the thoracic duct, the right lymphatic duct or through the numerous lympho-venous communications that exist throughout the lymphatic system. Thirty percent of women with negative axillary lymph nodes have distant metastases.
c. Carcinomas arising in the medial breast often metastasize to the internal mammary nodes. Thus the absence of metastases to the axilla does not exclude the possibility of lymphatic metastases.
d. The lymph node may contain no cancer cells because the woman has an effective host-tumor relationship. A powerful immune system may have destroyed or controlled the tumor cells that escaped and lodged in the lymph node.
e. Some occult tumor cells have become dormant because of a strong immune system. These tumor cells may remain dormant for long periods of time only to become activated and regain their lethal potential when, for some reason, the host's immune system becomes impaired (1).
f. Seventy percent of these women will survive for at least 10 years.

§12.05 CLINICAL SIGNIFICANCE OF A POSITIVE AXILLARY LYMPH NODE

a. A lymph node metastasis that is larger than 2 mm indicates that there is a poor host-tumor relationship. That is, the metastatic power of the tumor has overcome the immune resistence of the host (2).
b. Because of the interrelationship of the lymphatic and the vascular system, the presence of lymph node metastases indicates the presence of systemic disease. Seventy percent of these women will be dead within 10 years. Thirty percent will survive. Some say this is because these women have effective immune systems.
c. The tumor had the ability to metastasize to the regional lymph nodes. Not all tumors possess this ability, as we shall see in Chapter 13.

§12.06 CONCLUSION

The presence or absence of axillary lymph node metastases is the most powerful indicator of the prognosis of breast cancer. Metastasis to the axilla is not a time related event; it proves that this tumor possessed the ability to metastsize, not only to the axillary lymph nodes, but also to distant sites as well. Metastasis to the axilla is not an indication of a delay in diagnosis. It is proof that we are dealing with a biologically aggressive breast cancer. (See Chapter 13).

References

1. Fisher, Bernard. A Commentary on the Role of the Surgeon in Primary Breast Cancer. Breast Cancer Research and Treatment. 1:17-26, 1981.
2. Fisher ER. The Impact of Pathology on the Biologic, Diagnostic, Prognostic, and Therapeutic Considerations in Breast Cancer. Surg Clin N Am. 64(6):1073-1093, 1984.

CHAPTER 13: AXILLARY NODE METASTASES: DELAY IN DIAGNOSIS?

CHAPTER 13

AXILLARY NODE METASTASES: DELAY IN DIAGNOSIS?

§13.01 INTRODUCTION: STAGES DEFINED

For the sake of simplicity, in this chapter, we will define Stage I and Stage II breast cancer as follows:

Stage I --- Axillary lymph nodes negative.
Stage II -- Axillary lymph nodes positive.

The thought that the presence of axillary metastases indicates a delay in diagnosis is one of the common myths held by the general public. That is:

an early diagnsis = cure
late diagnosis = no cure.

Everyone is aware that the life cycle of all living things evolves around a series of predictable time-related events. We understand that when a seed is planted, in time it sprouts, matures, bears fruit, the seed matures, the plant withers, and finally dies. It is not surprising that the public assumes that all breast cancers are alike and that the events in the life cycle of a breast cancer, like the plant, are also predictable and time-related.

§13.02 PRESENCE OF AXILLARY METASTASES DOES NOT INDICATE A DELAY IN DIAGNOSIS

Mueller (1) has addressed this problem with the following statement:

> "Conventional wisdom holds that development, growth, and progression of breast cancer are a linear function, commencing with a small lesion in the breast, which enlarges and progresses to axillary lymph nodes and, ultimately, to distant sites."

Thus conventional wisdom tells us that if a breast cancer is diagnosed early the regional lymph nodes will be negative. If the cancer is diagnosed later the tumor will have spread to the regional lymph nodes or worse to distant sites.

Susan Love (2) also focused on this problem when she testified before the Senate Committee on Labor and Human Resources June, 1991 in Washington DC. Dr Love stated (2):

> "We have spent a lot of time, energy, and money touting 'early detection' and presenting it as if it were the answer. Unfortunately, we have misrepresented the situation through wishful thinking or just an attempt at simplification. We have acted as if all tumors go through progression from 1 cm. to 2 cm. and on and as if all tumors have the potential to be detected at a small size and therefore could be cured. Would that were true. What we are dealing with is a combination of a tumor and an immune system. Some tumors are very aggressive and will have spread before they are palpable. Thirty percent of nonpalpable tumors are found to have positive lymph nodes. Some tumors are very slow growing and will not have spread even though they have reached a large size."

Dr Love, referring to the problem caused by "conventional wisdom" stated succinctly, "*Would that were true.* Certainly, if breast cancer did progress in an orderly and predictable series of events our problems would be less complex. Unfortunately conventional wisdom is not correct. The problem is not that simple."

In reality, the presence of metastases to the axillary lymph nodes is not necessarily an indication of a delay in diagnosis. The fact that the tumor has metastasized to the axillary lymph nodes is proof that its genes have been altered in such a fashion that they are now able to manufacture the angiogenic factors, powerful proteolytic enzymes, and adhesion molecules that are necessary for the successful invasion and spread of the tumor via the lymph channels and blood vessels.

> Practice Note
>
> Tumors that remain confined to the breast do so, not by accident, but because their genes have NOT been "switched on" or altered to give the tumor the full metastatic power necessary to metastasize to the regional nodes and/or distant sites.

§13.03 MUELLER PROVIDES EVIDENCE THAT STAGE II BREAST CANCER IS NOT A LATE STAGE I

Those seriously interested in this problem should consult C. Barber Mueller's excellent article (1) "Stage II breast cancer is not simply a late stage I." Mueller provides convincing evidence that tumors that metastasize to the axillary lymph nodes are different from those tumors that remain confined to the breast. He concludes that the presence of lymph node metastasis is not simply due to a delay in diagnosis. He presented the following evidence to support his contention:

Evidence That Stage II Breast Cancer is Not a Late Stage I

1. Annual Death Rate (1) *See* Figures 13-1 and 13-2, infra.

	NSABP (3)	Connecticut Tumor Registry (4)
Stage I	5%	4.7%
Stage II	9%	8.0%

2. Tumor Size (1,5)

Stage I	2.4 cm
Stage II	3.2 cm

3. Lymphatic Invasion (1,5)

Stage I	infrequent
Stage II	frequent

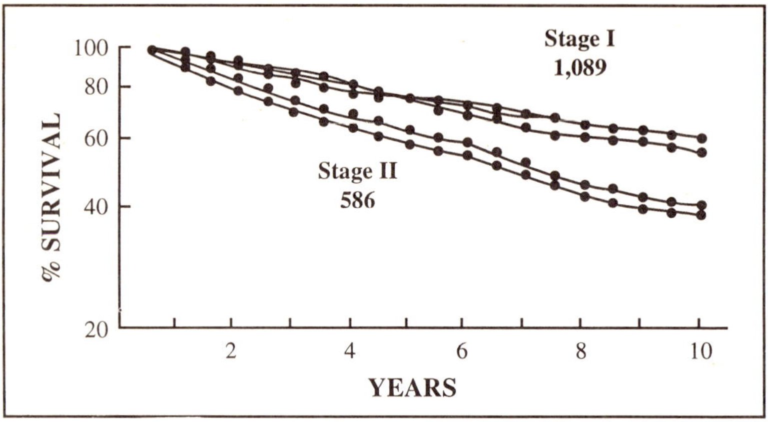

	Stage I	Stage II
T1/2 (Half death time)	12 Years	7.4%
Annual death rate	5%	9%

Figure 13-1. Survival Results from NSABP-BO4. Redrawn with additional derived data by Mueller CB. Stage II breast cancer is not simply a late Stage I. Surgery 104:631-638, 1988. Figure, 3 page 634. Reprinted courtesy of the author and publisher.

---

4. Local Recurrence (1)

Stage I infrequent
Stage II more common

5. Survival Curves (1) See Figure 13-3

a. If stage I and stage II tumors are members of a large homogeneous group of cancers, and
b. If stage II tumors (the dotted line) represent a late diagnosis of stage I tumors (the solid line), then
c. The survival curve of the node positive (dotted line) and the node negative curve (solid line) should continue on the same slope (should be parallel). They are not parallel (declining at the same rate).The annual death rate of the node positive group is almost twice that of the node negative group.

6. Errors Of Staging (1)

a. **Stage II breast cancers**—If the pathologist finds cancer in a lymph node he/she is rarely wrong. There should be no errors of this type.

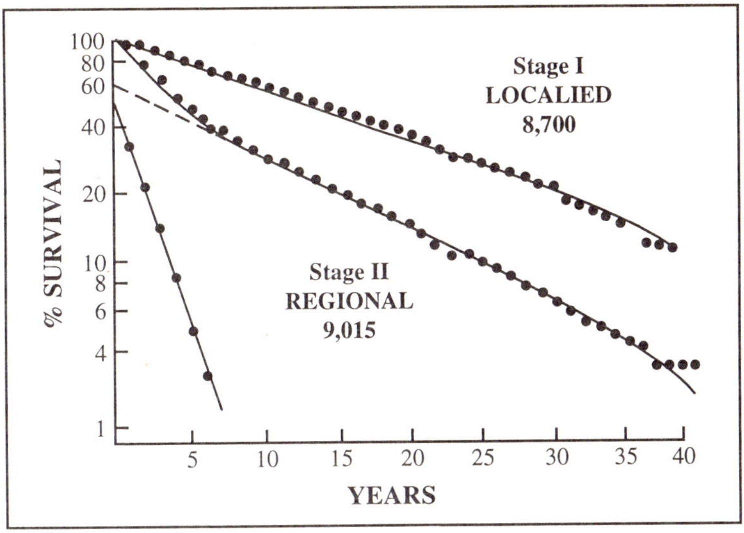

	Stage I	Stage II
T1/2 (Half death time)	11.8 years	8.54 years
Annual death rate	4.7%	8%

Figure 13-2. Survival Results Reported by the Connecticut Tumor Registry with Additional Derived Data by Mueller CB. Stage II breast cancer is not simply a late Stage I. Surgery 104:631-638, 1988. Figure 4 page 634. Reprinted courtesy of the author and publisher.

---

b. **Stage I breast cancers**—It is likely that some occult node metastases are overlooked by the pathologist. Removing these tumors with occult node metastases from the Stage I group would decrease the annual death rate of this group. Removing large medial lesions would have the same effect. Adding these tumors to the stage II group would not change the annual death rate of the node positive group. Thus errors of staging would increase the disparity of the annual death rates between these two groups. This would strengthen Mueller's contention that node positive breast cancers are biologically different from node negative breast cancers.

c. **Some stage I cancers unavoidably misclassified**—If stage I cancers consist of a group of so-called non-metastasizing tumors how can we explain the annual death rate of 4-5%? There are several reasons for this apparent anomaly:

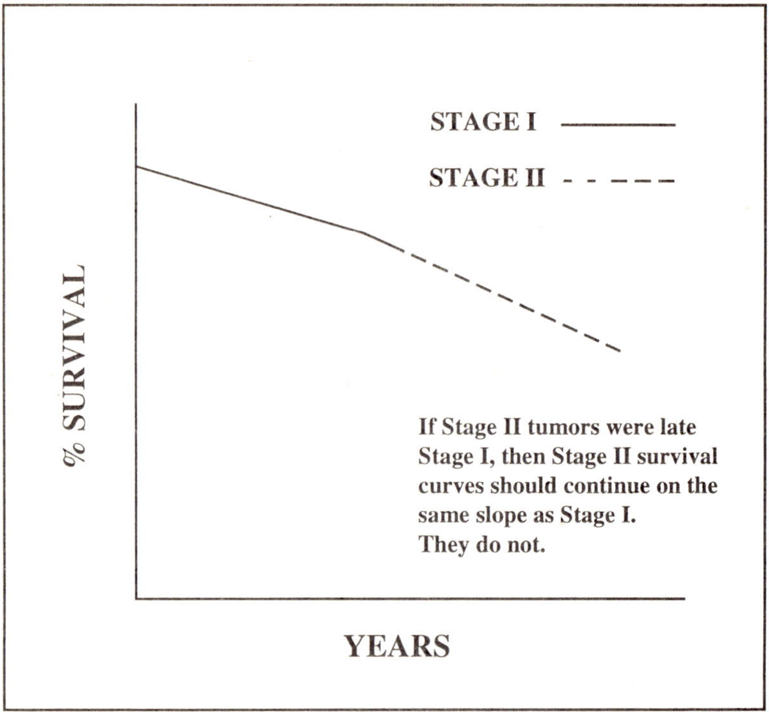

Figure 13-3. Stage II Breast Cancer is not Simply a Late I. (Redrawn from data derived from Figure 2 page 633 and Figures 3 and 4 page 634). Mueller CB. Stage II breast cancer is not simply a late Stage I. Surgery 104:631-638, 1988. Reprinted courtesy of the author and publisher.

---

1. The stage I group almost certainly contains a few stage II tumors whose nodal metastases were not detected.
2. Both groups are contaminated with a few early metastasizing breast cancers. Some of these cancers spread to distant sites without involving the regional lymph nodes.
3. Breast cancer is heterogeneous.

§13.04 CONCLUSION

There is powerful evidence that tumors that have metastasized to the regional lymph nodes or to distant sites are different from those tumors that remain confined to the breast. Additionally, the mere fact that these tumors have metastasized to the regional nodes proves that they have acquired the ability to manufacture the angiogenic factors, powerful proteolytic enzymes and adhesion molecules that are the basic requirements of successful invasion and metastasis.

Practice Note

Yes, node positive tumors are different, their genes function differently, they behave differently, and their mortality rates are different (70% vs 30%). The presence of axillary lymph node metastases is not an indication of a delay in diagnosis, rather it indicates the tumor possessed the ability to metastasize to the regional nodes via the lymphatics. Some tumors do not have this ability.

References

1. Mueller CB. Stage II Breast Cancer is Not Simply a Late Stage I. Surgery 104:631-638, 1988.
2. Love SM. quoted by Nancy Sharp, The Politics of Breast Cancer. Nursing Management. 22(9):24-28, 1991.
3. Fisher B, Fisher ER, Redmond C, et al. Ten Year Results From the National Surgical Adjuvant Breast and Bowel Project (NSABP) Clinical Trial Evaluating the Use of L-Phenylalanine Mustard (L-Pam) in the Management of Primary Breast Cancer. J Clin Oncol 4:929-941, 1986.
4. Metcalfe W. Accurate Representations, Comparisons and Predictions for Operable Breast Cancer. New York: Albert Einstein College of Medicine, 1981.
5. McDivitt RW, Stone KR, Craig RB, et al. A Proposed Classification of Breast Cancer Based on Kinetic Information. Cancer 57:269-276, 1986.

CHAPTER 14: THE CAMOUFLAGED TUMOR

CHAPTER 14

THE CAMOUFLAGED TUMOR

§14.01 INTRODUCTION

Since it has been well documented that when survival is measured from the onset of symptoms neither patient nor physician delay will alter outcome, why is it necessary to study tumor camouflaging? There are several reasons. First, negligence may be suspected when the clinician and/or radiologist is unable to detect a breast cancer until it attains a diameter of 2.0, 3.0, 4.0 cm or larger. Secondly, many have difficulty understanding why mammographers sometimes fail to image a clearly palpable breast cancer. Therefore, defense must understand the mechanism and significance of tumor camouflaging.

§14.02 GLOSSARY

[a] Tumor Camouflaging

The presence of some tumors is hidden or masked within the breast tissue in such a fashion that the tumors must grow longer and attain a larger diameter before they can be detected by mammography or palpation. In some cases, the tumor must attain a diameter of 3.0, 4.0, or even 5.0 cm before it can be identified. Some will never be detected by mammography.

Common causes of tumor camouflaging:

- dense breast
- density of breast and tumor similar

- vague tumor borders
- absence of tumor specific microcalcifications

[b] Threshold Size

The smallest size at which it is possible to detect a breast cancer by mammography and/or palpation. (See Chapter 15).

[c] Tumor Stroma

The benign tissue (connective tissue, blood vessels, fibrin-gel, inflamatory cells, etc.) in which the breast cancer cells are dispersed. The connective tissue provides scaffolding for the tumor cells. The blood vessels play an important role in nutrition, gas exchange and waste disposal for the cancer cells. Without stroma, breast cancers cannot grow beyond a diameter of 1.0-2.0 mm.

[d] Desmoplasia (Gr)

Defined as a band or ligament, refers to the formation of excess fibrous tissue. Excess production of fibrous tissue by the host is stimulated by proteins secreted by some cancer cells.

[e] Example of Tumor Camouflaging

Because of a family history of breast cancer both Nancy and Sue have been screened for breast cancer at six month intervals for the past three years. At the last screening examination Dr. ''A'' discovered a one centimeter cancer in Nancy's breast while Dr. ''B'' detected a three centimeter cancer in Sue's breast. Was Dr. ''A'' a more skillled diagnostician ? Not necessarily. Tumor camouflaging, rather than physician skill, determines the size at which most breast cancers can be detected.

§14.03 FREQUENCY OF TUMOR CAMOUFLAGING

Donegan (1) reported that 18% of 205 palpable tumors could not be visualized by mammography. Philip Strax (2) has stated that '' . . . it is generally agreed that up to 20% of cancers may not be apparent to the palpating fingers of even the most expert examiner.'' This impression is supported by studies of breast cancers detected only by mammograhpy and cancers detected soon after a negative clinical examination by an experienced clinician. The role of breast density in tumor camouflaging is illustrated by the fact that 74% of breast masses in the dense breasts of young women cannot be visualized by mammography (3). In the medical malpractice arena, significant tumor camouflaging is quite common. Studies of medical malpractice claims by the Physicians Insurers Association of America (PIAA) revealed that 68.2% of the mammograms were interpreted either as negative or equivocal [49.2% negative and 19% equivocal] (4). A 20-year Civil Court review of breast cancer litigation by Kern revealed that 80% of the mammograms were interpreted as normal (5). Mitneck (6) in a study of malpractice litigation in the state of New York reported that 37.5% of the mammograms were interpreted as normal.

The high incidence of ''false negative'' mammograms in breast cancers involved in malpractice litigation is secondary to selection bias. In the courtroom we are confronted with a group of women who have charged their physician with the failure to make a timely diagnosis of breast cancer. The inability of the mammographer to detect the cancers of 49 to 80% of these women indicates that we are dealing with a serious problem of tumor camouflaging. In a group of breast cancers with a high incidence of camouflaging, the mammographer may expect to encounter the following:

- A high incidence of ''false negative'' mammograms.
- Some mammographic shadows [of the breast cancers] will be so nebulous that they can be detected only in retrospect in serial mammograms. The inability to detect these lesions is not classifed as observer error by most mammographers.
- Some mammographic shadows [of the breast cancers] will be poorly defined and vague, secondary to similarites in the densities of the breast and tumor. Failure to detect these ill-defined shadows may be classified as observer error by many mammographers.
- Some breast cancers will be interval tumors.These rapidly growing, early metastasizing lesions, were not visible in the previous yearly screening mammograms because they were subthreshold in size [too small].

We classify these breast cancers as camouflaged tumors and realize that the degree of camouflaging can vary greatly. For example:

The Effect of Tumor Camouflaging on the Cancer Shadows in the Mammogram

Degree of Camouflaging	Mammographic Findings
100%	True false negative mammogram—* not considered radiologist error
80% +/-	Nebulous shadows seen in retrospect —should not be considered to be radiologist error
50-60% +/-	Ill defined shadows—observor error?

* Will include some cases of rapidly growing interval tumors that were too small to be visualized at the time of the previous screening examination. These should not be considered to be observor error.

§14.04 ROLE OF BREAST IN TUMOR CAMOUFLAGING

The breast itself contributes to the problem of tumor camouflaging. The density and consistency of the female breast, unlike most other solid organs in healthy individuals, varies strikingly from woman to woman. For example:

- High fat content [older women] --- breast soft, low density, and uniform in consistency.
- High glandular and fibrous tissure content [younger women] --- breast dense, firm, and rubbery.
- Irregular overgrowth of glandular, and/or fibrous tissue, and/or cyst formation --- breast diffusely or asymmetrically nodular.

The detectability of breast cancers varies from relatively easy [the low density fatty breast] to exceedingly difficult [the high density, nodular breast, and/or cystic breast]. Of course, when the density of the tumor and the breast are nearly identical the tumor will bc difficult or even impossible to detect by palpation and/or mammography.

- Location of tumor. Tumors situated deep in a dense breast or large dense breast will be more difficult to detect.

§14.05 ROLE OF TUMOR IN CAMOUFLAGING

Tumor cells are 70% water and have the consistency of a soft gel (7). When we diagnose a breast cancer we usually are not detecting the collection of soft tumor cells but rather the firm tumor-generated stroma within and sometimes surrounding the breast cancer.

[a] Tumor Stroma is Generated by the Tumor Cells Themselves (8,9)

At the outset, breast cancers contain no stroma (10,11,12). When the tumors atttain a diameter of 0.3 to 1.0 mm, some of the tumor cells secrete powerful proteins such as the vascular permeability factor, angiogenic factors, growth factors, etc. (10,11,12). One of these proteins [vascular permeability factor] causes the nearby capillaries to leak proteins into the surrounding tissue where the proteins clot and form a fibrin-gel (other angrogenic factors may also be involved). The fibrin-gel together with other proteins secreted by the tumor cells initiate a complex process which stimulates adjacent stroma elements (blood vessels, fibroblasts, inflammatory cells, etc.) to invade the fibrin-gel and establish a stroma for the tumor (8,9). As the tumor grows more and more stroma is created to provide scaffolding for the tumor and carry nutrition to and waste from the cancer cells. Without this supporting structure [stroma] the tumor cannot survive and grow (8,9).

[b] Consistency of Tumor Stroma Determines Threshold Size

Although the stroma of all breast cancers contains the same building blocks, some of the building blocks (usually connective tissue) can comprise as much as 90% or as little as 10% of the tumor (8,9). Since the concentration of connective tissue determines the density of the tumor some breast cancers possess a chameleon-like ability to mimic the density of almost any normal breast tissue. Thus the degree to which a tumor is camouflaged is genetically controlled by the genes of the tumor itself. It is not surprising that the progeny of a tumor generates a stroma which is identical to the parent tumor (8,9).

[c] The Size at Which it is Possible to Detect a Breast Cancer is Determined by the Density of the Tumor Stroma and the Nature of the Surrounding Breast

The degree of tumor camouflaging, of course, determines the size at which it is possible to detect the cancer [threshold size]. Therefore, the size at which a tumor can be detected is determined by the genes of the cancer itself, and the density of the surrounding breast. Both the degree of alteration of the genes of the cancer cell and the density of the breast are beyond the control of the physician. The phenomenon of tumor camouflaging creates a serious and all too common problem for those who screen for breast cancer.

[d] Absence of Tumor-Specific Microcalcifications

Some tumors stimulate the production of calcium deposits within the tumor which can be visualized in the mammogram as a small cluster of tiny specks of calcifications. These clusters of calcifications enable mammographers to identify many small breast cancers. Unfortunately the tumor cells of approximately 60-70% of breast cancers do not stimulate the production of tumor-specific microcalcifications (13). The absence of tumor-specific microcalcifications makes it impossible to detect some breast cancers by mammography.

§14.06 GENES OF TUMOR CELL DETERMINE PATTERN OF TUMOR INVASION AND DEGREE OF CAMOUFLAGING

[a] The Usual Pattern of Invasion

The cancer grows within the breast by slowly infiltrating and replacing the surrounding breast tissue with masses of cancer cells. Within the tumor, the normal breast structures (milk glands and ducts) are destroyed. Many tumor cells secrete proteins that generate a stroma with a high content of fibrous tissue within and sometimes surrounding the tumor. About one-third of cancers produce tumor-specific microcalcifications. All of these characteristics tend to increase the contrast between the tumor and the normal breast tissue. This helps the clinician identify these cancers.

[b] The Camouflage Pattern of Invasion (see also §14.08)

Although the infiltrating lobular carcinoma is a classic example of a camouflaged tumor, many breast cancers, including the infiltrating duct cell carcinoma, have this same capacity. These camouflaged tumors are characterized by one or more of the following:

1. Widely dispersed groups of cancer cells arranged in short rows that infiltrate but do not completely destroy or replace the breast structures.
2. Cells that frequently, instead of destroying the breast ducts, use the ducts as scaffolding along which to spread through the breast.
3. Tumors that stimulate little or no excess fibrous tissue within the tumor. As a result, the density of fibrous tissue within the cancer and the surrounding breast tissue may be similar. Thus the density of the tumor may be nearly the same or even less than the density of normal breast tissue.
4. Tumors that rarely stimulate the formation of tumor specific microcalcifications.

The net result is a classic camouflaged breast cancer. There is a lack of or minimal contrast between breast and tumor. The tumor borders are vague and indistinct. There may be no central tumor mass, just an indefinte area of thickening. Tumor-specific microcalcifications are absent.

§14.07 THE INFILTRATING DUCT CELL CARCINOMA (14,15)

The common infiltrating duct cell carcinoma not infrequently presents as a camouflaged tumor. It is dangerous, especially when situated in a dense breast. The density (hardness or firmness) of this tumor will vary significantly depending upon the composition of the tumor stroma. Tumors containing large amounts of fibrous connective stroma will be quite dense. When the density of the breast and tumor are similar, the cancer will be difficult to detect. When the tumor stroma contains little fibrous tissue, the tumors will be less dense and softer to the touch.

[a] Tumor Borders

Although most tumors will be stellate, serrated or circumscribed, a few tumors will have indistinct borders (15). These tumors may be more difficult to palpate and to visualize by mammography. See pattern of tumor invasion, §14.06.

[b] Intraductal Carcinoma Component (15)

About one-fourth of breast cancers contain significant amounts of intraductal carcinoma (16). In some, 33% to 99% of the cancer will consist of intraductal carcinoma. The intraductal component is thought by many [not all] to represent intraductal spread of the cancer. This pattern of growth can be difficult to detect unless microcalcifications are identifiable by mammography. Many invasive duct cell carcinomas have no areas of intraductal carcinoma. On the other hand, there are a number of carcinomas that are composed primarily of intraductal carcinoma and have only small areas of infiltrating duct cell carcinoma.

What is the clinical significance of this intraductal component? Consider the following illustration: A woman develops an invasive duct cell carcinoma which has the following composition.

1/3 invasive duct cell carcinoma
2/3 intraductal carcinoma.

The intraductal portion of the tumor is situated entirely within the ductal system and the proteins secreted by the tumor cells are unable to stimulate the tissues within and surrounding the tumor to produce excess fibrous tissue (desmoplasia). As a result it is not often possible to palpate this portion of the tumor. Thus, when the pathologist measures the tumor, the surgeon will be startled and dismayed to learn that the tumor is actually three times larger than he/she suspected (3.0 cm vs 1.0 cm). How could this be possible when the clinician was carefully examining this woman's breast at six month intervals? Simply because two-thirds of the tumor was not palpable. Thus, this was not a ''missed'' diagnosis but rather a cancer presenting with a camouflage problem in two-thirds of the tumor.

§14.08 THE INFILTRATING LOBULAR CELL CARCINOMA

[a] Introduction and Definition of the Problem

Grossly, these tumors often resemble the more common infiltrating duct cell carcinomas, especially when abundant fibrous tissue (desmoplasia) is present (17). Many, however, are remarkably different. For example, only 10-14% of all breast cancers can be classified as lobular (14) yet almost 50% of camouflaged breast cancers tend to be invasive lobular carcinomas (14). Why does the invasive lobular carcinoma so frequently present as a tumor that is masked or hidden from the physician's palpating finger and the radiologist's mammogram? Foote and Stewart (18,19) described the microscopic appearance of invasive lobular carcinoma as "... thread-like strands of small tumor cells loosely dispersed throughout the fibrous matrix" with "no tendency for the cells to simulate atypical lobules" (15,18,19). These strands are composed of rows of tumor cells, one behind the other (like peas in a pod), not unlike small groups of warriors stealthily creeping single file through a forest. Mendelson et al. (20) state that "The mammographic appearance (a poorly defined asymmetric density with architectural distortion) may reflect the behavior of the infiltrating lobular tumor cells, which travel in linear array (single file) along and around the arborizing ducts that serve as scaffolding for these small, malignant cells that permeate the parenchyma without a central nidus. When these strands of tumor cells are loosely dispersed throughout the fibrous tissue without forming a distinct border or a central tumor mass, they can be extremely difficult to detect. by palpation or mammography" (20). Indeed these tumors are truly camouflaged.

[b] Invasive Lobular Carcinomas Can be Difficult to Detect

These invasive lobular carcinomas are not only difficult to detect clinically, but they are equally confusing and misleading to the surgeon and the pathologists responsible for evaluating the gross specimen removed at the time of surgery. For example:

1. ***Visual inspection of the gross specimen (15,18,20)***
   At times this cancer will be invisible to the naked eye. There are no cysts, no hemorrhage, and no gross calcifications.
2. ***Palpation of the gross specimen (15,18,19)***
   Often palpation will reveal only a vague area of induration which has indistinct borders. Sometimes the only findings are areas of vague induration.
3. ***Mammography (20)***
   These lesions frequently present as asymmetric densities with indistinct, infiltrative, shaggy borders. At times, the tumors will have a low density with a somewhat wispy appearance. Translucent areas are sometimes seen within the tumor. About one-fourth of these tumors contain microcalcifications which are usually non-specific and associated with other benign or malignant histologies. Microcalcifications are not a distinguishing feature of invasive lobular carcinoma (20). Thus, some of these tumors can be difficult to detect by mammography and again qualify as camouflaged tumors.
4. ***Clinical examples of a camouflaged lobular carcinoma***
   Hilleren et al (21) studied 137 invasive lobular carcinomas and cited two excellent examples of tumor camouflaging:

   A. **Case # 1 presented with a metastatic supraclavicular lymph node**
      • Breast normal to palpation.
      • Mammogram suspicious for cancer.
      • Mastectomy --- infiltrating lobular carcinoma 10 cm in diameter with 10/14 nodes positive for cancer.
   B. **Case # 2 presented with a minimal (new) retraction of the nipple**
      • Breast examination revealed no palpable masses.
      • Mammogram revealed an area of architectural distortion beneath the areola which was not visible 18 months previously.
      • Mastectomy --- infiltrating lobular carcinoma 5 cm in diameter.

Certainly these tumors whose invasion produces only a vague induration with indistinct borders rather than a discreet mass are truly camouflaged tumors.

§14.09 SOME BREAST CANCERS MASQUERADE AS BENIGN TUMORS

These tumors can sometimes present as well-defined masses with:

- a thin radiolucent halo
- no architectural distortion
- no microcalcifications.

In other words, they are indistinguishable from a typical benign tumor by mammography. The following tumors have this capability (22).

- medullary carcinoma (the most common)
- colloid carcinoma
- occasionally a well-differentiated infiltrating duct cell carcinoma
- occasionally a well-differentiated lobular carcinoma
- intracystic carcinoma (quite rare).

§14.10 VISUAL AIDS

A verbal description of the problem of camouflaging has limitations. A simple visual presentaion more graphically presents the problem caused by camouflaging. See Figure 14-1 (23).

Suggestions for preparation of the poster board and questions:

1. Use a white or light gray 28 x 44 inch poster board.
2. Paint tumors dark gray.
3. Suggested tumor sizes, 0.3mm to 3.5 cm.
4. Use layers of white tissue paper to simulate breast density.

5. Place poster board on an easel 10 to 15 feet from the jury. (you may have to adjust the proper distance by trial and error).
6. Ask the jurors to identify the smallest tumor on the poster board.
   - without the tissue paper
   - with one layer of tissue paper in place
   - with two layers of tissue paper in place
   - with three layers of tissue paper in place.
7. With three or four layers of tissue paper in place, jurors should have difficulty identifying even the larger tumors.

Practice Note

Results of screening mammography confirm the importance of tumor camouflaging. The tremendous increase in the use of screening mammography has resulted in a dramatic increase in tumors with diameters less than 2.0 cm. (24). However, the numbers of tumors measuring 2.0 cm or more and those with regional and distant disease has not decreased (24). This, we are convinced, is because there is a significant group of camouflaged tumors that are difficult to detect by mammography.

§14.11 CONCLUSION

Contrary to conventional wisdom, the size at which it is possible to detect a breast cancer is not primarily dependent upon the skill of the physician. The size at which it is possible to detect the cancer [threshold size] is largely dependent upon two factors:

A. The density and consistency of the breast tissue in which the tumor is situated.
B. The genetic configuration of the tumor cell itself which determines:
   1. Histologic tumor type
   2. Density of tumor stroma
   3. Pattern of tumor invasion

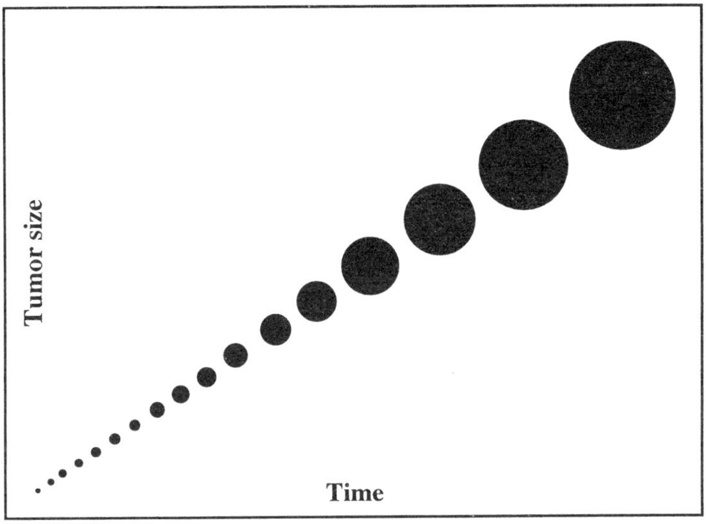

Figure 14-1. The Sliding Threshold Size of Breast Cancer. Watts, CF. Malpractice Defense: Breast Cancer. Medical Economics Books, 1990, Figure 13-1 page 97. Reprinted courtesy of author and publisher.

4. Presence or absence of tumor specific microcalcifications.

Tumor camouflaging, rather than physician skill, determines the size at which it is possible to detect most breast cancers.

References

1. Donegan WL. Evalulation of a Palpable Mass. Current Concepts, N Eng J Med 327(13): 937-942, 1992.
2. Strax, Philip. Imaging the Breast: a Perspective. Surg Clin N Am. 64(6):1061-1072, 1984.
3. Brenner RJ. Medicolegal Aspects of Breast Imaging: Variable Standards of Care Relating to Different Types of Practice. Am J Roentgenol 56:719-723, 1991.
4. Physicians Insurers Association of America Breast Cancer Study-1990. Public Relations, Donald J Sager and Associates Inc., 2 Park Avenue, New York, New York 10016, Telephone (212) 576-9800.

5. Kern KA. Causes of Breast Cancer Malpractice Litigation: A 20-Year Civil Court Review. Arch Surg 127:542-547, 1992.
6. Mitnick JS, Vasquez MF, Plesser KP, Roses DF. Breast Cancer Malpractice Litigation in New York State, Presented at the 79th Annual Meeting of the Radiological Society of North America, November 28-December 3, 1993. To be published in Radiology.
7. deDuve, Christian, *The Living Cell,* Vol I, page 19, Scientific American Books, WH Freeman Co, 1984.
8. Dvorak HF. Tumor Stroma. *Diagnostic Immunopathology,* edited by Colvin, Bhan, and McCluskey, Raven Press, New York, 1988, pages 401-419.
9. Dvorak HF. Tumors: Wounds That Do Not Heal. New Eng J Med 315:1650-1659, 1986.
10. Folkman J. Angiogenesis, in Cancer *The Outlaw Cell,* LaFond RE, Editor 2nd Ed., American Chemical Society, Washington, D.C., 1988 pages163-200.
11. Folkman J. Angiogenesis and its Inhibitors, in Important Advances in Oncology, DeVita, Helllman and Rosenberg, Eds, JB Lippincott, Philadelphia, 1985, Part 1, pages 42-62.
12. Folkman J. What is the Evidence That Tumors are Angiogenesis Dependent? J Natl Cancer Instit 2(1):January 3, 1990.
13. Kalisher, Lester. Factors Influencing False Negative Rates in Xeromammography. Radiology 133:297-301, 1979.
14. Holland R. So-called Interval Cancers of the Breast. Cancer 49:2527-2533, 1982.
15. Rosen PP. The Pathology of Breast Carcinoma. *Breast Diseases.* Harris, Hellman, Henderson, and Kinne, eds. JB Lippincott, 1987, pages 147-209.
16. Fisher ER, et al. The Pathology of Invasive Breast Carcinoma. A Syllabus Derived From Findings of the National Surgical Adjuvant Breast Project (protocol no. 4). Cancer 36:1-86, 1975.
17. Perez-Mesa, Carlos M. Gross and Microscopic Pathology, Cancer of the Breast, 3rd Ed. Donegan and Spratt, eds. WB Saunders 1988, pages 206-249.

18. Foote FW and Stewart FW. Lobular Carcinoma in Situ: A Rare Form of Mammary Cancer. Am J Pathol 17:491-497, 1941.
19. Foote, FW and Stewart, FW. A Histological Classification of Carcinoma of the Breast. Surgery 19:74-99, 1946.
20. Mendelson, Ellen B, Harris, Kathleen M., and Tobon, Hector. Infiltrating Lobular Carcinoma: Mammographic Patterns with Pathologic Correlation. A Pictorial Essay. Am J Radiol 153:265-271, 1989.
21. Hilleren DJ, Anderson IT, Lindholm K, and Linnell FS. Invasive Lobular Carcinoma: Mammographic Findings in a 10-Year Experience. Radiology 178:149-154,1991.
22. Wolfe, John. Xeroradiography of the Breast., 2nd Ed, Charles Thomas, 1983, pages 470-471.
23. Watts CF. *Malpractic Defense: Breast Cancer,* Medical Economics Books, Oradell, New Jersey, 1990.
24. Harris JR, Lippman ME, Veronesi U, Willett W. Medical Progress: Breast Cancer, Part I. N Engl J Med 327(5):319-328, 1992.

CHAPTER 15: TUMOR THRESHOLD SIZE

CHAPTER 15

TUMOR THRESHOLD SIZE

§15.01 INTRODUCTION

Although the drab term threshold-size sounds uninteresting, it is a concept which must be clearly grasped if we are to understand the vagaries of the clinical behavior of breast cancer. Excluding the early metastasizing breast cancer, threshold-size is one of the major factors which determines the likelihood of an unfavorable outcome.

§15.02 THRESHOLD SIZE; DEFINITIONS

[a] Definition of Threshold Size

Threshold size is the smallest size at which it is possible to detect a breast cancer by mammography and/or palpation.

[b] Threshold Size by Mammography

Threshold size by mammography is the smallest size at which it is possible to detect a breast cancer by mammography. Some breast cancers containing microcalcifications can be detected when only 2 or 4 mm in diameter and therefore have a small threshold size. Donegan reviewed 205 palpable breast cancers and reported that 18% could not be detected by mammography (1). Studies of malpractice claims suggest that, in this subset of women, the breast cancers were so effectively camouflaged that mammographers had difficulty in detecting 69-80% of these breast cancers (2,3). Thus, the threshold size of breast cancer by mammography varies from 2.0 mm to 4.0 cm or larger. Some breast cancers, even though clearly palpable, will not be visualized by x-ray.

[c] Threshold Size by Palpation

The threshold by palpation is generally agreed to be about 1 cm, however, many cancers situated in a dense breast cannot be palpated until they reach diameters of three or four centimeters, sometimes even larger.

[d] Pre–threshold Size

Tumors that cannot be detected by mammography or palpation, regardless of how large they are, must be classified as pre–threshold sized tumors. Most tumors remain pre–threshold in size by palpation for about 75% of their life cycle, that is, until they have undergone 30 net cell doublings and have attained a diameter of 1 cm. Many breast cancers, because of camouflaging, remain pre–threshold in size for longer periods of time. Some breast cancers remain pre–threshold in size until they attain diameters of 3.0 or 4.0 cm. By this time 80-90% of their life cycle has elapsed. They are in the terminal phase of their life cycle.

§15.03 FACTORS THAT INFLUENCE THE THRESHOLD SIZE

[a] The Density Factor

A small dense tumor in a soft fatty low density breast will readily be detected by mammography and palpation and will have a small threshold size. A large tumor without calcifications situated in a dense breast may not be detected by palpation until it is quite large. Some may never be detected by mammography even though they are clearly palpable. Thus these tumors will have large threshold sizes and can be classified as camouflaged tumors.

[b] The Absence of Microscopic Calcifications (Microcalcifications)

The absence of clusters of microscopic calcifications may make it difficult to detect many breast cancers, thus increasing their threshold size.

[c] The Pattern of Tumor Invasion

A unique pattern of invasion of some tumors results in vague indefinite tumor borders that increase the threshold size. See Chapter 14, The Camouflaged Tumor.

§15.04 CLINICAL SIGNIFICANCE OF A LARGE THRESHOLD SIZE

This discussion of threshold size may sound a bit academic to some, but it is not. The greater the threshold size, the longer the breast cancer must grow until it attains a diameter which is detectable by mammogaphy and/or palpation. Thus, the cancer has a longer sojourn time within the breast before it reaches threshold size. As a result, the cancer will undergo many more cell divisons during this prolonged sojourn time. Unfortunately the greater the number of cell divisons the greater the possibility of an error of cell division (a mutation). Errors of cell division not uncommonly produce highly lethal mutant clones of tumor cells that will eventually kill the patient.

§15.05 CONCLUSION

When the plaintiff alleges that an earlier diagnosis would have led to cure, in addition to stressing the time of metastasis, the defense should search for evidence that 12 months prior to detection this lesion was pre–threshold in size. The defense counselor should ask the following questions:

[a] Do the mammograms reveal findings consistent with tumor camouflaging that would increase the threshold size? (See Chapter 14).
- Absence of tumor-specific microcalcifications?
- Indistinct tumor borders?
- Density breast and tumor similar?
- Dysplasia of the breast?

[b] Does the gross and microscopic examination of the tumor reveal findings consistent with tumor camouflaging that would increase the threshold size?

- Tumor type - infiltrating lobular adenocarcinoma?
- A unique pattern of tumor invasion?
- A large intraductal carcinoma component?
- Other evidence of tumor camouflaging?

The jury should be reminded that all tumors remain pre–threshold in size by palpation for at least 75% of their life cycle. Additionally, all tumors remain pre–threshold in size by mammography for at least 60% of their life cycle. Some, about 10 to 18%, will remain pre–threshold for 80-90% of their life cycle. (See Chapter 14).

References

1. Donegan WL. Current Concepts: Evaluation of a Palpable Breast Mass. New Eng J Med, 327(13):937-942, 1992.
2. Physicians Insurers Association of America: Breast Cancer Study-1990. Copyright 1990 Physician Insurers Association of America.
3. Kern KA. Causes of Breast Cancer Malpractice Litigation: A 20-Year Civil Court Review. Arch Surg 127:542-547, May 1992.

CHAPTER 16: THE CANCER CONTROL WINDOW

CHAPTER 16

THE CANCER CONTROL WINDOW

§16.01 INTRODUCTION

The concept of the cancer control window will demonstrate clearly why some cancers are incurable (1-4). The Cancer Control Window (CCW) can be defined as that period of time that elapses from the moment that a breast cancer becomes detectable and the moment it metastasizes and becomes incurable. It is the window of time during which it is possible to diagnose and cure the cancer. When distant metastasis occurs before it becomes possible to detect the cancer by mammography and palpation, a cancer control window does not exist. Some refer to this as a negative cancer control window.

§16.02 FACTORS THAT ALTER THE SIZE OF THE CANCER CONTROL WINDOW

[a] Growth Rate and Lethal Potential of the Tumor

Rapidly growing aggressive cancers spread systemically early in the life cycle of the cancer and dramatically reduce thc size of the CCW. In many of these situations the window will be absent altogether.

[b] Tumor Camouflaging

A severe camouflaging problem produces a marked increase in the threshold size of a breast cancer which decreases the width and often eliminates the window.

[1] Mammography and the Cancer Control Window Ten to fifteen percent of breast cancers will never be visualized by mammography. As far as mammography is concerned, a cancer control window does not exist for these women. Some breast cancers cannot be identified until they reach a diameter of 3.0, 4.0 cm, or more. Again a cancer control window may not exist.

[2] Palpation and the Cancer Control Window Some breast cancers cannot be palpated until they reach a diameter of 4.0 or 5.0 cm or greater. A cancer control window does not exist for many of these women.

§16.03 CANCER CONTROL WINDOW: FISHER DOCTRINE

Proponents of Fisher's doctrine contend that there are two types of breast cancer. Some breast cancers have fairly stable DNA and neoplastic progression (metastasis) seldom occurs. These women rarely die of breast cancer. Local control will be the only problem for advanced cancers. The Cancer Control Window extends throughout the entire life cycle of the cancer.

Other breast cancers have great genetic instability. Neoplastic progression (the ability to metastasize) occurs at the first opportunity. Vascularization of the tumor provides that opportunity between the 10th and 20th doubling of the tumor when the cancer is only about 1 mm in diameter. These tumors metastasize before they can be detected by mammography. A cancer control window does not exist for these breast cancers.

§16.04 CANCER CONTROL WINDOW: INTERMEDIATE DOCTRINE

The proponents of of the Intermediate Doctrine agree that the clinical behavior of the majority of cancers can be explained by the Fisher

Doctrine. However, they contend that there is a third group of cancers that have moderately unstable DNA and undergo neoplastic progression (and metastasis) not only after they become detectable by mammography but also after they produce clinical symptoms. Thus, this hypothesis suggests that there is a window of opportunity for diagnosis and cure after these lesions become symptomatic and clinically detectable. This has not been proven.

§16.05 CONCLUSION

[a] Cancer Control Window: Author's Thesis

The concepts of the Fisher and Intermediate Doctrines are both partially correct. Many breast cancers (about 25% of all breast cancers) are so genetically unstable that neoplastic progression (and metastasis) occurs prior to the time these lesions can be detected by mammography. For these women, no CCW exists (as in the Fisher Doctrine). In the malpractice setting, where cancers with favorable outcomes are not encountered, this figure would be over 60%.

There is also a large group of cancers whose genes are only minimally unstable. These tumors, as in the Fisher Doctrine, seldom undergo the sequential alterations of their genes which are necessary to produce neoplastic progression. For these women, the CCW extends throughout the entire life of the tumor.

Practice Note

We are unable to exclude the possibility of a third group of breast cancers, as in the Intermediate Doctrine, whose genes are moderately unstable. Neoplastic progression (ability to metastasize) may continue to occur after the tumor becomes detectable by mammography. However, by the time these lesions become large enough to produce symptoms they are biologically old tumors that have completed 80% to 90% of their life cycles. They have entered the terminal phase of their existence. The tumor cells whose genes were unstable and susceptible to sequential alteration will have undergone neoplastic progression. Neither patient nor physician delay of diagnosis at this late stage will alter survival.

Our failure to lower the age-adjusted mortality rate of breast cancer since 1930 is proof that it is impossible to alter the survival of symptomatic tumors by decreasing the durations of symptoms (earlier clinical diagnosis). It is possible, but not proven, that the Cancer Control Window extends from the moment the cancer becomes detectable by mammography (2.1 mm) until the tumor becomes large enough to produce symptoms. Nevertheless, the studies of Charlson, et al, (5), Dennis et al. (6), Fisher et al. (7), Spratt (8), Skrabanek (9), and Plotkin and Blankenberg (10) all support our contention that decreasing the durations of symptoms will not alter the outcome of symptomatic breast cancers.

References

1. Spratt JS, Donegan WL, and Greenberg R. Screening and Follow-up. *Cancer of the Breast,* 3rd ed, Donegan and Spratt, WB Saunders, 1988, pp 558-590.
2. Spratt JS and Spratt SW. Medical and Legal Implications of Screening for Breast Cancer. Cancer 66:1351-1362, 1990.
3. Spratt JS, Donegan WL and Greenberg RH. Screening and Follow-up. *Cancer of the Breast,* 3rd ed, Donegan and Spratt, eds. WB Saunders, 1988. figure 19-4, page 566.
4. Spratt JS. The Relationship Between the Rates of Growth and the Intervals Between Screening Examinations for Effective Discovery. Cancer Detect Prev 4:301, 1981.
5. Charlson ME et al. Delay in the Treatment of Carcinoma of the Breast. Surg Gynecol Obstet 160:393-399, 1985.
6. Dennis CR et al. Analysis of Survival and Recurrence vs. Patient and Doctor Delay in Treatment of Breast Cancer. Cancer 35:714-720, 1975.
7. Fisher ER et al. A Perspective Concerning the Relation of Duration of Symptoms to Treatment Failure in Patients with Breast Cancer. Cancer 40:3160-3167, 1977.
8. Spratt JS. Realities of Breast Cancer Control, Public Expectations, and the Law. Surg Oncol Clin N Am 3(1): 25-34, 1994.
9. Skrabanek, Petr. False Premises and False Promises of Breast Cancer Screening. The Lancet, August 10, 1985 pages 316-319.

10. Plotkin D and Blankenberg F. Cancer Management Controversy. Breast Cancer—Biology and Malpractice. Am J Clin Oncol 14(3):254-266, 1991.

CHAPTER 17: THE INTERVAL TUMOR

CHAPTER 17

THE INTERVAL TUMOR

§17.01 INTRODUCTION

An interval tumor is defined as a breast cancer that surfaces within 12 months of a negative screening examination (1-4). The Physicians Insurers Association of America (PIAA) Breast Cancer Study-1990 (5) analyzed 273 paid malpractice claims for breast cancer and reported that 59% of the cancers in these cases surfaced within 12 months of a negative screening examination and 69% of the cancers were discovered by the claimant. Since the average breast cancer must grow for six to ten years before it can be detected these lesions were present within the breast at the time of the last negative screening examination. Why were they not detected?

§17.02 CLASSIFICATION OF INTERVAL TUMORS

Investigators (2,6,7) who have studied interval tumors have found a number of reasons why these tumors were not detected at the time of the last negative screening examination.

[a] Technical Errors (2,6,7)

Usually technical errors are secondary to poor quality films or failure to include the tumor in the imaging field. These occur at a rate of about 3-6%.

[b] Observer Errors (2,6,7)

These are the result of errors in observation and occur at the rate of about 26%.

[c] Subtle Mammographic Shadows (2,6,7)

These occur at the rate of approximately 33%. We classify these tumors as partially camouflaged tumors. These cancers, lacking tumor specific microcalcifications, were so well camouflaged within the dense breast and the density of tumor and breast were so similar that the resultant mammographic shadows were barely perceptible. Donegan (8) reported that 18% of 205 palpable breast cancers could not be detected by mammography at his center. True false negative mammograms, as in the Donegan series, are examples of breast cancers that are 100% camouflaged by mammography. Mammograms, which reveal only subtle breast cancer shadows, should be carefully evaluated since some experts may consider these lesions to be so nebulous that they could be diagnosed only in retrospect.

[d] True Interval Tumors (33%) (2,6,7)

The true interval cancers are another example of tumor camouflaging and occur at the rate of about 33%. However, in this case, the tumors are 100% camouflaged. These lesions were also present in the breast at the time of the last screening examination but were subthreshold in size and contained no tumor-specific microcalcifications. Although a few tumors can be detected when they are only 2.1-3.0 mm in diameter, the median size detected in mass screening programs is much larger. Spratt and Spratt (9) analyzed data from 30,000 mammograms of 10,180 women in the Breast Cancer Detection and Demonstration Project (BCDDP) in Louisville and reported: "The mean diameter of the first mammographic shadow in this study was 8.7 mm. . . . It should be emphasized that most tumors in the study were first detected at a larger size and were verified to be present [at the 8.7 mm diameter] only in retrospect."

Thus it is not uncommon for tumors as large as 8.7 mm in diameter to be 100% camouflaged within the breast. No breast cancer shadows will be visible in the mammogram because:

[1] Thcsc lesions were small (less than 8.7 mm in diameter).
[2] No tumor specific microcalcifications were present.
[3] The densities of tumor and breast were similar and borders indistinct.

These cancers that surface within 12 months of the negative screening examination are often rapidly growing aggresssive cancers. Heuser, et al. (10) have concluded "... that as many as 77% of all breast cancers may grow fast enough to grow from pre–threshold size detectability on mammograms to clinical detectable size in less than 12 months." Rapidly growing interval tumors with diameters of 3.0, 5.0 and 8.7 mm at the time of the last screening examination are dangerous tumors. Galante (11) has studied a large group of breast cancers and classified the doubling times as follows:

Classification	Frequency	Doubling Time
Fast	16%	< 30 days
Intermediate	42%	30.1 - 90 days
Slow	17.6%	90- ? days
Very slow	24.4%	immeasurable

Reprinted courtesy of Galante E Milan Italy: Personal Communication to Spratt and Spratt (11), Growth Rates, in *Diseases of the Breast,* 3rd Ed, Donegan and Spratt, eds, WB Saunders, 1988. Modified from Table 10-8, page 285 (12).

Arnerlov, et al. (13) calculated the doubling times of 158 breast cancers from serial mammograms. They reported that 33.5% had doubling times of 180 days or less while 13.9% had doubling times of less than 30 days. Thus it is well documented that many breast cancers can casily double their diameters two, three, or even four times within a period of 12 months. For a discussion of the defense based on doubling time arguments, see Chapter 19.

§17.03 GROWTH RATES: EXAMPLES OF INTERVAL TUMORS

When a breast cancer surfaces within 12 months of a negative screening examination, many women will assume that the cancer was "missed" at the time of the last examination. How could the doctor overlook a breast cancer with a diameter of one inch? Unfortunately, tumor camouflaging (Chapter 14) often makes it impossible to detect tumors with diameters of 3 to 10 mm or even as large as 2.0-4.0 cm. When these lesions happen to be rapidly growing cancers with considerable genetic instability (Chapter 10) there will be serious consequences. Consider the following examples:

[a] Tumor Doubling Time of 40 Days

diameter = 3.0 mm at time of the last negative screening examination

- net cell doubling time = 40 days
- 9 net cell doublings will occur in 360 days
- 3 net cell doublings = the diameter of the tumor will double
- therefore, the tumor diameter will double three times in 360 days, thus, if diameter at time of last screen = 3.0 mm
- at 120 days = 6.0 mm
- at 240 days = 1.2 cm
- at 360 days = 2.4 cm

[b] Tumor Doubling Time of 60 Days

diameter = 5.0 mm at the time of the last negative screening exam

- net cell doubling time = 60 days
- 6 net cell doublings will occur in 360 days.
- 3 net cell doublings = the diameter of the tumor will double
- therefore, tumor diameter will double twice in 360 days, thus, if diameter at time of the last screen = 5.0 mm
- at 180 days = 1.0 cm
- at 360 days = 2.0 cm

Thus, the combination of tumor camouflaging and a rapidly growing tumor with considerable genetic instability can create a situation with great lethal potential.

§17.04 FREQUENCY OF FALSE NEGATIVE MAMMOGRAMS

The incidence of false negative mammograms is, of course, much greater in the malpractice setting and many of these cancers can be classified as true interval tumors.

Frequency of False Negative Mammograms in the Malpractice Setting

Study	% of mammograms interpreted as normal
PIAA (5)	49.2%
Kern (14)	80.0%
Mitnick (15)	37.5%

Normally only about 10-15% of breast cancers cannot be visualized by mammography. However, in the malpractice situation we note that 37.5% to 80% of breast cancers could not be detected by mammography. Additionally, 59% surfaced within 12 months of a negative screening examination and 69% were discovered by the patient, see §17.01. And, of course, all had an unfavorable outcome. This tells us that the breast cancers we will encounter in the court room will have a high incidence of tumor camouflaging (37.5-80%) and all will have great lethal potential. Therefore, it is imperative that the jury understand the significance of tumor camouflaging, especially when it is associated with an aggressive cancer. This is something entirely beyond the control of the physician and/or the patient.

§17.05 MANY INTERVAL TUMORS ARE RAPIDLY GROWING AGGRESSIVE CANCERS

Spratt and Spratt (9,16,17) have stated "The acute interval surfacing tumors are distinctly different. Slow growing cancers have circumscribed margins and papillary intraductal growth. Fast growing tumors have anaplastic nuclear grade and absence of calcifications in both mammograms and histopathological sections. They are also present in women under 50 years of age and are associated with dysplastic breasts and a negative family history." Spratt continues, "This information has been accepted by some courts as refuting the idea that the alleged delay was responsible for a bad outcome.'' Certainly a profile of unfavorable prognostic factors such as anaplastic nuclear grade, lymphatic invasion at the periphery of the tumor, axillary lymph node metastases (10), high mitotic count, high S-phase, vascular invasion, and HER-2/neu amplification and/or protein overexpression would support the contention that the tumor was rapidly growing and had great lethal potential.

§17.06 CONCLUSION

The problems of the tumors missed at the time of the last screening examination can be summarized as follows:

a. Physician Error

1. Technical error

2. Observer error

b. Tumor Camouflaging

1. Partial tumor camouflaging

The tumor was camouflaged sufficiently to produce an indistinct, hazy and cloudy mammographic shadow. Some of these shadows can be correctly identified only in retrospect and should not be classified as observer error.

2. Complete tumor camouflaging

Some of these lesions are rapidly growing aggressive cancers that could not be detected at the time of the last screening because of small size, lack of tumor-specific microcalcifications, and a tumor density that did not significantly differ from that of the surrounding breast. Tumors A and B (§17.03, [a] & [b]) illustrate the problems caused by the camouflaging of rapidly growing cancers.

c. Rapidly Growing True Interval Tumors

1. Small tumor size

These rapidly growing cancers were simply too small to be detected at the time of the last screening examination.

Practice Note

Each interval tumor should be carefully evaluated. If a subtle breast cancer shadow was present in the mammogram 12 months previously, could it in all fairness, have been correctly interpreted prospectively? The plaintiff will have no difficulty in finding someone willing to state that the cancer should have been detected 12 months earlier. Therefore, we recommend the following:

1. Ask your radiologist to assemble a group of 12 mammograms from his/her teaching file.
2. Insert the plaintiff's mammogram (12 months prior to diagnosis) into this file.
3. All mammograms should be from the same mammographic unit with names and dates covered.
4. Have six or more radiologists interpret these blinded films. Record the results.
5. Then challenge the plaintiff to have his/her expert (one who has not had an opportunity to examine these films) prove in court, in the presence of the judge and jury, that this lesion should have been detected by the defendant. Few "experts" will be willing to take the risk of being humiliated in court.

References

1. DeGroote MD, et al. Interval Breast Cancer: A More Aggressive Subset of Breast Neoplasms. Surgery 94(4):543-547, 1983.
2. Holland R. So-called Interval Cancers of the Breast. Cancer 49:2527-2533, 1982.
3. Heuser L, et al. Relation Between Mammary Cancer Growth Kinetics and the Intervals Between Screening. Cancer 43:857-862, 1979.
4. Spratt JS et al. Geometry, Growth Rates, and Duration of Cancer and Carcinoma In Situ of the Breast Before Detection By Screening. Cancer Research 46:970-974, 1986.
5. Physicians Insurers Association of America: Breast Cancer Study-1990. Project Director, Sylvan H. Eisman, M.D., Pennsylvania Medical Society Liability Company.

6. Spratt JA, Fournier D.von, Spratt JS, and Weber EE. Mammographic Assessment of Human Breast Cancer Growth and Duration. Cancer 71(6):2020-2026, 1993.
7. Buchanan JB, Spratt JS, and Heuser LS. Tumor Growth, Doubling Times, and the Inability of the Radiologist to Diagnose Certain Cancers. Radiol Clin North Am. 21:115-126, 1983.
8. Donegan WL. Current Concepts: Evaluation of a Palpable Breast Mass. New Eng J Med, 327(13):937-942, 1992.
9. Spratt JS and Spratt JA. Growth Rates and the Cytokinetic Behavior of Breast Cancer. Presented at the University of Heidelberg, October 1986, personal communication.
10. Heuser LS, et al. The Association of Pathologic and Mammographic Characteristics of Primary Human Breast Cancer With 'Slow' and 'Fast' Growth Rates and With Axillary Lymph Node Metastases. Cancer 53:96-98, 1984.
11. Galante E. Milan Italy: Personal Communication to Spratt JS and Spratt JA. Growth Rates in *Cancer of the Breast,* 3rd ed, Donegan and Spratt, eds. WB Saunders, 1988, pp 284-285.
12. Spratt JS, Spratt JA. Growth Rates, pp 270-302 in *Cancer of the Breast,* 3rd ed, Donegan and Spratt, WB Saunders, 1988, Table 10-8, page 285.
13. Arnerlov C, et al. Breast Carcinoma Growth Rate Described by Mammographic Doubling Time and S-phase Fraction. Cancer 70:1928-1934, 1993.
14. Kern KA. Causes of breast cancer malpractice litigation—A 20-Year Civil Court Review. Arch Surg 127:542-447, 1992.
15. Mitnick JS, Vasquez MF, Plesser KP, Roses DF. Breast Cancer Malpractice Litigation in New York State. Presented at the 79th Annual Meeting of the Radiologic Society of North America, November 28-December 3, 1993, to be published in Radiology.
16. Spratt JS, et al. Acute Carcinoma of the Breast. Surgery Gynecology and Obstetrics 157:220-222, 1983.
17. Spratt JS. Discussion of a paper presented by DeGroote MD, et al. Interval Breast Cancer: A More Aggressive Subset of Breast Neoplasms. Surgery 94(4)543-547, 1983.

CHAPTER 18: THE TNM STAGING SYSTEM HAS MANY LIMITATIONS

CHAPTER 18

THE TNM STAGING SYSTEM HAS MANY LIMITATIONS

§18.01 INTRODUCTION

[a] Definition of TNM Staging (1,2), (See Table 18-1)

Early staging systems, such as the Manchester System and the Columbia Clinical Classification, measured only the clinical extent of the disease. In both the Manchester Stage I and the Columbia Stage A the primary tumor was operable and there was no clinical evidence of axillary metastases. In both the Manchester Stage II and the Columbia Stage B the primary tumor was still operable but there was clinical suspicion of axillary metastases. Both the Manchester and Columbia systems have serious faults. When the axilla is said to be clinically normal, there is a high rate of false negatives and when the axilla is said to clinically positive, there is a high rate of false positives. Attorneys for the plaintiff like the Columbia system because it considers only the clinical status and they can talk about the clinical status 12 months versus the clinical status at the time of surgery. They ignore the fact that they are using information from the pathology report to confirm the clinical stage prior to surgery.

The popular TNM Staging System was created in 1989 by merging the staging systems of the International Union against Cancer (UICC) and the American Joint Committee on Cancer Staging (AJC). This new system considers both the clinical status (cTNM) and the pathologic status (pTNM) of the tumor. Proponents use it to assist in selecting patients for various treatment modalities and as a prognostic indicator.

Critics fault it because of its complexity and because it does not consider tumor type and the biology of the tumor. Thus, the TNM staging system involves the classification of breast cancer solely on the basis of the anatomical extent of the disease. For example see Table 18-1 which follows:

Table 18-1

		1st ed (revised, 1973)	*2nd ed (1977)*	*2nd ed (revised, 1983)*	*3rd ed (1989)*
Primary Tumor (T)					
Tx		—— Primary tumor cannot be assessed ——			
T0		—— No evidence of primary tumor ——			
Tis		N/A	—— Paget disease without a tumor ——		
					Carcinoma in situ
T1		—— Tumor 2 cm or less in greatest dimension ——			
	T1a	No fixation to underlying pectoral fascia or muscle			0.5 cm or smaller
	T1b	Fixation to underlying pectoral fascia or muscle			Larger than 0.5 cm, but not larger than 1 cm
	T1c	—— N/A ——			Larger than 1 cm, but not larger than 2 cm
T2		Tumor larger than 2 cm but not larger than 5 cm in greatest dimension			
	T2a	No fixation to underlying pectoral fascia or muscle			N/A
	T2b	Fixation to underlying pectoral fascia or muscle			N/A
T3		—— Tumor larger than 5 cm in greatest dimension ——			
	T3a	No fixation to underlying pectoral fascia or muscle			N/A
	T3b	Fixation to underlying pectoral fascia or muscle			N/A
T4		Tumor of any size with extension to chest wall or skin (*Note:* chest wall includes ribs, intercostal muscles, and serratus anterior muscle, but not pectoral muscle)			
	T4a	—— Fixation to chest wall ——			
	T4b	Edema (including peau d'orange), ulceration of the skin of the breast, or satellite skin nodules confined to the same breast			
	T4c	—— Both T4a and T4b ——			
	T4d	N/A	—— Inflammatory breast cancer ——		
Regional Nodes (N)					
Nx		Regional lymph nodes cannot be assessed clinically ——			
N0		No palpable homolateral axillary nodes			No regional lymph node metastases
N1		Movable homolateral axillary nodes			Metastasis to movable ipsilateral axillary node(s)
	N1a	Nodes not considered to contain growth			N/A
	N1b	Nodes considered to contain growth			N/A
N2		Homolateral axillary nodes containing growth and fixed to one another or to other structures			Metastases to ipsilateral axillary lymph nodes fixed to one another or to other structures

Table 18-1 (continued)

<table>
<tr><th></th><th>1st ed (revised, 1973)</th><th>2nd ed (1977)</th><th>2nd ed (revised, 1983)</th><th>3rd ed (1989)</th></tr>
<tr><td>N3</td><td colspan="3">Homolateral supraclavicular or infraclavicular nodes containing growth, or edema of the arm</td><td>Metastases to ipsilateral internal mammary lymph node(s)</td></tr>
<tr><td colspan="5">Distant Metastases (M)</td></tr>
<tr><td>Mx</td><td colspan="4">Presence of distant metastases cannot be assessed</td></tr>
<tr><td>M0</td><td colspan="4">No distant metastases</td></tr>
<tr><td>M1</td><td colspan="3">Distant metastases</td><td>Distant metastases (including metastases to ipsilateral supraclavicular node(s)</td></tr>
<tr><td colspan="5">Stage Grouping</td></tr>
<tr><td>Stage 0</td><td colspan="3">N/A</td><td>TisN0M0</td></tr>
<tr><td>Stage I</td><td colspan="4">T1N0M0</td></tr>
<tr><td>Stage II</td><td colspan="3">T0N1M0
T1N1M0
T2N0M0
T2N1M0</td><td>N/A</td></tr>
<tr><td>Stage IIA</td><td colspan="3">N/A</td><td>T0N1M0
T1N1M0
T2N0M0</td></tr>
<tr><td>Stage IIB</td><td colspan="3">N/A</td><td>T2N1M0
T3N0M0</td></tr>
<tr><td>Stage III</td><td>Any T N2M0
Any T N3M0
T3 any N M0
T4 any N M0</td><td>T3N0M0
T3N1M0
T3N2M0
T1N2M0
T2N2M0</td><td>N/A</td><td>N/A</td></tr>
<tr><td>Stage IIIA</td><td>N/A</td><td>N/A
T1N2M0
T2N2M0
T3N0M0
T3N1M0
T3N2M0</td><td>T0N2M0
T1N2M0
T2N2M0
T3N1M0
T3N2M0</td><td>T0N2M0</td></tr>
<tr><td>Stage IIIB</td><td>N/A</td><td>N/A</td><td>T4 any N M0
Any T N3 M0</td><td>T4 any N M0
Any T N3 M0</td></tr>
<tr><td>Stage IV</td><td></td><td colspan="2">T4 any N any M
Any T N3 any M</td><td></td></tr>
<tr><td></td><td colspan="4">Any T any N M1</td></tr>
</table>

Table 18-1. Staging of Breast Carcinoma. Chapter 15, Staging and Prognostic Factors. *Breast Diseases,* Harris, Hellman, Henderson, and Kinne, editors, 2nd ed, JB Lippincott, 1991, Table 15-1, pages 328 and 329. Reprinted courtesy of authors and publisher.

T = tumor size
N = status axillary nodes
N_0 = negative lymph nodes
N_1 = one positive node
N_2 = two positive nodes, etc.
M = the presence or absence of distant metastasis

[b] Types of TNM Staging

[1] Clinical TNM (cTNM)

This is based on the clinical assessment of the patient prior to surgery.

[2] Pathologic TNM (pTNM)

This is based on examinaton of the tissues removed at the time of surgery and clinical data, laboratory tests, x-rays, scans, etc. performed at the time of and/or immediately following surgery. Obviously the cTNM and the pTNM cannot be compared. They are totally different.

§18.02 LIMITATIONS OF TNM STAGING

[a] Not Totally Accurate

The Yorkshire Cancer Group evaluated the TNM staging system and had this to say (3).

1. Tumor size (3)

Surgeons and pathologists agree in only 54% of the cases.
Surgeons and radiologists agree in only 39% of the cases.

2. Axilla (status of axillary nodes)

Clinically said to be negative --- wrong in 42% of the cases (3)
Clinically said to be positive --- wrong in 30% of cases (4)
Histologically said to be negative --- examination of nodes by serial sections reveal an error of +/− 20% (4).
Nodes negative clinically and histologically --- 20% to 30% of these women die of systemic disease. The metastatic tumor cells by-passed the lymph nodes (5).
Medial breast cancers tend to metastasize to the internal mammary nodes rather than the axillary nodes. Internal mam-

mary nodes are not often detected clinically or pathologically.

If clinical TNM stage (tumor size and node status) determined several days prior to surgery seldom agrees with the pathologic stage determined at the time of surgery, it is obvious that attempts to determine the TNM stage 12 months before surgery would be nothing more than sheer speculation.

[b] Ignores Histologic Type

Some histologic types such as tubular, medullary, mucinous, papillary, and adenocystic have a good prognosis. Others such as infiltrative duct cell carcinoma and invasive lobular carcinoma have a poor prognosis.

[c] Ignores Growth Rate and Aggressiveness of Tumor

The TNM staging system completely ignores the influence of growth rate, differentiation, and invasiveness of the tumor (1). See Chapter 23, Prognostic Factors. The TNM staging system does not consider the following factors:

1. ***Tumor type, §23.02[d].***
2. ***Microscopic examination of the tumor - §23.02[c], [d], [f] and §23.03[f]***

Histologic grade (HG)	lymphatic invasion
Nuclear grade (NG)	vascular invasion
Mitotic grade (MI)	tumor necrosis

3. ***Second generation prognostic parameters - Chapter 23***
   ER/PgR (estrogen receptor/ progesterone receptor).
4. ***Third generation prognostic parameters - See synopsis Chapter 23***
   Flow cytometery (ploidy and S-phase);
   EGFR (epidermal growth factor receptor);
   HER-2/neu gene amplification and/or overexpression;
   Cathepsin-D, high levels of;
   Angiogenesis, density of microvessels in tumor tissue; and
   New prognostic parameters, see Chapter 23 and/or consult your pathologist.

[d] Ignores the Biology and Natural History of Breast Cancer

1. *Breast cancer is a complex disease.*
2. *The progression of breast cancer is frequently not an orderly time related series of events.*
3. *Some cancers grow slowly and never metastasize.*
4. *Many cancers spread systemically long before they can be detected by mammography and/or palpation.*
5. *20% to 30% of women with systemic breast cancers do not have evidence of axillary metastasis.*

[e] Clinical TNM Staging (cTNM) Ignores the Phenomenon of Tumor Camouflaging

Tumor camouflaging may increase the threshold size of breast cancers to 2.0 cm, 3.0 cm, 4.0 cm or sometimes tumors as large as 8.0 centimeters (6). See also Chapter 14, The Camouflaged Tumor.

§18.03 TNM STAGING IS A USEFUL TOOL BUT NO SUBSITUTE FOR A COMPLETE BIOLOGICAL EVALUATION

The TNM staging system is a useful tool but it is no substitute for a complete and factual evaluation of the plaintiff's tumor which should include:

a. ***TNM Staging***
b. ***Histologic Tumor Type***
c. ***Histopathology of the Tumor***
   1. **Tumor grading**
      A. Histologic grade (HG)
      B. Nuclear grade (NG)
      C. Mitotic Index (MI)
      D. Tumor grade (a combination of HG, NG, & MI)

2. Adverse microscopic risk factors

A. Vascular and lymphatic invasion

B. Foci of tumor necrosis

d. Second and Third Generation Prognostic Parameters

There are some tests, not often used in the clinical setting because of their expense, that may be useful in establishing that the plaintiff's breast cancer was more aggressive than the average breast cancer. Consider the following:

[1] High S-phase fraction (§23.02 [h])
[2] HER-2/neu overexpression and/or amplification (§23.02 [i])
[3] Microvessel count (§23.02 [m])
[4] p53 over-expression of mutant protein (§23.02 [n])
[5] Consult your pathologists for the possibility of newer prognostic parameters.

Thus a careful consideration of tumor type, tumor grading, microscopic adverse risk factors, and molecular risk factors in addition to the TNM stage will enable the defense to assert that the plaintiff's breast cancer was indeed far more aggressive that one would suspect from the TNM stage alone.

§18.04 IN THE MALPRACTICE SETTING, CLINICAL BEHAVIOR IS MORE ACCURATE ASSESSEMENT THAN TNM

The clinical behavior of the tumor is not available to the clinician planning the early treatment program for primary breast cancer but should not be overlooked in the malpractice setting. The behavior of the tumor following surgery can provide convincing evidence regarding the lethal potential of the plaintiff's tumor.

The disease-free interval (DFI) is the interval of time between removal of the primary tumor and the first sign of recurrence and is an excellent gauge of the rate of growth and invasiveness of the cancer. A review of 800 untreated breast cancers reveals the median duration of life from the first symptom to death was 32.6 to 39.9 months (7,8,9). A few lived for only a few months while some lived for 30 years. Certainly a DFI of less than 30 months would suggest a rapidly growing cancer.

The R1-R2 Interval (10) is the length of time between the appearance of the first and second distant metastasis (recurrence).This is an indirect gauge of the growth rate of the tumor. A short R1-R2 interval was described as less than 6 months.

R1-R2 Interval	Median Survival
$<$ 6 mo	12 to 16 months
$>$ 6 mo	$>$ 40 months

Modifed from Pearlman and Jochimsen (10).

In all cases the clinical behavior of a patient's breast cancer must be considered. The tumor type, pathology, prognostic factors, etc. are all important, but the clinical behavior of the plaintiff's tumor must not be overlooked. Did the tumor metastasize to the axillary nodes? Did the tumor recur soon after surgery with evidence of systemic disease? Was the plaintiff's course rapidly downhill following recurrence? A "yes" answer to these questions indicates the patient's tumor was a rapidly growing aggressive breast cancer, a cancer that possessed great lethal potential. Unfortunately, careful examination of some very aggressive breast cancers will reveal little or no laboratory evidence of adverse prognostic risk factors as the result of sampling errors, see §23.01 [e]. However, the observation that the plaintiff quicky succumbed to a rapidly progressive cancer provides irrefutable evidence of a highly invasive, virulent breast cancer in a woman with little or no host immunity.

§18.05 PLAINTIFF MAY QUESTION THE VALUE OF THIRD GENERATION PROGNOSTIC FACTORS: SOME RESPONSES

a. Plaintiff may allege little is known about the predictive worth of these new factors.

Answer: A voluminous literature is rapidly accumulating and the techniques and reagents for performing these measurement are rapidly becoming standardized. (See Chapter 23).

b. Plaintiff may allege laboratory results are unpredictable.

Answer: The laboratory results do vary from laboratory to laboratory. This problem can be solved by having the test performed at a large reference laboratory interested in breast cancer. Most major medical schools have excellent laboratories or ask your pathologist what reference laboratory he/she uses for difficult cases.

c. Plaintiff may allege these tests do not add predictive power beyond that obtained from tumor size, node status, and the histopathology of the tumor.

Answer: The additional expense may not be cost-effective in the clinical setting. However, in the malpractice arena the discovery of one or more unfavorable third generation prognostic parameters will have significantly strengthened your conclusion that you are dealing with an aggressive tumor with great lethal potential.

§18.06 CONCLUSION: IT IS IMPOSSIBLE TO DETERMINE THE PATHOLOGIC TNM STAGE ONE YEAR PRIOR TO THE TIME OF SURGERY

The TNM staging system gains much of its predictive power from measuring lymph node status. It is useful in assisting in the selection of treatment modalities and in predicting prognosis. However, it is more accurate when tumor type, tumor grading, microscopic adverse risk factors, and tumor biology are also considered. Clinical staging systems such as the Columbia Clinical Classification have a high incidence false negatives and false positives when evaluating the axilla and are worthless when used to determine clinical staging 12 months prior to surgery. It is, of course, also impossible to determine the pathologic stage (pTNM) 12 months prior to surgery.

Practice Note

If we know the pathologic stage following surgery, is it possible to determine the pathologic stage 12 months prior to diagnosis and surgery? The answer is no, for several reasons. First, it is not possible to determine the pathologic stage without removal of the primary tumor and lymph nodes and, of course, it is impossible to do this retrospectively. Secondly, even in the best medical centers the clinical stage (determined just prior to surgery) and the pathologic stage determined immediately after surgery do not agree in about 50% of cases. Certainly attempts to predict the pathologic stage 12 months prior to surgery will be nothing more than sheer speculation.

References

1. Donegan, William. Staging and Primary Treatment. *Cancer of the Breast,* 3rd ed, Donegan and Spratt eds, WB Saunders, 1988, pages 336-402.
2. Harris, JR. Staging and Prognostic Factors. *Breast Diseases,* 2nd ed., Harris, Hellman, Henderson, and Kinne, eds., JB Lippincott, 1991, pages 327-346.
3. Yorkshire Breast Cancer Group: Critical Assessment of the TNM System in Breast Cancer. Br Med J. 281: 134, 1980.
4. Watts CF. Personal experience.
5. Harris JR and Hellman, Samuel. Biology: Natural History of Breast Cancer, in *Breast Diseases,* 2nd ed., Harris, Hellman, Henderson and Kinne, eds., JB Lippincott, 1991, pages 165-181.
6. Watts CF. Malpractice Defense: Breast Cancer. Medical Economics Books, 1990. Purchased by Blackwell Scientific Publications Inc., Cambridge, MA.
7. Wade P. Untreated Carcinomas of the Breast. British J Radiol 19:272, 1946.
8. Daland EM. Untreated Cancer of the Breast. Surg Gyn Obst 44:264.1927.

9. Haagensen CD. Disease of the Breast. Philadelphia. WB Saunders, 1950, page 411.
10. Pearlman NW and Jochimsen P. Recurrent Breast Cancer. Factors Influencing Survival, Including Treatment. J Surg Oncol 11:21-29, 1979.

CHAPTER 19: DOUBLING TIME DEFENSE

CHAPTER 19

DOUBLING TIME DEFENSE

§ 19.01 INTRODUCTION

The reader who is seriously interested in this subject is advised to review the section on cell kinetics (§8.01). The life cycle of breast cancer consists of approximately 40 net cell doublings. The idea of a net cell doubling time is conceptually correct and is an excellent teaching tool. However, employing the doubling time to extrapolate backwards to determine the date of a metastatic event is subject to a number of errors with which the defense must be thoroughly familiar. In our opinion, the doubling time defense will seldom be successful unless the jury has been properly educated regarding the biology and natural history of breast cancer.

In many situations a doubling time defense is not necessary, since, as we have stressed in previous chapters, by the time a breast cancer becomes large enough to produce symptoms, the tumors with genetic instability will have undergone neoplastic progression and metastasized. Symptomatic breast cancers are biologically old tumors and neither patient nor physician delay will alter symptoms since the prognosis has already been determined.

§19.02 CALCULATIONS FOR A DOUBLING TIME DEFENSE

A penny doubled every day for 30 days will yield one billion pennies or $1,000,000.00. Forty net cell doublings of a cancer cell will produce a tumor mass consisting of more than one-trillion cells which will, in most cases, results in the death of the patient. Thus, if we know the approximate number of cells in a metastasis and the approximate doubling time of the tumor it will be possible to extrapolate backwards and determine whether or not the metastasis arose during the 12 months preceding the diagnosis of the cancer. To do this we must:

a. **Accurately Determine the Size of the Metastasis**

b. **Determine the Number of Cancer Cells Within the Metastasis**

   Using the table in Chapter 8, calculate the number of tumor cells with the primary tumor. Ask your pathologist and/or oncologist for assistance.

c. **Use a Doubling Time of 100 Days to Extrapolate Backwards to Determine the Number of Cells Within the Metastasis One and Two Years Prior to the Time of Diagnosis: For Example:**

   1. **Calculation of a Doubling Time Defense for a Metastasis Containing One Billion Cancer Cells.**

Days prior to diagnosis	Number Cells in the Tumor
At time of diagnosis	one billion
100 days	500 million
200 days	250 million
300 days	125 million
400 days	60 million (rounded)
500 days	30 million
600 days	15 million
700 days	7.5 million
800 days	3.25 million

Thus, the metastatic event did not occur during the 12 months preceding the diagnosis of the breast cancer.

§19.03 CRITICS WILL CHARGE THE DOUBLING TIME DEFENSE IS SUBJECT TO MANY ERRORS

[a] There are Tremendous Variations in the Doubling Time of Breast Cancer

The doubling time of breast cancer varies tremendously. Spratt and Spratt have calculated that (1):

- With a doubling time of 9 days a cancer could grow from de novo to death of the patient within 365 days.
- With a doubling time of 18 days a cancer could grow from early threshold size (2 mm) to death within 365 days.

The Breast Cancer Diagnosis and Demonstration Project (BCDDP) was able to study serial mammograms of 32 breast cancers (1). They found the net cell doubling times to vary from 109 to 944 days. Spratt and Kaltenbach and Spratt (2) identified one cancer with a doubling time of only 23 days (2). Fournier reported the doubling times of 147 mammary cancers to range between 44 and 1869 days (3). Galante (4) has studied a large group of breast cancers and reported that 16% of breast cancers had doubling times less than 30 days while 24.4% had doubling times so prolonged that measurement was not possible.

Spratt and Spratt (1) concluded from their study of breast cancer that the growth rate of a large percentage of breast cancers is exceedingly rapid, especially in the early predictable phase of the tumor. Without serial measurements of the tumor over a period of 6-12 months, the selection of a doubling time will be at best a rough estimate. Spratt and Spratt have written an excellent chapter on the growth rate of breast cancer which appears in *Cancer of the Breast*, 3rd ed. by Donegan and Spratt (1). Readers interested in this subject should consult this chapter.

Comment

Yes, there are considerable differences in the doubling times of breast cancers. However, the metastases from tumors with prolonged doubling times will not surface for many years and these tumors will not be involved in litigation. The recurrences of rapidly growing cancers occur quite quickly and these tumors can be identified easily by the clinical behavior of the tumor, tumor grading, a high S-phase fraction, certain unfavorable microscopic risk factors such as tumor invasion of the vascular and lymphatic capillaries, and certain adverse molecular risk factors. (See Chapter 23). We have selected the doubling time for the average breast cancer, the type of a cancer that is commonly involved in litigation.

[b] Growth Characteristics of Breast Cancer Not Constant

[1] Linear Growth (1) During the prevascular phase, the small cluster of cancer cells is thought to increase its mass by a specific amount each day regardless of the size of the tumor. This type of growth is thought to occur when cell division is largely limited to the periphery of the tumor. See Prevascular phase §10.02 [d].

[2] Exponential Growth (1) Most breast cancers become vascularized when the tumors are 0.3 to 1.0 mm in diameter. With an established blood supply, all cells become well nourished and there is a sudden and temporary spurt in the growth of the tumor which is geometric or exponential in nature. For example, when the number of cells in a tumor increases from 10,000 to 20,000, to 40,000, to 80,000 etc. growth is said to be geometric or exponential. See §10.02 [a].

[3] Deceleratory Growth (Gompertzian) (1) Few cells can maintain geometric growth for long. As the tumor increases in size the growth rate gradually slows. The reason for this is not clear but such factors as growth inhibitory feedback may be one of the factors.

[4] Growth Spurts (1,5) Gompertzian growth may be interrupted by temporary growth spurts which may be secondary to loss of inhibitory feedback or other poorly understood factors.

[5] Irregular Growth (Plateaus of Slow or No Growth) (1,5) Plateaus of no growth or slow growth interspersed with periods of Gompertzian growth are not uncommon and may persist for months. The cause is uncertain but may be secondary to episodes of necrosis, spontaneous regression, errors of measurement of the tumor or other unknown factors.

The use of the doubling time defense assumes a constant linear or Gompertzian growth of the breast cancer. In reality, the doubling time of breast cancer varies from just a few days to over a year. Additionally, the growth rate of an individual cancer is not only constantly changing (linear, exponential, Gompertzian) during the life cycle of the tumor, but is further complicated by unpredictable plateaus of no growth or periods of rapid growth. In most cases, this totally destroys the accuracy of the doubling time defense.

Comment

The growth charactistics of the vast majority of breast cancers are quite predictable and consist of an early exponential phase followed by a long period of deceleratory growth. The tumors with periods of irregular growth, slow growth, or no growth tend to grow more slowly and are seldom involved in litigation. Rapidly growing tumors with extremely short doubling times can be identified by careful examination of the clinical history, tumor grading, a high % S-phase fraction, certain unfavorable microscopic risk factors as tumor invasion of vascular and lymphatic lymphatic capillaries, and various adverse molecular risk factors. (See Chapter 23).

[c] Precise Measurements of Tumor Size are Difficult to Obtain

Tumor size is not as easy to establish as one might think since tumors are usually spheroidal rather than circular. Tumor borders are often irregular and indistinct making the precise tumor diameter difficult to ascertain with accuracy and even small errors of measurement seriously impair the accuracy of the doubling time defense.

Comment

This is not a problem. Tumor diameters determined by gross and microscopic examination (before and after the sectioning of the tumor) in the pathology laboratory by a skilled pathologist are quite adequate.

[d] The Growth Fraction of the Tumor Varies

The portion of cells actively and constantly dividing is called the growth fraction (the remainder of the cells are dormant). The growth fraction of breast cancer is usually about 5% but this can vary. This is another source of error when calculating the onset of a metastatic event.

Comment

This is a theoretical objection which is not valid. The clinical history, percent S-phase fraction, and/or the mitotic index will provide reliable information concerning the growth fraction and the proliferation rate of the breast cancer.

[e] Tumors Contain Varying Amounts of Benign Stroma

When we are computing the onset of a metastatic event from a tumor with a diameter of 10 mm the doubling time defense assumes that the tumor contains 1 billion cells. For example:

If cancers consisted of nothing but cancer cells then:

# doublings	# tumor cells	tumor size
0	1	1/1,000,000 mm 3 (cubed)
10	1,000	0.1 mm
20	1,000,000	1mm
30	1 billion	10 mm (1cm)
40	1 trillion	10 cm (1 kilogram)

When we calculate the number of cancer cells within a tumor we are assuming that the tumor consists of nothing but tumor cells. This is not the case. Some tumors may contain as much as 90% stroma while others may contain as little as 10% stroma. Thus if we do not know the proportion of benign stroma within the tumor, our calculations of the number of tumor cells will be in error.

Comment

This is true, however, the amount of benign stroma can easily be ascertained by microscopic examination of the tumor. Knowing the percentage of benign stroma, it is simple to calculate the number of tumor cells within the cancer. Ask your patholgist or oncologist for assistance.

[f] Areas of Tumor Necrosis are a Source of Error

Another source of error is the presence of tumor necrosis or hemorrhage within the tumor. Necrosis and hemorrhage will decrease the number of viable tumor cells within the tumor.

Comment

This is not a problem. The amount of tumor necrosis, if any, can easily be determined by gross and microscopic examination of the tumor.

§19.04 PLAINTIFF WILL CHARGE IT IS IMPOSSIBLE TO EXTRAPOLATE BACKWARD AND ESTABLISH THE TIME OF ONSET OF A METASTATIC EVENT

When extrapolating backward to establish the time of a metastatic event, you are employing an estimated doubling time, although you really have no idea of the true length of the doubling time. Futhermore, you are using a vague estimate of the number of tumor cells within the tumor. And finally, you are totally ignoring the growth pattern of the tumor. With this information it is impossible to accurately establish the time of a metastatic event by backward extrapolation.

Comment

We are not attempting to determine the exact minute, hour, week or even the month of a metastatic event. We are attempting to determine the approximate year of an event. Extreme variations in the doubling times and growth rates can usually be recognized. It is obvious that tumors with long doubling times or prolonged periods of no growth or slow growth will not be encountered in the courtroom. The extremely rapidly growing tumors can easily be excluded by a review of the clinical history, tumor grading, unfavorable microscopic findings such as tumor invasion of the vascular and lymphatic capillaries, a high % S-phase fraction, and various unfavorable molecular risk factors. (See Chapter 23). We are calculating the doubling time defense for a typical breast cancer with its predictable growth pattern of early exponential and subsequent deceleratory growth. If used properly, and for short periods of time (12 to 18 months), the doubling defense will be quite accurate.

§19.05 WHEN SERIAL MEASUREMENTS OF THE TUMOR ARE AVAILABLE IT WILL BE DIFFICULT TO QUESTION THE VALIDITY OF THE DOUBLING TIME DEFENSE

[a] If serial measurements of the tumor or metastasis over a period of 6-12 months are available from mammograms or chest x-rays; and

[b] If you have a precise measurement of the tumor, that is, the width, length and depth; and

[c] If you can calculate from a microscopic examination of the tumor the approximate percentage of tumor cells versus benign stroma, then it is possible to determine the net cell doubling time for the tumor and the number of cancer cells within the tumor. If this data is used to extrapolate backward for a period no longer than 12-18 months your computations should be quite accurate.

§19.06 CONCLUSION

The doubling time defense is subject to a number or errors which limits its ability to predict the exact day, week, or month of an event. Nevertheless, the doubling time defense is still used by many defense attorneys. Certainly, if properly used, the doubling time defense should be able to predict whether or not an event occurred within a period of 12 to 18 months prior to the time of diagnosis. Dr. Plotkin describes his technique for using the doubling time defense in his commentary which follows Chapter 10, Appendix 10-2.

In general, the authors recommend a defense based upon:

[a] Education of the jury regarding the basic tenets of the biology and natural history of breast cancer.

[b] Education of the jury regarding the time of diagnosis as outlined in the Visual Aids of the Appendices for Chapters 6, 9, and 10.

[c] The doubling time defense can be employed as an adjunct to the education of the jury but, in our opinion, will be more effective if the jury understands the basic truths concerning the biology of breast cancer.

References

1. Spratt JS and Spratt JA, Growth Rates in *Cancer of the Breast,* 3rd ed, Donegan and Spratt, eds. WB Saunders, 1988, pp 270-302.

2. Spratt JS, Kallenbach ML and Spratt JA. Cytokinetic Definition of Acute and Chronic Cancer. Cancer Research 37:226, 1977.
3. Fournier DV, Weber E, Hoeffken W, et al. Growth Rate of 147 Mammary Cancers. Cancer 16: 961, 1963.
4. Galante E. Milan Italy: Personal communication to Spratt JS and Spratt JA, Growth Rates in *Cancer of the Breast,* 3rd ed, Donegan and Spratt, eds. WB Saunders, 1988, pp 284-285, table 10-8.
5. Retsky, Michael W et al. Is Gompertzian or Exponential Growth a Valid Description of Individual Human Cancer Growth? Medical Hypothesis 33(2):95-106, 1990.

CHAPTER 20: LIMITATIONS OF EARLY DIAGNOSIS

Chapter 20

LIMITATIONS OF EARLY DIAGNOSIS

§20.1 INTRODUCTION

Early diagnosis has and always will play an important role in the management of cancer but unfortunately it has not proven to be effective in lowering the mortality rates of all cancers. This is not surprising since the effectiveness of early intervention depends upon the inherent biology of the cancer and the ability of the screening programs to identify small cancers before they metastasize to distant sites. The steady decline in the mortality rate of cancer of the uterine cervix is secondary to early diagnosis which was made possible by the widespread use of the Papanicolaou test (Pap smear) (1). The Pap smear identifies many cervical cancers before they acquire the ability to metastasize. Early diagnosis of cancer of the endometrium of the uterus has been successful in reducing the mortality rate primarily because these cancers tend to be well differentiated and localized (1). On the other hand, the rapid growth and usually fatal course of small cell carcinoma of the lung thus far has not been altered by early diagnosis (2). For many years the American Cancer Society, all of our national Medical Societies and the mass media have extensively promoted the early diagnosis of breast cancer. Why, in spite of all our efforts, have we failed to improve the age-adjusted survival rate of breast cancer? There are a number of reasons, which are discussed throughout this book. A summary of these follows.

§20.02 FACTORS MITIGATING THE EFFECTIVENESS OF EARLY DETECTION

[a] Many Breast Cancers Metastasize before They Can be Detected by Mammography

Some breast cancers metastasize before detection by mammography is possible. Ten to 20% of breast cancers will not be visualized by x-ray because the lesions are 100% camouflaged. (See Chapter 14). Donegan (3) reported that 18% of clearly palpable breast cancers in one series could not be visualized by mammography. Additionally, some tumors are partially camouflaged and will be difficult to detect by x-ray.

[b] Most Breast Cancers Cannot be Detected by Palpation Until 75% of Their Life Cycle Has Elapsed

Unfortunately, almost all breast cancers remain camouflaged within the breast (pre–threshold in size) for the first 75% of their life cycle (until they reach a diameter of 1.0 cm and can be palpated). Others will remain camouflaged within the breast until these tumors attain diameters of 2.0, 3.0, or 4.0 cm or larger and 80 to 90% of their life cycle has elapsed. Reducing the durations of symptoms (earlier diagnosis) of these biologically old symptomatic tumors in the terminal phase of their life cycle will not alter the outcome (4,5). Those tumors with the ability to metastasize will have done so prior to the times these lesions became large enough to produce symptoms. (See Chapter 10).

[c] The Interval Tumor

Interval tumors are defined as breast cancers that surface within 12 months of a negative screening examination. These cancers were present within the breast at the time of the last screening examination but were too small to be detected. These rapidly growing tumors can easily double their diameter two, three or even four times within a period of 12 months and can surface as fairly large tumors. (See Chapter 17). These are dangerous tumors.

§20.03 CONCLUSION

The effectveness of early diagnosis is dependent upon the inherent biology of the tumor and tumor camouflaging rather than physician skill. For some breast cancers no matter how early the diagnosis or how high the standard of care, cure will not result.

References

1. Gusberg SB and Runowicz CD. Gynecologic Cancers, in *Clinical Oncology,* Holleb, Fink, and Murphy, eds., American Cancer Society, 1991, pp 481-497.
2. Faber LP. Lung Cancer, in *Clinical Oncology,* Holleb, Fink, and Murphy, eds., American Cancer Society, 1991, pp 194-212.
3. Donegan WL. Evalulation of a Palpable Mass: Current Concepts. N Eng J Med 327(13): 937-942, 1992.
4. Fisher ER, et al. A Perspective Concerning the Relation of Durations of Symptoms to Treatment Failure in Patients with Breast Cancer. Cancer 40:3160-3167,1977.
5. Spratt JS. Realities of Breast Cancer Control, Public Expectations, and the Law. Surg Oncol Clin N Am 3(1):25-34, 1994.

CHAPTER 21: SCREENING INTERVALS AND FOLLOW-UP

CHAPTER 21

SCREENING INTERVALS AND FOLLOW-UP

§21.01 INTRODUCTION

It has been well established that women with certain risk factors are more likely to develop breast cancer. These major risk factors are:

[a] Epithelial hyperplasia with atypia;
[b] Epithelial hyperplasia with atypia and a positive family history of breast cancer in one or two first degree relatives;
[c] Carcinoma-in-situ (duct cell or lobular);
[d] Family history of one or two first degree relatives with breast cancer, especially if the cancers were early onset or bilateral; and
[e] A personal history of breast cancer.

Recently these risk factors have become significant from the medical-legal standpoint (1). Women who develop early recurrence of their breast cancer often search for reasons why ''early diagnosis'' failed in their case. When these women learn that they had one or more of these risk factors they may question why a more aggressive screening program with more frequent screening intervals was not recommended. Bitterness and a malpractice claim are often the result.

§21.02 NO EVIDENCE THAT AGGRESSIVE SCREENING FOR HIGH-RISK WOMEN WILL REDUCE MORTALITY

All American women are at high risk for developing breast cancer since they have 1 chance in 9 of developing breast cancer by age 75. Even women with no known risk factors have 1 chance in 17 (5.9%) of developing breast cancer by age 75. Thus Berg (2,3) concluded that all women are at high risk of developing breast cancer. Eddy (2,4) observed that women with no risk factors have two-thirds of all breast cancers while the high-risk group has only one-third of the cancers. Therefore, all women should be advised to follow faithfully the screening guidelines of the American Cancer Society.

Berg (2,3) concludes that targeting the high-risk group for special screening would cause unnecessary anxiety in the women with high-risk factors and a false sense of security to those without risk factors. Alexander, et al. (2,5) specifically studied the use of risk factors in determining screening intervals. The results of their study were almost entirely negative. Spratt and Spratt (1) state "There are no controlled trials correlating screening strategies with benefit for the various subsets of risks reviewed."

Garber, Henderson, Love, and Gelman (6) reviewed aggressive screening programs for women thought to have truly genetic breast cancer histories with multiple relatives affected with early onset and/or bilateral breast cancers. These authors commented concerning the effectiveness of special screening programs for high-risk women.

> "It should be noted, however, that there are no data that demonstrate the effectiveness of this policy *[special screening]* in either improved detection or reduced breast cancer mortality. Mammography is often less sensitive in evaluating the denser breasts of younger women. Furthermore, it is plausible that the additional risk of the cumulative radiation exposure in young women who are otherwise at elevated risk would not be trivial."

Contrary to scientific data "conventional wisdom" hopefully suggests that women with increased risk factors will benefit from more intensive screening programs such as an early baseline mammogram with yearly mammograms thereafter, and breast examination at 4-6 months intervals.

Since there are no data that aggressive screening programs improve detection and reduce the mortality rate of breast cancer perhaps more potentially productive programs, such as the use of chemopreventative agents, should seriously be considered for women with a high risk of developing breast cancer. Breast cancer chemopreventative programs are currently undergoing evaluation in a large clinical trial.

§21.03 GUIDELINES FOR SCREENING WOMEN WITH HIGH-RISK FACTORS

[a] Mammograms

Garber, Henderson, Love, and Gelman 6) conclude:

> "We are not aware of any data to support the usefulness of mammography more frequently than annually for women with any degree of increased breast cancer risk."

We also have failed to find evidence supporting the use of mammograms more frequently than every 12 months for women with an increased risk of breast cancer.

[b] Physical Examinations

A frequency of every six months is thought to be adequate for women with high-risk factors. We have found that few women will continue a program of physical examinatin of the breast at 3 or 4 months interval for any length of time (7).

[c] Monthly Breast Self Examinations

It is difficult to document the true value of monthly breast self examination. However, it costs nothing and if conscientiously and regularly performed, may help. All women should be taught the technique of, and encouraged to perform, monthly breast self examinations.

§21.04 EARLY DETECTION OF LOCAL RECURRENCE FOLLOWING SURGERY DOES NOT INCREASE SURVIVAL

[a] Radical Mastectomy, Modified Radical Mastectomy, and Total Mastectomy

Traditionally these women have had physical examinations every six months and annual mammograms and chest x-rays. Tomin and Donegan (2,8) studied 1,230 women with a personal history of breast cancer and compared self surveillance and the traditional follow-up procedure. They were unable to show a survival benefit for the structured follow-up plans.

In our experience, local recurrence following these procedures almost always indicates the presence of systemic breast cancer (7). Earlier detection and treatment will seldom alter the ultimate outcome. The few patients that survive for 10 years do so because of the biology of the tumor rather than the time or the nature of the treatment (8,9,10).

[b] Breast Conservative Surgery (Lumpectomy With and Without Postoperative Radiation)

Local recurrence following conservative surgery does not always indicate the presence of distant metastasis. At least 50% of women whose local recurrences are treated with wide local excision or mastectomy will survive for five years. The question we must answer is, ''Does earlier detection and treatment of local recurrence following lumpectomy alter the final outcome''? Although some think that earlier detection of recurrence does benefit survival (10), consider the following:

Probability of Local Recurrence Following Lumpectomy (2,000 women) NSABP-B06 (11)

Procedure	% Local Recurrence	% 9 Year Survival
Lumpectomy alone	43%	59%
Lumpectomy + Rad	12%	60%
Total Mastectomy	low	63%

NSABP - National Surgical Adjuvant Breast Project

Rad = radiation therapy

Modified from Figure 1, page 328, Fisher B,et al., Lancet 338:327-331, 1991 (11).

Examination of this study reveals that (11):

1. The use of radiation following lumpectomy reduced the incidence of local recurrence from 43% to 12% but did not significantly alter the survival rate.
2. Substituting total mastectomy for lumpectomy eliminated virtually all of the local recurrences but again did not significantly alter the final outcome.
3. Fisher et al. report that women who have evidence of local recurrence following lumpectomy have a 3.41 times greater chance of harboring distant metastases.

Fisher, et al. (11) concluded that local recurrence following lumpectomy is a "marker" for the presence of systemic disease which was present at the time of the initial surgery. The local recurrence is not the cause of the systemic disease Thus, local recurrence is only a "marker" for a risk already present at the time of surgery (a 3.41 times greater chance of having systemic disease). Fisher's study demonstrated that when the breast is removed at the initial surgery the risk of local recurrence is greatly reduced but the final outcome is not significantly altered. Thus, earlier detection and removal of local recurrences following lumpectomy will not alter the final outcome.

§21.05 CONCLUSION

In view of the litigious nature of our society, when confronted with the woman with a high-risk of developing breast cancer, we would recommend the following for the physician:

a. Confirm the fact that your patient is really at high-risk by obtaining a second opinion.
b. Obtain a second opinion regarding the possibility of using chemopreventative agents, the feasiblity of bilateral subcutaneous mastectomy or prophylactic mastectomy with immediate reconstruction. These procedures, however, are seldom performed.

§21.06 ADDENDUM

There is increasing evidence that intensive follow-up programs for post-operative breast cancer patients do not increase survival. Ninety percent of all recurrences are discovered by the patient (12). Schapira and Urban (13) agree with Tomin and Donegan that a ''minimalist'' follow-up program is sufficient. And recently two large scale Italian trials (14,15) suggest that intensive follow-up programs are no better than surveillance by the family doctor.

References

1. Spratt JS and Spratt SW. Medical and Legal Implications of Screening for Breast Cancer. Cancer 66:1351-1362, 1990.
2. Spratt JS, Donegan WL, and Greenberg RA. Screening and Follow-up, in *Cancer of the Breast,* 3rd ed, Donegan and Spratt, WB Saunders, 1988, pp 558-590.
3. Berg JW. Clinical Implications of Risk Factors for Breast Cancer. Cancer 53:589-591, 1984
4. Eddy DM. Breast Cancer Screening. (Letter) J Natl Can Inst 81:234-235, 1989.
5. Alexander FE, Roberts NM, Huggins A, and Muir BB. Use of Risk Factors to Allocate Schedules for Breast Cancer Screening. J. Epidemiol. Community Health. 42:193-199, 1988.
6. Garber JE, Henderson IG, Love SM, and Gelman RS. Management of High-Risk Groups, in *Breast Diseases,* 2nd ed., Harris, Hellman, Henderson, and Kinne, eds., JB Lippincott Co. 1991, pp 152-163.
7. Watts, C.F. Personal experience of the author.
8. Tomin, R and Donegan, WL. Screening for Recurrent Breast Cancer—Its Effectiveness and Prognostic Value. J. Clin. Oncol., 5:62, 1987.
9. Recht A and Hayes D. Local Recurrence Following Mastectomy, in *Breast Diseases,* 2nd ed, Harris, Hellman, Henderson, and Kinne, pages 527-540, JB Lippincott Co., 1991.

10. Stotter, Anne, et al. Survival Following Locoregional Recurrence After Breast Conservation Therapy for Cancer. Ann Surg, 212(2):166-172, 1990.
11. Fisher, Bernard, et al. Significance of Ipsilateral Breast Tumour Recurrence After Lumpectomy. Lancet 338:327-331, 1991.
12. Spratt JS. Cost-Effective Follow-Up of Breast Cancer. (Letter). J Clin Oncol 12(9): page 1996, September 1994.
13. Schapira DV, Urban N. A Minimalist Policy for Breast Cancer Surveillance. JAMA 265-380-382, 1991.
14. GIVIO Investigators. Impact of Follow-Up Testing on Survival and Health-Related Quality of Life in Breast Cancer Patients. A Multicenter Randomized Controlled Trial. JAMA 271:1587-1592, 1994.
15. Del Turco MR, Palli D, Cariddi A, et al. Intensive Diagnostic Follow-Up After Treatment of Primary Breast Cancer: A Randomized Trial. JAMA 271:1593-1597, 1994.

CHAPTER 22: BIASES

CHAPTER 22

BIASES

§22.01 INTRODUCTION: STATISTICS DISTORTED BY BIASES

For years the medical literature and mass media have been flooded with reports of decreases in the mortality rate of breast cancer secondary to earlier diagnosis and/or various treatment innovations. These over-enthusiastic and inflated claims have created false hopes of cure for countless women. Alexander Walt, a prominent breast cancer expert, recently stated:

> "Sadly, despite our best efforts, we have not as yet produced data to show that we have improved the overall mortality rate [of breast cancer]. . . . Currently our muted triumphs lie mainly in the area of extended palliation and in the avoidance of unnecessarily destructive surgery."(1)

Thus far, improvements in the survival rate of breast cancer are limited largely to a special group of self-selected asymptomatic women whose cancers were detected by periodic screening with mammograms and small subsets of patients treated with postoperative adjuvant chemotherapy.

Therefore, when you encounter claims of cure or the possibility of cure that sound too good to be true remember the following:

> The magician creates illusions with smoke and mirrors. The unwary, over-enthusiatic clinician can create illusions (false claims) of cure when biases are allowed to contaminate his/her data.

When you suspect this possibility, ask your expert witness to consider the following biases. Does one or more of these impair the validity of the plaintiff's data?

§22.02 TYPES OF BIASES

Experts and the public have biases regarding various aspects of breast cancer. The following are suggestions for bringing out these biases and refuting them. Ask for the precise source of the opposing expert's data. Insist on a reference and obtain a copy for your expert witness. Discuss the possibility of the following biases with your expert witness.

[a] Biases Structured into the Study

1. Inadequate number of patients
2. Inadequate number of controls
3. Short follow-up
4. Selection bias
5. Eligibility bias

[b] Stage Creep (2,3)

Gelman and Zelen (3) have defined diagnostic bias (stage creep) as follows:

> As diagnostic and staging tests get better, each stage, except the worst, loses some bad prognostic patients and each stage except possibly the first gains some good prognostic patients; hence, survival appears to improve within each stage although the overall survival may stay the same.

Shifting patients from one group to the next can also cause stage creep.

[c] Lead Time Bias (3)

Periodic screening detects many cancers with occult systemic disease at an earlier stage in their life cycle. These patients, although not cured, live longer following diagnosis, thus improving the five year survival rate.

[d] Length Bias (3)

Slower growing tumors are more apt to be discovered at the time of yearly screening examinations. More rapidly growing tumors are more likely to surface between yearly screening examinations. Therefore, a study containing a preponderance of tumors discovered during routine screening examinations will have a better survival than a group of tumors surfacing between screening examinations (interval tumors).

[e] Overdiagnosis Bias (3)

Screening examinations with improved mammographic techniques detect many small breast cancers. Some of these small cancers may have little or no lethal potential. This falsely improves the survival rate of breast cancer.

[f] Other Biases

For a more detailed discussion of biases, consult the excellent article by Gelman and Zelen (3).

§22.03 EXAMPLES OF OVERDIAGNOSIS BIAS

Mass screening with more sensitive diagnostic mammographic techniques is detecting many small cancers and is partially responsible for the 23-32% increase in the incidence of breast cancer between 1973 and 1987 (1). Some of these small "cancers," however, may have less malignant potential than the cancers discovered in the 1930's and 1950's. Consider the following:

[a] Prostate Cancer

Autopsy studies reveal histologic evidence of prostate cancer in 14 to 46% of men over the age of 50 (4). Postmortem examination of men over the age of 70 who died of other causes revealed occult foci of cancer in 80% of the prostates (5). Yet the incidence of prostate cancer is only 87.7 per 100,000 male population (4). Thus it is obvious that although many lesions within the prostate gland histologically resemble adenocarcinoma, most never complete the steps necessary to acquire the ability to invade and metastasize (6). The majority remain latent.

[b] Breast Cancer

Nielsen et al (7) performed 83 consecutive autopsies in women older than 20 years and found 21 (25%) had invasive adenocarcinomas or premalignant lesions of the breast. These are the type of lesions which mass screening with mammography is detecting. Unfortunately, we know nothing about the natural history or biology of these small lesions which could not be detected in the past by conventional means. We suspect that, like the latent prostate cancers, many will never complete the necessary steps that will enable them to invade and metastasize. Thus the detection of small lesions histologically resembling invasive carcinomas could produce a serious overdiagnosis bias as well as a lead time bias. Mass screening with mammography may eventually lower the age-adjusted mortality rate of breast cancer but the authors suspect that it will be less than the 30% figure quoted by Tabar (8).

§22.04 CONCLUSION

Biases in the breast cancer literature are not uncommon. They can be quite subtle and difficult to detect. Defense should not hesitate to ask the expert medical witness for assistance in evaluating medical data presented by the plaintiff.

References

1. Walt Alexander. Breast Cancer: Totems, Taboos, Torts, and Tomorrow. Mayo Alumni 28 (2): 12-17 Spring 1992.
2. Donegan WL. Staging and Primary Treatment. *Cancer of the Breast,* 3rd ed. WB Saunders, 1988, pp 336-402.
3. Gelman R and Zelen M. Interpreting Clinical Data. In *Breast Diseases,* Harris, Hellman, Henderson, and Kinne, eds. JB Lippincott, 1987, pp 697-731.

4. Frank IN, Graham SD, and Nabors WL. Urologic and Male Genital Cancers, in *Clinical Oncology,* Holleb, Fink, and Murphy, eds., pp 271-290, American Cancer Society, 1991.
5. Paulson D. Diseases of the Prostate in *Clinical Symposia,* Ciba-Geigy 41(2):17, 1989.
6. Carter BS and Isaacs JT, Predisposing Factors to Prostate Cancer in *Endocrine Related Cancers,* # 4, ed., Stoll BA, ICI Pharma, ISSN0260-0897, Wilmington, Delaware 1989.
7. Nielsen M, Jensen J, and Andersen J. Precancerous and Cancerous Breast Lesions During Lifetime and Autopsy. Cancer 54:612-615, 1984.
8. Tabar L, Fagerberg G, et al. Viewpoint—Breast Cancer Treatment and Natural History: New Insights From Results of Screening. The Lancet. 339: Feb 15, 1992, pp 412-414.

CHAPTER 23: PROGNOSTIC FACTORS

CHAPTER 23

PROGNOSTIC FACTORS

23.01 GATHERING EVIDENCE OF TUMOR AGGRESSIVENESS

[a] Introduction

It is not enough to state that all breast cancers are not alike or that the plaintiff's clinical history suggested a tumor with great lethal potential. We must attempt to provide additional evidence that the plaintiff's breast cancer was indeed more aggressive than the average breast cancer. To do this, we must carefully examine the plaintiff's tumor for evidence of unfavorable prognostic factors. This can be a daunting task since investigators have discovered numerous prognostic indicators and the list is constantly growing. Unfortunately, some of these prognostic factors are weak, some overlap with others, a few are more predictive of response to drugs or hormones rather than prognosis, and many are expensive. Noel Weidner (1) reminds us that "There are well established prognostic tests that work quite well, but because they are older they tend not to be as newsworthy." Thus, defense should not ignore older tests such as tumor grading and certain adverse microscopic factors as blood and lymphatic capillary tumor invasion and tumor necrosis.

[b] Evaluation of the Routine Pathology Report

The busy pathologist, of course, is primarily concerned with whether or not the lesion is cancer and determining the precise histologic type of the cancer. He/she does not usually provide a detailed report regarding prognostic factors. Therefore, it is not surprising that a meticulous examination of the tumor may reveal significant information which was not provided in the routine pathology report.

The value of a careful microscopic examination of breast cancer by a skilled patholgist should not be underestimated. Noel Weidner (1) has this to say about this procedure. "The [microscopic] appearance of the tumor is in a sense the 'bottom line summation' of its genetic abnormalities. There's a great deal of information in the microscopic appearance of a tumor and anatomic pathologists can provide a wealth of information to clinicians and patients." Thus, the pathologist can be of great help to the defense.

[c] Meet With the Pathologist

1. ***Prepare a Check List of Unfavorable Prognostic Factors***
   Prepare a check list of prognostic factors and review each item with the pathologist. Request that each test be performed and discuss the significance of each.
2. ***Review the Items on the Check List With the Pathologist***
   A. Gross examination of tumor
      1. Tumor size
      2. Indistinct borders—Invasive?

   B. Histologic type of the plantiff's breast cancer
      1. Unfavorable tumor type?
      2. Intermediate tumor type?
      3. Favorable tumor type?
3. ***Microscopic Examination***
   A. Tumor grade
   B. Histologic grade
   C. Nuclear grade
   D. Mitotic grade or index
   E. Adverse microscopic risk factors
      1. Tumor invasion of blood capillaries; if negative ask that special stains be used to identify capillary walls.
      2. Tumor invasion of lymphatic capillaries; if negative ask that special stains be used to identify walls of lymphatic channels.
      3. Foci of tumor necrosis.
4. ***Molecular Prognostic Factors***
   A. Estrogen and progesterone receptors

B. DNA flow cytometry
1. ploidy
2. S-phase fraction

C. HER-2/neu oncogene
1. Overexpression
2. Amplification

5. *New Prognostic Factors*
   A. Mutant p53 Suppressor Oncogene Protein
   B. Angiogenesis (microvessel count)
6. *Ask Pathologist About The Recent Literature Concerning Prognostic Factors*

[d] Assemble a List of the Adverse Risk Factors Found in the Plaintiff's Breast Cancer

1. *Check the Appropriate Sections in this Chapter Regarding:*
   A. The rationale, history, and prognostic worth of each adverse prognostic factor discovered in the plaintiff's breast cancer.
   B. Gather information concerning the increased predictive power of combinations of negative prognostic discriminates.
2. *Ask the Pathologist About the Recent Literature Concerning Prognostic Parameters*

[e] Interpretation of Conflicting Laboratory Reports

When confronted with a clinically aggressive tumor whose laboratory reports yield both unfavorable and favorable prognostic determinants consider the following: In some respects the huge population of cancer cells within a breast tumor resemble the population of a large city. New York City, for example, contains many different ethnic groups while breast tumors contain a number of different groups [clones] of cells. Not uncommonly breast cancers contain:

- rapidly growing clones [groups] of cells while other clones may be growing slowly or not at all,

- some clones that possess the ability to metastasize to distant sites while other clones may lack this ability,
- some clones may contain estrogen receptors [estrogen receptor positive] while other clones may lack estrogen receptors [estrogen receptor negative],
- some clones may overexpress the HER-2/neu protein while other clones do not.

Thus it is not uncommon for biologically aggressive breast cancers to occasionally contain clones of cells that yield favorable prognostic factors. It is important to remember, however, that the clinical behavior of the tumor is determined by the behavior of the aggressive clones within the tumor. The clones of cells that express only favorable signs do not participate in the metastatic process. Therefore, when making your assessment of the aggressiveness of a breast cancer, ignore the favorable prognostic determinants and base your opinion upon the clinical behavior of the tumor and the profile of unfavorable prognostic determinants.

[f] Conclusion

Certainly adding several or more unfavorable prognostic factors to the aggressive history of the plaintiff's breast cancer will add considerable weight to your assertions that the plaintiff's breast cancer was more aggressive than the average breast cancer.

References

1. Weidner, Noel. Quoted by Tom Reynolds in Breast Cancer Prognostic Factors—The Search Goes On. News, News. J. Natl Can Instit 86(7):480-483, April 6, 1994.

§23.02 LYMPH NODE-NEGATIVE BREAST CANCER

[a] Introduction: Defending Use of Prognostic Factors

Although the absence of axillary lymph node metastases predicts a good prognosis, there are a number of unfavorable prognostic risk factors that may enable the defense to identify some node-negative women who have unusually aggressive breast cancers. Consider the following:

[b] Tumor Size (See also Chapters 11,14,15)

Although the size of a breast cancer may at times be secondary to physician delay, more often than not the tumor size is secondary to one or more of the following factors.

1. A tumor with a large threshold size as the result of a serious camouflaging problem.
2. A rapidly growing or biologic aggressive tumor (1).

Christine Carter, et al. (1) studied 24,740 breast cancer cases and concluded that tumor size and lymph node status are independent but additive prognostic factors. As tumor size increased, survival decreased even when lymph node status remained constant. For example:

5 Year Breast Cancer Survival of Lymph Node-Negative Patients

# Patients	Tumor Size	Relative Survival
5,278	< 2.0 cm	96.3%
6,927	2-5 cm	89.4%
809	> 5.0 cm	82.2%

Modified from Carter, et al. (1)
Cancer 63:181-187, 1989, Table 3.
Reprinted courtesy of author and publisher.

Carter, et al. also noted that the incidence (%) of axillary metastases increased dramatically with increasing tumor size.

Tumor Size and the Incidence of Axillary Node Metastases

Tumor Size	Axillary Metastases (%)
<0.5 cm	20%
1.0-1.9 cm	33%
2.0-2.9 cm	43%
3.0-3.9 cm	52%
4.0-4.9 cm	60%
>5.0 cm	70%

Modified from Carter (1)
Cancer 63:181-187, 1989, Figure 4, page 185.
Reprinted courtesy of author and publisher.

Thus, short-term studies (5 years) reveal that as tumor size increases, so does the incidence of systemic disease, but this is only part of the story. Long-term studies (18.2 years) of 474 patients by Rosen et al. demonstrate that the issue is more complicated (2). Using the methods of Brinkley and Haybittle (3) these authors compared the observed and expected survival curves of women with lymph node negative breast cancer. They observed that (4):

Expected Mortality Rate at 20 Years of Lymph Node-Negative Breast Cancer (474 patients)

Tumor Diameter	% Dead at 20 Years
1 cm or less	20%
1.2 -2.0 cm	30%

Source: McGuire WL et al. J Natl Can Inst 82(12):1006-1015, 1990 reference # 4.

The fact that 20% of lymph node-negative breast cancers with diameters of 1 cm or less have systemic disease is interesting because we know that the incidence of systemic disease is much higher in breast cancers with axillary metastasis. Consider these facts:

> 16 to 22% of breast cancers with a diameter of only 1 mm have been found to have evidence of axillary lymph node metastasis (5,6). See Chapter 10, Metastasis: When Does It Occur?

Therefore if we consider all cases of breast cancer (both node-negative and positive) we will discover that the incidence of incurable disease in breast cancers 1 cm or less is much greater than 20%, perhaps as high as 25-30%. Keep in mind, we are merely attempting to determine whether or not the plaintiff's breast cancer belongs to this group of early metastasizing breast cancers. It is also important to remember that all of the cancers with favorable outcomes (60% +/−) will have been excluded in the courtroom. Therefore, almost two-thirds of the cancers will have metastasized quite early in their life cycle.

References

1. Carter CL, Allen C, and Henson DE. Relation of Tumor Size, Lymph Node Status, and Survival in 24,740 Breast Cancer Cases. Cancer 63:181-187, 1989.

2. Rosen PP, Groshen S, Saigo PE, et al. Pathologic Factors in Stage I (T1N0M0) and Stage II (T1N1M0) Breast Carcinoma: A Study of 644 Patients With a Median Follow-up of 18 Years. J Clin Oncol 7:1239-1251, 1989.
3. Brinkley D and Haybittle JL. Long-Term Survival of Women With Breast Cancer. The Lancet 1:1118, May 19, 1984.
4. McGuire WL, et al. How to Use Prognostic Factors in Axillary Node-Negative Breast Cancer Patients. J Natl Can Instit 82(12):1006-1015,1990.
5. Kopald KH, et al. The Pathology of Nonpalpable Breast Cancer. The American Surgeon 56(12):782-787, 1990.
6. Margolis DS. Is Axillary Dissection Obligatory? Oncology Times 13(1):1-3, January 1991.

[c] Tumor Grading (Histologic Grade, Nuclear Grade, and Mitotic Grade)

Some not only have little confidence in the grading of tumors but seem to take perverse delight in belittling the value of tumor grading. If you plan to use grading (and we think you should) it is imperative that both defense and the medical witness become familiar with the history of tumor grading so that you will have confidence in its true worth.

For almost 100 years numerous observers recognized that the microscopic appearance of cancers correlated with clinical outcome . Broders in 1920, however, was the first to perceive the concept that epithelial tumors could be graded or classified according to the maturity of the cancer cells (1). In 1925, in an elegant paper, Greenough (2) was the first to report that the grading of breast cancers correlated with prognosis. In the 1950's, Bloom, and Bloom and Richardson personally graded over 1400 breast cancers and developed a practical system for the grading of breast cancers (3,4). They proved conclusively that grading, when performed by experienced pathologists, can accurately identify a group of women with an increased risk of relapse. The tumors were graded according to the degree of differentiation (maturity) of the tumor. The most differentiated tumors were graded I and had the best prognosis. The least differentiated tumors were graded III and had the worst prognosis. This system, still in use today, classified breast cancers according to:

Histologic grades (HG) I,II,III --- degree of tubule formation
Nuclear grades, (NG) I,II,III ----- immaturity of tumor nuclei
Mitotic grades (MG) I,II,III ------ frequency mitotic figures

Tumor Grade I,II,III --------------- considers histologic, nuclear and mitotic grades.

Tumor grading, however, never became popular for several reasons. First, knowing the prognosis of breast cancer had no clinical significance since no additional treatments were available. Secondly, most pathologists did not take the time to become proficient in the grading of breast cancers and as a result there was a problem of reproducibility. Today effective adjuvant chemotherapy programs are available and prognosis is important since women with a poor prognosis may benefit from postoperative adjuvant chemotherapy or hormonal therapy. Conversely, there is a need to identify women who are probably "cured" of their breast cancer and should be spared the rigors of adjuvant chemotherapy. As a result there has been a resurgence of research regarding the effectiveness and technique of, and alternatives to, tumor grading.

[1] Tumor Grade Tumor grade measures the maturity of all cytologic features of breast cancer (HG, NG, and MG) and has been evaluated in thousands of cases for over 60 years. Again and again it has, in experienced hands, proven to be an accurate predictor of prognosis. See articles by Bloom, Bloom and Richardson, and Henson and Ries (3,4,5,6).

[2] Histologic Grade Recent evidence suggests that histologic grade adds little or nothing to the predictive value of nuclear grade (7,8).

[3] Nuclear Grade In the hands of experienced pathologists nuclear grade has proven to be a powerful predictor of the prognosis of node-negative breast cancer. In recent years many pathologists have included an evaluation of the frequency of mitotic figures. It is imperative, however, that the pathologist have special training and interest in this procedure. Fisher, et al. (9) have modified nuclear grade as follows (9):

Nuclear grade good ----- formerly nuclear grades I and II

Nuclear grade poor ----- formerly nuclear grade III.

Fisher, et al (9) reported a survival difference of 22% at 8 years between nuclear grade good and nuclear grade poor in 950 node-negative women. For example:

Nuclear Grade	8-Year Survival Rate (%)
Good	86%
Poor	64%

Modified from Fisher et al. Cancer 65:2121-2128,1990 (9).
Reprinted courtesy of author and publisher.

When Fisher et al. (9) added histologic tumor type (23.02[d]) to nuclear grade the results were as follows. (See also Tumor.)

Nuclear Grade	Tumor Type	8 Year Survival Rate (%)
Good	Favorable	94%
Poor	Unfavorable	54%

Modified from Fisher et al. Cancer 65:212-2118,1990 (9).
Reprinted courtesy of author and publisher.

Fisher, ". . . observed a very strong association between nuclear grade and tumor cell area or perimeter in 200 consecutive cases from this protocol examined by computerized digital morphometry." If you are unable to obtain a satisfactory nuclear grade, nuclear morphometry could be a good alternative.

Thus nuclear grading in the hands of an experienced pathologist has been proven to be a powerful predictor of the prognosis of breast cancer. When used in combination with histologic tumor type it is even more powerful. *(See Tumor Type, this chapter)*

References

1. Broders AC. Squamous Epithelioma of the Lip. JAMA 74(10):656-664, 1920.
2. Greenough FB. Varying Degrees of Malignancy in Cancer of the Breast. J Cancer Res 9:453-463, 1925.
3. Bloom HJG. Prognosis in Carcinoma of the Breast. Brit J Cancer 9(3):259-288, 1950.
4. Bloom HJG and Richardson, WW. Histological Grading and Prognosis of Breast Cancer. A Study of 1409 Cases of Which 350 Have Been Followed for 15 Years. Br J Cancer 11:359-377, 1957.
5. Henson DE. The Histological Grading of Neoplasms. Arch Pathol Lab Med 142:1091-1096, 1988.
6. Henson DE and Ries MS, et al. Relationship Among Outcome, Stage of Discasc and Histologic Grade for 22,616 Cases of Breast Cancer. Cancer 68:2142-2149, 1991.
7. Bacus SS, et al. Biologic Grading of Breast Cancer Using Antibodies to Proliferating Cells and Other Markers. Am J Pathol 135(5):783-792, 1989.

8. Lash RH et al. Partial Mastectomy: Pathologic Findings and the Prognosis. Hum Pathol 17:813-822, 1986.
9. Fisher ER, Redmond C, Fisher B, Bass G, et al. Pathologic Findings from the National Surgical Adjuvant Breast and Bowel Project (NSABP). Prognostic Discriminants for 8-Year Survival for Node-Negative Invasive Breast Cancer Patients. Cancer 65:2121-2128, 1990.

[4] Mitotic Grade or Index Numerous investigators have observed that breast cancers containing numerous mitotic figures have a high rate of relapse (1,2,3). The problem has been that many breast cancers with few detectable mitotic figures also frequently relapse. How can we explain this? (4,5):

A. Counting the number of mitotic figures in 10 high power fields of an ordinary light microscope can be time-consuming and tedious.
B. The determination is subjective.
C. Nuclear artifacts such as pyknosis and karyorrhexis can be mistaken for mitotic figures. This is not a problem for experienced pathologists.
D. There may be a problem of sampling error.
   1. Some areas of the tumor grow faster.
   2. Some tumors contain larger amounts of benign stromal cells than tumor cells. This can make mitotic counts relatively meaningless (5).
   3. Mitoses are so scarce in some breast cancers that many hours are required to measure the mitotic index (5).

Bacus, et al. (4) examined breast cancers in which the pathologist found few mitotic figures. They then stained sections of the tumors with the monoclonal antibody Ki-67, which identifies a nuclear protein which is present only in cycling cells, and found a high percentage of proliferating tumor cells. Thus a mitotic count is more apt to be falsely low than falsely high. Why is this true? The length of the cell cycle is about 48 hours (5) Sisken studied the cell cycle from three breast cancer cell lines and found that histologically recognizable mitoses (M-phase) were present for only 30, 47, and 68 minutes (6). Thus, many dividing cells may never be recognized in ordinary microscopic sections. However S-phase, as determined by flow cytometry identifies all cells that are manufacturing DNA in preparation for cell division. The S-phase lasts approximately 19 hours (5). Thus, S-phase is a more accurate measurement of the rate of cell division since the number of cells in S-phase is 20 times greater than the number of cells in the actual process of cell division (mitosis). Therefore S-phase counts have a great statistical advantage over M phase counts (5).

S-phase is being used with increasing frequency as a measure of the proliferation rate of breast cancer. It is usually used in combinations with other risk factors. (See flow cytometry this chapter and the appendix)

> Practice Note
>
> When the mitotic count is high use it. When it is low it may be falsely low, therefore, order an S-phase determination.

References

1. Bloom HJG. Prognosis in Carcinoma of the Breast. Brit J Cancer 9(3):259-288, 1950.
2. Bloom HJG and Richardson WW. Histological Grading and Prognosis of Breast Cancer. A Study of 1409 Cases of Which 350 Have Been Followed for 15 Years. Br J Cancer 11:359-377, 1957.
3. Schnitt SJ, et al. Pathologic Predictors of Early Local Recurrence in Stage I and II Breast Cancer Treated by Primary Radiation Therapy. Cancer 53:1049-1057, 1984.
4. Bacus SS, et al. Biologic Grading of Breast Cancer Using Antibodies to Proliferating Cells and Other Markers. Am J Pathol 135(5):783-792, 1989.
5. Meyer JS. Cell Kinetics of Breast and Breast Tumors. *Cancer of the Breast*, 3rd Ed, Donegan and Spratt, WB Saunders, 1988, pp 250-269.
6. Sisken JE, Bonner SV, Grasch, BD, et al. Alterations in Metaphase Durations in Cells Derived from Human Tumors. Cell Tissue Kinetics. 18:137, 1985.

[d] Histologic Tumor Type

Some tumor types are more aggressive than others and have a higher rate of relapse. Fisher, Redmond, Fisher and Bass (1), studied the prognostic discriminants for eight-year survival of 950 node-negative breast cancer patients. They found that the histologic type significantly influenced the risk of relapse and death. The authors assigned a relative risk factor of 1.00 to the most common breast cancer, infiltrating duct cell carcinoma NOS (not otherwise specified). Cancers with a risk factor of less than 1.00, therefore, would have a lower risk of relapse and death, and those with a value greater than 1.00 would have a higher risk of relapse and death. The authors classified their breast cancers as follows:

Prognostic Groups	# of patients	Relative Risk Factor*
Unfavorable		
Invasive duct cell (NOS)	263	1.00
Atypical medullary	60	1.08
Intermediate		
Medullary	78	0.58
Lobular	117	0.55
NOS combinations	274	0.49
Favorable		
Mucoid	35	0.08
Tubular	91	0.20
Papillary	32	0.45

* Risk of developing distant recurrence

Source: Fisher, Redmond, Fisher, & Bass Table 2, page 2123, Cancer 65:2121-2128, 1990. Reprinted courtesy of author and publisher.

Fisher et al. (1) also noted nuclear grade and tumor type were much more powerful predictors of prognosis when used together than when used separately. For example:

Eight-Year Survival (%) and Nuclear Grade and Tumor Type

Histologic Tumor Type	Nuclear Grade Good/# Patients		Nuclear Grade Poor/# Patients	
Not considered	86%	(580)	64%	(370)
Favorable	94%	(136)	70%	(22)
Intermediate	85%	(307)	75%	(162)
Unfavorable	81%	(137)	54%	(186)

Source: Fisher, Redmond, Fisher, Bass et al. Cancer 65:2121-2128, 1990. Modified from Table 2, page 2123. Reprinted courtesy of author and publisher.

Practice Note

Thus both tumor type and nuclear grade are separately predictive of prognosis but when both are used together they are more powerful predictors of outcome. Therefore, defense should assemble not only a list of unfavorable prognostic factors found in the plaintiff's cancer but also a list of combinations of unfavorable prognostic indicators such as tumor type and nuclear grade. Assemble as many as possible. Even though the predictive power of some may overlap, a greater number will provide more predictive power.

Many infiltrating duct cell carcinomas have a significant component of intraductal carcinoma. Fisher's group found that the tumor type (but not the extent) of this intraductal component influenced prognosis. Again these authors assigned a relative risk value of 1.00 to an infiltrative duct cell carcinoma with an adenocystic intraductal carcinoma component. Thus:

Infiltrative Duct Cell Carcinomas

Intraductal Component	# of Patients	Relative Risk of Relapse*
Adenocystic	138	1.00
Solid	113	1.82
Papillary	17	2.49
Comedo	43	4.11
Combinations	238	1.58

* Risk of developing distant recurrence and death

Source: Fisher, Redmond, Bass et al. Cancer 65:2121-2128, 1990. Modified from Table 2, page 2123. Reprinted courtesy of author and publisher.

Practice Note

Thus infiltrative duct cell carcinomas (NOS) with intraductal components that can be classified as comedo, papillary or solid have a greater risk of distant recurrence. That is, they tend to be more aggressive.

References

1. Fisher ER, Redmond C, Fisher B, Bass G et al. Pathologic Findings from the National Surgical Adjuvant Breast and Bowel Projects (NSABP). Prognostic Discriminants for 8-

Year Survival for Node-Negative Invasive Breast Cancer Patients. Cancer 65:2121-2128, 1990.

[e] Nuclear Morphometry (Computerized Digital Morphometry)

The terms nuclear morphometry and computerized digital morphometry sound formidable until we consider the derivation of the word morphometry. The word morphometry is derived from two Greek words:

Morphe (Gr) = form
Metron (Gr) = measure.

For more than 100 years, pathologists have been vaguely aware that the microscopic appearance of cancer sometimes correlated with its clinical behavior. However, it was not until 1925 that Greenough, in a brilliant paper, demonstrated a powerful correlation between the microscopic appearance of the breast cancer cell and survival (1). Greenough was the first to specifically state that the degree of variation in the size and shape of the breast cancer cell* and/or nucleus, the degree of nuclear hyperchromatism** and the frequency of mitotic figures correlated with the risk of treatment failure.

* The diameter of the nucleus is usually measured since the cell wall is often indistinct and difficult to identify.

** With common H/E stains the nuclear content, (which is largely DNA and is snow white) takes on a deep purple hue. Early cytologists who knew nothing of DNA called this deep-staining nuclear material chromatin (chromatin (Gr) = color) because it had the most color of any material within the cell. Hyperchromatism refers to an increase in the amount, density, and/or pattern of the nuclear chromatin (DNA) (2).

Nuclear morphometry was created when the first attempts were made to measure the size and shape of tumor nuclei from enlarged photomicrographs of breast cancer tissue. Today a VCR is used to capture the greatly enlarged image of the breast cancer through the microscope. The image is then projected on a video digitizing board of a computer. If necessary, the image can be enhanced and further magnified. Using a mouse the examiner can measure the perimeter of the breast cancer cell and/or nucleus. The computer can measure 256 shades of gray and can substitute 256 different colors for these shades of gray. This enables the examiner to measure the density and variations in the density and pattern of the nuclear chromatin (DNA).

Since many have complained that nuclear grade is unreliable because of the subjectivity of its assessment, Fisher et al. (3) compared the predictive power of tumor cell area or perimeter versus nuclear grade in 200 consecutive cases of breast cancer. They observed a very strong correlation between the predictive power of nuclear grade and tumor cell area or perimeter. Although tumor cell area or perimeter offered no additional information beyond that of nuclear grade it would appear that tumor cell area or perimeter could be used instead of nuclear grade. Since tumor cell area or perimeter can be determined with great accuracy the problem of subjectivity and reproducibility would thus be eliminated. In the future, morphometric findings may replace histologic and nuclear grading.

Practice Note

If you encounter difficulty in obtaining a satifactory nuclear grade do the following:

1. Contact a pathologist who has a special interest and expertise in the grading of breast cancer, or:
2. Contact a reliable reference laboratory regarding the feasibility of computerized digital morphometry.

References

1. Greenough FB. Varying Degrees of Malignancy in Cancer of the Breast. J Cancer Res 9:453-463, 1925.
2. de Duve, Christian. A Guided Tour of the Living Cell, Volume 2, page 284, Scientific Library, Scientific American Books, Inc., New York, 1984.
3. Fisher ER, Redmond C, Fisher B, Bass G et al. Pathologic Findings From the National Surgical Adjuvant Breast and Bowel Project (NSABP). Prognostic Discriminants for 8-Year Survival for Node-Negative Invasive Breast Cancer Patients. Cancer 65:2121-2128, 1990.

[f] Lymphatic and Vascular Tumor Invasion

Women whose tumors contain evidence of lymphatic and/or vascular peritumoral invasion have a significantly higher incidence of recurrence and death (1,2). Therefore, if your pathologist has not found evidence of peritumoral lymphatic and vascular invasion ask that he/she employ elastic stains to identify the walls of blood vessels and immunohistochemical stains to identify the endothelium of small lymphatics and blood vessels (1). Lymphatic and vascular invasion are definitely unfavorable prognostic factors and will add considerable weight to your prognostic profile.

Practice Note

Small blood and lymph capillaries can be difficult to identify. Therefore, if no evidence of invasion is found ask that special tests be done to identify these small and fragile structures.

References

1. Hutter RVP. The Role of the Pathologist in the Management of Breast Cancer. Ca-A Cancer Journal for Clinicians, 45(5):283-299, September/October 1991.
2. Rosen PP and Groshen S. Factors Influencing Survival and Prognosis in Early Breast Carcinoma (T1N0M0-T1N1M0), Surg Clin North America. 70(4):937-962, 1990.

[g] Estrogen Receptor Protein (ER) and Progesterone Receptor Protein (PgR)

The medical literature concerning the predictive value of the hormone receptors (ER and PgR) is confusing and difficult to interpret. There are a number of reasons for this (1).

1. Many of the studies are retrospective.
2. The numbers of women in many of the studies are small.
3. The period of observation is frequently short.
4. Both ER and PgR are weak discriminants of prognosis.
5. The receptor assay values vary from laboratory to laboratory.

However, a critical analysis of the literature suggests that the following conclusions are valid: First, estrogen receptor negative tumors grow faster and metastasize sooner than estrogen positive tumors. Secondly, the disease free-survival (DFS) of ER + tumors is considerably greater than ER- tumors at 12, 24, and 36 months. After 36 months, however, the survival curves start to merge (2) and at five years the survival differences are 10% or less (3). Other studies reveal that the differences in DFS disappear with time although a small survival advantage persists for the ER + tumors. Recurrent ER + tumors respond to hormonal manipulation and thus live longer but ultimately die of breast cancer. This creates the illusion of a better overall survival (4,5). Of course, the quality of life is better for those who respond to hormonal therapy.

It is generally agreed that the long-term prognostic power of the negative ER/PgR status is minimal when used alone. However, most also agree that when negative ER status is included in a profile of other unfavorable prognostic factors, overall predictive power will be slightly improved. The presence or absence of an estrogen receptor is a good predictor of response to hormonal manipulation but a poor predictor of long-term survival.

References

1. Chevallier B, et al. Prognostic Value of Estrogen and Progesterone Receptors in Early Breast Cancer. Cancer 62:2517-2524, 1988.
2. Sainsbury JR, et al. Epidermal Growth Factor Receptor Status as Predictors of Early Recurrence and Death From Breast Cancer. The Lancet, June 20, 1987, pp 1389-1402.
3. Osborne CK. Prognostic factors. Oncology Viewpoints, Special Issue, Adjuvant Therapy In Node-Negative Breast Cancer, LP Communications, Inc. New York, New York, December, 1988, p 12.
4. Osborne, CK. Receptors, in *Breast Diseases,* Harris, Hellman, Henderson, and Kinne, eds. JB Lippincott, 1987, pages 210-232.
5. Howell A, Barnes DM, Harland RNL, et al. Steroid Hormone Receptors and Survival After First Relapse in Breast Cancer. Lancet 1:588-591, 1984.

[h] DNA Flow Cytometry

DNA flow cytometry measures the amount of DNA in each individual tumor nucleus. From this information we can calculate the number of cells that are actively synthesizing DNA [in the S-Phase of the cell cycle] in preparation for cell division [mitosis]. This provides us with an approximation of the proliferation rate [growth rate] of the cancer. Additionally, we learn about the ploidy [the DNA content] of the breast cancer cell. That is, to what extent the DNA content was altered at the time the breast cell was transformed into a malignant cell or later by mutation. Thus we can learn whether the DNA content of the breast cancer is diploid [normal or nearly normal] or aneuploid [abnormal].

Diploid --- Tumor cells contain a normal or near normal amount of DNA.

Aneuploid --- Tumor cells contain an abnormal amount of DNA. Most commonly, the DNA content is increased, less frequently the DNA content is decreased.

The early literature concerning the prognostic worth of S-phase and ploidy is confusing and conflicting. However, recent improvements in methodology, larger sample sizes, improved modeling techniques and other innovations have greatly improved the accuracy of flow cytometry.

[1] Ploidy (1) Some investigators report that aneuploid tumors have a poorer survival rate than diploid breast cancers. Others are unable to confirm these findings. Merkel et al. (2) found the survival rates of diploid patients to be slightly better than the survival of aneuploid patients but the difference was not statistically significant. For example:

Ploidy and Eight-Year Disease-Free Survival (DFS)
280 Infiltrating Duct Cell Carcinomas

Ploidy	8-Year DFS	Statistical Significance
Diploid	87%	not significant
Aneuploid	74%	not significant

Modified from Merkel DE, Winchester DJ, Goldschmidt RA, et al. DNA Flow Cytometry and Pathologic Grading as Prognostic Guides in Axillary Lymph Node-Negative Breast Cancer. Cancer 72; 1926-1932, 1993, Table 1, page 1928. Reprinted courtesy of author and publisher.

However, since the reliability of flow cytometry is steadily improving, we suggest that you check with a reference laboratory or your expert witness regarding the current status of ploidy as a prognostic determinant in node-negative breast cancer.

[2] S-phase (1) Fraction The % S (synthesis) -phase fraction is a measure of the number of tumor cells (%) that are manufacturing DNA, that is, they are preparing for cell division by manufacturing DNA. Thus, the % S-phase fraction is a measure of the proliferative or growth rate of a cancer. The number of tumor cells undergoing mitosis is also a measure of the proliferation rate, but the S-phase fraction is more accurate. McGuire and Clark have this to say about S-phase (1):

> "What does the S-phase fraction provide about node-negative breast cancer? First, we know that patients with micrometastatic disease and a high S-phase fraction are more likely to have recurrent disease and die earlier. Simply put, things happen faster in patients with fast growing tumors. Second, and of more biologic relevance, a high S-phase may be an important signal that as yet unidentified genes associated with metastasis have been turned on or that genes that suppress invasion or metastasis have been turned off. For example, high rates of proliferation have been associated with overexpression of the HER-2/neu oncogene and loss of the p53 tumor suppressor gene."

Clark et al. (3) were able to identify high and low risk groups in both diploid and aneuploid node-negative breast cancers using a low cut-off of < 4.4% S-phase for diploid tumors and a < 7.0 % S-phase cut-off for aneuploid tumors.

Clark, Dressler and Owens (4) evaluated the predictive power of a combination of S-phase and ploidy. For this purpose, they divided S-phase into two groups:

low S-phase ----- 6.7% or below*
high S-phase ---- above 6.7% *

Using this classification they determined:

DNA Content	Patients	6 Year DFS**
Diploid/ low S-phase	112	88%
Diploid/high S-phase	15	56%
Aneuploid/any S-phase	233	71%

Modified from Figure 2 page 631, Clark GM, Dressler LG Owens MA, et al. N Engl J Med 320:627-633, 1989 (4). Reprinted courtesy of author and publisher.
* This percentage may vary from laboratory to laboratory
** DFS = disease free survival

In this study a high S-phase did identify a high-risk group within the diploid group of tumors but gave no additional information in the aneuploid group of tumors.

Other investigators (4,5,6) confirm that a high S-phase fraction will discriminate between a high- and low-probability of relapse in both lymph node negative and lymph node-positive breast cancer. Merkel et al. (2) using a cutoff of 9% S-phase concluded that histopathologic grading [histologic grade and nuclear grade] and flow cytometric determination of S-phase appear to provide additive prognostic information for patients with early invasive duct cell carcinoma [lymph node-negative breast cancer]. For example:

Five-Year Disease-Free Survival
Histologic (HG) or Nuclear Grade (NG) and S-phase Fraction
280 Lymph Node-Negative Breast Cancers

Tumor Grade	S-Phase	Five-Year Disease-Free Survival (%)
Low-grade 1	S-phase did not alter outcome	95%
High-grade 2 or 3	Low S-phase < 9%	84%
High-grade 2 or 3	High S-Phase > 9%	70%

Modified from Merkel DE, Winchester DJ, Goldschmidt RA, et al. DNA Flow Cytometry and Pathologic Grading as Prognostic Guides in Axillary Lymph Node-Negative Breast Cancer. Cancer 72; 1926-1932, 1993, Table 1, page 1928. Reprinted courtesy of author and publisher.

Merkel et al. (2) conclude ". . . S-phase determination and grading can provide complimentary information and together permit a more accurate description of the natural history of node-negative breast cancer." Of course, this is precisely the information we want in the malpractice setting.

It is important to remember that the cut-off points used to separate low S-phase from high S-phase vary from laboratory to laboratory. Therefore, if you plan to establish the prognostic worth of an S-phase determination for a particular tumor, select a reliable reference laboratory that has established the prognostic significance for the high and low S-phase cut-offs used at their laboratory.

Practice Note

Lynn Dressler (7) states that the combination of poor nuclear grade and a high S-phase fraction is a more powerful predictor than nuclear grade alone. In §23.02[d] we learned that a combination of poor nuclear grade and unfavorable histologic type was a powerful predictor of prognosis. Thus the combination of poor nuclear grade, high S-phase fraction and unfavorable histologic type might be a better predictor of prognosis.

Reference

1. McGuire WL and Clark GM. Prognostic Factors and Treatment Decisions in Axillary Node-Negative Breast Cancer. New Eng J Med 326(26):1756-1761, 1992.
2. Merkel DE, Winchester DJ, Goldschmidt RA, et al. DNA Flow Cytometry and Pathologic Grading as Prognostic Guides in Axillary Lymph Node-Negative Breast Cancer. Cancer 72;1926-1932, 1993.
3. Clark GM, Mathieu MC, Owens MA, et al. Prognostic Significance of S-Phase Fraction in Good-Risk, Node-Negative Breast Cancer Patients. J Clin Oncol 10:428-432, 1992.
4. Clark GM, Dressler LG, Owens MA, et al. Prediction of Relapse or Survival in Patients With Node-Negative Breast Cancer by DNA Flow Cytometry. N Engl J Med 320:627-633, 1989.
5. McGuire WL, Tandon AK, Allred C, Chamness GC, and Clark GM. Commentaries: How to Use Prognostic Factors in Axillary Node-Negative Breast Cancer Patients. J Natl Can Instit 82:(12) 1006-1015, 1990.
6. Owens MA, Beardsley S, Wenger CR, et al. DNA Flow Cytometry Correlates With Other Prognostic Factors for Breast Cancer. Breast Cancer Research and Treatment. 14:(abstr 8) 134, 1989.
7. Dressler, Lynn. Quoted by Tom Reynolds. Prognostic Indicators—The Search Goes On. News, News. J Nat Can Instit 86(7):480-483, April 6, 1994.

[i] HER-2/neu Proto-Oncogene (also known as C erb-B2)

[1] Introduction and Discussion of Terminology For a number of years investigators have suspected, but could not prove, that the study of oncogenes might enable the clinician to predict the clinical course of breast cancer. However, in the past several years Slamon et al. (1) and others have demonstrated that the amplification of the HER-2/neu oncogene predicted an increase in the mortality rate of lymph node-positive breast cancer. Recently articles by Paik et al (2) and Allred et al (3) reported that improvements in technology now suggest that the oncogene erb B-2 (also known as HER-2/neu) may be a powerful predictor of the prognosis of both lymph node-positive and lymph node-negative cancer (4).

It will be easier to understand these new developments if we briefly review the role of the oncogene in breast cancer. A small segment of normal DNA which carries a specific genetic message for the cell is called a **gene**. A gene that assists in the control and modulation of the normal process of cell division is called a **mitogene or a proto-oncogene** (5). A mitogene (proto-oncogene) is a normal gene whose genetic message codes for a protein that helps the cell maintain an orderly process of cell division. The process of cell division is complicated and "... many different kinds of mitogenes exist, with varying roles in regulating mitosis" (5). Normally the mitogene controls cell division in the following manner. Within the nucleus of the cell, the mitogene produces a **messenger protein (mRNA)** which carries a "blue print" or code for the manufacture of a protein which will in some way be capable of modulating cell division. The messenger protein (mRNA) diffuses from the nucleus into the cytoplasm of the cell and congregates in the "factory region" of the cell (the endoplasmic reticulum and the Golgi apparatus).

Here the messenger protein (mRNA) supervises the production of a protein that precisely matches the protein coded by the mitogene. This specific protein product of the mitogene (the protein expression product) will play an active role in maintaining an orderly process of cell division.

When the DNA of a normal mitogene (proto-oncogene) is altered or damaged by a carcinogen, radiation, virus or aberration of cell division (mutation) the final protein product will be altered or produced in unusually large quanities. The mitogene (proto-oncogene) has become an **oncogene**. The altered DNA of the oncogene now codes for an abnormal messenger protein (mRNA) that directs the cell to manufacture an abnormal final protein product or an abnormally large quantity of the normal protein product. This abnormal final protein product promotes uncontrolled cell growth. A **cancer** has developed. It is intriguing that investigators have noted a remarkable similarity between the structure of the oncogene HER-2/neu and the powerful growth factor receptor EGFR (epidermal growth factor receptor) (1).

[2] Detecting the Presence of an Oncogene or its Protein Products in Breast Cancer The presence and/or abnormal function of an oncogene can be detected in breast cancer tissue in several ways.

[A] Gene amplification When a mitogene (proto-oncogene) is transformed into an oncogene it acquires the ability to make copies of itself, sometimes 20 or more copies. Tests are now available (Southern blot analysis) that can detect the presence of the HER-2/neu oncogene in breast cancer. Slamon er al (1) reported that the presence of five or more copies of the HER-2/neu oncogene in breast cancer predicts an increase in the likelihood of relapse of the lymph node-positive breast cancer.

[B] mRNA (messenger RNA) Tests also are available that can measure the presence and the amount of messenger protein (mRNA) of a specific oncogene. These tests may not be available in the clinical setting as yet.

[C] Protein overexpression The presence and amount of the final protein product of the oncogene HER-2/neu and/or its copies can be detected within the cell membranes of some breast cancer cells with the use of monoclonal antibodies and special staining techniques (2). Check with a reference laboratory for availability.

[3] Clinical Significance (1,2,3,4) The terminology used in the discussion of oncogenes can be confusing, even intimidating, to the non biologist. Initially the genes **neu, c erb-B, and HER-2** were each found to correlate with the behavior of breast cancer (1). Later it was discovered that all three genes were identical. Thus, in the current medical literature the terms HER-2/neu and c erb B2 are interchangeable.

[A] HER-2/neu protein overexpression In the past, the clinical significance of the protein overexpression of the HER-2/neu oncogene was controversial. Recently, however, an immunohistochemical assay has been developed which uses a monoclonal antibody that specifically

identifies the protein expression product of the HER-2/neu oncogene (2). It is now possible to examine large numbers of formalin-fixed, paraffin-embedded breast cancers for evidence of the protein expression product of HER-2/neu (2). Paik et al. report that the formalin fixation and paraffin embedding of breast cancer tissue does not impair the specificity of this immunohistochemical assay. This is good news for the defense attorney since archival paraffin blocks of breast cancer tisssue should be available in almost all situations.

Paik et al. (2) analyzed 292 formalin fixed and paraffin embedded breast cancers with an immunohistochemical assay which used a monoclonal antibody specific for the protein product of erb B-2 oncogene. Tumor cells that contained this protein were recognized by distinct cell membrane staining. The cell membranes of cancer cells that did not contain the protein of erb B-2 did not take the stain. Paik, et al. (2) concluded that:

1. Overexpression of the HER-2/neu protein is found in about 21% of breast cancers and these women have been found to have an approximate doubling of the mortality rate, regardless of the lymph node status (2).
2. The survival rate of patients with nuclear grade poor was uniformly poor regardless of the presence or absence of the protein product of erb B-2. This suggested to the authors that there is an interaction between nuclear grade poor and HER-2/neu protein overexpression.

Practice Note

Paik et al. (2) reported the presence of the erb B-2 protein in the cell membranes of breast cancers that were both **node-negative** and **nuclear grade good** in a small group of women who had an extremely high mortality rate (five times higher than cancers in which the erB-2 protein was not found!)

Allred et al. (3) studied breast cancer tissue from 355 node negative women whose tumors were **less than 3.0 cm in diameter and ER+**. The authors concluded that the overexpression of the protein for HER-2/neu oncogene in pure invasive duct cell cancers predicted a decrease in probability of a five-year disease-free survival from 75% to 40%.

Therefore, if you encounter a woman whose breast cancer proves to be (4):

- Axillary lymph node-negative,
- A pure invasive duct cell carcinoma with no intraductal component,
- Tumor size < 2 cm,
- ER +, and
- Nuclear grade good,

you will be told that you are dealing with a breast cancer that has an excellent prognosis (A five-year disease-free survival of 85% or better). This is true, but let's look at it another way. In spite of the absence of adverse risk factors, 15 to 20% of these tumors are aggressive and will recur and ultimately kill the patient. How can we identify this small group of aggressive breast cancers? Paik et al. (2), Allred et al. (3), and McGuire et al. (4) suggest that it may be possible to identify this small subset of highly lethal tumors by the overexpression of HER-2/ neu protein. When confronted with this type of situation do the following:

1. Obtain copies of the Paik et al., Allred et al., and McGuire et al. articles.
2. Ask your medical expert to send breast cancer tissue to a reputable reference laboratory for measurement of the protein expression product of HER-2-neu oncogene.
3. If these results are positive, you may argue that this cancer had five times greater risk of recurrence than a cancer with no evidence of overexpresssion of the HER- 2/neu protein.
4. If these results are negative, this woman will still have a 15% chance of developing a recurrence within five years.

[B] Amplification of the HER-2/neu oncogene Slamon et al. (1) have reported the the amplification of the oncogene HER- 2/neu (greater than 5 copies) in the lymph node-positive breast cancer predicts a high risk of relapse of the cancer. Therefore it might be wise to check with your expert medical witness and/or a reference laboratory regarding the current status of the prognostic significance of amplification of the HER-2/neu oncogene in node-negative breast cancer.

References

1. Slamon DJ, Clark GM, Wong SG, Levin WJ, Ullrich A, and McGuire WL. Human Breast Cancer: Correlation of Relapse and Survival With Amplification of the HER-2/neu Oncogene. Science 235:177-181, 1987.
2. Paik S, Hazan R, Fisher ER, Sass RE, Fisher B, Redmond C, Schlessinger J, Lippman ME, and King CR. Pathologic Findings From the National Surgical Adjuvant Breast and Bowel Project: Prognostic Significance of erbB-2 Protein Overexpression in Primary Breast Cancer. J Clin Oncol 8:103-112, 1990.
3. Allred D, Clark G, Tandon A, et al. HER-2/neu Expression Identified a Group of Node-Negative Breast Cancer Patients at High Risk for Recurrence. Presented at the American Society of Clinical Oncology Annual Meeting, Washington DC, May 20-22, 1990.
4. McGuire WL, Tandon AK, Allred C, Chammness GC, and Clark GM. Commentaries: How to Use Prognostic Factors in Axillary Node-Negative Breast Cancer Patients. J Natl Can Instit 82:(12) 1006-1015, 1990.
5. Gordon, Hymie. Oncogenes. Mayo Clin Proc 60:697-713, 1985.

[j] Cathepsin-D (1-7)

[1] Presence May Indicate Metastasis Overexpression of the proteolytic enzyme Cathepsin-D by breast cancer cells has been demonstrated to be an independent predictor of early recurrence and death from lymph node-negative breast cancer (1-7). McGuire (1,8) has suggested that Cathepsin-D may play a role in the metastatic process of breast cancer by stimulating cell growth and facilitating the process of invasion and metastasis.

Breast cancer patients whose tumors have high levels of Cathepsin-D have a 3.9 times greater risk of recurrence and death (8). Tandon et al. (7) have reported:

Lymph Node-Negative Breast Cancer
Cathepsin-D Levels, Ploidy and Recurrence Rate*

	5 year recurrence rate*
Diploid	22%
(with high or low Cathepsin levels)	
Aneuploid	
Low levels Cathepsin-D	29%
High levels Cathepsin-D	60%

*Actuarial 5-yr recurrence rate

Modified from Tandon AK, et al. N Eng J Med 1990 (7), Figure 4, page 300. Reprinted courtesy of author and publisher.

Thus if you encounter a lymph node-negative breast cancer that developed distant metastasis soon after surgery and/or had a rapidly downhill course, consider the possibility of an aneuploid tumor with high levels of Cathepsin-D.

[2] Conclusion The recent literature concerning the prognostic worth of Cathepsin-D is controversial. Consult with your pathologist about the most recent information on this factor.

References

1. McGuire WL and Clark GM. Prognostic Factors and Treatment Decisions in Axillary Node-Negative Breast Cancer. New Eng J Med 326(26):1756-1761, 1992.
2. Rochefort, Henri, et al. Structure, Function, and Regulation and Clinical Significance of the 52 K Pro-cathepsin-D Secreted by Breast Cancer Cells. Biochemie 70:943-949, 1988.
3. Spyratos, Frederique et al. Cathepsin-D: An Independent Prognostic Factor for Metastasis of Breast Cancer. The Lancet November 11, 1989, pp 1115-1118.
4. Maudelonde, Thierry et al. Immunoenzymatic Assay of M, 52,000 Cathepsin-D in 182 Breast Cancer Cytosols: Low Correlation With Other Prognostic Parameters. Cancer Research 48:462-466, 1988.

5. Capony F et al. Increased Secretion, Altered Processing, and Glycosylation of Pro-cathepsin-D in Human Mammary Cells. Cancer Research 49:3904- 3909, 1989.
6. Ingle, James. Assessing the Risk of Recurrence in Breast Cancer. Editorial. N Engl J Med 322(5):329-331, 1990.
7. Tandon AK, Clark GM, Chammness GC, et al. Cathepsin-D and Prognosis in Breast Cancer. N Engl J Med 322:297-302, 1990.
8. McGuire WL. Quoted by Stockwell S. in Three Studies Mark Cathepsin as a Relapse Marker. Oncology Times, April 1990, pp 28-29.

[k] Race

Many have observed that black women have a poorer survival rate than Caucasians. Fisher, Redmond, Fisher, and Bass studied 950 women with node-negative breast cancer (Stage I) breast cancer (1). They found race to be an important prognostic factor. For example:

5- and 8-Year Survival According to Race (lymph node-negative breast cancer)

		Survival (%)	
Race	# patients	5 years	8 years
white	897	89%	79%
black	71	74%	64%

Source: Fisher, Redmond, Fisher and Bass, 1990 (1) Modified from Table 4, page 2125. Reprinted courtesy of author and publisher.

Crowe et al. reported that this is especially true for node-negative black women with ER-tumors. More detailed data are not available because of the difficulty in obtaining sufficient numbers of black women.

References

1. Fisher ER, Redmond C, Fisher B, Bass G et al.: Pathologic Findings from the National Surgical Adjuvant Breast and Bowel Projects (NSABP). Prognostic Discriminants for 8-Year Survival for Node-Negative Invasive Breast Cancer Patients. Cancer 65:2121-2128, 1990.

2. Crowe JP Jr, Gordon NH, Hubay CA, Pearson OH, Marshall JS, McGuire WL. The Interaction of Estrogen Receptor Status and Race in Predicting Prognosis for Stage I Breast Cancer Patients. Surgery 100(4):599-605, 1986.

[l] p53 Tumor Suppressor Gene

In a recent interview (1) Ann Thor suggests that mutation of the tumor suppressor gene p53 may help identify the 20-30% of node-negative women who will die of breast cancer. Thor stated that accumulations of mutant p53 mutant protein in breast tumors may be a predictor of shortened survival in both node-negative and node-positive breast cancer. She cautions, however, that although the mutant p53 protein may have a promising future, it is not yet ready for the clinic. Much more work needs to be done. We recommend that you ask your expert witness about the current status of the p53 mutant protein.

References

1. Thor AD. Quoted in an interview in Researchers Make Slow Progess in Establishing Prognostic Indicators for the Clinic, J Natl Can Instit 85(6):428-429, March 17, 1993.

[m] Tumor Angiogenesis (Microvessel Count)

[1] Generally McGuire recently stated that a good prognostic indicator "... should possess clear biologic significance" (1). Certainly the measurement of the intensity of angiogenesis within a breast cancer should have biologic significance. In §10.02 and §10.06 we discussed the biologic significance of angiogenesis, the various mechanisms by which it facilitates metastasis, and the role of angiogenesis throughout the life of a breast cancer.

Weidner et al. (2,3) have reported that the density of microvessels in areas of breast cancer with the most intense neovascularization provides significant prognostic information concerning overall survival and disease-free survival of early breast cancer. Fortunately for the defense attorney, this information can be obtained from archival paraffin blocks of breast cancer tissue. Archival breast cancer tissue is stained with factor VIII antigen using standard immunoperoxidase staining techniques. The tiny microvessesl can be identified by the brown-red stained endothelial cells. Weidner et al. (2) studied the correlation of the density of microvessels in archival breast cancer tissue with the frequency of metastasis. They observed:

# Microvessesls per 200x hpf	% with Metastasis
0-33	14%
34-67	45%
68-100	71%
>100	100%

Weidner N, Semple JP, Welch WR, and Folkman J. Tumor Angiogenesis and Metastasis: Correlation in Invasive Breast Carcinoma. N Engl J Med 324:1-8, 1991, Figure 3, page 5. Reprinted courtesy of author and publisher.

Other studies support Weidner's findings (4).

Weidner et al. (3) conclude that:

- Microvessel counts provide highly significant information concerning the overall and disease-free survival of early breast cancer.
- Adding microvessel counts to the number of involved lymph nodes provides information over and above that provided by the number of involved lymph nodes alone.
- Adding microvessel counts to other prognostic factors also provides additional information.

[2] Conclusion Microvessel counts provide independent and highly significant prognostic information concerning overall survival and disease-free survival in all breast cancer patients, **both node-positive and node-negative.** Although the use of microvessel counts as a prognostic indicator is relatively new, knowledge concerning its worth is rapidly accumulating. We think it has great potential and agree with Page and Dupont that it should be valuable in some patient subgroups (5).

Practice Note

Current literature continues to be favorable concerning the prognostic power of the microvessel count; therefore, we recommend that you consult your pathologist and/or expert witness regarding the availability and feasibility of obtaining microvessel counts of the most intense areas of neovascularization of the plaintiff's breast cancer.

References

1. McGuire Wl. Breast Cancer Prognostic Factors: Evaluation Guidelines. J Natl Cancer Instit 83:154-155, 1991.
2. Weidner N, Semple JP, Welch WR, and Folkman J. Tumor Angiogenesis and Metastasis: Correlation in Invasive Breast Carcinoma. N Engl J Med 324:1-8, 1991.
3. Weidner N, Folkman J, et al. Tumor Angiogenesis: A New Significant and Independent Prognostic Indicator in Early-Stage Breast Cancer. J Natl Can Instit 84(24):1875-1887, 1992.
4. Bosari S, Lee Ak, DeLellis RA et al. Microvessel Quantitation and Prognosis in Invasive Breast Carcinoma. Hum Pathol 23:755-761, 1992.
5. Page DL and Dupont WD. Breast Cancer Angiogenesis: Through a Narrow Window. J Natl Can Instit 84(24):1850-1851, 1992.

§23.03 THE LYMPH NODE-POSITIVE BREAST CANCER

[a] Introduction

[1] Axillary Lymph Node Metastasis is a Powerful Prognostic Factor Metastasis to the axillary lymph nodes is the single most powerful predictor of the outcome of breast cancer. For example:

10-Year Relapse Rate of Breast Cancer

# of Positive Lymph Nodes	10-Year Relapse Rate (%)
0	30% +/−
1-3	65-67% (1)
4+	84-86% (1)
10+	90% + (1)

Therefore, it is important to take advantage of this powerful prognostic factor when you assemble your prognostic profile. To do this, however, you must first dispel the common myth that the presence of axillary lymph node metastasis is an indication of a delay in diagnosis.

[2] Axillary Lymph Node Metastasis is not an Indication of a Delay in Diagnosis Unfortunately some physicians, resistant to change, still cling to the outdated and scientifically disproven concepts of the biology of breast cancer first espoused by William Halsted and Sampson Handley some 90 years ago (2). They still consider breast cancer to be a group of homogeneous tumors that grow in a time-related sequence of events. These physicians consider breast cancers to be (2):

- A group of homogeneous tumors that,
- Progressively grow over time, and then,
- Spread to the axillary lymph nodes.
- If the nodes are not removed the cancer will spread systemically to produce incurable disease.

Edwin Fisher (2) in an excellent paper has summarized the currently accepted scientifically proven concepts of the biology of breast cancer. He states "... the most salient shortcoming of the conventional concept of tumor biology [is] the failure to recognize the significance of *host response* and *tumor characteristics* in its equation" (my italics). Fisher is saying that breast cancers are a heterogeneous group of neoplasms. Some grow slowly, are only minimally invasive, and have low lethal potential. Others grow more rapidly, are more aggressive, and possess moderate to great lethal potential. Fisher continues, "Although it cannot be denied that primary tumors take time to grow, relating regional and subsequently systemic spread to time is, according to more moderate tenets and experiences, not only misleading but inaccurate." He is saying that the presence of axillary metastases is not a time-related event but an indication that the growth potential of the tumor was greater than the resistance of the host.

C. Barber Mueller (3) in a thoughtful and provocative paper agrees with Fisher that the final outcome of breast cancer is secondary to factors other than the time of diagnosis and extent of surgery. Mueller is convinced that tumors that metastasize to the axillary lymph nodes are different from tumors that do not metastasize to the regional nodes. They are different in that they possess the metastatic and invasive power to spread to the regional lymph nodes. Tumors that do not metastasize to the regional lymph nodes lack the ability to metastasize. We are dealing with two different tumors. (See Chapter 13)

[3] An Example of Lethal Power of the Tumor Versus Host Immunity A simple illustration may help the jury understand that lymph node metastases is not a time-related event, that is, an indication of a delay in the diagnosis of the breast cancer. In our illustration the host defense and the various breast cancers will be represented by football teams. Consider the following:

The Football Teams	Represented By	Relative Strength
The home team		
Host defense	A college team	2
The visiting teams		
A slow growing cancer	A high school team	1
An average cancer	A college team	2
An aggressive cancer	A professional team	4

Assume that one touchdown against the host defense team = a metastasis to the regional axillary lymph nodes or to a distant site.

Visiting Team		Home Team	% Teams Able to Score During First 5 Minutes
High school team	vs	Host defense	0%
College team	vs	Host defense	15-30%
Professional team	vs	Host defense	100%

Our illustration clearly illustrates that the ability or the inability to score a touchdown is not time-related but secondary to the differences between the power of the host defense team versus the power of the visiting teams. The host defense in our illustration was a constant factor as it usually is in the majority of the women who develop breast cancer. The only variability was the aggressive power of the cancers (the visiting teams) just as we encounter it in clinical practice.

Practice Note

When the the plaintiff uses the presence of metastasis to the axillary nodes as proof that the diagnosis was not timely, don't be defensive, go on thc offense. Do the following: First, read the articles by Fisher and Mueller. Second, reread Chapter 10. Third, use the football illustration, or a similar analogy to demonstrate that the development of regional and systemic disease are not simply time-related events but rather are dependent upon the differences between the strength of the host defense and the aggressiveness and metastatic potential of the breast cancer.

References

1. Bonadonna G and Valagussa P. Editorial: Dose-intense Adjuvant Treatment of High-Risk Breast Cancer. J Natl Can Instit. 82(7):542-543, 1990.
2. Fisher E. The Impact of Pathology on the Biologic, Diagnostic, Prognostic, and Therapeutic Considerations in Breast Cancer. Surg Clin N Am. 64(6):1073-1093, 1984.
3. Mueller, C Barber. Stage II Breast Cancer Is Not Simply a Late Stage I. Surgery 104:631-638, 1988.

[4] It is Possible to Identify High- and Low-Risk Patients within the Node-Positive Group Proven axillary metastasis is the single most powerful predictor of outcome of breast cancer and as additional nodes become involved with tumor the risk of relapse rapidly escalates. Therefore, it is possible to identify women within the positive node group who have low and high risks of relapse and death. Consider the following:

A. **Low risk of treatment failure**
   - Node metastases less than 2 mm in diameter --- These women have the same frequency of relapse and death as women who have lymph node-negative breast cancer, that is, about 30% at 10 years (1,2).

B. **Intermediate risk of treatment failure**
   - 1-3 positive axillary lymph nodes --- These women have a 65-67% chance of relapse and death at 10 years (3).

C. **High risk of treatment failure**
   - 4 or more positive axillary lymph nodes --- These women have an 84-86% chance of relapse of death at 10 years (3).

D. **Highest risk of treatment failure**
   - 10 or more positive axillary lymph nodes --- These women have greater than 90% chance of relapse and death at 10 years (3).

References

1. Fisher ER and Palekan AS, Rockette H et al. Pathologic Findings From the National Surgical Adjuvant Breast Project (Protocol #4) V. Significance of Axillary Nodal Micro and Macrometestases. Cancer 42:2032-2038, 1978.

2. Fisher B, Bauer M, Wickerham DL et al.: Relation of Number of Positive Axillary Nodes to the Prognosis of Patients With Primary Breast Cancer. An NSABP Update. Cancer 52:1551-1557, 1983.
3. Bonadonna G and Valagussa P. Editorial: Dose-intense Adjuvant Treatment of High-Risk Breast Cancer. J Natl Can Instit. 82(7):542-543, 1990.
4. Fisher E. The Impact of Pathology on the Biologic, Diagnostic, Prognostic, and Therapeutic Considerations in Breast Cancer. Surg Clin N Am. 64(6):1073-1093, 1984.

Additionally, within each of the above positive nodal categories it is possible to identify women who are at increased risk of relapse and death by using a profile of unfavorable prognostic factors. None of these unfavorable factors is as powerful as lymph node status but when used in combinations can add significant prognostic power to your evaluation. The factors that are presented in the following section should be considered.

[b] Tumor Size

Tumor size is also a reliable predictor of treatment failure in the lymph node-positive woman. Christine Carter et al. (1) examined the relation of tumor size and lymph node status to the survival of 24,740 breast cancer patients. They found that tumor size and lymph node status were **independent** and **additive** prognostic indicators of survival. Survival decreased when tumor size increased even though the lymph node status was held constant. For example:

Lymph Node-Positive Breast Cancer
(One to three positive nodes)
Relation of Tumor Size and Survival

Tumor Size	# of Patients	5-Year Survival (%)
< 0.5 cm	53	95.3%
0.5-0.9 cm	140	94.0%
1.0-1.9 cm	1,574	86.6%
2.0-2.9 cm	1,897	83.4%
3.0-3.9 cm	1,185	79%
4.0-4.9 cm	540	69.8%

Modified from Carter et al. (Tables 3 & 4) Cancer 63:181-187, 1989 (1). Reprinted courtesy of author and publisher.

Larry Norton (2) assigns a 10% risk of relapse for each centimeter of tumor diameter when attempting to plan a course of management for his lymph node-negative patients. From Carter's data (see above) we can see that there was a 6% risk of relapse for the first centimeter of tumor diameter and thereafter an 8-10% increase for each additional diameter. These data would indicate that Norton's estimate of a 10% risk of relapse for each additional centimeter of tumor would also hold for node-positive breast cancer. Therefore, we recommend adding 6-10% for each centimeter of tumor diameter to the risk of relapse calculated for the number of positive axillary lymph nodes.

To those who state that tumor size cannot be used in the malpractice setting because large tumor size is an indication of a delay in diagnosis we have this to say: Large tumor size is most commonly secondary to:

1. A camouflage problem that prevents early detection of the tumor by the patient, the physician, and at times even the mammographer.
2. A rapidly growing tumor.
3. A combination of a camouflage problem and a rapidly growing aggressive breast cancer.

Before preparing this portion of your defense reread Chapters 11, 14. and 16.

References

1. Carter CL, Allen C, Henson DE. Relation of Tumor Size, Lymph Node Status, and Survival in 24,740 Breast Cancer Cases. Cancer 63:181-187, 1989.
2. Norton, Larry. An Interview by Ted Bosworth. Special Report—Chemotherapy for Node-Negative Breast Cancer? Evaluating Prognostic Factors. Oncology Times. 14(1):p 21, January 1992.

[c] Tumor Grading (See §23.02[c] for additional background)

[1] Introduction Tumor grading is based upon certain microscopic features of the cancer such as:

1. Histologic grade—an estimation of the degree of maturity of the tubule formation, maturity of the tumor nuclei, and

frequency of mitotic figures. (1 = mature, 2 = intermediate, 3 = immature)

2. Nuclear grade—measures the maturity of the cancer nuclei, and some pathologists include the frequency of mitotic figures. Graded 1 to 3 as for histologic grading.
3. Mitotic Index or Grade—measures the frequency of mitotic figures within the most actively growing region of the tumor.
4. Tumor grade—is a combination of histologic, nuclear and mitotic grades. Tumor grade is preferred by many investigators and has been proven to be a reliable predictor of prognosis for over 40 years.

The recent literature (1,2) continues to reinforce the value of tumor grading. Henson from the National Cancer Institute reported that the grading of breast cancer provides prognostic information in addition to that provided by stage (lymph node status and tumor size). He concluded that the grading of breast cancer can substantially improve the prediction of outcome that is predicted by lymph node status (1). This is additional support for the concept that combinations of risk factors are more predictive of outcome. Unfortunately, most investigators agree that expertise of tumor grading is not widespread since few pathologists have interest in this area (1,2). Thus, if you plan to incorporate tumor grading in your defense try to find a pathologist who has a special interest in this phase of pathology and read the excellent articles by Henson (1) and Henson and Ries et al. (2).

[2] Histologic Grade Henson (1) and Henson et al. (2) studied 22,616 breast cancer patients and reported that tumor grading further divides the survival of node-positive patients into subsets with varying survival rates. For example, in the node-positive patients the 10-year survival rate was as follows: histologic stage I (71%), histologic stage II (57%), and histologic stages III and IV (43 & 42%) (2).

These authors (2) recommend combining grades III and IV. They conclude that as breast cancers increase in size (and extent) they become less differentiated and suggest that this may explain the correlaton of size and prognosis.

[3] Lymph Node Status, Tumor Size and Mitotic Index Van Der Linden et al. (4) report that breast cancers containing more than 9 mitotic figures per 10 high-power fields have a significantly increased risk of recurrence. For example, cancers with less than 9 mitoses per 10 high-power fields had a 48-month disease-free survival of 90%, while those with greater than 9 mitoses per 10 high-power fields had a 48-month disease-free survival of only 60%. These same authors also reported that combinations of lymph node status, tumor size, and the mitotic index were more powerful predictors of prognosis than lymph node status alone (4).

[4] Lymph Node Status, Tumor Size and Tumor Grade In England, Blaney (5) , Haybittle et al. (6), and Todd JH et al. (7) have found that lymph node status, tumor size and tumor grade (Nottingham Index) were much more powerful predictors of outcome than lymph node status alone. Once again we have support for the value of combinations of risk factors. The Nottingham index is determined by the following formula.

Index = 0.2 x Size of tumor in cm + Grade + Stage (nodal status)

The following information will be needed for the calculation:

- Tumor size in centimeters
- Histologic grade (Bloom-Richardson)
- Stage (nodal status)
  - All axillary nodes negative
  - Lower axillary nodes positive
  - Higher axillary nodes or mediastinal nodes positive.

The Nottingham prognostic index can, if properly used, easily identify women whose cancers were more aggressive than the average breast cancer.

For additional information or assistance in calculating the Nottingham Index for the plaintiff's breast cancer contact one of the English authors.

References

1. Henson DE. The Histological Grading of Neoplasms. Arch Pathol Lab Med 142:1091-1096, 1988.
2. Henson DE and Ries MS et al. Relationship Among Outcome, Stage of Disease and Histologic Grade for 22,616 Cases of Breast Cancer. Cancer 68:2142-2149, 1991.
3. Osborne CK. Prognostic Factors. Oncology Viewpoints: Special Issue, Adjuvant Therapy in Node-Negative Breast

Cancer. Society of Clinical Oncologists. p 12, LP Communications Inc., New York, N.Y., 1988.

4. Van Der Linden JC, Baak JP, Hermans J, and Meyer CJL. Prospective Evaluation of Prognostic Value of Morphometry in Patients With Primary Breast Cancer. J Clin Pathol 40:302-306, 1987.
5. Blamey RW, et al. A Prognostic Index in Breast Cancer—Tested and Confirmed. Abstract. Breast Cancer Treatment and Research. 4:335, 1984.
6. Haybittle JL, Blamey RW et al. A Prognostic Index in Primary Breast Cancer. Br J Cancer 45:361-366, 1982.
7. Todd JH et al. Confirmation of a Prognostic Index in Primary Breast Cancer. Br J Cancer 56:489-492, 1987.

*[5]Nuclear Grade** Nuclear grade, which usually includes an evaluation of nuclear maturity and the frequency of mitotic figures, is a reliable predictor of outcome for both the node-positive and the node-negative patient. Some are of the opinion that nuclear grade, when used alone, is a reliable predictor of treatment failure and that the addition of histologic or tumor grade does not increase its predictive power. However, Lynn Dressler states that the combination of a poor nuclear grade and a high S-phase fraction are more powerful predictors of prognosis than nuclear grade alone (1).

Nuclear grade has one problem, which is that some pathologists are reluctant to assess nuclear grade because of inexperience and the concern about the subjectivity of their results. Fisher et al. (2) have had a vast experience with the grading of breast cancer. They state that only a modest period of training will enable the pathologist to obtain accurate and reproducible results. However, if you have difficulty obtaining a reliable nuclear grade consider having the nuclear grade determined by a pathologist who has expertise in this area or order a computerized digital morphometry of the plaintiff's breast cancer. Fisher et al. (2) compared the predictive ability of nuclear grade with tumor cell area or perimeter as determined by computerized digital morphometry. Tumor cell area or perimeter gave no added information beyond that from nuclear grade, but

*For a more complete discussion of nuclear grade see §23.02 [c][3].

Fisher et al. found a very strong correlation between nuclear grade and tumor cell area or perimeter. Therefore, if you have trouble obtaining a nuclear grade try to obtain tumor cell area or perimeter from the plaintiff's archival breast cancer tissue. If this procedure cannot be performed in your community ask your pathologist to recommend a good reference laboratory.

References

1. Dressler, Lynn. Quoted by Tom Reynolds in Breast Cancer Prognostic Factors—The Search Goes On. News, News, J Natl Can Instit 86(7):480-483, April 6, 1994.
2. Fisher ER, Redmond C, Fisher B, Bass G et al.: Pathologic Findings From the National Surgical Adjuvant Breast and Bowel Projects (NSABP). Prognostic Discriminants for 8-Year Survival for Node-Negative Invasive Breast Cancer Patients. Cancer 65:2121-2128, 1990.

[6] Mitotic Grade or Index Mitotic grade or index is a measure of the frequency of mitotic figures in the most anaplastic and rapidly growing region of the tumor. The mitotic index tells us how rapidly the tumor is growing and is usually reported as:

Grade I ---- 0-10 mitotic figures per 10 high-power fields (hpf) of an ordinary light microscope.
Grade II --- 11-20 mitotic figures per 10 hpf.
Grade III -- >20 mitotic figures per 10 hpf.

Others report mitotic grade in this way:

Grade I ---- 1 mitotic figure per one hpf in the most actively growing area of the tumor.
Grade II --- 2 mitotic figures per one hpf in the most actively growing area of the tumor.
Grade III -- 3 mitotic figures per one hpf in the most actively growing area of the tumor.

For many years it has been well known that breast cancers containing frequent mitotic figures have a higher incidence of relapse and death. We recommend that your mitotic count be performed in the most actively growing area of the tumor. Before interpreting the mitotic index please read §23.02[c][4]. If the mitotic count is low, and often it will be falsely low, be certain to include an S-phase determination in the prognostic profile. The S-phase fraction also tells us the percentage of cells preparing to undergo cell division (the proliferation rate).

[d] Lymphatic Peritumoral Invasion

When lymphatic peritumoral invasion is found in node-positive breast cancers, there is a significantly increased incidence of recurrence and death (1). Unfortunately it is often difficult to identify small lymphatic channels with ordinary stains. Therefore, if you are seriously interested in the possibility of lymphatic invasion request that your pathologist use immunohistochemical staining to identify the lymphatic endothelium (2). This will make it possible to detect many lymphatic channels that otherwise would have been overlooked.

[e] Blood Vessel Invasion

Recurrence and death from breast cancer is significantly higher when peritumoral blood vessel invasion is found in women with node-positive breast cancer (1). Small blood vessels can be difficult to identify with ordinary stains. Therefore, ask your pathologist to use elastic stains to identify the walls and immunohistochemical stains to identify the endothelium of the small blood vessels (2).

[f] Tumor Necrosis

Multiple foci of tumor necrosis within a breast cancer occur when the tumor is growing so rapidly that it outgrows its blood supply. This is an unfavorable prognostic finding (1).

References for [d], [e], & [f]

1. Rosen PP and Groshen S. Factors Influencing Survival and Prognosis in Early Breast Carcinoma (T1N0M0-T1N1M0), Surg Clin North America. 70(4):937-962, 1990.

2. Hutter RVP. The Role of the Pathologist in the Management of Breast Cancer. Ca-A Cancer Journal for Clinicians. September/October. 41(5), 283-299, 1991.

[g] Estrogen and Progesterone Receptors

Estrogen receptor negative tumors grow more rapidly and metastasize sooner than estrogen receptor positive tumors. The increase in metastasis is especially evident in estrogen receptor negative tumors of women who have greater than three positive lymph nodes. Two-thirds of these women develop recurrence within two years (1). Long-term survival studies, however, suggest that after 3-5 years the survival curves of ER + and ER − tumors begin to merge (1). Some have even suggested that the increased survival rate of ER + patients is an illusion created by the favorable response of the ER + breast cancer metastases to endocrine therapy (1). If the estrogen receptor status was negative, this fact should be included in your prognostic profile since it provides evidence that the plaintiff's cancer was a more rapidly growing tumor.

The epidermal growth factor receptor has been found to have an inverse correlation with the estrogen receptor. When one is known the other adds little additional information. Thus if the estrogen receptor status is not available one could order the epidermal growth factor receptor (2).

References

1. Osborne CK. Receptors. In *Breast Diseases*, Harris, Hellman, Henderson, and Kinne, eds. JB Lippincott, Philadelphia, 1991, pp 301-325.
2. Norton, Larry. An interview by Ted Bosworth. Special Report-Chemotherapy for Node-Negative Breast Cancer? Evaluating Prognostic Factors. Oncology Times. 14(1):p 21, January 1992.

[h] DNA Flow Cytometry

[1] Ploidy DNA Flow Cytometry DNA Flow Cytometry measures the DNA content of the tumor nuclei (ploidy), and the number of tumor cells that are synthesizing DNA (% S-phase) in preparation for cell division. Although some (1,2,3) agree that diploid (normal amount of DNA) tumors and tetraploid tumors (double the normal amount of DNA) have a better prognosis than aneuploid tumors (with an increased amount of DNA but less than double the normal amount), most recent studies fail to find a significant difference in the prognosis of diploid and aneuploid tumors (4). Most, however, agree that node-positive breast cancers with a high S-phase have an increased risk of recurrence and death.

[2] S-Phase Fraction Tumors with a low S-phase have a better prognosis. Small tumors tend to have a low S-phase which tends to increase as the tumor enlarges. It is not known whether tumor size and S-phase are independent prognostic factors (4).

References

1. Hutter RVP. The Role of the Pathologist in the Management of Breast Cancer. Ca-A Cancer Journal for Clinicians. September/October. 41(5):283-299, 1991.
2. Rosen PP and Groshen S. Factors Influencing Survival and Prognosis in Early Breast Carcinoma (T1N0M0-T1N1M0). Surg Clin North America. 70(4):937-962, 1990.
3. Henderson J Craig. Prognostic Factors, pp 332-346 in *Breast Diseases*, Harris, Hellman, Henderson, and Kinne, eds. JB Lippincott Co., 1991.
4. Norton, Larry. An interview by Ted Bosworth. Special Report—Chemotherapy for Node-Negative Breast Cancer? Evaluating Prognostic Factors. Oncology Times. 14(1):p 21, January 1992.

[i] HER-2/*neu* Oncogene (see also §23.02[i] for additional background)

Should you desire to further document the lethal potential of the lymph node-positive woman consider the HER 2/neu oncogene.

[1] Amplification Slamon, et al. (1,2) have reported that amplification of the HER-2/neu proto-oncogene is present in about 41% of primary breast cancers. They studied the correlation of survival and

relapse in patients with amplification of the HER-2/neu oncogene. They conclude that (1):

> "The current study indicates that amplification of the HER-2/neu gene is a significant predictor of both overall survival and time to relapse in node-positive patients with breast cancer. Amplification of the gene retains its prognostic significance in multivariate analysis, even when adjustments are made for other known prognostic factors. Moreover, amplification of HER-2/neu has greater prognostic value than most currently used prognostic factors, including progesterone and estrogen receptors, and *is equivalent to and independent of the best known prognosticator—the number of positive lymph nodes*" (Emphasis added.)

These same authors (2) found that the degree of amplification (that is, a greater gene copy number) was associated with a a poorer prognosis. For example, breast cancers with no amplification of the HER-2/neu oncogene had an 84-month disease-free survival of 48% while those with greater than 5 copies of the HER-2/neu oncogene had an 84-month disease-free survival of only 30%.

[2] Overexpression of the HER-2/neu Oncogene Recent studies by Paik et al. (3) report that overexpression of the neu protein is associated with poor survival regardless of the lymph node status. Interestingly, women with nuclear-grade good breast cancers and overexpression of the neu protein had an unusually high rate of relapse and death.

Practice Note

Both amplification and overexpression of the HER-2/neu oncogene appear to be as powerful as lymph node status in identifying women with a high rate of relapse and death from breast cancer. Amplification of the HER-2/neu oncogene (>5 copies) is a powerful predictor of an unusually poor prognosis in lymph node-positive breast cancer. Its prognostic power is equivalent to positive lymph node status. It is not used routinely in the clinical management of breast cancer because of the power of node status. However, in the malpractice setting it is a powerful tool in assessing the lethal potential of a tumor. By all means ask your expert witness and/or a reliable reference laboratory regarding the current status of these powerful prognostic factors.

References

1. Slamon D, Godolphin W, Jones L et al. Studies of the HER 2/neu Proto-oncogene in Human Breast and Ovarian Cancer. Science 244:707-712, 1989.
2. Slamon DJ, Clark GM, Wong SG, Levin WJ, Ullrich A, and McGuire WL. Human Breast Cancer. Correlation of Relapse and Survival With Amplification of the HER-2/neu Oncogene. Science 235:177-181, 1987.
3. Paik S, Hazan R, Fisher ER, Sass RE, Fisher B, Redmond C, Schlessinger J, Lippman ME, and King CR. Pathologic Findings From the National Surgical Adjuvant Breast and Bowel Project: Prognostic Significance of erbB-2 Protein Overexpression in Primary Breast Cancer. J Clin Oncol 8:103-112, 1990.

[j] Cathepsin-D

Although the use of Cathepsin-levels has great potential for determing the prognosis of breast cancer it will be of little or no help in the immediate future since there are conflicting reports regarding its prognostic worth in node-positive breast cancer. Additionally, appropriate cut-off levels for the determination of low- versus high-risk have not yet been established (1). Consult your expert witness regarding the present status of Cathepsin-D as a prognostic determinant in axillary lymph node-positive disease.

References

1. Henderson J Craig. Prognostic Factors, pp 332-346 in *Breast Diseases*, Harris, Hellman, Henderson, and Kinne, eds. JB Lippincott Co., 1991.

[k] Host Immunity

Host immunity plays a powerful and usually unrecognized role in the clinical behavior of breast cancer. In one recently completed double blinded, mass screening trial, one arm consisted of women with clinically normal axilla who underwent total mastectomy with no treatment of any kind to the axilla. From the radical mastectomy arm of the trial we know that 40% of the women with untreated clinically negative axilla harbored clinically undetectable axillary metastases. Yet only 16% of these women who did not undergo axillary dissection developed clinical axillary metastases within a period of 10 years. The axillary metastases were removed only when they became clinically apparent. Amazingly, the mortality rates of the two groups were identical. The immune system of the host destroyed or controlled the axillary metastases in two-thirds of thesc women (1). This is a powerful demonstration of host immunity.

Long-term studies reveal that about one-third of women who have survived breast cancer for more than 20 to 30 years had proven axillary lymph node metastases at the time of diagnosis and surgery (2). These women apparently possessed effective immune systems. The vast majority of these women were treated with radical mastectomy without chemotherapy as were almost all others in that time frame. Some may have had postoperative radiation.

References

1. Fisher E.R The Impact of Pathology on the Biologic, Diagnostic, Prognostic, and Therapeutic Considerations in Breast Cancer. Surg Clin N Am. 64(6):1073-1093, 1984.
2. Rosen PP and Groshen S. Factors Influencing Survival and Prognosis in Early Breast Carcinoma (T1N0M0-T1N1M0). Surg Clin N Am. 70(4):937-962, 1990.

[l] Clinical Behavior of the Plaintiff's Breast Cancer

Obviously, if the tumor relapses soon after surgery with evidence of distant metastases, we are dealing with a tumor with proven invasive and metastatic potential. A short disease-free interval, less than 2-3 years, indicates that the tumor was biologically aggressive and that the metastasis arose more than 12 months prior to the time of diagnosis and excisioin of the primary tumor. A rapid down-hill course following the appearance of the first evidence of recurrence is additional evidence of a lethal tumor. This type of tumor, the early metastasizing breast cancer, often spreads to distant sites during or shortly after the period of vascularization before the tumor attains a size detectable by mammography. Those that do not metastasize before they can be detected by mammography do so prior to the time the tumor becomes large enough to produce symptoms. (See Chapter 10)

[m] Tumor Angiogenesis (Microvessel Count)

McGuire recently stated that a good prognostic indicator ". . . should possess clear biologic significance." (1) Certainly the measurement of the intensity of angiogenesis within a breast cancer should have biologic significance. In Chapter 10, we discussed the biologic significance of angiogenesis, the various mechanisms by which it facilitates metastasis, and the role of angiogenesis throughout the life of a breast cancer.

[1] Density of Microvessels a Good Prognostic Indicator Weidner et al (2,3) have reported that the density of microvessels in areas of breast cancer with the most intense neovascularization provides significant prognostic information concerning overall survival and disease-free survival of early breast cancer. Fortunately for the defense attorney, this information can be obtained from archival paraffin blocks of breast cancer tissue. Archival breast cancer tissue is stained with factor VIII antigen using standard immunoperoxidase staining techniques. The tiny microvessels can be identified by the brown-red stained endothelial cells. Weidner et al. (2) studied the correlation of the density of microvessels in archival breast cancer tissue with the frequency of metastasis. They observed:

# Microvessels per 200x hpf	% with Metastasis
0-33	14%
34-67	45%
68-100	71%
>100	100%

Weidner N, Semple JP, Welch WR, and Folkman J. Tumor Angiogenesis and Metastasis: Correlation in Invasive Breast Carcinoma. N Engl J Med 324: 1-8, 1991, Figure 3, page 5. Reprinted courtesy of author and publisher.

Others studies support Weidner's findings (4).
Weidner et al. (3) conclude that:

- Microvessel counts provide highly significant information concerning the overall and disease-free survival of early breast cancer.

- Adding microvessel counts to the number of involved lymph nodes provides information over and above that provided by the number of involved lymph nodes alone.
- Adding microvessel counts to other prognostic factors also provides additional information.

*[2] **Conclusion*** Microvessel counts in the area of the most intense neovascularization provides independent and highly significant prognostic information concerning overall and disease-free survival survival in all breast cancer patients, **both node positive and node negative.** Although the use of microvessel counts as a prognostic indicator is relatively new, knowledge concerning its worth is rapidly accumulating. We think it has great potential and agree with Page and Dupont that it should be valuable in some patient subgroups (5). Therefore, we recommend that you consult your pathologist and/or expert witness regarding the availability and feasibility of obtaining microvessel counts of the most intense areas of neovascularization of the plaintiff's breast cancer.

References

1. McGuire WI. Breast Cancer Prognostic Factors. Evaluation Guidelines. J Natl Cancer Instit 83:154-155, 1991.
2. Weidner N, Semple JP, Welch WR, and Folkman J. Tumor Angiogenesis and Metastasis—Correlation in Invasive Breast Carcinoma. N Engl J M 324:1-8, 1991.
3. Weidner N, Folkman J et al. Tumor Angiogenesis: A New Significant and Independent Prognostic Indicator in Early-Stage Breast Cancer. J Natl Can Instit 84(24):1875-1887, 1992.
4. Bosari S, Lee AK, DeLellis RA et al. Microvessel Quantitation and Prognosis in Invasive Breast Carcinoma. Hum Pathol 23:755-761, 1992.
5. Page DL and Dupont WD. Breast Cancer Angiogenesis: Through a Narrow Window. J Natl Can Instit 84(24):1850-1851, 1992.

[n] p53, Tumor Suppressor Gene

In a recent interview (1) Ann Thor suggests that mutation of the tumor suppressor gene p53 may help identify the 20-30% of node-negative women who will die of breast cancer. Thor stated that accumulations of mutant p53 mutant protein in breast tumors may be a predictor of shortened survival in both node-negative and node-positive breast cancer. She cautions, however, that although the mutant p53 protein may have a promising future it is not yet ready for the clinic. Much more work needs to be done. We recommend that you ask your expert witness about the current status of the p53 mutant protein.

References

1. Thor AD. Quoted in an interview in Researchers Make Slow Progess In Establishing Prognostic Indicators For The Clinic, J Natl Can Instit 85(6):428-429, March 17, 1993.

§23.04 CONCLUSION

The authors recommend that the following factors be carefully considered when gathering information concerning the aggressiveness of the plaintiff's cancer. Read the appropriate sections in this chapter concerning each factor before discussing them with your expert witness.

- Tumor type §23.02 [d]
- Clinical history §18.04 and §23.02 [l]
  - Rate of progression of the disease
  - Extent of distant metastasis
  - Time of first recurrence (the DFI)
- Lymph node metastasis Chapter 13 and §23.02 [a]
- Tumor grading §23.02 [c] and §23.03 [c]
  - Nuclear grade
  - Mitotic grade or index
- Unfavorable microscopic risk factors §23.02 [f] and §23.03 [d]
  - Tumor invasion of vascular capillaries
  - Tumor invasion of lymphatic capillaries
  - Foci of tumor necrosis
- DNA flow cytometry §23.02 [h] and §23.03 [h]

Ploidy
S-phase fraction (more important than ploidy)
HER-2/neu oncogene §23.02 [i] and §23.03 [i]
Overexpression of protein product
Amplification of the HER-2/neu oncogene
Microvessel count §23.02 [m]
Consult pathologist regarding feasibility

CHAPTER 24: SILICONE GEL BREAST IMPLANTS

CHAPTER 24

SILICONE GEL BREAST IMPLANTS

§24.01 INTRODUCTION

This brief summary regarding the use of medicinal grade silicone in breast implants will introduce the defense attorney to the silicone gel breast implant controversy. In the invited commentary presented in Chapter 25, Dr. Albert Cram and Dr. John Canady, experienced plastic and reconstructive surgeons, will share with us their clinical experience and expertise in the use of silicone gel implants for breast cosmetic augmentation and breast reconstruction.

The overwhelming majority of women with breast implants were happy with their implants. They obtained significant physical and emotional benefit from these devices and serious complications were rare. Yet, on April 16, 1992, Dr. David A Kessler (1), commissioner of the Food and Drug Administration, announced that silicone gel breast implants would no longer be available for cosmetic augmentation of the breast. The FDA charged that adequate data to demonstrate the safety and effectiveness of these devices do not exist (1). Marcia Angell (2) aptly described the results of Kessler's mandate "... the FDA's decision has given rise to great fears among the 1 million now living with implants—fears that in many women are out of all possible proportion to what is known about the risks. The results are hundreds of high-stakes court cases...." Jack Fisher (3) commented as follows: "The attitude of the FDA and its actions this past year have depended largely on the exaggerated claims of consumer advocacy groups and on poorly documented assertions.'' Furthermore, Fisher (3) stated the FDA, in making its decision, ignored the position statements of ''The American Medical Association, American College of Surgeons, American College of Radiology, American College of Rheumatology, Society of Surgical Oncologists, and the American Society of Plastic and Reconstructive Surgery.'' Dr. Fisher (3) continued, ''After the moratorium on the use of breast implants was announced by Dr. Kessler on January 6, 1992, a torrent of legal activity began. The American Trial Lawyers Association conducts regular seminars for plaintiff's attorneys, assisted by selected data provided by Dr. Wolfe of Public Citizen, an organization that conducts no scientific research of its own, yet offers scientific judgements.'' Critics charged that silicone gel implants not only increased the risk of breast cancer but caused delays in diagnosis that decreased the likelihood of cure. Additionally, the controversy has been fueled by the media's publicity of anecdotal reports which allege a cause and effect relationship between silicone gel implants and numerous autoimmune disorders.

When preparing a rebuttal to charges that there is a causal relationship between silicone gel breast implants and systemic disease, the defense should not underestimate the plaintiff. He/she may well have been educated by consumer advocacy groups such as The Public Citizens Health Group which was founded by Ralph Nader. This group is said to have assembled and sold at cost ($750.00) a 4,000 page report on breast implant scientific and medical research to an estimated 50 plaintiffs' attorneys (4). Kits have been prepared for trial attorneys on the proper conduct of product liability suits involving silicone gel implants. Symposiums on breast implant litigation are held in major cities at frequent intervals. Many attorneys are attending lectures such as (5):

- ''Breast Implants: Types, Uses and Risks''
- ''Long-Term Effects of Silicone Breast Implants''
- ''The Pathologic Effects of Silicone Breast Implants''
- ''The Relationship Between Silicone Implants and Autoimmune Diseases.''

Therefore, the defense must clearly understand the mechanism and clinical significance of capsular contracture, silicone ''bleed,'' implant rupture, and the anecdotal reports of autoimmune disorders that do occur in some women with silicone gel implants. Additionally, defense must be able to prove that silicone gel implants do not cause cancer of the breast or delay the diagnosis of breast cancer. But first, we must become familiar with the compound called silicone and its many uses in medicine.

References

1. Kessler, David A. Special Report—The Basis of the FDA's Decision on Breast Implants. New Eng J Med 326(25):1713-1715, June 18, 1992.
2. Angell, Marcia. Breast Implants—Protection or Paternalism? New Eng J Med 326(25):1695-1696, June 18, 1992.
3. Fisher, Jack C. Sounding Board. The Silicone Controversy—When Will Science Prevail? New Eng J Med 326(25):1696-1698, June 18, 1992.
4. National Women's Health Resource Center, 2440 M Street N.W., Washington DC, 20037, Special report, 14 (2): page 7, reprinted May 1,1992.
5. Symposium on Breast Implant Litigation, Law Journal Seminars Press, The Plaza Hotel, New York City, June 1, 1992.

§24.02 GLOSSARY

Chemical structure of the silicone polymer—Si0(CH3)2.

Polymer length (polymer [G] = part)—The longer the chain of simple repeating molecules, the more solid the product. The shorter the chain, the more liquid the product.

Silica—(SiO_2), silicon dioxide, a biologically active compound that excites intense fibrosis and possibly systemic sclerosis. Critics often charge that because silicone contains SiO_2 (silica) it is a dangerous product. This is not true. The silica is tightly bound within the silicone polymer and cannot be released.

Silicon—(Si) a non metallic element (atomic number 14) found extensively in the earth's crust in silica and silicates

Silicone—polydimethylsiloxane is a compound containing silicon, carbon, oxygen and hydrogen. It is manufactured by reducing silica ($Si0_2$) with methyl chloride (CH_3Cl) which is the hydrochloric acid ester of methyl alcohol. The resulting compound is then hydroxylated to produce polydimethylsiloxane (silicone). This mixture is then heated in the presence of a catalyst to obtain the various viscosities of silicone (a process called fumarization (1) which cross links the polymers making the silicone more solid). The silicone for the shells for both the gel and saline implants, as well as the solid silicone devices, is hardened by fusing silicone gel with 30% fumed silica (2,3,4,5). Thus, the concentration of silica is higher in the implant shells (for both gel and saline breast implants) and the solid silicone implants such as heart valves, shunts, and lens implants than in silicone gel itself (2).

Silicone gel implants—silicone gel, consisting of a matrix of silicone polymers permeated by silicone oils, contained within a vulcanized silicone outer shell (6).

§24.03 MEDICINAL USES OF SILICONE

Medicinal grade silicone is used in many ways. Silicone was used medically in World War II when syringes were lubricated with liquid silicone so they would function properly in combat (7). In 1955, an intracranial shunt using silicone was used to drain excess fluid from the brain in hydrocephalus. In 1962, the first silicone gel breast implant was introduced. Since then, 1 to 2 million women (includes implants for reconstruction following cancer surgery) have received silicone gel breast implants and the majority are happy with the results. The following is a partial list of the many uses for silicone in medicine today:

- Breast implants
- Tubing for renal dialysis
- Oxygenator lining
- Surgical drains
- Penile implants
- Testicular implants
- Skin lotions and creams
- Lubrication of syringes and blood pumps
- Intraocular lens implants following cataract surgery
- Encasements for cardiac pacemakers
- Lubrication of surgical material
- Tubing for administration of parenteral fluids and blood
- Tubing cardio-pulmonary bypass procedures

References

1. Bridges AJ and Vasey FB. Silicone Breast Implants: History, Safety, and Potential Complications. A Review Article. Arch Intern Med 153:2638-2644, 1993.
2. Schusterman, Mark A, Kroll SS, Miller MJ et al. Incidence of Autoimmune Disease in Patients After Breast Reconstruction With Silicone Gel Implants Versus Autogenous Tissue: A Preliminary Report. Annals of Plastic Surgery 31:1-6, 1993.
3. Kossovsky N, Heggers JP, and Robson MC. The Bioreactivity of Silicone, in *CRC Critical Reviews in Biocompatibility,* Williams DF, ed. Boca Raton, Fl: CRC Press, 1987, pp 53-85.
4. McGrath MH, Burkhardt BR. The Safety and Efficacy of Breast Implants for Augmentation Mammaplasty. Plast Reconstr Surg 74:550-560, 1984.
5. Dunn KW, Hall PN, and Khoo TK. Breast Implant Materials: Sense and Safety. British Journal of Plastic Surgery 45:315-321, 1992.
6. Independent Advisory Committee on Silicone Gel-filled Breast Implants. Special Article. Summary of the Report on Silicone Gel-filled Breast Implants. Canadian Medical Association Journal. 147(8):1141-1146, 1992.
7. Fisher, Jack C. Sounding Board. The Silicone Controversy—When Will Science Prevail? New Eng J Med 326(25):1696-1698, June 18, 1992.
8. Angell, Marcia. Breast Implants—Protection or Paternalism? New Eng J Med 326(25):1695-1696, June 18, 1992.

§24.04 CAPSULAR CONTRACTURE

[a] In General

All breast implants are foreign bodies and the body reacts by producing a dense layer of fibrous tissue which creates a capsule which surrounds the implant. When the capsule shrinks (contracts), the breast becomes more firm. Capsular contracture may simply represent the normal response of the body to a foreign body. However, myofibroblasts, hematoma, infection, and silicone bleed have been suggested as possible causes (1). The precise cause is not known. Although capsular contraction may cause annoying breast firmness, the capsule serves a useful purpose since it holds the implant in place and provides a barrier to the migration of silicone gel should the implant leak or rupture (1).

[b] Clinical Significance

Woods et al. (2) have had a vast experience with silicone gel implants and agree that capsular contractures may cause firmness, discomfort, and in a few, unsightly distortion of the breast but stress this is not a health hazard. In their experience ". . . the overwhelming majority of the patients who have this problem can be dealt with satisfactorily by surgery. For those who continue to have problems after corrective surgery, the solution is to remove the implants." Woods et al. (2) emphasize that in their experience this is rarely a serious problem.

References

1. Hidalgo DA. Are Breast Prostheses Safe for Use in Breast Reconstruction? Yes. Important Advances in Oncology—1993, Devita, Hellman, and Rosenberg, eds. JB Lippincott Co, 1993 pp 179-188 (an excellent review article).
2. Woods JE, Arnold PG, Meland NB, Clay RP, Petty PM, and Bite U. Breast Implant Complications: Fact and Fiction—Speaking Out—The Post Bulletin, Rochester, Minn., Friday, March 20, 1992.

§24.05 SILICONE GEL "BLEEDING"

[a] Diffusion of Particles

Although initially the vulcanized solid outer silicone shell of the silicone gel implant was thought to be impermeable, it is actually a semipermeable membrane through which small amounts of silicone can diffuse (1,2). The new "low bleed" silicone gel implants introduced in 1980, however, have significantly reduced "gel bleeding" (2). The diffusion of small silicone particles occurs in microscopic amounts and does not result in a measurable change in the volume of the implant even after long periods of time (1). Fisher (2) reminds us that the diffused particles of silicone are hydrophobic and have difficulty migrating through the aqueous environment of the extracellular tissues. Thus, it is not surprising that the diffused silicone particles remain within the fibrous implant capsule and the inner 1-2 mm of the capsule itself. Jennings et al (3) examined implant capsular tissue with a scanning electron microscope and electron dispersive x-ray analysis and reported that the migration of the diffused silicone was limited to the inner 1-2 mm of the fibrous implant capsule "and in many cases much less" than 1 mm. Unless forcibly injected into the body under pressure silicone cannot and does not gain entry to the blood and spread throughout the body. Occasionally, however, microscopic particles of silicone are ingested by macrophages and carried to the regional lymph nodes through the lymphatics (4).

[b] Clinical Significance

The silicone that "bleeds" through the semipermeable implant shell remains within the implant capsule and is only able to penetrate the inner 1-2 mm of the implant capsule. The microscopic amounts of silicone particles ingested by macrophages and occasionally carried by the lymph to the regional nodes do no harm. Hidalgo (1) states that silicone gel "bleed" has been studied extensively and is not believed to be a health risk. Woods et al. (5) have observed no symptoms or health hazards secondary to silicone bleeding in their series of more than 1700 breast implants.

References

1. Hidalgo DA Are Breast Prostheses Safe for Use in Breast Reconstruction? Yes. Important Advances in Oncology—1993, Devita, Hellman, and Rosenberg, eds. JB Lippincott Co, 1993 pp 179-188 (an excellent review article).
2. Fisher, Jack C. Sounding Board. The Silicone Controversy—When Will Science Prevail? New Eng J Med 326(25):1696-1698, June 18, 1992.
3. Jennings DA, Morykwas MJ, DeFranzo AJ et al. Analysis of Silicone in Human Breast and Capsular Tissue Surrounding

Prostheses and Expanders. Ann Plast Surg 27:553-558, 1991.

4. Hausner RJ, Schoen FJ, and Pierson KK. Foreign Body Reaction to Silicone Gel in Axillary Lymph Nodes After an Augmentation Mammaplasty. Plast Reconstr Surg 62:381-384, 1978.
5. Woods JE, Arnold PG, Meland NB, Clay RP, Petty PM, and Bite U. Breast Implant Complications: Fact and Fiction—Speaking Out—The Post Bulletin, Rochester, Minn, Friday, March 20, 1992.

§24.06 MASSIVE INTRAVENOUS INJECTIONS OF SILICONE SELDOM CAUSE HARM

[a] In General

Both Hidalgo (1) and Fisher (2) report that the hematogenous spread of silicone is not uncommon (3,4,5). Fisher (2) stated "The administration of drugs and parenteral fluids as well as hemodialysis and cardiac-bypass technology depends upon liquid silicone. Over time patients with insulin-dependent diabetes and those who depend upon dialysis accumulate substantial bodily exposure to silicone. Yet no systemic illness attributable to silicone has been reported in diabetes or in patients undergoing long-term dialysis." Additionally, Fisher (2) estimates that an insulin-dependent diabetic may over many years inject 25,000 to 50,000 microdroplets of silicone and that all of us continually consume or inspire microdroplets of silicone from foods, beverages or cosmetics without ill effects. Leong et al (3) studied the spallation and migrations of silicone from blood-pump tubing in patients on hemodialysis and commented: "Considering the long-term and massive exposure to synthetic dialysis materials, remarkably few instances of toxicity in the clinical situation have been reported."

[b] Clinical Significance

It is interesting that toxicity seldom results when massive amounts of silicone are distributed throughout the body during hemodialysis. Consumer advocacy groups that charge silicone spreads throughout the body ignore the fact that silicone is hydrophobic and cannot migrate for more than 1-2 mm through the aqueous environment of the tissues surrounding the implant shell. However, assuming for the moment that silicone could spread to distant sites through the reticuloendothelial system, the amount of silicone involved would be infinitesimal compared to that which occurs during hemodialysis and would do no harm.

References

1. Hidalgo DA. Are Breast Prostheses Safe for Use in Breast Reconstruction? Yes. Important Advances in Oncology—1993, Devita, Hellman, and Rosenberg, eds. JB Lippincott Co, 1993 pp 179-188 (an excellent review article).
2. Fisher, Jack C. Sounding Board. Thc Silicone Controversy—When Will Science Prevail? New Eng J Med 326(25):1696-1698, June 18, 1992 (an excellent review article).
3. Leong ASY, Disney APS, and Gove DW. Spallation and Migration of Silicone From Blood-pump Tubing in Patients on Hemodialysis. N Engl J Med 306:135-140, 1982.
4. Parfrey PS, O'Driscoll JB, and Paradinas FJ. Refractile Material in the Liver of Hemodialysis Patients. Lancet 1:1101-1102, 1981.
5. Valentin N, and Vilhelmsen R. Blood and Tissue Silicone in Extracorporeal Circulation. J Cardiovasc Surg 17:20-26, 1976.

§24.07 SILICONE GRANULOMAS

The plaintiff may charge that granulomas that sometimes occur near ruptured or leaking implants are an indication of an immune response. This is not true. Foreign body granulomata sometimes develop as the body surrounds and isolates diffused micro-particles of silicone. They do no harm and are most commonly seen in patients who have had their implants changed several times (1). Dunn et al. (2) state that since granulomatous reactions occur in response to both biocompatible as well as immunogenic materials their clinical significance is equivocal. Travis et al. (3) have reviewed the literature on this subject.

References

1. Hidalgo DA. Are Breast Prostheses Safe for Use in Breast Reconstruction? Yes. Important Advances in Oncology—1993, Devita, Hellman, and Rosenberg, eds. JB Lippincott Co, 1993, pp 179-188.
2. Dunn KW, Hall PN, and Khoo TK. Breast Implant Materials: Sense and Safety. British Journal of Plastic Surgery 45:315-321, 1992.
3. Travis WD, Balogh K, and Abraham JL. Silicone Granulomas: Report of Three Cases and Review of the Literature. Hum Pathol 16:19-27, 1985.

§24.08 IMPLANT RUPTURE

The media and advocacy groups allege that implant rupture is not only common but has catastrophic local and systemic effects. Manufacturers report that implant rupture occurs in about 1% of cases. The FDA (1) implied the incidence of implant rupture to be about 4 to 6%. However, Dowden and Yetman at the Cleveland Clinic (2) estimate that "About 3% of implants over the past 30 years have required replacement for breakage."

[a] Types of Rupture

1. Silent Rupture (intracapsular rupture)—The implant shell is ruptured or leaking but the fibrous implant capsule remains intact. The silicone gel remains confined within the implant capsule.
2. Gross Rupture (extracapsular rupture)—Both the implant shell and the contracted fibrous implant capsule are ruptured. Silicone gel escapes into the adjacent tissure at the site of the capsule rupture. Gross rupture is uncommon.

[b] Causes of Implant Rupture (3,4)

1. Blunt trauma.
2. Closed capsulotomy—In some studies, 50% of the patients with ruptured implants have a history of a failed closed capsulotomy procedure (3). During this procedure, which is now condemned by many, external force is applied to the

breast in an effort to rupture the contracted fibrous capsule surrounding the implant. Unfortunately, this excessive pressure may rupture both the capsule and the implant.

3. Surgical trauma—during insertion of implant through a small opening.
4. Failure of the implant itself—incidence unknown, but is less in newer implants.

[c] Symptoms of Rupture (4)

1. Silent Rupture—few if any symptoms and difficult to detect with mammography.
2. Gross Rupture—Both the implant shell and the fibrous capsule of the implant are ruptured. The gel surrounds the implant and may extend into the adjacent tissues, resulting in a change in the contour of the breast and/or a mass adjacent to the implant, and sometimes produces breast tenderness, or even breast pain or a burning sensation.

[d] Diagnosis of a Ruptured Implant

1. Mammograms—The majority of ruptured implants have a thick dense fibrous wall which may interfere with the use of mammography. However, de Camara et al. (4) reported that retrospectively 16 of 20 ruptures could be detected by mammography. Prospectively this detection rate probably could not be duplicated (5).
2. Sonography—Most (6) agree that sonography may fail to detect subtle discontinuities in the implant and/or capsular shell, however, it has been useful in detecting some ruptures and silicone granulomas (7).
3. Magnetic Resonance Imaging (MRI)—Early evaluation of MRI has shown good sensitivity and specificity in detecting implant complications (7). Ahn et al. (6) studied 200 women with implant-related symptoms and were disappointed with the accuracy of breast palpation and mammography. These same authors (6) then examined 100 women with breast implant-related complaints and reported that MRI was able to consistently distinguish between intra and extra capsular rupture. They reported the following:

Accuracy of MRI in Detection of Implant Rupture

False Negative Diagnosis	3.75%
False Positive Diagnosis	3.75%

Modified from Ahn et al. (6).

[e] Treatment of a Ruptured Implant

When a diagnosis of a ruptured implant is made, the implant and as much as possible of the escaped gel should be removed. Some surgeons also perform a capsulectomy (removal of the thick contracted implant capsule) (4,8). In one series, (4) the surgeon reinserted implants in 32 of 34 patients (two patients refused another implant). In most cases, the surgeon will immediately insert a new ''low bleed'' implant.

[f] Clinical Significance of a Ruptured Implant

Caffee (5) states that we realize that silicone ''bleed'' contributes to the generation of capsular contracture but we have not detected any other ill effects. The spillage of silicone gel into the implant capsule and/or into the surrounding tissues does increase the local foreign body reaction but has no systemic effect. Fisher (9) in his excellent review article states ''. . . no systemic medical illnesses have been attributed to either symptomatic or silent [implant] rupture.'' Dowden and Yetman (2) state ''. . . there is no evidence that a leakage or broken implant poses any danger to the health of the patient. In the United States no cases of 'silicone poisoning' have been reported with any use of silicone.'' Woods et al. (10) related their experiences with rupured implants and the so-called implant leakage in more than 1700 patients. The following is paraphrased from Woods' et al. excellent article ''Implant Complications: Fact and Fiction'' (10):

> In the majority of these patients there are absolutely no symptoms related to rupture or ''leakage'' and in fact rupture is usually undetected even by mammography. In our experience, ruptured implants are found as a coincidence at the time of release or treatment of capsular contracture or when exchanging an implant because of breast firmness. Because the implant is surrounded by an intact fibrous capsule the gel simply lies free within the fibrous capsule which surrounds the leaking or ruptured implant and does not travel to other parts of the body.

Through the years we have removed many ruptured implants, not because of symptoms, but simply in the process of releasing capsular contractures or exchanging the implants. We have not seen any serious consequences in patients with ruptured implants. Silicone gel is readily removed from the pocket, and has rarely been associated with any postoperative problems. We believe that when ruptures are known to exist, it is appropriate to remove the implants.

References

1. Kessler, David A. Special Report—The Basis of the FDA's Decision on Breast Implants. New Eng J Med 326(25): 1713-1715, June 18, 1992.
2. Dowden RV and Yetman RJ. Mastectomy with Immediate Reconstruction: Issues and Answers. Cleve Clin J Med 59:499-503,1992.
3. Peters W and Pugash R. Ultrasound Analysis of 150 Patients with Silicone Gel Implants. Ann Plast Surg 31:7-9, 1993.
4. de Camara DL, Sheridan JM, and Kammer BA. Rupture and Aging of Silicone Gel Breast Implants. Plast Reconstr Surg 91(5):828-834, April 1993.
5. Caffee, H Hollis. Discussion of de Camara et al., Rupture and Aging of Silicone Gel Breast Implants. Plast Reconstr Surg 91(5):828-834, April 1993, pp 835-836.
6. Ahn CY, Shaw WW, Narayanan K et al. Definitive Diagnosis of Breast Implant Rupture Using Magnetic Resonance Imaging. Plast Recontr Surg. 92:681-691, 1993.
7. Russell, David A. Personal communication January 19, 1994.
8. Coccaro SF, Dealing with the Ruptured Implant. Letter. Plast Reconstr Surg 92(3):557, Sept 1993.
9. Fisher, Jack C. Sounding Board. The Silicone Controversy—When Will Science Prevail? New Eng J Med 326(25):1696-1698, June 18, 1992 (an excellent review article).
10. Woods JE, Arnold PG, Meland NB, Clay RP, Petty PM, and Bite U. Breast Implant Complications: Fact and Fiction—Speaking Out—The Post Bulletin, Rochester, Minn. Friday, March 20, 1992.

§24.09 CANCER IN THE AUGMENTED BREAST: IS EARLY DETECTION POSSIBLE?

Kessler (1) has charged that the presence of a silicone implant within the breast complicates the usc of mammography for the detection of breast cancer. Clark et al. (2) have addressed the problem of the diagnosis and prognosis of cancers arising in the augmented breast. A review of the literature revealed only 66 cases (3,4,5). This is not surprising since many cases are not reported (6). Evaluation of the reported cases, however, revealed no evidence to suggest that patients with augmented breasts had more advanced disease. An earlier series of 20 patients (7) suggested that cancer was more difficult to detect and more advanced but as the series matured this could not be substantiated.

Clark et al. (2) compared 33 breast cancers discovered in augmented breasts with 1735 cancers from a cancer registry. A Lorad mammographic unit, Eklund views (8) after 1988, and sonography were routinely used to detect these cancers. They found that in spite of the limitations in imaging of the augmented breast these patients had smaller tumors with a lower incidence of nodal metastasis than those in the control population. Clark et al. (2) combined the data from three studies (3,4,5) published during the past 10 years and concluded that ". . . the pathologic stage at diagnosis is clearly comparable to that of the non-augmented breast.

Cancers in the Patient With Augmented Breasts
Combined patients in Literature (2)

Study	n	Invasive	In situ	Nodal Involvement
Liebman and Kruse (5)	11	8%	3%	4/10 (40%)
Deapen and Brody (3)	21	17%	2%	7/19 (37%)
Silverstein et al. (4)	35	32%	3%	15/32 (47%)
Clark, current study (2)	33	27%	6%	6/31 (19%)
Total	100	84%	14%	32/92 (35%)

Modified from Clark et al. Cancer 72:2170-2174,1992 (Table 7, p. 2174).

Jack Fisher (9) states that the American College of Radiology (10) believes that an adequate examination can be achieved with commonly available techniques. David A. Russell (6), an experienced midwest mammographer, strongly concurs with the American College of Radiology (10).

References

1. Kessler, David A. Special Report—The Basis of the FDA's Decision on Breast Implants. New Eng J Med 326(25): 1713-1715, June 18, 1992.
2. Clark CP, Peters GN, and O'Brien KM. Cancer in the Augmented Breast: Diagnosis and Prognosis. Cancer 72:2170-2174, 1993.
3. Deapen DM, and Brody GS. Augmentation Mammoplasty and Breast Cancer: A 5-Year Update of the Los Angeles Study. Plast Reconstr Surg 89:660-665, 1992.
4. Silverstein MJ, Gierson ED, Gamagami P, Handel N and Waisman JR. Breast Cancer Diagnosis and Prognoses in Women Augmented with Silicone Gel-filled Implants. Cancer 66:97-101, 1990.
5. Leibman AJ, and Kruse B. Breast Cancer: Mammographic and Sonographic Findings After Augmentation Mammoplasty. Radiology 174:195-198, 1990.
6. Russell, David A. Personal communication January 19, 1994.
7. Haycs H Jr, Vandergrift J, and Diner WE. Mammography and Breast Implants. Plast Reconstr Surg 82:1-8, 1988.
8. Eklund GW, Busby RC, and Job JS. Improved Imaging of the Augmented Breast. AJR 151:468-473, 1988.
9. Fisher, Jack C. Sounding Board. The Silicone Controversy—When Will Science Prevail? New Eng J Med 326(25):1696-1698, June 18, 1992 (an excellent review article).
10. Eklund GW. Statement for American College of Radiology at FDA Advisory Panel for General and Plastic Surgical Devices. Gaithersburg, Md., Nov 12, 1991, Rockville, Md, Food And Drug Administration, 1991.

§24.10 INCIDENCE OF CANCER IN THE AUGMENTED BREAST

Berkel et al. (1) studied the incidence of breast cancer in 11,670 women who had undergone breast augmentation. This cohort was compared with 13,557 women who were diagnosed with breast cancer during the same period of timc. Eighty-six cancers were expected in the augmented women but only 41 cancers were observed. Thus the standarized incidence rate of 47.6% was significantly lower than in the control population. Bryant et al. (2) recently reviewed Berkel's data and identified a number of biases that resulted in an underestimation of the standarized incidence rate in Berkel's study. A revised standarized incidence ratio will be published in the near future. However, Berkel et al. (1) concluded that ". . . (we) did not find an increase risk of cancer among the women who received implants, although the length of the follow-up (13.3 years) and, the completeness of the follow-up, and the size of the cohort (11,690 women) would have allowed the detection of such a risk."

A review of the literature by Berkel et al. (1) found only four other other studies (3,4,5,6) that addressed the incidence of cancer in the augmented breast. In one of these studies, Deapen et al. (3) found a standardized incidence rate of 57% in a cohort of 3,111 women who had undergone augmentation mammoplasty and were followed for an average of 6 years. The only other studies (4,5,6) were actually surveys among plastic surgeons inquiring about the freqency of cancers in women with implants. These surveys all failed to discover an increased frequency of breast cancer in women who have undergone augmentation mammoplasty with silicone gel implants.

Although breast cancers do occur in women who have silicone gel breast implants, a causal relationship between silicone and adenocarcinoma of the breast has never been demonstrated (7).

It is interesting that when materials such as cellophane, Dacron, Teflon, nylon, silk, polyvinyl chloride, and silicone are placed subcutaneously in rats, a fibrous capsule does not form around the material, but soft tissue sarcomas sometimes arise in the tissue adjacent to the implanted material (8,9,10). However, in humans implanted silicone is surrounded by a dense fibrous capsule and neither sarcomas or carcinomas arise in the adjacent breast tissue (8). There is no evidence that silicone breast implants cause adenocarcinoma of the breast in humans (8).

Woods et al. (11) have performed more than 1700 subcutaneous mastectomies (many for women with a high risk of breast cancer). During this procedure, 90-95% of the breast tissue is removed and a silicone implant is inserted. These authors report than during the 28-year period in which this procedure has been performed at the Mayo Clinic only six women have develped breast cancer. This is far below the expected rate of breast cancer and strongly suggests that there is no increased risk of breast cancer from silicone breast implants.

References

1. Berkel Hans, Birdsell DC, and Jenkins H. Breast Augmentation: A Risk Factor for Breast Cancer? N Engl J Med 326:1649-1653, 1992.
2. Bryant H, Brasher P, Van De Sande J, and Turg J. Review of methods in "Breast Augmentation: A Risk Factor for Breast Cancer?" N Eng J Med 330(4):293, Jan 27, 1994.
3. Deapen DM, Pike MC, Casagrande JT, and Brody GS. The Relationship Between Breast Cancer and Augmentation Mammaplasty: An Epidemiologic Study. Plast Reconstr Surg 77:361-367, 1986.
4. Synderman RK and Lizzardo JG. Statistical Study of Malignancies Found Before, During or After Routine Breast Plastic Operations. Plast Reconstr Surg 25:253-256, 1960.
5. Harris HI. Survey of Breast Implants From the Point of View of Carcinogenesis. Plast Reconstr Surg 28:81-83, 1961.
6. DeCholnoky T. Augmentation Mammaplasty Survey of Complications in 10,941 Patients by 265 Surgeons. Plast Reconstr Surg 45:573-577, 1970.
7. Dunn KW, Hall PN, and Khoo TK. Breast Implant Materials: Sense and Safety. British Journal of Plastic Surgery 45:315-321, 1992.
8. Hidalgo DA. Are Breast Prostheses Safe for Use in Breast Reconstruction? Yes. Important Advances in Oncology—1993, Devita, Hellman, and Rosenberg, eds. JB Lippincott Co, 1993 pp 179-188.
9. Oppenheimer BS, Oppenheimer ET, Danishefsky I et al. Further Studies of Polymers as Carcinogenic Agents in Animals. Cancer Res 15:333-340, 1955.

10. Oppenheimer BS, Oppenheimer ET, and Stout AP. Sarcomas Induced in Rodents by Imbedding Various Plastic Films. Science 118:305-306, 1953.
11. Woods JE, Arnold PG, Meland NB, Clay RP, Petty PM, and Bite U. Breast Implant Complications: Fact and Fiction—Speaking Out—The Post Bulletin, Rochester, Minn. Friday, March 20, 1992.

§24.11 DO SILICONE GEL IMPLANTS CAUSE AUTOIMMUNE DISEASE?

[a] Anecdotal Reports

One of the most serious concerns regarding breast implants are the anecdotal reports that allege a relationship between silicone and autoimmune disease. When interpreting these reports, we must remember that the key word is "anecdotal" which is defined as a "short account of a real or fictitious event." Anecdotal reports provide no scientific evidence to support the data which they present. There now have been more than 120 anecdotal reports of autoimmune disorders in women with silicone gel implants through 1991. Many allege a cause and effect relationship between silicone breast implants and a variety of autoimmune diseases such as:

Scleroderma	Systemic lupus erythematosus
Rheumatoid arthritis	Inflammatory polyarthritis
Sjogren's syndrome	Mixed connective tissue disease
Adult Still's disease	Myositis.

A special committee of the Canadian Medical Association (3) carefully analyzed the more than 120 anecdotal reports published through 1991 and found a number of deficiencies in these reports (3):

1. Poor, vague or absent case definiton.
2. Failure to apply conventional diagnostic criteria.
3. Inconsistency in the definition of "human adjuvant disease."
4. Forty-six of the 120 cases involved Japanese who had undergone liquid injection for breast augmentation. Only 2

were reported after 1969 and in only 14 was the injected liquid silicone.

5. In two cases silicone bone prostheses were used and in neither was the word autoimmune disease mentioned.
6. Disease status at the time of implantation was not determined in many of the cases.
7. Lack of a consistent latency period between implantation and the onset of the autoimmune disease.
8. Removal of the implant was not consistently associated with relief of symptoms.
9. Selection bias—Facilities known to have a special interest in a particular problem attract patients with that problem.

The above findings and conclusions of the special committee of the Canadian Medical Association (3) agreed with a special report of a group in the British Department of Health and Social Security:

> The reported cases of so-called autoimmune disease in women with implants are far less numerous than would be expected in women without implants. The reported number even if multiplied 10-fold to account for under-reporting of disease would not equal the expected incidence (3).

[b] Recent Scientific Studies

A number of animal studies are attempting to determine if silicone can initate a cell mediated delayed hypersensitivity response to unrelated antigens. Subcutaneous injections of silicone, pulverized gel, and implant envelope in rats, guinea pigs, and mice have provided no convincing evidence that there is an increased risk of autoimmune disease in women with breast implants. Others are comparing serum from women with silicone gel implants with serum from women without implants for evidence of immune perturbation. These investigators have and continue to search for such factors as antinuclear antibodies, C-reactive proteins, complement measurements, antibodies to type I collagen, and HLA type, etc. As yet they have found no convincing evidence that women with breast implants are at increased risk for autoimmune diseases.

Some have theorized that macrophages ingest silicone and loosen it from its bonds to silica dioxide. The silica dioxide (silicon) is then free to stimulate an immune reaction. This has not been proven (2). Others argue that there may be an atypical autoimmune response in some women with silicone gel breast implants (5) and/or that silicone implants in genetically susceptible hosts may pose a significant risk for immunopathology (3). Again, these theories have not been proven.

Two recent review articles by prominent rheumatologists (4,5) found no data which support a direct link between silicone and connective tissue disease. Both, however, indicated the need for additional studies to exclude the possibility of a link in rare individuals. Since the literature on this subject is rapidly expanding the defense should contact the manufacturer of the suspect device for an update of the most current literature.

References

1. Independent Advisory Committee on Silicone Gel-filled Breast Implants. Special Article. Summary of the Report on Silicone Gel-filled Breast Implants. Canadian Medical Association Journal. 147(8):1141-1146, 1992.
2. Vargus A. Shedding of Silicone Particles From Inflated Breast Implants (letter). Plast Reconstr Surg. 64:252, 1979.
3. Vojdani A, Campbell A, Brautbar N. Immune Functional Impairment in Patients With Clinical Abnormalities and Silicone Breast Implants. Toxicology and Industrial Health. 8(6):415-429, 1992.
4. Sergent JS, Fuchs H, and Johnson JS. Silicone Implants and Rheumatic Diseases. In Kelly WN, Harris ED, Ruddy S and Sledge C, eds. Textbook of Rheumatology, 3rd ed, Update 4, pp 1-15, WB Saunders, Philadelphia, 1993.
5. Bridges AJ, and Vasey FB. Silicone Breast Implants: History, Safety, and Potential Complications. A Review Article. Arch Intern Med. 153:2638-2644, 1993.

[c] Incidence of Autoimmune Disorders in Women Without Breast Implants

In many instances the best defense against anecdotal reports alleging a causal relationship between silicone and autoimmune disorders will be well-planned epidemiologic studies. Some have been completed and many are now in progress. It is estimated that breast implants have been inserted in approximately 1-2,000,000 women. In a population of 1-2,000,000 females without breast implants we would expect to encounter many cases of autoimmune disorders. For example (1).

Incidence of Autoimmune Disease in a Female Population Without Breast Implants*

	# per 100,000 population	# per million population	# per 2 million population
Rheumatoid arthritis (1,2)	1,000	10,000	20,000
Systemic lupus erythematosus (1,3)	250	2,500	5,000
Scleroderma (1,4)	2	10	20

*The incidence of fibrositis, the most common musculoskeletal disease in women under the age of 40, is not included in the above table since the exact incidence is not known (1,5).

Sergent (1) reminds us that we "must remember that all the diseases under discussion are more common in women." Thus to prove silicone induces autoimmune disease it must be demonstrated that autoimmune disorders are more common in women with silicone gel implants than in the general female population. As we shall see this has not been done.

References

1. Sergent JS, Fuchs H, and Johnson JS. Silicone Implants and Rheumatic Diseases, in *Textbook of Rheumatology*, 3rd ed, Update 4, Kelly WN, Harris ED, Ruddy S and Sledge C, eds, pp 1-15. WB Saunders, Philadelphia, 1993.
2. Harris, ED. The Clinical Features of Rheumatoid Arthritis, in *Textbook of Rheumatology*, 3rd ed, Update 4, Kelly WN, Harris ED, Ruddy S and Sledge C, eds. WB Saunders, Philadelphia, 1993.
3. Shur PH. Clinical features of SLE, in *Textbook of Rheumatology*, 3rd ed, Update 4, Kelly WN, Harris ED, Ruddy S and Sledge C, eds. WB Saunders, Philadelphia, 1993.

4. Seibold JR. Connective Tissue Diseases Charactrized by Fibrosis, in *Textbook of Rheumatology*, 3rd ed, Update 4, Kelly WN, Harris ED, Ruddy S and Sledge C, eds. WB Saunders, Philadelphia, 1993.
5. Goldenberg DL. Fibromyalgia Syndrome (Fibrosits). Mediguide Inflamm Dis 7:1, 1988.

[d] Epidemiologic Studies

The following are brief abstracts of some of the epidemiologic studies that have, or are now addressing, the alleged causal relationship between silicone gel breast implants and autoimmune disorders. Since additional surveys are in progress, or planned, the defense should contact the manufacturer of the suspect device for information regarding the most recent epidemiologic reports.

- Weisman MH, Veccione TR, Albert D et al., Connective tissue disease following breast augmentation: A preliminary test of the human adjuvant disease hypothesis. Plast Reconstr Surg 82:626, 1988.

Surveyed by mail 378 patients who had undergone augmentation with silicone gel implants and could find no evidence of a specific inflammatory rheumatic complaint in the 125 that responded to the survey.

- Schusterman, Mark A, Kroll SS, Miller MJ et al., Incidence of autoimmune disease in patients after breast reconstruction with silicone gel implants versus autogenous tissue: a preliminary report. Annals of Plastic Surgery 31:1-6, 1993.

The authors prospectively examined the incidence of autoimmune disease in women with cancer who underwent reconstruction between January 1986 and March 1992. Silicone gel implants were used for 250 of the women while 353 women did not receive a silicone implant. One patient from each group developed a documented autoimmune disorder requiring treatment. Both were mild. There was no evidence of implant rupture or other complicaions. The authors concluded the incidence of autoimmune disease in mastectomy patients receiving silicone gel implants is not different than in patients who had reconstruction with autogenous tissue.

- Wigley FM, Miller R, Hochberg MC, and Steen V. Augmentation mammoplasty in patients with systemic sclerosis: data from the Baltimore Scleroderma Research Center and Pittsburgh Data bank, presented at the American College of Rheumatology, San Antonio, Texas, November 7-11, 1993.

The authors examined a large registry of 741 women with scleroderma. Seven had history of a silicone breast implants. The frequency of implants (1%) in this group paralleled the rate of 1% in the general female population. They failed to find support for the hypothesis linking scleroderma and silicone breast implants.

- Gabriel SE, Melton LJ, Woods JE, Kurland LT. Mayo Clinic, Rochester MN, Silicone-containing breast implants and connective tissue diseases: A population-based retrospective cohort study (abstract) presented at the American College of Rheumatology, San Antonio, Texas, November 7-11, 1993.

The medical records of 824 women with silicone gel breast implants and 1634 age matched women without implants were compared. All of the age-matched controls had medical evaluations within two years of the women with breast implants. The average duration of follow-up was eight years for both groups. Among the women with breast implants there was one case of rheumatoid arthritis, one case of Sjogren's syndrome and no cases of progressive systemic sclerosis, systemic lupus erythematosus, or myositis. There was no excess risk for connective tissue disease in women with breast implants compared to age-matched controls. The authors concluded these data did not support a causal relationship between silicone gel breast implants and subsequent connective tissue disease.

- Goldman JA, Lamm SH, Cooper WL, and Cooper L. Rheumatological Clinic at Emory University. Breast implants are not associated with an excess of connective tissue disease. Presented at the American College of Rheumatology, San Antonio, Texas, November 7-11, 1993.

The diagnostic records of 6,325 patients in a single rheumatology practice were reviewed for differences in the frequency of rheumatologic diagnostic mentions among women with breast implants compared to women without breast implants. Among patients seeking a rheumatological consultation those with a history of breast implants were no more likely to have a diagnosis of a connective tissue disease than compared to a control group, whether the analysis was matched or unmatched.

- Dugowson CE, Daling J, Koepsell TD, Voigt L, and Nelson JL. Silicone breast implants and risk for rheumatoid arthritis. University of Washington, Pacific Medical Center and Fred Hutchinson Cancer Research Center, Seattle, WA. Carin E. Dugowson, Division of Clinical Research Center, Seattle WA. Presented at a recent meeting of the American College of Rheumatology, 1993.

As part of a prospective case-control study of risk for rheumatoid arthritis (RA) we recruited 349 women with new onset RA and 1456 similarily aged control women. The controls were recruited cooperatively with a breast cancer study and for that reason all were asked about breast implants. To help determine if implants are a risk factor for RA we sent questionnaires to the RA cases about the history of breast implants prior to their reference date. For cases, this was the date of the first physician visit for what was ultimately diagnosed as RA: for controls, this was a date randomly chosen from the distribution of reference dates for cases. The data from the 300 returned questionnaires did not support an increased risk of rheumatoid arthritis among women with silicone breast implants.

- Feller AM, and Biefel K. Division of Plastic Surgery and Reconstructive Surgery, Klinikum rechts der /sar, Technische Univ., Munich, Germany. Presented at a Berlin Congress, 1993.

Three hundred and ten implanted females were given questionnaires, physical examinations, and serologies for 30 immunological parameters. No statistically significant changes in laboratory values and no evidence of causal relationship between implants and disease.

- Alasia ST*, Ambroggio GP**, DiVittrio S, Sismondi P*** et al. Autoimmune connective tissue diseases and silicone implants. *Plastic Surgery Traumatological Center, Turin; **Rheumatology Dept, Molinette Hospital, Turin; ***Oncological Gynecology University, Turin.

The authors compared the clinical course of 102 patients with silicone implants and a control group for 2 to 17 years. No increase in the incidence of autoimmune disease was observed in the implant group.

- von Hesler FW, von Finckenstein J, Bohmert H. Klinikum Groshadern, LMU-Munchen, Munchen, Germany. Are there systemic side effects after silicone gel breast implants?

Questionnaires were sent to 687 patients who had received breast implants and 467 responded. Examinations and serologies of all symptomatic respondents (121) revealed no significant differences blood counts, electrolytes, renal and hepatic function, rheumatoid factor, C-reactive protein, antinuclear antbody, or antimitochrondial antibody.

- Englert, Australia. Case control study of scleroderma. Reported in November 1993 at a Plastic Surgery Meeting in Australia.

No excess of scleroderma compared to the controls.

- In progress. by Schottenfeld of University of Michigan.

A case control design study of scleroderma and undifferentiated Connective Tissue Disease. First part due in December 1993. Eventually will include 9% of the population of the United States.

- Peters WJ, Keystone D. Lee P et al. (Department of Surgery, University of Toronto) Silicone gel implants and connective tissue disease. Presented at the annual meeting of the American College of Rheumatology, November 9, 1993. San Antonio.

These authors demonstrated that the laboratory data from 200 women with intact implants and 29 with ruptured implants were similar to 100 control patients of the same age and who did not have implants. Peters was quoted as saying that this data ''strengthens the concept that there is no conclusive evidence that silicone implants are related to the development of connective disorders'' (PR Newswire, November 16, 1993).

- Dr Hochberg. of the University of Maryland presented a paper on the incidence of scleroderma in women with silicone breast implants at the meeting of the American College of Rheumatology at San Antonio, Nov 7-11, 1993 (PR NEWSWIRE)

These authors studied a group of women with scleroderma and compared them to a large control of women without connective tissue disease. They discovered that the frequency of silicone implants in the scleroderma population was no more and possibly less than in the group of women without connective tissue disease. The final study is expected to gather nationwide data from 1,000 women with scleroderma and a control group of about 2,000 women.

[e] Summary of Epidemiologic Studies

These studies provide sound scientific evidence that silicone gel breast implants do not cause systemic disease or increase the risk of breast cancer. A similar picture is emerging for connective tissue disease. However, since there are many large epidemiologic studies now in progress the defense should contact the manufacturer of the suspect device for an update on the current status of these studies.

§24.12 REPORT OF THE COUNCIL ON SCIENTIFIC AFFAIRS, AMA

The Council on Scientific Affairs of the American Medical Association has prepared a follow-up report on the silicone gel breast implant controversy which was published in the Journal of The American Medical Association on December 1, 1993. This report provides an excellent summary of the chemical profile of silicone gel implants and supports the conclusions made in this chapter regarding:

- Silicone gel bleed
- Contracture of the fibrous implant capsule
- Carcinogenesis and silicone implants
- Diagnosis of cancer of the breast in women with implants
- Silicone and immune disorders

This excellent report should be read by all who become involved in litigation regarding silicone gel breast implants.

References

1. Council Report: Silicone Gel Breast Implants, Council on Scientific Affairs, American Medical Association. J.A.M.A. 320(21):2602-2606, Dec 1, 1993.

§24.13 CONCLUSION

The vast majority of women are happy with their breast implants. The most common complication, capsular contracture, is not serious. The body normally walls off all foreign bodies with scar tissue and breast implants are no exception. When the scar tissue capsule surrounding the implant shrinks, the breast may become firm, uncomfortable, or even slightly distorted. Most capsular contractures do not require treatment, but surgical release of the contracture is available and usually solves the problem. If not, the implant can be removed.

The gel which diffuses from an intact implant or escapes from a failed implant is confined within the scar tissue capsule which envelops the implant and does not spread throughout the body. Ruptured implants and the surrounding gel are simply removed and a new implant is inserted. Experienced surgeons who collectively have inserted thousands and thousands of implants have observed no ill effects or health hazards from leaking or ruptured implants.

Contrary to what some critics charge, there is no evidence that silicone gel implants cause adenocarcinoma of the breast and the diagnosis of cancer is not delayed by the presence of an implant.

In a population of 1-2,000,000 women without implants there will be significant numbers of women who develop autoimmune disorders. Epidemiologic studies reveal that the incidence of autoimmune diseases in women with silicone gel implants is no greater than in women without breast implants. There is no proof that silicone gel implants cause any serious disease.

The decision of the FDA banning the use of silicone gel implants for cosmetic augmentation should be rescinded.

CHAPTER 25: SILICONE AND PUBLIC HEALTH: PLASTIC SURGEONS' VIEWPOINT

CHAPTER 25

SILICONE AND PUBLIC HEALTH: PLASTIC SURGEONS' VIEWPOINT

By: **Albert E. Cram,** MD, FACS, Professor of Surgery and Director, Division of Plastic and Reconstructive Surgery, University of Iowa Hospitals, University of Iowa College of Medicine

John W. Canady, MD, Assistant Professor of Plastic and Reconstructive Surgery, University of Iowa College of Medicine

§25.01 INTRODUCTION

It is somewhat ironic that an implantable substance with the general safety record of silicone is to be the subject of at least two chapters in a book on medical malpractice defense. The presence of silicone in materials encountered in everyday life and its use in the practice of medicine is so widespread that the adjective ubiquitous is appropriate. Some of the basic science regarding silicon, silica and silicone has been covered in the previous chapter. In this chapter we will be referring almost exclusively to the polymer silicone. Despite its long record of use and apparent safety, this material has become the culprit in the largest class action settlement ever negotiated. Presided over by Federal Judge Samuel Pointer, the settlement provides $4.2 billion in compensation for women with breast implants who develop any of seven conditions (1).

The settlement concerns only product liability on the part of manufacturers.

It appears that some potential plaintiffs are being advised to bypass the global settlement and pursue their case against the manufacturers individually. On those grounds alone there may be sufficient opportunity to test defense strategies. In addition, it is possible that some women will pursue individual medical malpractice claims against physicians. This is certainly of concern to plastic surgeons and all the more so because the global settlement appears to preclude enjoining the manufacturers when a claim of product liability is leveled against the physician.

This chapter would be simpler to write if the issues were not so broad, if the biologic sciences involved were more easily quantifiable, and our understanding of the nuances was more complete. We will attempt to improve the readers' understanding of the basic issues and will present (with as little bias as we are able) a body of knowledge that we believe may be useful in defending against malpractice claims involving silicone.

§25.02 BASIC CHEMISTRY OF SILICON

Silicon is the basic element. It is one of the more common elements of our planet and is perhaps best well known to us in its silicon dioxide form. Sand is probably the most common form of silicone-containing molecule and we are all exposed to it in this form. Glass and a number of other useful items are formed from silica compounds. Talcum powder commonly applied to chafed and irritated infant skin contains silica, as does the powder used to lightly dust surgical gloves. There are numerous proprietary medications, both prescription and non-prescription, which contain silicone moieties perhaps best known in the antacid formulations for "heartburn."

The form of silicon of greatest interest to us, however, is the combination of the basic Si atom with two methyl groups and an atom of oxygen. This basic molecule known as dimethylsiloxane can be polymerized and, depending on increasing chain length, may be a fluid, a gel, or a solid. The shorter the chain of dimethylsiloxane units the more fluid the product. The most common examples would include silicone lubricants, which are commonly used in the household and in the work place. These short-chain liquids are often delivered an atomized spray and depending on particle size, might gain access to the body via direct injuries to skin or through dermatologic diseases. In addition, where spray atomization produces extremely small particle size such as in some hair sprays, the dimethylpolysiloxane might enter the body via the respiratory tract.

Many baby bottle nipples and pacifiers utilized throughout the United States are composed, at least in part, of polydimethylsiloxane elastomers. It is certain that all humans have exposure to silicon and in modern industrialized nations it is highly unlikely that there are any individuals who have not been exposed to the silicone polymers at the very least by ingestion and in many cases by exposures which would include deposition within the soft tissues of the body.

The medical uses of silicone include the use of liquids, gels, and solid polymers. The best known but least common forms of implantable silicone are breast prostheses, testicular prostheses and penile prostheses. Of these devices the breast prosthesis has been in use the longest—for approximately the last thirty-five years. Other commonly implanted solid form uses of silicone include medical tubing, prosthetic joints, hydrocephalic shunts, implanted drug delivery systems and as a protective coat around heart pacemakers. It is interesting that the FDA approved the use of Norplant®, which uses a dimethylsiloxane compound outer shell, shortly after it called for a moratorium on breast implants. The population receiving Norplant® is the same sex and generally the same age group as those who have received and continue to request breast implants.

Most of the injection needles used in the modern practice of medicine have a silicone liquid coating, as do the catheters inserted into blood vessels to measure pressures, most commonly in the intensive care unit setting. The syringes utilized by diabetics for insulin injection also contain a thin film of liquid silicone. This coating prevents the insulin from sticking to the syringe and ensures that the patient gets the desired dose of insulin at each administration. Diabetics who inject themselves twice daily over a period of 10-15 years have varying amounts of liquid silicone within the soft tissues at their injection sites. Given the wide exposure to many forms of dimethylsiloxane polymers, it is curious that groups other than breast implant patients have not come forward with symptoms similar to those of the breast implant plaintiffs' group.

The symptoms noted by breast implant patients are similar but not identical from patient to patient. The majority of patients seen in the senior author's practice have usually complained of pain in the breast surrounding one or both implants. A variety of vague muscular or joint related aches and pains, and complaints of easy fatigability are among the more common complaints. In what I would classify as a second tier of commonality are complaints of short-term memory loss and a ''metallic'' taste in the throat. In the third tier, a variety of unusual and occasional bizarre symptoms are related. Prior to 1990, only the complaint of chest pain at the site of the implant was common and this complaint was almost without fail accompanied by evidence on physical examination of significant peri-prosthetic capsular contracture. The anecdotal experience related here should not be mistaken for controlled scientific experiments, but anecdotal observations have certainly proved helpful to the plaintiff's bar. Perhaps the clinical observations in our practice may suggest useful lines of inquiry for defense in silicone-related cases.

The author's practice is in a university-based referral center. As the publicity surrounding the silicone controversy gained widespread media exposure, we experienced an initial surge of inquiries from patients we had never seen or previously treated regarding implant-related risks. A majority of these early calls related anxiety over media reports of ''a ticking time bomb in their chest,'' but many had experienced no adverse symptoms related to their implants. Many had been in place for between 10-15 years. The majority of these patients were satisfied by a telephone consultation in which we offered examination but also related to the patients the FDA's own position that at present the risk of implant removal exceeded the known risks of keeping the implants if the patient was asymptomatic.

When large jury awards began receiving media attention, there was a second wave of inquiries from patients, the majority of which had received their implants in other medical centers. Most of these patients have been seen and examined by the authors. The most consistent complaint seen has been discomfort surrounding the implant and physical examination often reveals capsular contracture as the potential explanation for their symptoms. Anxiety has been noted in all of the patients seen. Patients with significant joint pain or firbromyalgia-like symptoms have been referred to Rheumatology. History, physical examination and laboratory workups with a variety of blood tests have failed thus far to identify any patient with a diagnosable connective tissue or autoimmune disorder.

Many of our patients have been primarily concerned that their implant might be ruptured and if examination and a variety of imaging tests appear negative for rupture, the majority of these patients have appeared to be reassured and have not sought further consultation or treatment. Most of the patients in whom there was some reasonable doubt about implant integrity have chosen to undergo implant removal. Approximately half of these patients have chosen to replace gel-filled implants with saline-filled silicone implants. In our limited and very anecdotal experience there has not been a consistent trend toward improvement of the complaints of easy fatigability, joint and fibromuscular pain, nor has there been a consistent improvement in chest wall pain. The stated duration of symptoms in this group of patients is quite variable and it seems unusual that many of the patients did not seek medical attention for their symptoms prior to the publicity associated with the implant controversy. A review of all medical records should help to identify the time at which symptoms become severe enough to cause the patient to seek medical attention.

§25.03 PHYSIOLOGIC RESPONSE TO FOREIGN BODY

Invasion of animal or human soft tissue by foreign material elicits a specific defensive response which may vary slightly in its expression among the species but which follows a general physiologic theme. There is an initial response aimed at stopping the bleeding associated with either accidental or elective surgical tissue injury and a general inflammatory response is set in motion. The aim of this response is to repair the injury and to prevent infection. White blood cells are attracted immediately to the area of injury and form the first line of internal defense against infection. If the number of bacteria present in the wound exceeds the capability of this defensive mechanism, an infection of the area surrounding the foreign body is inevitable. Redness and swelling will usually be apparent within a 24-hour period and in the majority of cases the infection will persist, even if treated with antibiotic, until the foreign body is removed.

If the body's defense against infection is able to prevail, the initial inflammatory cell response is followed by the migration of cells called fibroblasts which begin to wall off the foreign body from the surrounding soft tissue by making collagen. In essence, the body makes a scar around the foreign material, whether it be a surgically implanted vascular prosthesis, a breast prosthesis, a wooden splinter or a splinter of glass from an automobile accident. The stronger the inflammatory response, the more exuberant the formation of the scar. The body builds a protein wall around the foreign material and maintains this wall, usually referred to as a capsule, so long as the foreign body remains in the soft tissue.

Within the population of fibroblast cells in the body there are some specialized fibroblasts referred to as myofibroblasts. These cells have an ability to cause the scar to contract and they are felt to be responsible for the capsular contracture which is often seen around breast prostheses. Because the breast prosthesis is soft and pliable, the tightening of the capsule around the implant can cause distortion of implant shape. In severe cases the implant may be displaced from its original position. The same mechanisms doubtless occur around wood splinters and solid heart pacemaker implants but these materials are solid enough to resist distortion by the weaker force exerted by the capsule.

It is generally assumed that the pain many patients have in association with a tight soft-tissue capsule is due to the capsule but pain is not a universal finding in patients with significant capsular contracture causing implant distortion. The true incidence of significant capsular contracture is unknown but figures as high as 75% have been reported in mastectomy reconstruction (2). Figures in cosmetic augmentation are lower but a 30-40% incidence is not an uncommon figure.

§25.04 CAPSULAR CONTRACTURE—ETIOLOGY AND TREATMENT

[a] Diagnosis

The diagnosis of capsular contracture around a breast prosthesis is made by physical examination. Capsules are often graded by a scheme devised by Dr. Baker (3). Capsules are classed in increasing severity as Baker Grade I, II, III, or Grade IV. Baker Grade I and II capsules are often subtle changes noted only by the examining physician. Many patients with this milder form of capsular contracture are asymptomatic and totally satisfied with their implant. Baker Grade III and IV capsules are more often symptomatic. The patients are usually aware of an abnormality and in the more severe cases the distortion would be obvious even to a casual observer. Patients with this severity of capsule formation generally request some form of treatment.

Onset of the tight capsule may occur very early in the postoperative period or can be delayed for many years. Often the problem of a tight symptomatic capsule is found only on one side in cases where bilateral implants have been inserted. This would seem to preclude a systemic abnormality in healing as the etiology. The cause of capsular contracture is unclear but a number of theories have been advanced to explain its development. There is anecdotal evidence that bleeding in the tissue around the implant increases the risk of tight capsule formation. A very low-grade infection has also been cited as a possible cause for tight capsule formation and either of these explanations would be compatible with the development of a tight capsule on one side while the opposite periprosthetic capsule remained soft and pliable. Although one cannot rule out with certainty an immune cause in bilateral implant capsular contracture, it does seem unlikely that a systemic reaction by the body's immune system would affect only one of two identical foreign body implants.

[b] Prevention

Attempts to modify capsule formation and prevent the tight periprosthetic capsular contracture have led many surgeons to recommend methodical massage. It has also been accepted practice by many plastic surgeons to place steroids either in the implant where the construction of the implant allowed insertion of saline and medication or through direct insertion of steroid into the pocket created for placement of the implant. Steroids decrease the body's inflammatory reaction and it is felt that this may help to prevent the formation of tight capsules. Unwanted side effects of steroid have led other surgeons to forgo this potential preventative measure. Despite many anecdotal reports of the efficacy of massage or steroid application, there are no good double-blind studies to prove unequivocally the efficacy of these treatments.

[c] Treatment

Once an established capsular contracture has developed, there are basically three treatment options. If the patient is asymptomatic and is satisfied with the breast shape and consistency, one option is to forgo any attempts at therapy. If the patient does desire treatment, one time-honored approach has been the technique of closed capsulotomy (4). In this technique, pressure is applied to the breast and the underlying implant in an attempt to rupture the soft tissue capsule. Although many capsules have been successfully treated by this technique, there is the obvious potential risk of rupturing the implant outer shell as well as the body's soft tissue capsule. Although this technique was widely applied in the past, its use is less prevalent today.

The third option with regard to capsular contraction treatment is operative. The implant and its surrounding soft-tissue capsule is usually approached through the previous incision used for implant insertion. The soft-tissue capsule may either be incised with the capsule being left in place following this division of its fibers (open capsulotomy) or the entire capsule may be excised and the implant placed in a fresh soft-tissue pocket. This technique is referred to as capsulectomy. Both the closed and open capsulotomy techniques as well as capsulectomy may provide successful treatment but all of these techniques are followed by a healing response on the part of the body and in some cases there is a recurrent tightening of the newly healed capsule. Capsular contracture remains the primary known complication of breast implant surgery.

§25.05 IMPLANT RUPTURE

Loss of integrity of the outer shell can potentially occur any time from the moment of insertion to many years following insertion. In most cases, rupture of the implant during insertion is immediately recognized by the surgeon. The implant shell and its inner silicone gel can then be removed and a new implant placed. Despite the relatively strong outer silicone elastomer shell, application of adequate force can cause rupture. Direct trauma to the chest wall in falls, motor vehicle accidents, physical assaults, during therapeutic closed capsulotomy and even during mammography have been reported as causes of implant shell rupture. If implant rupture occurs very early before the inflammatory response has had time to build an outer soft tissue scar the gel may travel through soft tissue planes. Ultimately, this will be treated by the body as a foreign body in its new location and the gel will be enclosed in a new collagen scar. Some of the specialized white cells of the body may ingest small droplets of silicone and this may explain how silicone is occasionally found in lymph nodes draining a particular area of the body where silicone gel has migrated. This is seen most commonly in the axillary lymph nodes which drain the breast. Although the presence of silicone in lymph nodes has been noted in scientific papers and by the media, there is no evidence that this phenomena is associated with any disease process.

§25.06 GEL BLEED

The mechanism of gel bleed in silicone gel implants has been covered in Chapter 24. Although the newer implants are often referred to as "low bleed," one can identify some microscopic silicone in the inner layers of the soft tissue capsule in almost all capsulectomy specimens (5). The articles previously cited in Chapter 24 by Fisher and Hausner are pertinent here. In admittedly anecdotal personal experience, there has been no significant correlation between patients' symptoms and the observed amount of gross "silicone gel bleed." There has also been no good correlation between silicone bleed and capsular thickness. Some of the thickest capsules I have personally observed have been around saline-filled breast implants.

Since January of 1992 when the FDA requested a moratorium on the use of silicone gel-filled implants, the use of saline-filled implants has increased. Some surgeons had used these implants preferentially even prior to the moratorium. The outer shell of such implants still consists primarily of the polysiloxane moiety and from a potential immunogenic standpoint is basically identical to the gel-filled implant outer shell. Following insertion of a saline-filled implant, the body's reaction is identical to that seen following an insertion of a gel-filled implant. The scar the body builds around the saline-filled implant, like that of the gel-filled implant, may remain soft and pliable or may go on to form a capsular contraction. Anecdotally, some of the worst capsular contractions I have seen have been in saline-filled implants. In my personal experience, the formation of calcium deposits around the implant in the soft-tissue capsule has been more common in the saline-filled implant than in the gel-filled.

As noted previously, when a gel-filled implant ruptures, if the soft tissue capsule is well formed, the rupture may be undetectable on clinical examination and can be difficult even using multiple imaging techniques. In contrast, rupture of the saline-filled implant results in the loss of saline within the soft-tissue capsule. Since the body is primarily composed of saline, this fluid is easily absorbed and there is very early and significant change in breast shape with loss of the saline-filled implant integrity. Neither the patient nor the physician has any difficulty making the diagnosis of implant rupture in these cases. A very slow leak of a saline-filled implant such as through a defective one-way valve may be more difficult for the patient to detect as the change may occur over a much longer period of time and therefore be less noticeable to the patient. Most patients experiencing rupture of a saline implant do request replacement with a new implant.

Saline implant outer shell technology is leaning toward a thicker outer shell but we can be certain that these manmade implants will not invariably last for the patient's entire lifetime. The normal activities of breathing and arm and chest motion, as well as external pressures applied over the implant, will in some cases weaken the outer shell to the point where trauma may produce rupture. There is insufficient data to predict the probable average lifetime of currently available saline-filled implants.

The FDA has initiated the process of reviewing saline-filled silicone breast implants. The Global Settlement appears to include patients who have saline-filled silicone outer shell implants. Given the approval of Norplant by the FDA, it seems unlikely they can justify removing the saline-filled implants from the clinical armamentarium, but at the time of this writing the issue certainly remains in doubt. From a purely theoretical standpoint, it is difficult to imagine that the body's immune system can distinguish between the dimethylpolysiloxane molecules derived from the implant shell from those of the inner gel.

§25.07 IMMUNE RESPONSE TO SILICONE

In the 35 years that silicone gel-filled elastomer envelope-type breast prosthesis have been available in the United States, approximately 1 to 2 million women have had them implanted for breast augmentation and reconstruction (6). In January, 1992, after hearing of case reports of autoimmune and connective-tissue disease following use of these devices, the United States Food and Drug Administration called for a moratorium on the use of these types of breast implants. It is extremely important to note that at the time of the moratorium, there were no well controlled studies available which implicated breast implants as a cause of any of these disease processes. In fact, Dr. John Sergent, who at the time was president of the American Academy of Rheumatology, went on record publicly saying that he was not aware of any proof of a cause and effect relationship between silicone implants and rheumatic disease.

From a scientific viewpoint, case reports like the ones precipitating the moratorium provide the weakest evidence for cause and effect relationships (7). They do, however, provide insight into isolated patient outcomes. It is tempting to apply these experiences of individual patients to the population as a whole, but there is no scientific basis for this type of comparison. This section will review the nature of these diseases and summarize the scientific literature, both pro and con, which has developed since this controversy began. It should be kept in mind that an immune response is not synonymous with autoimmune disease.

[a] Autoimmune and Collagen-Vascular Diseases

Autoimmune and collagen-vascular diseases comprise a wide spectrum of disease processes with clinical names such as rheumatoid arthritis, vasculitis, myositis, lupus, scleroderma, systemic sclerosis, and others. In essence, these diseases are caused by a failure of the body's immune system to recognize itself. This ability to recognize what is "self" and what is not is the cornerstone of the body's ability to ward off disease and infection without consuming itself in the process.

The terminology for this class of disease can be confusing. Autoimmune Disease, Connective Tissue Disease, and Collagen Vascular Disease are all used interchangeably in describing this classification of disease process. This may be incorrect in the strictest sense. In common usage even within the medical community, however, they generally refer to the same classification of disorders. The term "Human Adjuvant Disease" is defined by the presence of six conditions: autoimmune disease-like symptoms and signs developing in a patient after plastic surgery involving injection of foreign substances; injection into the body of paraffin, silicone, or other immunogenic substance; foreign body granulomas observed histopathologically; and the presence of autoantibodies (8).

Two examples of this "self" versus "other" phenomenon familiar to almost everyone include the hard, woody reaction to a thorn or splinter which has been under the skin for some time. In this case, the body is trying to wall off the invading material because it has correctly recognized that this foreign substance is not properly part of the body ("host"). Another type includes the inflammatory reaction of rejection which occurs when the host rejects a transplanted organ. The inflammatory reaction in the body occurs when a large number of cells from the tissues and blood stream are mobilized to surround and consume an invading or offending agent.

These cells are capable of releasing some of the most potent and toxic substances known to mankind. This is an extremely good situation for the body if an invading substance or agent is harmful and thus correctly identified, neutralized, and consumed. However, if the identification process is faulty, these toxic substances will be released inappropriately and are capable of causing serious harm or death to the host.

The process of the body attacking itself results in an autoimmune phenomenon which is frequently labeled clinically by one of the names mentioned previously. This is admittedly an oversimplified approach, but it is the basis for of the autoimmune diseases attributed to silicone. The proponents of a causal link between silicone and autoimmune diseases hypothesize that the silicone or some compound containing portions of silicone sensitize the body and trigger the problems caused by the autoimmune phenomenon.

[b] Evidence of a Connection Between Autoimmune Processes and Silicone

As previously mentioned, the literature that exists in this area consists mainly of case reports and anecdotal accounts. The articles cited will be discussed in light of their scientific merit and similarity or differences to the way silicone breast implants were most commonly utilized clinically at the time of publication of the article.

Kumagal, Abe, and Shiokawa published an article in *Arthritis and Rheumatism* in 1979 regarding human adjuvant disease following cosmetic surgery. These patients were treated with injectable paraffin and "related substances" for breast and nasal augmentation. There is no mention of the purity or exact composition of the substances injected. The authors cite an article by Miyoshi (9) in which a single patient experienced improvement in symptoms following removal of the foreign substance by bilateral mastectomies (breast removal).

Van Nunen et al. describe three patients with "autoimmune connective tissue disease" which developed within 30 months after cosmetic mammary augmentation with gel-filled prosthesis (10). They admit that any causal relationship between implantation and the development of a connective tissue disease is entirely circumstantial. In their discussion, they point out that elastomeric silicone has been extensively used in medicine. Artificial heart valves, prosthetic finger joints, arteriovenous shunts for dialysis patients, and ventricular shunts for hydrocephalics (11). They point out that there have been no reports of connective tissue disease after implantation of such materials. Further, they state that there have been no reports of exacerbations of existing disease of this type by these devices.

Articles such as these provide poor evidence for a causal relationship for silicone as it was and is used in the United States. Free injection of silicone into the breast tissue, as described by Kumagal et al., has not been utilized by legitimate practitioners for many years and is now widely condemned in training programs across the country. It is unclear in articles such as this exactly what substance was used, its purity, or the techniques used during its introduction. Van Nunen et al. clearly are reporting a *finding*, not a causal relationship, and make a point of this several times in their paper.

Other articles (12) provide a review of some of the foreign literature but are, again, strictly a clinical study, reporting only case reports and observations. Quoting some of the material already cited here, they admit that the most notable associations were between progressive systemic sclerosis and paraffin injected freely into the breast tissue. For reasons discussed in the review of the original cases, this is simply not a valid comparison.

Two other articles have appeared in the dermatological literature regarding resolution of scleroderma or progressive systemic sclerosis-like illnesses occurred after removal of implants (13, 14). These two articles, which summarize the clinical course of only three patients, again provide comparisons between non-homogenous groups. In Bozena et al's paper, one of the patients had silicone freely injected into her breast tissue and the second patient had had a biopsy which was not diagnostic of any autoimmune disease. The patient in the article by Sahn et al. had known exposure to other possible etiologies (causative mechanisms) of scleroderma in her past. The authors are left to correctly state in their discussion that "how the liquid or gel form of silicone produces a systemic reaction is unclear."

Any type of silicone, even "medical grade" silicone, can cause *local* mild inflammatory reactions. This is not a new phenomenon. A basic defense mechanism is the ability to wall off foreign or "non-self" material. This encapsulation may involve the classic characteristics of inflammation: erythema or redness, swelling, and pain. All implants of foreign material will cause a fibrous encapsulation. Some authors have suggested that leakage of silicone from the implant envelope may be related to the formation of the capsule around the prosthesis (15). Other data, however, makes this relationship much less clear. In a study in which microscopic examination of the tissue making up the capsule was performed, no correlation was found between silicone droplets and capsule formation (16).

In summary, although there is certainly evidence of the coexistence of autoimmune type diseases and breast implants in the same patient, there is absolutely no evidence that breast implants cause the autoimmune disease. The numbers of well documented cases of patients with breast implants and autoimmune disease is very small compared to the total number of women with implants in place. It is unscientific, and, in fact, unfair, to take the individual patient reports outlined in this section and apply them in any manner to the population as a whole.

[c] Evidence Against a Causal Relationship Between Silicone and Autoimmune Disease

The articles in this group generally have been published more recently than those cited above. Admittedly, some have been motivated by a desire to defend the use of silicone gel implants. Nevertheless, they deal with large numbers of patients, involve specialists from different fields (plastic surgery and rheumatology), and they look at a number of autoimmune diseases.

A study from Missouri of 156 women looked at symptoms of joint swelling, muscular pain, and connective tissue disease (17). Some patients had some laboratory studies which were consistent with some of the autoimmune connective tissue diseases studied. Their overall diagnostic work up did not meet the American College of Rheumatology criteria for either rheumatoid arthritis or systemic lupus erythematosus. The authors concluded that most women with silicone breast implants and symptoms of rheumatic disease have normal results of common immunologic tests. There was a subset of 10 women who had unusual autoantibodies which the authors felt might suggest that some women with silicone breast implants may develop atypical immunologic reactions. They admit that the significance of this finding is not clear and they make no attempt to say that there is a cause and effect relationship between breast implants and rheumatic diseases.

Another study looked at 658 patients undergoing breast reconstruction after mastectomy. Three hundred eight implants were used in the 250 patients undergoing reconstruction with this technique. The incidence of autoimmune disorders was compared to a group of 353 women undergoing reconstruction with their own tissue. The main outcome measure was documented diagnosis of autoimmune disorder by a Board-certified rheumatologist. One patient in *each* group had a documented occurrence of an autoimmune syndrome requiring therapy. Both of these cases were mild and were treated with steroids which were ultimately discontinued. The conclusion of the study was that the incidence of autoimmune disease in mastectomy patients receiving silicone gel implants is *not* different that in patients who had reconstruction with autogenous tissue (18).

An article in 1989 looked at the relationship between systemic sclerosis following augmentation mammoplasty with silicone implants (19). This paper studied only four patients and the authors reached a conclusion that the chronic inflammatory reaction surrounding some elastomer-silicone-gel breast implants may play a role in the development of systemic sclerosis. The authors contradict this conclusion as they go on to review the literature on systemic sclerosis after augmentation mammaplasty.

They found 16 cases of systemic sclerosis after augmentation mammaplasty, with 9 of these patients receiving implantation in the United States. If the assumption is made that over one million women in the United States have had breast augmentation with implants, this gives an apparent prevalence ratio (the number of women who have a disease at any given time) of 9:1,000,000. The authors then correctly note that this prevalence does *not* represent a significant increase over the reported age- and sex-specific incidence rates for systemic sclerosis. It can be correctly stated from the findings of this study and the review of the literature that there is no evidence that there is an increase in systemic sclerosis in women who have undergone breast augmentation with silicone gel implants.

The association between rheumatoid arthritis, another connective tissue disorder, and silicone breast implants has been examined in two studies. One study found that in 349 women with recent-onset rheumatoid arthritis, there were fewer arthritic complaints among women who had undergone implantation (20). Another study examined 6,325 rheumatic disease patients and found no excess frequency of any connective tissue disorder, including rheumatoid arthritis, among women with silicone breast implants (21).

The most recent article to dispute a causal link between silicone and autoimmune disease appeared in the New England Journal of Medicine on June 16, 1994 (22). These authors conducted a population-based, retrospective study to examine the risks of connective tissue diseases and other disorders after breast implantation. A total of 749 women who had received breast implants were followed for an average of 7.8 years and were compared to a group of 1498 community controls (did not have implants) followed for an average of 8.3 years. A connective tissue disease was diagnosed in 5 of the women who had breast implants and 10 women in the group who did not have breast implants also had a diagnosis of connective tissue disease during the time they were followed.

Signs or symptoms of arthritis were present in twenty-five of the women with implants and in thirty-nine of the women who did not have implants. It is apparent by these data that neither the diagnosis of connective tissue disease nor the signs and symptoms of arthritis were statistically significantly more prevalent in women with implants. Only the symptom of morning stiffness was found to be statistically increased among women with implants. The authors' conclusion in this study was that they had found no association between breast implants and the connective tissue diseases and other disorders studied.

[d] Summary

Clearly there is dispute in the literature regarding the association of silicone breast implants with the development of autoimmune or connective tissue disorders. Every scientific study cited in this chapter has certain limitations and none stands alone as a definitive text on the problem. In our opinion, there is no current evidence to suggest a causal relationship between silicone breast implants and the development of autoimmune disease. We fully recognize that some women may develop autoimmune diseases following augmentation or reconstruction with silicone implants, but we also recognize that women develop these diseases without undergoing augmentation. The exact role of silicone in this process is not known now, and it certainly was not known prior to the time of the FDA moratorium.

More scientific data will undoubtedly be forthcoming. Additional data which have been presented at various medical meetings have yet to be subjected to the peer review process of publication. There is a feeling among both plastic surgeons and some rheumatologists that this emerging epidemiologic evidence suggests that there is little or no association between silicone implants and the development of connective tissue disease (23). As more data become available, the role, if any, of silicone in this disease process may become more clear.

§25.08 CONCLUSION

[a] Breast Implants and Cancer Risk

The lack of any association between breast implants and an increased risk of breast cancer is well covered in Chapter 24. All studies done to date have failed to identify any increase in the risk of breast cancer among patients with implants. In fact, the majority of studies have noted development of breast cancer in fewer patients than expected when implant patients are compared to matched non-implant controls (24).

[b] Unresolved Issues

Contraction of the soft-tissue capsule around the foreign body implant remains the greatest problem associated with either silicone gel or saline-filled silicone implants (25). Other well-documented problems associated with implants are infection of the implant, necessitating removal, and implant rupture. The question of auto-immune or connective tissue disorders in association with breast implants is not yet resolved. Suggestions that there is a relationship between the implant and autoimmune or connective-tissue disease is raised primarily by anecdotal reports. As noted in this chapter, there is a slowly growing body of evidence that the incidence of such diseases is not higher in the implant population than would be expected in the normal female population of the same age. It will be ironic if research currently in progress ultimately is able to exonerate silicone. There is significant risk that by the time an adequate data base can be built and analyzed through basic and clinical research studies, there may no longer be any implant manufacturers. The anecdotal reports and several very large judgments, combined with the public's perception of the Global Settlement, have become a heavy weight indeed on the scales of justice. The dry statistical evidence which might exculpate silicone will have far less jury appeal than the anecdotal but gripping human drama that most jurors will already have seen on their favorite talk show program. Nevertheless, the evidence is mounting and the well-prepared defense attorney can expect an ever-increasing supply of ammunition for his/her cause.

References

1. Global Settlement Update: Special Bulletin: American Society of Plastic and Reconstructive Surgeons, Inc., April 1, 1994.
2. McCraw JB, Maxwell GP. Clinics in Plastic Surgery: October 1988, pp 717-726.
3. Little G and Baker JL. Results of Closed Compression Capsulotomy for Treatment of Contracted Breast Implant Capsules. Plastic and Reconstructive Surgery, 65:30, 1980.
4. Baker JL Jr, Bartels RJ and Douglas WM. Closed Compression Technique for Rupturing a Contracted Capsule Around a Breast Implant. Plastic and Reconstructive Surgery, 58:137, 1976.
5. Thomsen JL, Christensen L, Nielsen M et al. Histologic Changes and Silicone Concentrations in Human Breast Tissue Surrounding Silicone Breast Prostheses. Plastic and Reconstructive Surgery, 85:38-41, 1990.
6. Deapen May. New England Journal of Medicine 1,2.
7. Collins. New England Journal of Medicine.
8. Sahn EE, Garen PD, Silver RM, Maize JC. Scleroderma Following Augmentation Mammaplasty—Report of a Case and Review of the Literature. Arch Derm 126:1198-1202.
9. Jap Med J 2122:9-14, 1964.
10. Post Mammaplasty Connective Tissue Disease Arthritis and Rheumatism, 25:6, 964-697, 1982.
11. Mitchel RM: Surgery, Art or Science? Med J Aust 2:5-9, 1975.

12. Clinical Spectrum of Connective Tissue Disease After Cosmetic Surgery. Kumgai, et al., Arthritis and Rheumatism 27:1 1-12, 1984.
13. Scleroderma Following Augmentation Mammaplasty. Sahn, et al. Arch Derm 126:1198-1202, 1990.
14. Human Adjuvant Disease Following Augmentation Mammaplasty. Bozena et al. Arch Derm 124:1383-1386, 1988.
15. Barker DE, Retsky MI, Schultz SS. ''Bleeding'' of Silicone From Bag-gel Breast Implants, and its Clinical Relation to Fibrous Capsule Reaction. Plast Reconstr Surg 61: 836-841, 1978.
16. Gayou RM. A Histological Comparison of Contracted and Non-contracted Capsules Around Silicone Breast Implants. Plast Reconstr Surg 63: 700-709, 1979.
17. Bridges AJ, Conley C et al. A Clinical and Immunological Evaluation of Women with Silicone Breast Implants and Symptoms of Rheumatic Disease. Annals of Int Med. 1993, 118: 929-936.
18. Schusterman MA, Kroll SS, Reece GP et al. Incidence of Autoimmune Disease in Patients After Breast Reconstruction with Silicone Gel Implants Versus Autogenous Tissue: A Preliminary Report. Annals of Plastic Surgery 31:1, 1-6, 1993.
19. Varga J, Schumacher R, Jimenez SA. Systemic Sclerosis After Augmentation Mammaplasty with Silicone Implants. Annals of Int Med. 1989, 111:377-383.
20. Dugowson CE, Daling J, Koepsell TD, Voigt L, Nelson JL. Silicone Breast Implants and Risk for Rheumatoid Arthritis (abstract). Arthritis Rheum 35 (suppl 9):S66, 1992.
21. Goldman JA, Lamm SH, Cooper W, Cooper L. Breast Implants are not Associated with an Excess of Connective Tissue Disease (abstract). Arthritis Rheum 35 (suppl 9):S65, 1992.
22. Gabriel SE, O'Fallon WM, Kurland LT et al. Risk of Connective-tissue Diseases and Other Disorders After Breast Implantation. NEJM, vol 330,24: 1697-1702.
23. Sanchez-Guerrero J., Schur PH, Sergent JS, Liang MH. Silicone Breast Implants and Rheumatic Disease—

Clinical Immunologic, and Epidermologic Studies. Arthritis & Rheumatism 37:2; 158-168, 1994.

24. Berkel H, Birdsell D, Jenkins H. Breast augmentation : A Risk Factor for Breast Cancer? New England Journal of Medicine 325:1649-1653, 1992.
25. Federal Register. Volume 56, No. 69, April 10, 1991.

GLOSSARY

–A–

ADHESION MOLECULE. Some tumor cells display specific proteins on their surface (adhesion molecules) which enable them to adhere to the adhesion molecule receptors on the surface of endothelial cells forming the lining of the blood capillaries, and other tissues such as basement membranes. Once fixed to the endothelial cell the tumor cell is able to make contact with the underlying basement membrane, destroy a small segment of the membrane, and escape from the blood stream into the parenchyma of a distant organ. Tumor cells can also use adhesion molecules to adhere to adhesion molecule receptors on the membranes surrounding the post capillary venules and gain entrance to the blood stream.

ANAPLASTIC. Immature, undifferentiated; poorly differentiated and immature cancer cells tend to be more aggressive and have greater lethal potential.

ANEUPLOID. A cancer cell containing an abnormal amount of DNA; usually an increase in amount, although a few tumors contain a less than normal amount of DNA. Some (not all) aneuploid tumors have a greater lethal potential than diploid tumors.

ANGIOGENESIS. The development of new blood vessels.

ANGIOGENIC FACTORS. Proteins or other agents that stimulate the formation of new blood vessels.

ATYPIA. Epithelial cells that are irregular and do not conform to the shape of a normal epithelial cell. The term epithelial hyperplasia with atypia suggests that some of the cells resemble cancer cells but no evidence of invasion could be identified. These lesions are thought to be a premalignant phase of breast cancer.

–B–

BASEMENT MEMBRANE. A thin membrane composed of a dense meshwork of carbohydrates and proteins which ensheathes the small capillaries and post capillary venules. It does not contain pores or channels which will permit the passage of a tumor cell or a white blood cell. To gain entrance to the blood stream the tumor cell must adhere to a receptor on the surface of the basement membrane. Once fixed to the basement membrane the tumor cell releases its powerful enzymes which disintegrate a tiny section of the basement membrane creating a defect through which the tumor cell can gain entry to the blood stream.

BIAS, LEAD TIME. Screening mammography detects many tumors *with systemic disease* at an earlier phase of their life cycle. These women live longer following detection (and may have a five- or ten-year survival) but eventually die of their cancer. *See Chapter 22.*

BIAS, LENGTH. Rapidly growing aggressive breast cancers tend to surface between negative screening examinations. Slowly growing cancers are more often detected at the time of the routine screening examinations and tend to have a better survival rate. Thus, screening programs which include only cases discovered during the routine screening examination will have a better survival rate. This is called length bias. *See Chapter 22.*

BIAS, OVER-DIAGNOSIS. Screening asymptomatic women with mammograms not infrequently detects small "look-like cancers" that have little or no lethal potential. Many of these lesions would never have become clinically overt during the life of the patient. This falsely impoves the survival rate. *See Chapter 22.*

BIAS, SELECTION. Investigators sometimes unconscioulsy eliminate women with unfavorable cancers. Eliminating these cancers, of course, falsely improves the survival rate. *See Chapter 22.*

BIOLOGIC PREDETERMINATION. The DNA of the breast duct cell must sustain a series of sequential alterations before it acquires full lethal potential. When this occurs early in the life cycle of the breast cancer, the tumor will have metastasized to distant sites before it can be detected by mammography. Thus, the outcome is predetermined before it is possible to detect the cancer.

–C–

CAMOUFLAGED TUMOR. Some breast cancers are hidden or masked within the breast and cannot be detected by mammography and/or palpation. This common and serious problem is secondary to one or more of the following; (a) density of tumor and breast are similar; (b) absence of tumor microcalcifications; (c) a unique pattern of tumor invasion which creates vague and indistinct tumor borders.

CANCER CONTROL WINDOW. That period of time between the moment a cancer becomes detectable (threshold size) and the time that it metastasizes to distant sites. It is the window of opportunity during which it is theoretically possible to cure the cancer. *See Chapter 22.*

CAPILLARY. The small blood vessel that connects the terminal arteries to the veins returning blood to the heart. Metastasis is thought to occur just beyond the junction of the capillary and the small veins (in the post capillary venule). *See also lymphatic capillary.*

CHROMOSOME. A long coiled and twisted strand of DNA that contains genetic information. There are 46 chromosomes in all human cells except the ovum and sperm which contain 23.

COLUMBIA CLINICAL CLASSIFICATION. A clinical staging system, primarily of historical interest. *See §18.01[a].*

CURE, CLINICAL. When, after a long follow-up a patient dies without clinical or post-mortem evidence of breast cancer recurrence, she is said to have had a clinical cure of breast cancer. *See Chapter 9.*

PERSONAL CURE. Those women who die from causes other than breast cancer and without evidence of recurrent breast cancer are said to have had a personal cure. *See Chapter 9.*

STATISTICAL CURE. When the risk of death from breast cancer, as demonstrated by the relative survival curve, is the same as in the general female population. *See Chapter 9.*

CYTOMETRY. *See flow cytometry and §23.02[h] and §23.03[h].*

–D–

DESMOPLASIA. An overgrowth of fibrous tissue within and surrounding the tumor secondary to proteins secreted by the tumor cells. The degree of desmoplasia determines the density of the tumor.

DIAMETER, DOUBLING. When the tumor undergoes three net cell generations or doublings, there will be an eight-fold increase in mass and a doubling of the diameter of the tumor.

DIPLOID. A cell that has two normal sets of chromosomes (normal amount of DNA). The DNA index of a diploid cell is 1.0. Diploid tumors tend to have a better survival than aneuploid tumors but in breast cancer the difference is not statistically significant.

Hypodiploid. A hypodiploid tumor cell has less DNA than a normal cell (DNA index less than 1.0) and often has a poor prognosis.

Hyperdiploid. The DNA content is greater than normal.

DISEASE FREE INTERVAL (DFI). The length of time between the removal of the breast cancer and the first sign of recurrence of the cancer. A short disease-free interval is an indication of a rapidly growing aggressive cancer.

DNA. Deoxyribonucleic acid. An acid consisting of a long linear combination of nucleotides (adenine (A), cytosine (C), guanine (G), and thymine (T) which are strung together on a long strand (backbone) of sugar and phosphate like beads on a string. These four subunits form the letters (A,C,G,T) in the alphabet which record the genetic information for all organisms except for the RNA viruses. DNA is present in all of the cells in the human body.

DNA FLOW CYTOMETRY. *See Flow Cytometry.*

DNA INDEX. The amount of DNA within the nucleus of cell. Normal cells have a DNA Index of 1.0. Cancer cells often have a DNA Index greater than 1.0 since the nucleus contains an abnormal amount of DNA. Some cancer cells may contain less than the normal amount of DNA and would, therefore, have a DNA Index of less than 1.0. Some cancers with an abnormal amount of DNA have greater lethal potential. During the process of cell division the DNA Index increases from 1.0 to 2.0 and returns to 1.0 when the cell divides.

DOUBLING TIME. The time required for a tumor to double the number of tumor cells within the tumor. Three net cell doublings of a tumor results in an eight-fold increase in mass and a doubling of the tumor diameter. The life cycle of a breast cancer consists of 40 doublings, since this will produce a mass of tumor large enough to cause the death of the patient.

DOUBLING TIME DEFENSE. *See Chapter 19.*

DYSPLASIA. An overgrowth of benign tissue which is sometimes premalignant.

–E–

EMBOLUS. A tumor can spread to regional or distant sites as a single cell or a small cluster of tumor cells (tumor emboli). Some refer to this as the shedding of cancer cells. *See Shedding.*

ENZYME. A protein capable of accelerating a chemical reaction.

EPITHELIAL CELL (EPITHELIUM). The cells lining the external and internal surfaces of the body. The cells lining the milk glands and ducts of the breast are epithelial cells.

ESTROGEN AND PROGESTERONE RECEPTORS. Normal breast cells and some breast cancer cells contain special proteins called estrogen and progesterone receptors. When estrogen and progesterone enter the cells containing these receptors they attach to and activate these receptors thus initiating certain vital functions within the cell. Tumor cells that contain estrogen and progesterone receptors tend to be more mature, grow more slowly and respond to hormonal manipulation. Tumor cells without or low levels of these receptors (estrogen receptor negative and progesterone receptor negative) tend to grow more rapidly.

–F–

FIBROCYTE OR FIBROBLAST. A connective tissue cell.

FISHER DOCTRINE. *See §7.03*

FLOW CYTOMETRY. A suspension of tumor nuclei is created by separating the nuclei from the cell cytoplasm mechanically and/or enzymatically. The DNA within the tumor nuclei is then stained with a fluorescent dye which is activated when exposed to a laser beam of light. The suspension of tumor cells is then forced through the cytometer under pressure in such a manner that the cell suspension is broken into fine droplets each containing a single tumor nucleus.As the tumor nuclei pass through the laser light beam the computer measures the precise degree of fluorescence of each nucleus. From flow cytometry we determine:

1. The % S-phase fraction. As the breast cancer cells prepare for cell division they manufacture DNA. These cells, therefore, contain a greater than normal amount of DNA and are said to be in the synthesis phase of cell divison (S-phase fraction). The percent of S-phase tumor cells is an excellent measure of the growth rate of a breast cancer.
2. The DNA content of each tumor cell. Thus we learn whether the tumor nuclei contain a normal amount of DNA (diploid) or whether they contain an abnormal amount of DNA (aneuploid). Some aneuploid tumors grow more rapidly and tend to be more aggressive. *See also §23.02[h] and §23.03[h].*

–G–

GENE. A small segment of DNA that carries a specific genetic message.

GROWTH RATES. *See §8.02[d].*

–H–

HALSTED DOCTRINE. *See §7.02.*

HER-2/neu ONCOGENE. *See §23.02 [i]* and *§23.03 [i].*

HETEROGENEOUS. Composed of dissimilar parts.

HISTOLOGIC GRADE. *See §23.02[c][2] and §23.03[c][2].*

HISTOLOGY. Microscopic anatomy of a tissue.

HYPERDIPLOID. *See diploid.*

HYPODIPLOID. *See diploid.*

HYPERPLASIA. An abnormal overgrowth of tissue, usually benign.

HYPERTETRAPLOID. *See tetraploid.*

–I–

IMMUNOHISTOCHEMICAL TESTS. Chemical tests that employ monoclonal or polyclonal antibodies to identiy certain tumor antigens on the surface of cancer cells.

INCIDENCE. The ratc of occurrence of a disease. The incidence of breast cancer has been increasing since 1930 secondary to bettter reporting of cases, earlier detection (lead time bias), a more benign form of the disease as the result of dramatic changes in our methods of the detection of breast cancer, and a true increase in incidence as the result in changes in the life-style of most women. *See Chapter 6.*

INTERMEDIATE DOCTRINE. *See §7.04.*

INTERVAL TUMOR. A breast cancer that surfaces within 12 months of a routine negative screening examination. *See Chapter 17.*

–K–

KARYORRHEXIS. The rupture of a cell nucleus with dispersion of the chromatin from the cell nucleus. Can be mistaken for a mitotic figure.

–L–

LEAD TIME BIAS. *See bias.*

LENGTH BIAS. *See bias.*

LYMPHATIC CAPILLARY. The smallest lymph vessel, consists of a single layer of endothelial cells ensheathed with a few scattered connective tissue fibers. Since there are no pericytes or basement membranes these structures easily collect the excess water, proteins, gases, etc. from the extracellular space. Unfortunately their flimsy structure makes them an easy target for cancer cells.

LYMPHATIC SYSTEM. The capillary lymphatics collect excess water, electrolytes, gases, large protein molecules, etc. (lymph) from the extracellular tissues and transport the lymph to the blood stream via the thoracic duct and right lymphatic duct. There are many lympho-venous communications between the vascular and the lymphatic systems. Cancer cells can easily pass from one system to the other. Thus the two systems should be considered as one large system. For example, more than 70% of women with lymph node metastases also have systemic breast cancer.

–M–

MACROPHAGE. A large white cell that can ingest necrotic tissue, debris, and kill bacteria.

MALEVOLENT. Malignant, some breast cancers since 1930 are said to have become increasingly less malevolent, that is, more benign. *See Chapter 6.*

MANCHESTER STAGING SYSTEM. A clinical staging system, primarily of historical interest. *See §18.01[a].*

MATRIX. The substance which binds together the various structures, molecules, and water within the cell.

METASTASIS. The spread of a cancer cell or small cluster of cancer cells via the blood and/or lymph to distant sites where, if the proper growth factors are present the tumor cells will grow and establish a nodule of cancer cells.

MICROVESSEL COUNT. *See Angiogenesis §23.02 [m].*

MITOTIC INDEX. The number of mitotic figures of cells undergoing division in 10 high power fields of an ordinary light microscope. *See §23.02[c][4] and §23.03[c][6].*

MITOSIS. The act of cell division.

MUTATION. (L) to change. Refers to the change in the genetic message of the tumor cell by a single or a series of sequential alterations of the DNA of the cell.

MYOFIBROBLAST. A contractile fibroblast.

–N–

NECROSIS. The death of cells and/or tissue. *See §23.03[f].*

NEOPLASTIC PROGRESSION. Tumor cells that have sustained a series of sequential alteration of their DNA and have developed full lethal potential (metastasis) and are said to have undergone neoplastic progression.

NUCLEAR GRADE. *See §23.02[c][3] and §23.03[c][5].*

NUCLEAR MORPHOMETRY. A photomicrograph is enlarged and projected onto a screen where the nuclear diameter and area can be determined. The mean nuclear diameter, nuclear area, and mitotic index all correlate with prognosis. *See §23.02[e].*

NSABP. The National Surgical Adjuvant Breast Protocol. A non profit research organization which conducts large prospective, randomized clinical trials to evaluate various treatment modalities for breast cancer.

–O–

ONCOGENE. A unit of genetic information (gene) that specifies a protein that controls or modulates normal cell division should properly be called a mitogene. When the DNA of the mitogene is altered (mutated) it may produce abnormal proteins or larger amounts of the normal protein that promote disorderly cell division and this is the first step in the formation of a cancer. The mitogene has become an oncogene. *See §23.02[i] and §23.03[i].*

OSMOSIS. The diffusion of fluids and small particles through membranes or porous materials.

–P–

p53 TUMOR SUPPRESSOR GENE. *See §23.02 [l].*

PLOIDY. A Greek word meaning a fold. Therefore, ploidy refers to the gross configuration of the DNA. Tumors with a greater amount of DNA than normal are called aneuploid, those with a normal amount of DNA are said to be diploid. Diploid tumors tend to be less aggressive.

PRETHRESHOLD SIZE. *See threshold size and Chapter 15.*

PROGESTERONE RECEPTOR. Normal breast duct cells contain a protein complex that attaches to progesterone within the nucleus of the cell or transports progesterone to thc nucleus where it initiates a vital celluar function. Some tumor cells also contain progesterone receptors. *See § 23.02[g].*

PROTEASE. A powerful enzyme which destroys proteins. Proteolytic enzymes secreted by cancer cells breaks down proteins in the surrounding tissues which enables the tumor to invade the local tissues and eventually gain entrance to the blood and/or lymph. *See §8.03[c][2].*

PROLIFERATION RATE. The growth rate of a cancer, commonly measured by the mitotic index, the thymidine labeling index, or the S-phase fraction determined by flow cytometry. Tumors that are growing more rapidly than the average breast cancer tend to be more aggressive (but not always).

PROTO-ONCOGENE. Proto (Gr, first). That which precedes the oncogene. Another term for mitogene, a unit of genetic information that produces proteins that control and modulate the normal process of cell divison. When the DNA of the proto-oncogene or mitogene is altered an abnormal protein or an abnormal amount of normal protein is produced. Both the abnormal protein product or unusually large amounts of normal protein will disrupt the normal process of cell divison. The proto-oncogene has become an oncogene and the process of cell divison will be disorderly. A cancer has been created. *See §23.02[i].*

PYKNOSIS. The shrunken nucleus of a degenerating cell. Can be mistaken for a mitotic figure.

–R–

RELATIVE SURVIVAL RATE. *See §9.02[c].*

R1-R2 INTERVAL. The interval between the first and second metastasis. A short R1-R2 interval suggests a rapidly growing aggressive tumor.

–S–

SELECTION BIAS. *See bias and Chapter 22.*

SHEDDING. The escape of cancer cells or small clusters of cancer cells into the blood or lymph. Formerly thought to be a passive process but we now know it is an active process requiring active participation by the tumor cell. *See §10.03[a],[b].*

S-PHASE FRACTION. Cancer cells whose DNA is in the synthesis phase (in the process of doubling the DNA prior to cell division) are said to be in the S-phase of the cell cycle. Determination of the S-phase fraction is one of the most accurate gauges of the proliferation or growth rate of breast cancer. *See §23.02[h].*

STAGE CREEP. As our diagnostic tests improve we are able to detect distant metastases at an earlier stage. These patients are then shifted to the next stage with more serious disease. This improves the survival rate of each stage but the overall survival remains the same. *See Chapter 22.*

STAGING SYSTEMS. *See Chapter 18.*
Columbia Clinical Classification. §18.01[a]. Manchester Clinical Staging System §18.01[a]. TNM Staging System §18.01 to §18.06.

STROMA, TUMOR. The supporting tissue framework of the breast (connective tissue, blood vessels, fibrin gel, inflammatory cells, water, etc.). The stroma provides the scaffolding for the tumor cells. The blood vessels play an important role in the nutrition, gas exchange, and waste disposal for the tumor cells. Without stroma tumors cannot grow beyond a diameter of 1-2 mm.

–T–

TETRAPLOID. Normal cells have a diploid (two-fold) content of DNA (DNA Index 1.0). Tetraploid tumor cells have double the amount of DNA (DNA Index 2.0).

Hypertetraploid. Tumor cells that contain more than double the amount of DNA of a diploid or normal cell. The DNA Index would be greater than 2.0.

THRESHOLD SIZE. The smallest size at which it is possible to detect a breast cancer, thus, we talk of the threshold size of breast cancer by mammography and/or by palpation.

Threshold Size by Mammography—the smallest threshold size by mammography is about 2.1 mm.

Threshold Size by Palpation—the average threshold size by palpation is about 10 mm (1 cm).

Prethreshold Size—a tumor that is too small to be detected by mammography and/or palpation. Breast cancers remain prethreshold in size by palpation for the first 75% of their life cycle. Virtually all breast cancers remain prethreshold size by mammography for more than 50% of their life cycle.

THYMIDINE LABELING INDEX (TLI). One of the most accurate measurements of the proliferation rate of breast cancer. It is determined as follows:

1. The amino acid thymine is unique that it is found only in DNA.
2. However, thymine cannot enter the cell nucleus unless it is attached to a sugar.
3. Therefore, a sugar is attached to thymine and it becomes thymidine.
4. Thymidine is tagged with a radioactive tracer (H3) and placed on a thin slice of fresh tumor tissue. The thin slice of tumor tissue covered with radioactive thymidine is incubated for several hours so that the tumor cells undergoing cell division will incorporate thymidine into the DNA of their nuclei.
5. The tissue is removed from the incubator and flooded with water to wash away the radioactive thymidine that was not taken up and incorporated into the DNA of the tumor nuclei during the period of incubation.
6. The thin slice of tumor tissue is then covered with a photographic emulsion and placed in a dark container for several

days. During this time the radioactive material in the newly formed DNA will develop the photographic emulsion overlying the nuclei containing radioactive DNA.

7. The percentage of cells in the S-phase of cell division in determined by countng the number of nuclei containing silver.

The thymidine labeling index (TLI) is seldom used in the clinical or medical malpractice setting since it requires fresh tumor tissue. However, it is one of the most accurate ways to measure the proliferation rate of breast cancer and serves as a standard against which we can compare other tests. For example, tumors with a poor nuclear grade and a high thymidine labeling index have a high risk of developing recurrence. This tells us that poor nuclear grade and a high S-phase fraction or a high mitotic index would also predict an unfavorable outcome.

TNM STAGING SYSTEM. A staging system which measures the extent of the breast cancer by recording the diameter of the tumor (T), the number of axillary lymph nodes containing metastases (N), and the number of distant metastases (M). Thus an early breast cancer might be $T_1N_0M_0$ while a more advanced tumor might be $T_2N_2M_0$, and a far advanced tumor could be $T_2N_4M_2$. There are both clinical (cTNM) and pathologic (pTNM) staging sytems. *See Chapter 18.*

TUMOR GRADING. *See §23.02[c][1] and §23.03[c].*

TUMOR STROMA. *See Stroma.*

TUMOR DIAMETER. A large tumor diameter sometimes but not always indicates a poor prognosis. *See Chapter 11, Tumor Size.* Three net cell tumor doublings result in an eight-fold increase in mass and a doubling of the diameter of the tumor.

–V–

VENULE. The small veins that collect blood from the arterial capillaries. The post capillary venule is thought to be the site at which cancer cells gain entrance to the blood stream.

INDEX
LEGAL SECTION

References are to Page Numbers

P

Q

INDEX
MEDICAL SECTION

References are to Sections

C

R

T

- Definition of the word "cure"
- Long-term survival data (30 years)
- Doubling time of many cancers 365 days or longer

Appendix - 10-1

- History of development of lumpectomy
- Survival rate of lumpectomy vs. total mastectomy
- Survival rates of breast cancer
- Long term survival (30 years) studies of breast cancer
- Age-adjusted mortality rate of breast cancer since 1930
- If survival is measured from the onset of symptoms, increasing the durations of symptoms does not alter the survival rate
- Animal models reveal that many cancers metastasize soon following the vascularization of the tumor
- Tumor capillaries are quite "leaky" and are easily penetrated by the cancer cell
- Conclusion visual aids: breast cancers metastasize prior to the time they become large enough to produce symptoms
- Once a myth is entrenched in the minds of the medical community it is difficult to expel

Appendix - 10-2 by David Plotkin and Francis Blankenberg

- Is breast cancer curable?
- Doubling times of breast cancer
- Breast cancer survival
- Diagnosis of primary and metastatic breast cancer
  Discussion of time of origin of distant metastases that surface within five years of removal of primary tumor
- Fusion of multifocal sites of breast cancer
  Explains why some tumors not detected until they are quite large
- Long term survival studies
- Major mammographic screening studies